Digital Media Law

Digital Media Law

Ashley Packard

A John Wiley & Sons, Ltd., Publication

Blackwell Publishing was acquired by John Wiley & Sons in February 2007. Blackwell's publishing program has been merged with Wiley's global Scientific, Technical, and Medical business to form Wiley-Blackwell.

Registered Office
John Wiley & Sons Ltd, The Atrium, Southern Gate, Chichester, West Sussex, PO19 8SQ, United Kingdom

Editorial Offices
350 Main Street, Malden, MA 02148-5020, USA
9600 Garsington Road, Oxford, OX4 2DQ, UK
The Atrium, Southern Gate, Chichester, West Sussex, PO19 8SQ, UK

For details of our global editorial offices, for customer services, and for information about how to apply for permission to reuse the copyright material in this book please see our website at www.wiley.com/wiley-blackwell.

The right of Ashley Packard to be identified as the author of this work has been asserted in accordance with the UK Copyright, Designs and Patents Act 1988.

Library of Congress Cataloging-in-Publication Data

Packard, Ashley.
  Digital media law / Ashley Packard.
    p. cm.
  Includes bibliographical references and index.
  ISBN 978-1-4051-8169-3 (hardcover : alk. paper) — ISBN 978-1-4051-8168-6 (pbk. : alk. paper)   1. Digital media—Law and legislation—United States.   2. Internet—Law and legislation—United States.   3. Telecommunication—Law and legislation—United States.
4. Freedom of expression—United States.   5. Digital media—Law and legislation.   I. Title.
  KF2750.P33 2010
  343.7309'9—dc22

2010003746

A catalogue record for this book is available from the British Library.

Set in 10.5 on 13 pt Minion by Toppan Best-set Premedia Limited
Printed and bound in Malaysia by Vivar Printing Sdn Bhd

01   2010

Contents

Preface

It is time to stop thinking about media law as though it were the exclusive domain of traditional media organizations. Our global shift to digital media has precipitated a shift in information control. Meanwhile the affordability of digital media and their ease of use has democratized media production. With the right equipment, anyone can produce a website, listserv, blog or video with the potential to reach a mass audience. When *anyone* can become a media producer, *everyone* should know something about media law – both to protect their own rights and to avoid violating the rights of others.

This text focuses on digital media law, which like digital media, is characterized by its general applicability. The information presented here is applicable to professionals in fields such as publishing, public relations, advertising, marketing, e-commerce, graphic art, web design, animation, photography, video and audio production, game design, and instructional technology among others. But it is equally relevant to individuals who use digital media for personal interests – either to express themselves through social networking sites, blogs, and discussion boards or to engage in file trading or digital remixing.

As a field, digital media law is also characterized by its global impact. Digital media are borderless. Material uploaded to the Internet enters every country. Material broadcast via satellite reaches across entire continents. What does not travel internationally, however, is the First Amendment. American publishing companies and writers have been sued in courts all over the world for publishing information on the Internet that violated the laws of other countries. Foreign courts will apply their laws to material that is accessible within their borders through the Internet or via satellite if they perceive that material to have caused harm there. Producers of digital media need to understand how jurisdiction is determined and when foreign law can be applied to them.

Digital Media Law focuses on issues that are particularly relevant to the production and use of digital media. Its cases and controversies are based on freedom of expression, information access and protection, intellectual property, defamation, privacy, indecency, and commercial speech in the context of new media. This growing area of law also encompasses regulations imposed on the content and operation of telecommunications, such as broadcast, cable and satellite media, cellular communications, and the Internet. The material is framed to appeal to the broad audience of future media producers in communication and digital media disciplines. Current examples bring legal concepts to life. The text is also accompanied by a website (www.DigitalMediaLaw.us) that provides updated information about new court decisions and legislation, links to cases, and supplementary material.

Chapter 1 provides an introduction to the legal system and a guide to locate primary sources of law. Use it to gain a basic understanding of law before moving on to other topics.

Chapter 2 explores the First Amendment. Speech is presumed to be protected in the United States unless proven otherwise. This chapter addresses the extent of that protection and its limitations.

Chapter 3 covers telecommunications law, including regulations for broadcast media, cable, direct broadcast satellite, and phone service. It explores the varying levels of First Amendment protection that apply to different media and the Federal Communications Commission's efforts to adapt its rules to converging technologies.

Chapter 4 discusses the Internet's regulatory structure and explains the difference between domestic and international concepts of net neutrality. It describes statutes in place to combat cybercrime and also introduces the concept of virtual law.

Chapter 5 provides an introduction to the legal area of procedure called conflict of laws. It explains how jurisdiction, choice of law, and enforcement of foreign judgments applies to transnational conflicts involving digitally disseminated content.

Chapter 6 describes federal and state guarantees of access to information and protections for information sources. This area of law, which has always been of particular significance to traditional journalists, is now increasingly important to bloggers and podcasters.

Chapters 7 and 8 provide an overview of intellectual property law. Chapter 7 explains copyright law, a field that applies to every digital media producer's work. Chapter 8 describes patent law, trademark protection, trade secret protection, and cybersquatting legislation.

Chapter 9 addresses defamation law, which has always been the bane of traditional media, but is now increasingly applied to "average people" who post damaging accusations on websites, blogs, and listservs. It explains how U.S. libel law differs from that of other countries and the impact that difference has on the treatment of plaintiffs and defendants.

Chapter 10 explores protections for privacy, scattered among state and federal statutes, common law, and state constitutions. It addresses rights to privacy in the marketplace, work, home, and electronic communications.

Chapter 11 delves into the regulation of sex and violence. In particular, it explores varying protections accorded indecency v. obscenity and how states have tried to apply these theories to control violence in media.

Chapter 12 explains differences in First Amendment protection accorded to commercial speech v. political speech. It describes the efforts of regulatory agencies to control deceptive advertisements, spam, and antitrust violations.

Acknowledgments

A collaborative effort is required to bring a project like *Digital Media Law* to life. Without the talented editorial and production staff at Wiley-Blackwell, it would still be just a file on my computer. I am particularly grateful to my editors, Elizabeth Swayze and Margot Morse, for guiding me through the book's publication process. Their experience, enthusiasm, and humor made my job much easier. I also want to thank my copy-editors, David Williams and Michael Coultas, as well as the Wiley-Blackwell production editors, graphic designers, and marketing specialists, whose expertise and professionalism shows in the final product.

My sincere appreciation goes to the manuscript's reviewers, Robert Kerr of University of Oklahoma, Barry Berlin of Canisius University, Anthony Fargo of Indiana University, and Thomas Schwartz of Ohio State University. All respected scholars in the field of communication law, their insight and suggestions made my work better.

Others, who may not realize the integral role they played in this book, include my former law professors at the University of Missouri, William Fisch, Martha Dragich, and Sandra Davidson. I hope I can inspire the same appreciation of media law in my students that they did in me.

And, most importantly, I want to express my gratefulness for the collaborative effort that took place at home. While my attention was consumed by matters of media law, my husband, Chris, and daughter, Eliza, kept everything else under control. They truly made this book possible.

1

Introduction to the Legal System

It makes no sense to dive into a particular area of law without understanding the basic structure of the legal system and its terminology. This chapter describes the primary sources of law in the United States and provides a guide to find them. It explains the structure of the federal and state court systems, the basic differences between civil and criminal law, and the role of judicial review in the United States. It can be used to establish a foundation before proceeding to other chapters and as a reference later when you need to review a particular concept.

The Meaning of Law

Before discussing how law is made, it might be helpful to define it generally. Law is a system to guide behavior, both to protect the rights of individuals and to ensure public order. Although it may have a moral component, it differs from moral systems because the penalties for its violation are carried out by the state.

Digital media law encompasses all statutes, administrative rules, and court decisions that have an impact on digital technology. Because technology is always changing, digital media law is in a state of continuous adaptation. But its basic structure and principles are still grounded in the "brick and mortar" legal system.

Sources of Law in the United States

All students are taught in civics class that there are three branches of government and that each serves a unique function in relation to the law. The legislative branch makes law. The judicial branch interprets law. And the executive branch enforces law. Although this is true, it is also a little misleading because it suggests that each branch is completely compartmentalized. Actually, all three branches make law.

The legislative branch produces statutory law. The executive branch issues executive orders and administrative rules. The judicial branch creates common law and law of equity. In the United States, sources of law include constitutions, statutes, executive orders, administrative agencies, federal departments, and the judiciary. The most important source of law, however, is the U.S. Constitution.

Constitutions

A political entity's constitution is the supreme law of the land because it is the foundation for government itself.[1] The constitution specifies the organization, powers, and limits of government, as well as the rights guaranteed to citizens. Because the legislative, judicial, and executive branches of government draw their power from the U.S. Constitution, they cannot act in opposition to it. It is only through a three-fourths vote from the states that the Constitution may be altered.

In addition to the federal Constitution, there are 50 state constitutions. States are sovereign entities with the power to make their own laws. However, their laws must operate in accord with their own constitutions and the federal Constitution. The U.S. Constitution also requires that states give "full faith and credit" to each other's laws and judicial decisions.

Statutes

When we think about the word "law," we generally have in mind the statutes passed by our elected representatives as part of city councils, county commissions, state legislatures, and the U.S. Congress. These laws, called ordinances at the city level and statutes at the state and federal level, are meant to serve as guidance to people before they act. Criminal law, in particular, must give people fair warning that an act is illegal before punishing them for violating it, so it is always statutory.

Statutes are intended to address potential social needs and problems, so they are written broadly to apply to a variety of circumstances. But their broad language sometimes creates confusion regarding the meaning of particular terms. In such cases, it falls to courts to interpret their meaning. Courts do this by looking at the statutory construction of laws, otherwise known as their *legislative history*. When laws are passed, they go through a series of committees. Each committee files a report, documenting its actions related to the law. This history of the legislative process usually includes the legislators' intent regarding the law's scope and interpretation. Judges may review the reports to find out what was discussed when legislators were hammering out the legislation and how they intended it to be applied.

As you read federal statutes, you will notice that many of them apply to activities carried out through "interstate or foreign commerce." For example, the federal stalking statute applies to anyone who uses "a facility of *interstate or foreign commerce* to engage in a course of conduct that causes substantial emotional distress."

Likewise, federal law prohibits the transmission of obscene materials through *interstate and foreign commerce*. This phraseology is added to bring activities within the federal government's jurisdiction. The federal government does not have police powers as states do. So it regulates illegal activity through its exclusive jurisdiction over commerce. Article 1, Section 8 of the U.S. Constitution gives Congress the power "To regulate Commerce with foreign Nations, and among the several States …" Application of the term "commerce" does not mean that money must change hands. When the Constitution was written, commerce was also used in a non-economic context to refer to conduct. Congress applies the term loosely to conduct that crosses state and national borders. Activities carried on within a single state must be regulated under state law.

Executive orders

Within the executive branch of government, mayors, governors, and presidents have the power to issue *executive orders*, which are legally binding. Some executive orders are issued to fill in the details of legislation passed by the legislative branch. For example, if Congress passes a bill requiring action on the part of federal agencies without providing sufficient information about how its mandate is to be implemented, the president may issue an executive order specifying procedure.

In other cases, executives issue orders of their own accord to promote their policies or to regain order in the event of a threat to security. Following a natural disaster like a hurricane, for example, a governor may issue a state of emergency, which would empower him or her to make binding rules for a certain period of time.

Executive orders are passed without the legislature's consent, but the legislature may override them with enough votes. Congress could override a presidential executive order, for example, with a two-thirds vote.

Administrative agencies and federal departments

Also within the executive branch, independent administrative agencies and federal departments are empowered to make administrative rules that carry the force of law.

Independent administrative agencies   Independent administrative agencies are so named because, although they are part of the executive branch of government, they carry out the mandates of the legislative branch in specific government-regulated industries. Agencies monitor technical areas of law thought to be better handled by specialists than members of Congress. Not only do they have the power to make rules and enforce them with fines and other retaliatory measures, but federal agencies also serve a quasi-judicial function. Their administrative courts are the first to hear cases related to violations of agency rules.

Congress passed the *Administrative Procedures Act* in 1946, to specify the proto-col for agency rule-making and enforcement.[2] One of the Act's purposes is to keep agency rulemaking open to provide opportunities for public participation. To that end, the law requires agencies to publish notices of proposed rulemaking, opinions, and statements of policy in the Federal Register. Administrative rules are later codi-fied in the Code of Federal Regulations.

Another purpose of the Administrative Procedures Act is to keep the process for rulemaking and adjudication across agencies relatively consistent by prescribing uniform standards and a mechanism for judicial oversight. A federal court may set aside an agency decision if the rule is "arbitrary and capricious, an abuse of discre-tion, or otherwise not in accordance with the law."[3] It is not the court's role to substitute its judgment for the agency's, but to ensure that when an agency creates a new rule or modifies established policy that it articulates "a satisfactory explana-tion for its action including a 'rational connection between the facts found and the choice made.'"[4] A court may conclude that an agency action is arbitrary and capri-cious if it has

- relied on factors Congress did not intend it to consider;
- failed to consider an important aspect of the problem;
- offered an explanation for its decision that contradicts evidence before the agency; or
- is too implausible to be ascribed to a difference in view or agency expertise.[5]

Independent agencies most likely to be involved with digital media law are the Federal Communications Commission and Federal Trade Commission. The Federal Communications Commission regulates interstate and international communica-tion emanating from the United States. The Federal Trade Commission enforces fair advertising, consumer protection, and antitrust rules.

Federal departments   Federal departments also make administrative rules, but do not act independently of the executive branch of government. Their leaders are appointed by the president and make up the president's cabinet. The federal depart-ments most likely to be involved with digital media law are the Departments of Commerce and Justice. The Department of Commerce fosters economic develop-ment and technological advancement. Among its many bureaus is the National Telecommunications and Information Administration, which acts as the adminis-trative branch's policy advisor for telecommunication issues. It also serves as the contracting agency for the Internet Corporation for Assigned Names and Numbers (ICANN), the nonprofit corporation responsible for the management and coordi-nation of Internet domain names and addresses. The Department of Justice, led by the Attorney General, supervises federal law enforcement. As such, it is involved in the prosecution of crimes, such as incitement to violence, fraud, threats, and distribution of obscenity, that may be carried out through digital media. The Justice Department also represents the United States in civil suits against the government. Cases challenging U.S. law before the Supreme Court frequently include the Attorney General's name as one of the parties.

Common Law and Law of Equity

In all legal systems, the role of courts is to determine whether law is applied appropriately in particular cases. But in common law legal systems, like those of England and its former colonies, courts have the power to make law. In the United States, courts have the power to strike down laws that are unconstitutional as well. Common law legal systems inherited two forms of judge-made law from England – *common law* and *law of equity*.

Common law is customary law that has evolved through the common practices of a people. In theory, judges find or discover common law, but in practice they actually make it. Its history dates back to twelfth-century England. King Henry II appointed judges who would ride out to English territories, divided into *circuits*, judging cases that had accumulated in each village or town. The judges applied laws developed through the central court, called the King's Bench. As they did so, local customs were replaced by a national common law.

Circuit judges applied the common law equally, but equal application does not always ensure a fair outcome. When the rules became too rigid, the common people appealed to the king for mercy. The king referred them to his chancellor, who opened the Court of Chancery to issue equitable relief when it seemed appropriate. The Court of Chancery became a court of equity.

Judges still have the power to grant equitable relief, although they rarely do so in separate courts anymore. Nor is the law of equity a separate legal system. Equity is a supplement to common law that provides remedies common law cannot. Common law has the power to compensate a person for harm after the fact, but no mechanism to prevent an action likely to cause harm. For example, there is no relief under common law to prevent a person who has obtained an illegal copy of a yet-to-be-released feature film from putting it on the Internet. Once it has been published on the Internet, the person who uploaded it can be sued or punished, but by that time the market value of the film may have plummeted. Equity fills the gap. Using the law of equity, a judge can impose a restraining order or injunction to prevent the thief from acting before the harm occurs.

Precedents

The decisions that judges make in common law systems form precedents that later courts follow as law. The practice of following precedents is known as *stare decisis* (pronounced stair-ee da-sy-sis), which literally means "let the decision stand." The part of the case that sets the precedent is called the *holding*. This is the court's actual decision regarding the specific facts of the case. In some cases, a court will be very helpful by saying, "We hold that … ," but other times you have to sift though a lot of text to find the golden nugget.

Collateral statements made by judges are referred to as *obiter dictum* or "dicta." This is all the rest of the text in a judicial opinion. Dicta (which often encompass a lot of analogies, opinions, and explanation) can be interesting, but are not legally binding. Dicta may be used to understand a court's reasoning and provide an indication of how it might rule in the future.

In a decision from an appellate court, which involves a panel of judges, the precedent or holding comes in the part of the opinion issued by the court's majority. When judges on the panel support the conclusion rendered in the *majority opinion*, but for different reasons, they issue a *concurring opinion* that supplies an alternative analysis. Judges who disagree with the majority's conclusion issue a *dissenting opinion*. Concurring and dissenting opinions are published with the majority opinion, so someone reading the case can acquire a full understanding of the court's reasoning. Occasionally, an appellate court will release a *plurality opinion*, in which there is majority support for a conclusion but no majority support for a rationale supporting the conclusion. The plurality's opinion is the rationale that received the most support. Plurality opinions are narrowly interpreted. Only those aspects of the plurality opinion that draw support from concurring judges are binding.

Court precedents are either binding or persuasive. A *binding precedent* is one that a court must follow. A *persuasive precedent* is one that a court may use as guidance but also has the prerogative to reject. Whether a precedent is binding depends on the court's jurisdiction and hierarchy. *Jurisdiction* refers to the forum in which the case will be decided. There are two separate systems of jurisdiction – the federal system and the state system. A decision from a higher court always binds a lower court in the same jurisdiction.

Modifying, distinguishing, and overruling precedents

The concept of stare decisis may lead one to assume that common law courts are always bound by earlier precedents. In fact, they are not. The law is a lot like a coral reef. Precedents build upon one another in some areas, while in other areas they remain relatively consistent or may even be torn down.

Courts have the option of modifying, distinguishing, or overruling precedents. Courts *modify* a precedent when they adapt it to fit a new situation. For example, courts had to modify "print-based" precedents to fit the first copyright cases related to the Internet. Courts *distinguish* a precedent when they determine that it does not fit the particular case or situation under analysis. For example, when the Supreme Court reviewed the Communications Decency Act, a law intended to control indecency on the Internet, the government tried to persuade the Court that the Act's restrictions on Internet speech were analogous to restrictions imposed on "dial-a-porn" that had already been upheld. The Court distinguished the dial-a-porn precedent from the Internet case because they dealt with different media. Courts *overrule* precedents when they decide that the precedents are no longer good law. For example, the Supreme Court decided in 1915 that films were public spectacles unworthy of First Amendment protection.[6] The Court reversed its opinion in 1952, deciding that films, like other media, are a form of protected expression.[7]

The Difference Between Common and Civil Law Legal Systems

Common law legal systems are unique to England and her former colonies. Civil law systems are actually more common. Civil law is used in most of Europe, all of Central and South America, parts of Asia and Africa, and in some states within common law countries, such as Louisiana in the United States and Quebec in Canada.[8] Judges do not make law in civil law systems. They rely exclusively on statutory law, usually set down in codes that are cohesively structured. Civil law is based on deductive logic. There is one rule of law and decisions for cases are drawn from the rule. In contrast, common law relies on inductive logic. The rule is based on a general conclusion from a number of cases.

Not only is civil law the dominant legal system, it is also the oldest. Its heritage can be traced back to the early Roman Empire. In the sixth century, the Emperor Justinian amassed all law into a unified code called the *Corpus Juris Civilis*. More commonly known as the Justinian code, it included a dictate that rejected precedent. It stated that "decisions should be rendered in accordance, not with examples, but with the law."[9] This policy can be traced back to Roman tradition, in which judges were appointed on a case-by-case basis and magistrates were appointed for no more than one year. As such, their individual decisions were not accorded much weight.[10]

As an alternative to stare decisis, civil law judges follow the doctrine of *jurisprudence constante*. The doctrine of jurisprudence constante does not require judges to follow earlier precedents; nevertheless, judicial deference to earlier decisions is commonplace. "Under civil law tradition, while a single decision is not binding on courts, when a series of decisions form a 'constant stream of uniform and homogenous rulings having the same reasoning,' jurisprudence constante applies and operates with 'considerable persuasive authority.'"[11]

The Structure of Court Systems

A court's jurisdiction and hierarchy within the system determines whether the decision it renders will be a binding precedent. So a basic knowledge of the structure of court systems is essential before reading particular cases. In the United States there are two court systems: the federal system and the state system. Whether a case enters the federal or state system depends on the issue and parties involved.

The federal court system

Federal courts address cases that involve constitutional questions, federal statutes, and treaties. They also hear bankruptcy cases and diversity cases, which involve parties from different states, if the amounts in controversy exceed $75,000.

The federal court system includes the U.S. Supreme Court, U.S. Courts of Appeals, U.S. District Courts and bankruptcy courts. Congress has also created legislative courts with reduced powers. These include the U.S. Court of Military Appeals, U.S. Tax Court and U.S. Court of Veterans Appeals.

The point of entry for a case in the federal system is the *district court*. This is the trial level (that comes closest to television depictions of trials), where one judge sits on the bench, witnesses take the stand, and a jury examines the evidence to determine the facts of the case. The federal system is divided into 94 judicial districts, each staffed with multiple judges. Each state, along with the District of Columbia and U.S. territories, includes at least one district. Larger states, like Texas, may include as many as four districts located in different parts of the state.

Above the trial level is the appellate level. Courts of appeals review lower court decisions to make sure the law was applied correctly. A panel of judges – usually three – examines the case to make sure judicial rules were followed, that proper witnesses were allowed, and that juries received correct instructions. A court of appeals normally does not re-examine the facts of a case. If, in the course of its review, an appellate court finds that a fact is still in dispute that could materially affect the outcome of the trial, it will send the case back (called *remanding* it) for a retrial to resolve the issue. Because there are no witnesses at the appellate level – only transcripts, lawyers, and judges – courtroom drama is considerably diminished.

Federal courts of appeals are divided into autonomous circuits. A decision from an appellate court is binding within its own circuit, but it does not bind courts in other circuits. There are 13 federal circuits within the United States. Eleven of them are drawn from clusters of states and U.S. territories.

First Circuit	Maine, Massachusetts, New Hampshire, Puerto Rico, Rhode Island
Second Circuit	Connecticut, New York, Vermont
Third Circuit	Delaware, New Jersey, Pennsylvania, Virgin Islands
Fourth Circuit	Maryland, North Carolina, South Carolina, Virginia, West Virginia
Fifth Circuit	Louisiana, Mississippi, Texas
Sixth Circuit	Kentucky, Michigan, Ohio, Tennessee
Seventh Circuit	Illinois, Indiana, Wisconsin
Eighth Circuit	Arkansas, Iowa, Minnesota, Missouri, Nebraska, North Dakota, South Dakota
Ninth Circuit	Alaska, Arizona, California, Guam, Hawaii, Idaho, Montana, N. Mariana Islands, Oregon, Washington
Tenth Circuit	Colorado, Kansas, New Mexico, Utah, Oklahoma, Wyoming
Eleventh Circuit	Alabama, Florida, Georgia

The other two federal circuits, which are located in Washington, D.C., are related to specific topics. The U.S. Court of Appeals for the District of Columbia Circuit hears appeals from administrative agencies. The U.S. Court of Appeals for the Federal Circuit hears appeals in specialized cases. These include cases on patent law or cases that come from the Court of International Trade and the Court of Federal Claims.

In exceptional cases, the judges sitting on a circuit court of appeals may, at the request of one of the litigants or a circuit judge, vote to vacate a three-judge panel's decision and review the case *en banc*. In an en banc hearing, the full court sits to rehear and decide the case. Such reviews are rarely granted unless the panel's judgment was out of sync with the court's earlier decisions or the case involves a legal question of particular importance.

Decisions rendered by federal circuit courts may be appealed to the U.S. Supreme Court, which binds every lower court on constitutional and federal law. The Supreme Court hears very few cases comparatively, usually between 80 and 100 a year. When it agrees to hear a case, it grants a *writ of certiorari*.[12] The Court grants certiorari only to those cases that pose a significant legal issue. The Supreme Court has original jurisdiction (the right to be the first to hear a case) in two types of cases: those involving ambassadors and those in which the United States is a party. In all other cases, it has appellate jurisdiction. As with courts of appeals, cases involve written briefs and oral arguments presented by attorneys, but no witnesses or juries. Court justices issue written opinions, explaining their decisions, months after hearing the case.

The Supreme Court has nine members – eight justices and a chief justice. They are Chief Justice John Roberts and Justices Ruth Bader Ginsburg, Sonia Sotomayor, Clarence Thomas, Stephen Breyer, Antonin Scalia, John Paul Stevens, Anthony Kennedy, and Samuel Alito. Occasionally, one of the justices will have a conflict of interest that makes it inappropriate to hear the case. For example, he or she may have a prior relationship with one of the parties. In such a case, the justice will voluntarily remove him or herself from the case, a process known as *recusal*. This would leave eight justices to decide the case. In the event of a tie, the lower court's decision would stand.

The state court system

As sovereign entities, states constitute jurisdictions of their own. Although a lower court is bound by the decisions of a higher court within its own state, it is not required to follow the decisions of courts in other states. If, however, a court is dealing with an issue on which there is no case law in its state, the court will examine the way other states have addressed the issue and potentially adopt another state court's approach if it is persuasive.

At the state level, cases enter trial courts of limited or general jurisdiction. *Courts of limited jurisdiction*, which account for 90 percent of all courts in the United States, handle small cases involving misdemeanor behavior in criminal matters and sums under $10,000 in civil matters. Most common are justice of the peace courts, magistrate courts, municipal courts, city courts, county courts, juvenile courts, and domestic relations courts.[13] More serious criminal and civil cases are tried in *courts of general jurisdiction*. These courts are usually divided into districts or circuits based on existing political boundaries for counties or groups of counties. They are commonly called district, circuit, or superior courts.

The decisions of lower courts may be appealed to intermediate appellate courts, usually called courts of appeals. Most states have one appellate court, but larger states like California have regional appellate courts. Because it is assumed that all cases deserve at least one appeal, intermediate appellate courts have little discretion over whether to accept cases from the trial level.

Each state also has a court of last resort, usually called its supreme court. These courts, which usually have three to nine judges sitting en banc, are the final arbiters on state law. Most courts of last resort sit in states with intermediate appellate courts and therefore have the power to exercise discretion over the cases they choose to hear.[14] Like the U.S. Supreme Court, they generally elect to review only those cases that involve important policy issues.

Types of Law

Within the common law system, there are two different types of law: criminal law and civil law. The term civil law can be confusing because it has two meanings. As discussed earlier, civil law refers to a type of legal system that is distinct from the common law system used in the United States. Within the United States, the term civil law more commonly characterizes law that regulates relationships between private parties. Criminal law, prosecuted by the government, is probably more familiar to you because it is more commonly depicted in books, movies, and television. Unfortunately, these dramatic representations tend to gloss over the specifics.

Criminal law

Criminal law addresses violations against the state (government) that, even if directed toward an individual, are considered an offense to society as a whole. It may include the commission of an illegal act (like computer fraud or cyberstalking) or the omission of a duty (through negligent conduct, for example) that causes public harm. A state may sanction the violation of a criminal law by fines or imprisonment as long as the punishment, like the crime, was clearly outlined in a statute passed by a legislative body before the act occurred.

Grand juries and preliminary hearings   The Fifth Amendment guarantees a grand jury hearing to anyone accused of a federal crime. Most grand juries consist of 16 to 23 citizens pulled from voter registration lists, who are empanelled for a period ranging from one month to one year. The federal prosecutor submits his or her evidence to the jury, which determines whether there is probable cause to believe the accused committed a federal crime. The accused is not present at the time. If, after hearing the evidence, the jury is convinced there is probable cause to warrant a trial, it will issue a formal accusation of a felony, called an *indictment*, against the accused. Grand jury hearings and records are closed to the public. The Supreme Court has provided three justifications for this secrecy:

> (1) disclosure of pre-indictment proceedings would make many prospective witnesses "hesitant to come forward voluntarily, knowing that those against whom they testify would be aware of that testimony"; (2) witnesses who did appear "would be less likely to testify fully and frankly as they would be open to retribution as well as inducements"; and (3) there "would be the risk that those about to be indicted would flee or would try to influence individual grand jurors to vote against indictment."[15]

States have the option of using preliminary hearings led by a judge as an alternative to a grand jury hearing. The accused may be present at a preliminary hearing and may even present evidence in his or her favor, although most elect not to at that time. Preliminary hearings are also open to the public.

Arraignments   Once a grand jury or judge has determined there is probable cause for a trial, the accused goes before a judge, where he or she is read the formal charge and issues a plea in a proceeding called an *arraignment*. It is important to understand the distinction between an arrest and an arraignment to avoid publishing inaccurate information that could lead to a defamation suit. Only after an arraignment is it correct to publish that someone was "charged" with a crime. If the defendant's plea is "guilty," the judge may issue a sentence. If the plea is "not guilty," a trial date is set. At the state level only 10 percent of cases actually make it to trial. Most are *plea bargained* before trial, meaning the prosecutor and defendant agree to a deal that usually involves some form of leniency in exchange for a guilty plea.

The Sixth Amendment to the Constitution guarantees "a speedy and public trial" by an impartial jury in all criminal prosecutions. In the Speedy Trial Act of 1974, Congress interpreted the term "speedy" to mean that a trial must ensue within 100 days after criminal charges are filed or the case must be dismissed. States have enacted similar measures.

The jury   Potential jurors are subjected to a process called *voir dire* (pronounced vwahr deer) to assess their suitability for jury service. During this period, the prosecution and defense ask potential jurors questions regarding their knowledge and attitudes about the case, as well as any relevant personal experiences or connections that might influence their decision. A common misperception is that potential jurors must not have heard anything about the case to be selected. That is not a requirement. It is only necessary that potential jurors believe themselves to be capable of impartiality. During the selection process, each side is given a number of peremptory challenges, which are opportunities to strike a person from the jury pool for no specific reason. These are useful when a potential juror displays no overt biases, but the attorney still has a bad feeling about the person. Peremptory challenges may not, however, be used to strike a juror on the basis of race or gender.[16] Strikes for cause are unlimited. Attorneys do not have to use one of their peremptory strikes to exclude a juror who displays an obvious bias regarding the case.

In a federal criminal trial, a jury must have 12 members who reach a unanimous decision. At the state level, a jury may be smaller and a slight variation in votes is acceptable. It is the jury's job to decide the facts of the case and render a verdict. It is the judge's job to make sure proper procedure is followed during the trial and to instruct the jurors about the meaning of the law and how it is to be applied. In most states, and at the federal level, the judge imposes the sentence.[17] However, some states place this responsibility on the jury.

Grounds for appeal   Approximately one-third of criminal verdicts are appealed. The appeal must be based on the contention that the law was misapplied, not that the facts were misinterpreted. Acceptable reasons might be that inadmissible evidence was allowed, jury selection was flawed, or the judge's instructions were incorrect. A successful appeal usually results in a new trial.

Civil law

Civil law involves disagreements between people or organizations in which the court's role is to help settle the dispute. This may involve the issuance of an injunction that requires someone to do something or prohibits someone from doing something, or the imposition of a fine. It does not involve imprisonment. On rare occasions, a state may be a party to a civil suit, but this is the exception rather than the rule.

Civil cases are more common than criminal cases.[18] They generally involve disputes over contracts, the ownership or use of property, inheritance, domestic relations (involving marriage, divorce, child custody), and torts. A tort is a civil wrong resulting from conduct that causes injury. Torts associated with digital media law include defamation, invasion of privacy, and infringement of intellectual property, among others.

Civil procedure   Civil procedure differs from criminal procedure in a number of respects. First, there is no prosecutor in civil cases. One party (the *plaintiff*) brings a suit against another party (the *defendant* or *respondent*). The plaintiff must have *standing* – a personal stake in the outcome of the case – in order to initiate the suit. Without standing, there is no real controversy between the parties for a court to settle. Second, the standard of proof required to win a civil case is less stringent than in criminal cases. It is usually sufficient for a plaintiff to show that the "preponderance of evidence" demonstrates the defendant's guilt. Plaintiffs are not required to demonstrate guilt beyond a reasonable doubt, the standard used in criminal trials. Third, due process protections are weaker in civil trials. The court is not required to provide an attorney for a defendant who cannot afford one, for example. Also, although the Seventh Amendment guarantees the right to a jury in a civil trial, the litigants have the right to waive that option in favor of a bench trial, in which the judge determines the facts of the case in addition to deciding questions of law.[19] When juries are used, they are normally smaller than those used in criminal trials.

To initiate a suit, the plaintiff or the plaintiff's attorney files a petition, called a *complaint*, outlining the circumstances that led to the dispute, the damages alleged and the compensation expected. After receiving a summons, announcing the suit, the defendant or defendant's attorney may file a *motion* with the court to strike parts of the suit that are improper or irrelevant or to dismiss it entirely because it was improperly filed or because there is no sound basis for the suit.[20] If the court rejects the defendant's motions, the defendant will have to respond to the suit. The response, called the defendant's *answer*, may contain an admission, denial, defense, or counterclaim.[21]

At that point, the trial will enter a *discovery* phase in which the litigants gather and share information related to the dispute. Although surprises make good drama in television courtrooms, they are not appreciated in real trials. Opposing parties are obligated to disclose their evidence to each other before the trial. Pre-trial discovery, which is used in civil and criminal trials, gives each side the opportunity to search for new information to explain or rebut the opposing party's evidence, and minimizes opportunities to falsify evidence.[22] In civil trials, putting all of the evidence out on the table also encourages settlements before the case can go to trial. Litigants use a variety of tools for discovery. One of the most common is the *deposition*. In a deposition, potential witnesses describe what they know, under oath, before the trial begins. Depositions normally occur in one of the attorney's offices. All parties are notified in advance so they can be present to hear the witness's testimony. The counsel for both the plaintiff and the defendant may question the witness during a deposition. Information is also gathered through *interrogatives*, which are questionnaires that the opposing party answers under oath. Each party is also entitled to request the opposition's list of witnesses to be called at trial, a summary of anticipated expert testimony, and any documents that may be used in the case as evidence.

Summary judgment   Either party in the trial may motion for a summary judgment in his or her favor. A *summary judgment* is a ruling that all factual issues have been discovered and the case can be decided on the facts without a trial. If, after considering the pleadings, depositions, answers to interrogatories, affidavits, and admissions on file, the judge determines that there is no genuine issue of material fact and that as a matter of law the motioning party is entitled to a judgment, the judge may render a summary judgment in the case.[23] If the court refuses to issue a summary judgment, the case will go to trial.

If the district court issues a summary judgment and the opposing party believes material facts remain that justify a full trial, he or she may appeal the summary judgment. An appellate court may choose to review *de novo* (anew) the evidence leading to the district court's summary judgment. If it does so, it will review the evidence in the light most favorable to the nonmoving party.

Remedies   If a case involves an issue of equity, a judge may issue a *preliminary injunction* to prevent one party from doing something that harms the other party until the case can be considered fully at trial. Before granting an injunction to a plaintiff, the court must be satisfied that (1) there is a substantial likelihood that the plaintiff would win a case against the defendant if it were to go to trial; (2) that the plaintiff would suffer "irreparable harm" without the injunction; (3) that the harm the plaintiff suffers would be worse than any harm the defendant would suffer from the injunction; and (4) that the injunction would not harm the public's interest.[24] If a full trial justifies the preliminary injunction, the court will replace it with a *permanent injunction*.

If, on the other hand, the damage is already done and the judge or jury finds that the defendant is responsible, the defendant may be punished with a monetary fine. Civil juries issue two types of damage awards: compensatory and punitive. *Compensatory damages* compensate the victim for actual loss. *Punitive damages*, which may be awarded in addition to compensatory damages, serve as punishment and to set an example for future offenders.

Doctrine of respondeat superior   The civil liability doctrine of *respondeat superior* allows plaintiffs to sue not only the person directly responsible for a tort, but those who may be tangentially responsible. Literally it comes from the ancient idea that the master is responsible for the servant. In modern times, it means the employer is responsible for the employee. People take advantage of the doctrine of respondeat superior when they are looking for deeper pockets. This means that if you are employed by a company, your company may also be liable for your actions if you violate the law. If you own a company, it means that you may be liable for your employees' actions and should have a good errors and omissions insurance policy.

Appeals   If the losing party feels that the court's judgment was reached in error because the law was somehow misapplied, he or she can ask the court to set aside its verdict. If the court refuses to do so, the losing party may appeal the decision. A losing party who is legally entitled to a review will become the *appellant*, while the opposing party becomes the *appellee*. If the higher court's review is discretionary, the losing party may petition for a writ of certiorari, a court order granting a review. The party requesting the review will be the *petitioner*. The opposing party will be the *respondent*. Case names are likely to change on appeal. A lawsuit brought by Jones against Smith will begin life as *Jones v. Smith*. If Smith loses and initiates an appeal, the case name will switch to *Smith v. Jones*.

The significance of judicial review

The power of judicial review refers to a courts' authority to review the decisions of other branches of government. Judicial review is the power of a court to declare a law unconstitutional – in effect, to strike it down. Theoretically, any federal court in the United States has this power, but lower courts are reluctant to use it because it is guaranteed to lead to an appeal and embarrassment if the decision is overturned.

Although the framers of the Constitution never specifically granted the Supreme Court the power of judicial review, the Court nevertheless decided it must have that authority in *Marbury v. Madison* (1803).[25] The case involved a judicial appointment that President Adams made before leaving office following his loss to Thomas Jefferson. Several of Adams' judicial appointees were confirmed by the Senate, but Adams' secretary of state did not have time to issue their commissions before leaving office. When Jefferson assumed the presidency, he asked his new secretary of state, James Madison, not to issue the commissions because he wanted to appoint his own judges to the bench. William Marbury, who was in line for a federal judgeship, asked the Supreme Court to issue a *writ of mandamus*, a court order compelling a public official to do his duty, to force Madison to turn over the commission. Congress gave the Supreme Court the power to issue writs of mandamus in the Judiciary Act of 1789. But the Constitution does not give the Supreme Court original jurisdiction in such matters. Facing an untenable position, the Court concluded that the law must be unconstitutional and therefore invalid. In terms of constitutional law, the decision is the most important the Supreme Court has ever made. Shortly after, in *Martin v. Hunter's Lessee* (1816), the Court also held that it had the power to determine whether the decision of a state's legislature is constitutional.[26]

The Supreme Court's assertion of judicial review was controversial because it vested the one branch of government that is not democratically elected with the greatest power. However, the Court has used that power to protect minority rights that might otherwise have been trampled by the majority. Judicial review is particularly important to media law. Without it, courts would not have the power to strike down laws that impinge upon the First Amendment. Having that power over states also means that the Court can prevent 50 inconsistent laws.

How to Find the Law

To be confident of your knowledge of the law, you need to know how to find it. Fortunately, most legal resources are now available through computerized databases and the Internet. Below are the primary sources of law and directions to read citations used with them.

Constitutions   Constitutions are the ultimate source of law for a political body. The U.S. Constitution can be found online through the Government Printing Office website at http://www.gpoaccess.gov/constitution/index.html. State constitutions can be found online at http://www.constitution.org/cons/usstcons.htm. Citations indicate the applicable jurisdiction in abbreviated form, article, section (indicated by §) and clause:

Jurisdiction	Article	Section	Clause
U.S. Const.	art. III	§ 2	cl. 2
N.Y. Const.	art. I	§ 9	cl. 2

Federal and state codes   Federal, state, and municipal laws are arranged topically in codes. Federal statutes are amassed in the United States Code (U.S.C.), which is divided into 50 titles, categorized by subject. Title 17, for example, contains copyright law. Citations indicate the title of the U.S. Code, the section number, and the date of the compilation:

Title	Code	Section	Date
17	U.S.C.	§ 106	(2000)

The U.S. Code is published every six years. In between editions, the government releases annual supplements. The official version is available through the Government Printing Office website at http://www.gpoaccess.gov/USCODE/index.html. Annotated versions of the U.S. Code, such as the U.S. Code Annotated (U.S.C.A.) and the U.S. Code Service (U.S.C.S.), are available through commercial databases like Westlaw and Lexis-Nexis. The citations are similar, but the publisher is often included with the compilation date:

Title	Code	Section	Publisher and Date
17	U.S.C.A.	§ 106	(Thomson/West 2000)
17	U.S.C.S.	§ 106	(LexisNexis 2000)

State codes also come in official and commercial annotated versions, e.g. the Iowa Code and the Iowa Code Annotated. Citations to state codes include the name of the code, the section number and the date of the compilation:

Iowa Code § 321 (2005)
Iowa Code Ann. § 321 (Thomson/West 2005)

State statutes can be found easily through commercial databases like Lexis or Westlaw, but are also available on the Internet though Cornell's Legal Information Institute at http://www.law.cornell.edu/statutes.html.

Administrative regulations and executive orders   Federal agency rules, proposed rules, and notices, as well as executive orders and other presidential documents, are published daily in the Federal Register (abbreviated as either FR or Fed. Reg.), which can be found at http://www.gpoaccess.gov/fr/. Citations to agency notices include the volume number, abbreviation for Federal Register, page number, and publication date:

Vol.	Publication	Page	Date
73	FR	143	(June 30, 2008)

Citations to executive orders include the same information preceded by the executive order number:

Exec. Order No. 13,462, 73 FR 11805 (March 4, 2008)

Federal department and agency rules published in the Federal Register are eventually codified in the Code of Federal Regulations (C.F.R.), located at http://www.gpoaccess.gov/CFR/. The C.F.R. is divided into 50 titles related to specific subject areas. Citations include the title, abbreviation for Code of Federal Regulations, section number, and date.

Title	Code	Section	Date
16	C.F.R.	§ 255.1	(2008)

Court opinions Court decisions are initially released as slip opinions, published on court websites, arranged by date or docket number. Eventually, these decisions are collected in bound volumes called case reporters that are paginated, annotated, and accompanied by topical digests. The commercial services that produce case reporters sell access to the same information through Westlaw and Lexis-Nexis. These searchable, full-text databases are expensive, but often available to college students free through their university libraries. Findlaw.com offers searchable versions of slip opinions for free.

Supreme Court decisions are published in United States Reports (U.S.), the official case reporter for Supreme Court decisions, and the commercial reporters Supreme Court Reporter (S.Ct.), U.S. Law Week (USLW), and United States Supreme Court Reports, Lawyers' Edition (L.Ed. or L.Ed.2d). Oral arguments can be heard online through the Oyez Project at http://www.oyez.org.

Citations to Supreme Court cases provide the case name, volume, abbreviated name of the reporter, beginning page of the case, and date the case was decided. It is sufficient to reference a case by its official citation, but some authors and courts supply parallel citations to make a case easier to find:

Case name	Vol.	Reporter	Page	Year
ACLU v. Reno,	521	U.S.	844	(1997)
ACLU v. Reno,	117	S.Ct.	2329	(1997)

U.S. Court of Appeals opinions are reported in the Federal Reporter (F., F.2d, F.3d). Volumes for 1950–93 are online at http://bulk.resource.org/courts.gov/c/F2/. Citations include the case name, volume, abbreviated name of the reporter, beginning page of the case and, in parentheses, the circuit in which the case was decided and date:

Case name	Vol.	Reporter	Page	Circuit and Year
Taubman Co. v. Webfeats,	244	F.3d	572	(7th Cir. 2001)

Selected U.S. District Court opinions appear in the Federal Supplement (F. Supp.). Citations include the case name, volume, abbreviated name of the reporter, beginning page of the case and, in parentheses, the district in which the case was decided and date:

Case name	Vol.	Reporter	Page	District and Year
Doe v. MySpace,	474	F.Supp.2d	843	(W.D. Tex. 2007)

State court opinions appear in regional reporters that collect opinions from several states. These include West's Atlantic Reporter, North Eastern Reporter, North Western Reporter, Pacific Reporter, South Eastern Reporter, South Western Reporter, and Southern Reporter. The citation 807 A.2d 847 (Pa. 2002), for example, indicates that the opinion appears in volume 807 of the Atlantic Reporter, 2nd series, on page 847, and that the case was decided by the Pennsylvania Supreme Court in 2002. Some states also have their own reporters.

Secondary sources   Secondary sources of information, such as law review and journal articles, can provide helpful background and analysis to understand a legal issue. Digital versions of law reviews are available by subscription through Westlaw, Lexis-Nexis and Hein Online. Findlaw.com compiles some full text versions of law reviews at http://stu.findlaw.com/journals/general.html.

A law review citation includes the author's name, article title, journal volume, abbreviated journal name, page on which the article begins, and date of publication. A second page number refers to a specific citation in the text:

Dan Hunter, Cyberspace as Place and the Tragedy of the Digital Anticommons, 91 CAL. L. REV. 439, 491 (2003)

This citation indicates that the article "Cyberspace as Place and the Tragedy of the Digital Anticommons" written by Dan Hunter, appears in volume 91 of the California Law Review, printed in 2003, beginning on page 439, with a particular reference on 491.

Some helpful sites with government information

Library of Congress, http://www.loc.gov, for copyright information.

Library of Congress Thomas, http://thomas.loc.gov/home/thomas.ht, for pending bills and legislative history.

U.S. Patent and Trademark Office, http://www.uspto.gov, for trademarks and software patents.

U.S. Federal Communications Commission, http://www.fcc.gov, for telecommunications regulations.

U.S. Federal Trade Commission, http://www.ftc.gov/, for advertising and antitrust rules.

U.S. Department of Justice, http://www.usdoj.gov, and the *Federal Bureau of Investigation*, www.fbi.gov, for information on computer and other federal crimes.

Questions for Discussion

1. What are the four sources of law in the United States? Which is paramount and why?
2. How do hierarchy and jurisdiction determine whether a precedent is binding or persuasive?
3. How do common law and civil law legal systems differ?
4. What is the significance of judicial review and how does it make the U.S. legal system different from other common law legal systems?

2

Freedom of Expression

No other country in the world is more protective of expression than the United States. In fact, some countries believe the United States takes speech protection too far, protecting expression at the expense of other equally important rights, such as personal rights to reputation and privacy. It should not be surprising that nations balance speech protections differently. Each nation forms its concepts of what is acceptable in terms of expression based on its own cultural and political heritage. Countries such as France and Germany, for example, developed a particular sensitivity to the dangers of hate speech following their experiences with Nazism during the 1930s and 1940s. European countries in general are more sensitive to defamation. Their social structures grew out of feudalism during the middle ages and subsequent class divisions that extended through the nineteenth century. Historically, an accusation that marred the reputation of a member of the aristocracy was likely to result in a duel. Strict laws against defamation reduced violence. In contrast, American colonists represented a range of social strata, looking for religious, economic, and expressive freedom. The founding fathers incorporated these values into the U.S. Constitution.

This chapter will explore the First Amendment, the primary means through which expression is protected in the United States. It will consider the varying levels of protection accorded to different media; categories of speech without protection; and the legitimate scope of time, place, and manner restrictions. It will also address questions specifically related to Internet speech, such as whether the Internet is a public forum, computer code is considered speech, and student websites are protected.

The First Amendment

Protection for free expression in the United States draws its power from the First Amendment to the constitution, which says:

Congress shall make no law respecting an establishment of religion, or prohibiting the free exercise thereof; or abridging the freedom of speech, or of the press; or the right of the people peaceably to assemble, and to petition the Government for a redress of grievances.

In those 45 words, the founding fathers integrated a number of rights: the right to freely exercise one's religious beliefs, protection against state establishment of religion, protection for freedom of speech and the press, the right to assemble freely and with it an implied freedom of association, and the right to petition for a redress of grievances.

The First Amendment's protection for speech and press is foundational to U.S. media law. It distinguishes our national approach to such issues as defamation, hate speech, and obscenity from those of other commonwealth and civil law countries. Other nations have included protections for expression in their constitutions, but no guarantee of speech and press freedom is as broadly stated as the First Amendment.

Ironically, the First Amendment's breadth is sometimes a source of confusion. The Supreme Court and Congress have struggled with its admonition "to make no law abridging freedom of speech."[1] On first reading the language seems clear enough, but it is actually quite open to interpretation. Judges and scholars have debated its meaning for two centuries. What exactly does freedom of speech mean? What does abridgement mean? How far can Congress go before it abridges freedom of speech? Advances in technology have also put the words "or of the press" in doubt. When the founding fathers wrote the First Amendment, the meaning of press was clear: books and newspapers. In the twentieth century, the meaning of press expanded to include radio, film, and television. In the twenty-first century, should it now encompass websites, web logs, pod casts, vod casts, videos on YouTube, and social networking sites?

There is also the question of how closely the text should be followed. First Amendment absolutists, like Justices Hugo Black and William Douglas, interpreted the admonition to make "no law" respecting speech or the press to mean no law whatsoever.[2] Others have felt that the right of expression must be balanced against other rights and societal interests.

The First Amendment's Purpose

No matter how literally the First Amendment is interpreted, one thing is clear: it does not protect all expression. A common misconception is that the First Amendment protects anything we have to say, anywhere we want to say it. Actually, the First Amendment *only protects against government suppression* of expression. It does not prohibit private suppression of expression. If, in a fit of anger, you were to post an announcement on your website that your boss looks like a baboon's rear and later find yourself out of a job, you could not turn to the First Amendment for recourse. Nor could you count on it to protect your expression on someone else's private property – including private onramps to the Internet. If your posts venture into offensive territory, your web host is entitled to ask you to remove the speech. If you refuse to do so, the company may do it for you.

The First Amendment protects speech from government suppression at the city, state, and federal level. Because the First Amendment states "*Congress* shall make no law," the Supreme Court initially interpreted the First Amendment to apply only to the federal government.[3] Circumstances changed, however, when the Fourteenth Amendment was ratified in 1866. The Fourteenth Amendment says:

> No State shall make or enforce any law which shall abridge the privileges or immunities of citizens of the United States; nor shall any State deprive any person of life, liberty, or property, without due process of law; nor deny to any person within its jurisdiction the equal protection of the laws.

In 1925, the Supreme Court modified its position.[4] The Court determined that the Fourteenth Amendment's concept of liberty incorporates freedom of expression and that through the Fourteenth Amendment the First Amendment applies to the states.

The Fourteenth Amendment binds the states to other guarantees in the Bill of Rights as well, under the theory that it incorporates the "fundamental principles of liberty and justice which lie at the base of all our civil and political institutions."[5] This notion has come to be known as the *incorporation doctrine*. In the landmark case *Gideon v. Wainwright* (1963), Justice Black outlined the amendment's scope:

> This Court has looked to the fundamental nature of original Bill of Rights guarantees to decide whether the Fourteenth Amendment makes them obligatory on the States. Explicitly recognized to be of this "fundamental nature" and therefore made immune from state invasion by the Fourteenth, or some part of it, are the First Amendment's freedoms of speech, press, religion, assembly, association, and petition for redress of grievances. For the same reason, though not always in precisely the same terminology, the Court has made obligatory on the States the Fifth Amendment's command that private property shall not be taken for public use without just compensation, the Fourth Amendment's prohibition of unreasonable searches and seizures, and the Eighth's ban on cruel and unusual punishment.[6]

Through the Fourteenth Amendment, the First Amendment also applies in U.S. territories, such as Puerto Rico and Guam,[7] and to aliens legally residing in the United States.[8] The Supreme Court has not incorporated the full Bill of Rights into the Fourteenth Amendment. Rights that the justices do not consider to be "fundamental" remain outside the amendment's reach. These include the Second, Third, and Seventh Amendments and the Fifth Amendment's requirement of grand jury indictments.

Prohibition on prior restraint

Constitutional historians have noted that the founding fathers' understanding of press freedom when the Bill of Rights was written probably mirrored the English definition presented in the authoritative legal text used at the time, William Blackstone's *Commentaries on the Laws of England.*[9] Blackstone interpreted freedom of the press to mean freedom from prior restraint. In other words, he understood it to mean the freedom to publish without prior censorship, but not freedom from punishment after the fact. There is support for the contention that the founding fathers also understood freedom of the press to refer to prior restraint. The First Amendment was ratified in 1791. Only seven years afterward, many of the same men who voted to ratify the Bill of Rights passed The Sedition Act of 1798. The Sedition Act made it a crime to "write, print, utter or publish … any false, scandalous and malicious writing or writings against the government of the United States, or either house of the Congress of the United States, or the President of the United States."[10] Although the meaning of the First Amendment was narrowly understood when it was first written, historian Leonard Levy observes that "it was boldly stated, and that the bold statement, the principle of unqualified free speech, was written into fundamental law and was meant to endure."[11] Levy notes that a broad libertarian theory of expression did emerge within a decade after the constitution's ratification – a contention supported by the fact that the Sedition Act was allowed to expire in 1801.

It was not until the twentieth century that the power of the First Amendment began to take hold. The Supreme Court confirmed that "The chief purpose of the guarantee of freedom of the press is to prevent previous restraint on publication" in the landmark case *Near v. Minnesota* (1931).[12] J.M. Near and Howard Guilford were editors of a scandal sheet called *The Saturday Press*, which vilified Jews and Catholics, among others. Shortly after the first edition was published, Guilford was shot. Near did not think authorities were doing enough to find his assailant and used his paper to make his opinions known. He accused the chief of police of conspiring with Minneapolis gangsters and the local prosecutor of ignoring the matter. Minnesota had an abatement statute against "malicious, scandalous or defamatory newspapers, magazines or periodicals" and used it to enjoin publication of Near's paper. The Supreme Court's opinion, written by Justice Hughs, stated "it has been generally, if not universally, considered that it is the chief purpose of the guaranty [of freedom of the press] to prevent previous restraints upon publication."[13] The Court overturned the state statute as a violation of the First Amendment, concluding that prior restraint would only be allowed in four exceptional cases:

(1) obstruction of military recruitment or the publication of sailing dates, the number or location of troops;

(2) obscenity;

(3) incitements to violent overthrow of government; and

(4)   protection of private rights according to equitable principles. (For example, prior restraints have been upheld in order to protect defendants' rights to a fair trial or plaintiffs' rights to protect their intellectual property.)

Courts have interpreted *Near* to mean that few circumstances other than national security can justify prior restraint on the press. In *New York Times Co. v. United States* (1971), the Supreme Court lifted an injunction barring the *New York Times* from printing the Pentagon's classified record of the Vietnam conflict (otherwise known as the Pentagon Papers) because the government had not met the heavy burden required to warrant an injunction.[14] In a concurring opinion, Justice Stewart explained that publication would not clearly result in "direct, immediate, and irreparable damage to our Nation or its people."[15] But in *United States v. The Progressive*, a federal district court concluded that the *Near* standard was met when it enjoined a magazine from publishing directions to make a hydrogen bomb.[16] Even though the information was available in the public domain in bits and pieces, the court believed that, when synthesized, it was too dangerous. The injunction was lifted later, however, when other publications printed the secret.

   The Supreme Court declared that "prior restraints on speech and publication are the most serious and the least tolerable infringement on First Amendment rights" in *Nebraska Press Association v. Stuart* (1976).[17] The case involved a lower court's attempt to impose a gag order on the media to limit the potential damage of excessive press coverage on the defendant's right to a fair trail. The Supreme Court limited the circumstances in which a judge could issue a prior restraint to prevent excessive media coverage to situations in which no other alternative could curb the damaging effect of the publicity and a restraining order would actually be effective.[18]

Types of prior restraint orders

Prior restraint orders come in three forms: temporary restraining orders, preliminary injunctions, and permanent injunctions. A *temporary restraining order* (TRO) is intended to supply immediate relief. An aggrieved party files a complaint with a court, applying for an order to stop someone from engaging in an action that if continued will result in "irreparable injury" before the matter can be heard in a formal court proceeding. Because the defendant is not present to defend his or her actions, the court may require the plaintiff to pay a bond to mitigate against any harm that may ensue to the defendant from the TRO if the plaintiff has misrepresented the circumstances. Along with the TRO, the court establishes a hearing date, so the defendant can come before the court to contest the order. At the hearing, the court may replace the TRO with a *preliminary injunction* if the plaintiff establishes both the potential for irreparable harm and the likelihood of winning a suit at trial. The court will also establish a trial date to determine whether issuing a permanent injunction is appropriate. A *permanent injunction*, established after a trial, is a court's final order to enjoin an action permanently.

Normally, the purpose of a temporary restraining order is to preserve the status quo until the court has time to give the matter due consideration. But, according to the U.S. Court of Appeals for the Sixth Circuit, a temporary restraining order "is a different beast in the First Amendment context."[19] In the context of press freedom, the status quo is to "publish news promptly that editors decide to publish. A restraining order disturbs the status quo and impinges on the exercise of editorial discretion."[20] Therefore, a court is obligated to deal with them on an emergency basis. Furthermore, while the criteria a court normally considers before issuing a restraining order include the potential for irreparable harm and the requesting party's likelihood for success on the merits of the suit, in a First Amendment context, "the hurdle is substantially higher: publication must threaten an interest more fundamental than the First Amendment itself."[21]

This guideline is easier for courts to follow when the defendant in danger of censorship is a traditional medium. Courts have been less willing to protect Internet sites that purport to share news, but lack institutional credibility. After international cries of censorship, a federal district court lifted a TRO against the whistleblower website Wikileaks.org and a permanent injunction against its Internet host. WikiLeaks posted documents leaked by a former employee of Julius Baer Bank's Cayman Islands branch, which suggested that some of its clients were involved in money laundering and tax evasion schemes. The Swiss bank filed suit against the website and its web hosting company, Dynadot, in San Francisco, alleging they had engaged in unlawful and unfair business practices under California law and violated the privacy of the bank's clients.[22] Judge Jeffrey White of the U.S. District Court for Northern California signed off on a permanent injunction settlement between Dynadot and Julius Baer, in which Dynadot agreed to disable the WikiLeaks site and lock the domain name to prevent WikiLeaks from moving to another server.

In February 2008, the judge realized that the injunction was not only too broad, but ineffective. In a decision to lift the injunction, he explained that the broad injunction had the opposite effect intended. Not only was the material mirrored on websites all over the world, but the media attention garnered by the injunction increased public awareness that it was available online. In addition to First Amendment concerns, the court realized that its jurisdiction over the case was questionable. When the proceeding began, it was clear that the plaintiff was Swiss. However, it was assumed that the owner of the WikiLeaks domain was a California resident. Only after issuing the TRO against WikiLeaks did the court learn that the defendant was a citizen of Australia and a resident of Kenya. U.S. courts have no jurisdiction over aliens.[23] The court suggested that the permanent injunction it had imposed on Dynadot was not the least restrictive means to protect the bank clients' privacy and that assuming it still had jurisdiction, something more limited, like redaction of their identifying information from the leaked documents, might be more appropriate.

This case highlights a particular characteristic of the Internet that makes censorship ineffective. The phenomenon is known as the Streisand Effect. The term refers to the likelihood that legal action to censor information will draw greater attention to it. Coined by Mike Masnick, the CEO of TechDirt, the Streisand Effect alludes to a lawsuit Barbara Streisand launched against an amateur photographer who inadvertently posted a picture of her home on the web. The defendant, Kenneth Adelman, photographed the California coastline from a helicopter for an environmental project to document coastal erosion. He took 12,000 aerial photos in all. When he put them on the web, he was not aware that Streisand's house was visible in image 3,850. She sued for $10 million for violating a California "anti paparazzi" law and her privacy rights. The media attention from the case peaked the interest of Internet users who downloaded the images en masse.[24] A Los Angeles Superior Court Judge dismissed the suit because it restricted Adelman's speech rights on a matter of public concern. The image is still accessible and now labeled as the Streisand Estate.[25]

© 2002–2009 Kenneth & Gabrielle Adelman, California CoastalRecords Project, www.California coastline.org
Barbra Streisand's lawsuit over an aerial photo of her estate posted on the Internet prompted even more people to search for it.

Expanding the Meaning of the First Amendment

Throughout the twentieth century, protection for expression expanded beyond restrictions on prior restraint. As lawmakers began to understand that statutes could be applied in a variety of ways to restrict speech, they began to interpret the First Amendment as a protection against censorship after the fact, undue burdens on expression, and discriminatory applications of speech regulations. First Amendment cases based on such issues involve *applied challenges* to laws, based on their interference with a particular person's protected speech. The Supreme Court has also recognized facial challenges to laws that violate the First Amendment. A *facial challenge* to a particular statute is based on the argument that regardless of whether the litigant's speech is protected in the particular situation, the statute itself should be struck down because, as written, it has the potential to interfere with or "chill" the protected speech of others – either by limiting more speech than necessary to accomplish its purpose or by leaving people confused by ambiguous wording regarding what is prohibited.

Doctrines of overbreadth and vagueness

The Supreme Court has developed the doctrines of Overbreadth and Vagueness to address facial challenges to laws restricting speech. The *overbreadth doctrine* entitles a court to strike down a law that covers more protected speech or expressive conduct than necessary to accomplish its intended purpose. The Supreme Court explained the doctrine's purpose in *Virginia v. Hicks* (2003):

> We have provided this expansive remedy out of concern that the threat of enforcement of an overbroad law may deter or "chill" constitutionally protected speech – especially when the overbroad statute imposes criminal sanctions … Many persons, rather than undertake the considerable burden (and sometimes risk) of vindicating their rights through case-by-case litigation, will choose simply to abstain from protected speech, … harming not only themselves but society as a whole, which is deprived of an uninhibited marketplace of ideas. Overbreadth adjudication, by suspending all enforcement of an overinclusive law, reduces these social costs caused by the withholding of protected speech.[26]

A court will not invalidate a statute lightly, however. In *Broadrick v. Oklahoma* (1973), the Supreme Court explained that "the overbreadth of the statute must not only be real but substantial as well, judged in relation to the statute's plainly legitimate sweep."[27] When overbreadth is not significant, the Court prefers to uphold the statute but narrow its interpretation.

Unlike the overbreadth doctrine, the *vagueness doctrine* is not specific to First Amendment cases. The Constitution's Fifth and Fourteenth Amendments include the right to due process of law. Due process requires that people be given fair warning regarding conduct that is deemed illegal. An ambiguously written law that fails to do that may be struck down as unconstitutionally vague. The Supreme Court has said that a law is unconstitutionally vague if persons of "common intelligence must necessarily guess at its meaning and differ as to its application."[28] When the challenged law concerns a fundamental right, like expression, the Court demands a higher degree of clarity. Aside from its potential to chill protected speech, a vague law is dangerous because it is subject to discriminatory enforcement by officials who interpret it as they see fit.

The vagueness doctrine is frequently coupled with the overbreadth doctrine in First Amendment cases. For example, in *Reno v. ACLU* (1997), the Supreme Court determined that a provision of the Communications Decency Act banning the Internet transmission of indecent and patently offensive materials to minors was both vague and overbroad.[29] It was vague because the terms *indecent* and *patently offensive* were not defined. It was overly broad because while it was meant to protect minors from indecent speech, it would also suppress speech that adults have the right to send and receive, when less restrictive options were available. Other provisions of the Act remain in place. Congress normally incorporates a severability clause in legislation that allows a court to sever parts of a law it finds unenforceable while retaining the rest of the statute.

Limitations on Protection

Despite the First Amendment's broad application and wording, expression is not completely protected from government suppression. The level of protection for expression varies somewhat depending on the medium used. Categories of speech perceived to be of no value or likely to cause imminent harm garner little or no protection. The time, place, and manner of expression may be controlled when the expression occurs on government property, particularly if it does not comport with the intended use of the property. The government also has more leeway to regulate expressive or symbolic speech and student speech.

Medium specific protection

The Supreme Court does not grant equal First Amendment protection to all media. It bases the level of protection allotted to each form on its distinct characteristics. Print media, which require no special accommodations, get maximum protection from government intervention. Broadcast media, which require use of the public spectrum, operate under government constraints. They must be licensed to operate by the Federal Communications Commission and are subject to content restrictions based on their pervasiveness and accessibility to children. Cable, which relies on public rights of way for its lines, is obligated to carry signals from local broadcast stations, but as a subscription-based medium, it is generally free from content restrictions. Satellite, another subscription medium, must reserve some of its capacity for educational programming and local stations, but its own content is protected from censorship.

Initially the government was unsure about how to characterize the Internet. It is largely print-based, but it also carries audio and video and provides the immediacy of phone service. In reaction to a flawed Carnegie Mellon study spotlighted on the cover of *Time* magazine, which suggested that 83 percent of the images on Usenet groups contained pornography, Congress imposed restrictions on the Internet that would be unconstitutional for print media.[30] It modified the Telecommunications Act to treat cyber porn like dial-a-porn, requiring websites with indecent content to verify that their users were adults via a credit card, debit account, or adult access code, as 900 numbers must do. In 1997, the Supreme Court struck down the legislation, observing that the government's comparison was flawed.[31] It concluded that like print, the Internet is worthy of full First Amendment protection.[32]

© 2009 Time Inc. Reprinted through the courtesy of the Editors of TIME Magazine.
Time magazine's July 1995 cover story "Cyber Porn" prompted Congress to attempt to regulate Internet indecency through the Communications Decency Act, which was later held to be unconstitutional.

Categorical speech protection

A basic assumption in a liberal democracy is that government should not interfere with speech unless it poses a legitimate threat of harm. There are categories of speech that the Supreme Court considers unworthy of First Amendment protection because they carry this potential. These are areas of expression whose value appears to be so slight that they deserve no special consideration. Among them are incitement to violence, criminal solicitation, fighting words, true threats, obscenity, false

commercial speech, and in some cases, libel. Restrictions related to these categories
of speech are discussed in later chapters.

Levels of Judicial Review

Barring an exception for unprotected categories of speech, the government cannot
restrict speech based on its content. In First Amendment cases when courts suspect
that the regulation challenged was put in place to restrict the expression of a particular idea or viewpoint, they subject the regulation to strict scrutiny, the highest
level of judicial review. *Strict scrutiny* demands that content-based regulations be
narrowly tailored to serve a compelling government interest. It is one of three levels
of review that courts impose on government regulations and policies that burden
speech. A mid-tier level of review known as *heightened* or *intermediate scrutiny* is
generally applied to cases involving restrictions that burden speech, but which are
not intended to target a particular idea or point of view. Under heightened scrutiny,
a content-neutral regulation must serve an important government interest and
restrict no more speech than necessary to achieve that interest. When legislative
actions or agency regulations are challenged as arbitrary or capricious, courts
impose a lower level of judicial scrutiny known as the *rational-basis test*. The test
considers whether the government can supply a rational basis for the regulation
and whether the regulation serves a legitimate state interest.

Time, place, and manner restrictions

As the trustee of public property, the government attempts to balance speech interests against its own interest in using public property for its intended purpose. When
speech occurs on public property that is not reserved for speech purposes, the
government may impose nondiscriminatory restrictions on the time, place, and
manner in which the speech is conducted. The Supreme Court suggested that the
question to consider in assessing time, place, and manner restrictions is "whether
the manner of expression is basically incompatible with the normal activity of a
particular place at a particular time."

Forum analysis   The Supreme Court has adopted a forum analysis to assess the
constitutionality of regulations that constrain speech on public property.[33] It identifies three forum tiers for public property: the traditional public forum, the designated public forum, and the nonpublic forum.[34]

   Traditional public forums include public spaces that have traditionally been open
for speech – like parks, street corners, sidewalks, and the steps of city hall. According
to Justice Owen Roberts, these places "have immemorially been held in trust for
the use of the public and, time out of mind, have been used for purposes of assembly, communicating thoughts between citizens, and discussing public questions."[35]

In a traditional public forum, government restrictions on speech are subject to strict scrutiny.

Designated or limited public forums are public places like fairgrounds, town halls, and some public school facilities that government entities have opened to the public as a place for expressive activity.[36] Once public property has been intentionally opened for expressive activity, the government must make it available on a nondiscriminatory basis. But it may still impose reasonable time, place, and manner restrictions in keeping with the property's primary use.

Courts subject "time, place, and manner" restrictions on speech in limited public forums to intermediate scrutiny. They assume that the government may enforce certain restrictions if the following conditions are met:[37]

- The law must be content neutral, both on its face and in the manner in which it is applied.
- The law must not constitute a complete ban on communication. Alternative options must be available to the speaker.
- The law must be narrowly tailored to further a substantial state interest and restrain no more expression than necessary to further that interest.

Consider, for example, a regulation that bans public demonstrations in a neighborhood park between the hours of 10 p.m. and 8 a.m. During daylight hours groups are allowed to engage in expressive activities, but after 10 the park closes for the night. The time constraint may have the unintended effect of limiting expression, but it is not intended to target particular expression, so the regulation would be considered content neutral. It does not impose a complete ban on speech, because groups are free to demonstrate during daylight hours. It also serves an important purpose – ensuring people who live around the park a peaceful period in which to sleep – that is both unrelated to suppression of speech and narrowly tailored to accomplish that goal.

Nonpublic forums include public areas designated for purposes other than expression, such as airport concourses, polling places, subway stations, prisons, and military bases, which have never been opened for speech purposes. Government has the right to restrict speech in these areas.

Is the Internet a public forum?   The question of whether the Internet constitutes a public forum is open for debate. It certainly is a "space" open to the public where information is exchanged. On the other hand, Internet servers are by and large privately owned. An Internet service provider, like Verizon, is well within its rights to withdraw service from any subscriber who violates its rules. Domains ending in .com, .org, .kids, and many of the .edu's are also privately controlled, entitling their owners to remove comments made on interactive sites that they find offensive.

California courts have interpreted the Internet to be a public forum. One appellate court said "Under its plain meaning, a public forum is not limited to a physical setting, but also includes other forms of public communication such as electronic communication media like the internet."[38] Another held that "a website that is accessible free of charge to any member of the public, which provides a forum where members of the public may read the views and information posted, and also post their opinions on the site is deemed to be a public forum."[39]

However, despite its conviction that the Internet is entitled to full First Amendment protection, the Supreme Court has been reluctant to recognize the Internet as a public forum. In *United States v. American Library Association* (2003), the Supreme Court rejected a district court's use of public forum analysis that had concluded the public has a right of access to public library computers, and through them, to the Internet.[40] The case concerned the constitutionality of the Children's Internet Protection Act, which Congress enacted in 2000 to require libraries that receive public funding to install software on their computer terminals to block indecent speech. The Supreme Court did not consider the Internet to be a traditional public forum and would not recognize library terminals as a designated public forum without the government's express intent to transform them into such.

In fact, the Supreme Court has been reluctant to apply forum analysis to any medium. In *Denver Area Educational Telecommunications Consortium v. FCC* (1996), it refused to apply forum analysis to public access cable channels. In the case, which concerned a First Amendment challenge to restrictions on indecency, Justice David Souter said "As broadcast, cable, and the cybertechnology of the Internet and World Wide Web approach the day of using a common receiver, we can hardly assume that standards for judging the regulation of one of them will not have immense, but now unknown and unknowable, effects on the others."[41] The justices were reluctant to apply forum analysis to a "new and changing area."

In his dissent, Justice Kennedy countered that forum analysis was appropriate despite the newness of the medium because, "Minds are not changed in streets and parks as they once were. To an increasing degree, the more significant interchanges of ideas and shaping of public consciousness occur in mass and electronic media."[42]

Lower courts have been willing to entertain the notion that the Internet might be a public forum, but have not found it to be so. In *Putnam Pit v. City of Cookeville* (1998), the Sixth Circuit weighed the question of whether a local publisher was entitled to a link on to the city's website to his publication. Geoffrey Davidian, the publisher of The Putnam Pit, argued that by granting links to anyone who requested one on the city website, the city of Cookeville, Tennessee, had created a designated public forum. After reviewing Supreme Court forum analysis, the court stated that a public forum was a place "which by long tradition or by government fiat has been devoted to assembly and debate …"[43] It concluded that the city website did not allow for "open communication or the free exchange of ideas between members of the public" and therefore was a nonpublic forum.[44] The court based its determination on a two-part test that considered whether the city made the website available to an entire class of speakers and whether it was legitimate to limit speech occurring on the website to "that which is compatible with the forum's purpose."[45] The court observed that links had been granted on a case-by-case basis and deferred to the city administrator's contention that the site's purpose was to provide information about jobs, taxes, and other municipal news.

Must a forum be a place?   The conceptual relationship between the Internet and forum analysis is complicated by the traditional assumption that a forum is a place defined in the sense of real property. This is usually the case. However, it is not axiomatic. A forum also may be a publication or a program that fosters expression (like a mail system,[46] a charitable contribution program,[47] or a Student Activities Fund). For example, in *Rosenburger v. Rector and Visitors of the University of Virginia*, the Supreme Court described the university's Student Activities Fund as "a forum more in a metaphysical than in a spatial or geographic sense, but the same principles are applicable."[48]

Of course, the Internet is not a place. It is a collection of wires and routers and computer servers that transfer bits of data back and forth. Nevertheless, people conceive of it as a place when they refer to it as "cyberspace," a term coined by William Gibson in his 1984 novel *Neuromancer*. This metaphor has a powerful hold on the Internet. When we go online, we visit websites, chat rooms, home pages, simulated worlds, and online communities.[49] Justice O'Connor made this observation in *Reno v. ACLU* when she said, "cyberspace undeniably reflects some form of geography; chat rooms and Web sites, for example, exist at fixed 'locations' on the Internet."[50]

Expressive conduct

Although we normally think of communication as verbal, communication can also be nonverbal. Sit-ins and flag burning, for example, are both forms of expressive conduct meant to communicate a message. So was the 1996 decision by thousands of website operators to blacken their home pages in protest of the Communications Decency Act. But, at the same time, it cannot be assumed that all acts are intended to communicate a message. The act must be evaluated in context. The Supreme Court developed a test for symbolic speech in 1974. Courts are required to consider *whether the intent to convey a particularized message was present, and whether the likelihood was great that the message would be understood by those who viewed it.*[51] The test has since been modified. After reviewing a case that involved a homosexual group's denial of entrance into a parade, the Court pointed out that although there is no particular message in a parade, parading is certainly a "form of expression." A "narrow, succinctly articulable message is not a condition of constitutional protection."[52]

The government has more leeway to regulate symbolic speech than pure speech. The landmark case on expressive conduct is *United States v. O'Brien* (1968).[53] In that case, David O'Brien and three of his friends were arrested and convicted for violating an amendment to the Selective Service Act that prohibited the mutilation or destruction of a draft card. The defendants argued that burning their draft cards was a gesture meant to show their disgust for the Vietnam War and that the true purpose of the law was to prohibit that form of political expression. The government argued that the law was drafted to improve the administration and operation of the selective service system, an important government objective that had no relationship to suppression of particular expression. The Supreme Court devised a test for regulations suppressing symbolic speech, that relies on an alternatively phrased version of intermediate scrutiny. If the following questions can be answered in the affirmative, the regulation can stand:

1.   Did Congress have the Constitutional authority to enact the regulation?
2.   Does the regulation further a substantial government interest?
3.   Is the government interest served by the regulation unrelated to the suppression of free expression?
4.   Is the incidental restriction on free expression no greater than what is essential to the furtherance of that interest?

Is computer code speech or conduct?   Some forms of expressive speech contain *both* speech and nonspeech elements. The U.S. Court of Appeals for the Second Circuit classified the posting and linking of computer code as expressive conduct rather than pure speech in *Universal City Studios, Inc. v. Corley* (2001).[54] The appellants, Eric Corley and his company 2600 Enterprises, published a magazine and website targeted to computer hackers. On the website, Corley posted a copy of the computer program "DeCSS" that can be used to circumvent the CSS encryption technology movie studios like Universal have placed on DVDs to prevent unauthorized viewing and copying. When Universal got a preliminary injunction requiring Corley to take the program down, he complied but linked to another site with the program. Universal got a permanent injunction that also barred Corley from linking to other sites with DeCSS. The injunction was based on the anti-trafficking provisions of the Digital Millennium Copyright Act, which make it illegal to circumvent technologies designed to prevent access to a copyrighted work.[55]

Corley challenged the injunction and the DMCA as a violation of the First Amendment. The court acknowledged that computer code and computer programs are forms of speech covered by the First Amendment. However, because a program can function without additional human action, the court concluded that it contains both speech and nonspeech components:

> Computer programs are not exempted from the category of First Amendment speech simply because their instructions require use of a computer. A recipe is no less "speech" because it calls for the use of an oven, and a musical score is no less "speech" because it specifies performance on an electric guitar. Arguably distinguishing computer programs from conventional language instructions is the fact that programs are executable on a computer.[56]

The *Corley* court noted that the scope of protection for speech generally depends on whether the restriction is "content based" or "content neutral" and that the government's motive is usually the controlling factor in making that determination. It concluded that the DMCA and injunction were not motivated by DeCSS's capacity to convey information, but rather its capacity to instruct a computer to decrypt CSS. The court applied the same reasoning to hyperlinks, concluding that they have both a speech and nonspeech component. The hyperlink conveys information that is protected speech, but it also has the functional capacity to bring the content of the linked page to the user's computer screen.

Student speech

Supreme Court cases regarding student speech rights have been limited to the consideration of speech on school property and at school-sanctioned events. Lower courts have considered cases involving off-campus student expression, however, and found it to be protected.[57] Internet posts – made off school property but accessible on campus – fall into a gray area in between on- and off-campus speech. Most courts consider student websites to be protected off-campus speech.[58] Some, however, have upheld disciplinary actions against students if there is a "sufficient nexus between the web site and the school campus to consider the speech as occurring on-campus."[59]

In determining whether that nexus exists, courts rely on the Supreme Court's holding in *Tinker v. Des Moines Independent School District* (1969), a case that involved a silent protest of the Vietnam War by students wearing black armbands. In *Tinker*, the Court famously declared that students do not shed their constitutional rights to freedom of speech at the schoolhouse gate.[60] It said that speech would be upheld unless it *materially disrupts class work or involves substantial disorder* or *invades the rights of others*. These criteria have become the watchwords for student online speech.

The first case to consider student speech online was *Beussink v. Woodland R-IV School District* (1998).[61] A Missouri high school student developed a website that was critical of his school and its administrators. As is common with these kinds of sites, it also included profanity. The student had no intension of sharing the site's content with people at school, but a conflict with a friend led the other student to "out" the website during a computer class. School administrators suspended Beussink for 10 days. The unexcused absences dropped his GPA. Beussink challenged the suspension as a violation of his First Amendment rights. A federal district court held that his site was constitutionally protected because it did not create substantial disruption in the school or interfere with school activities. The court said "[d]isliking or being upset by the content of a student's speech is not an acceptable justification for limiting student speech under *Tinker*."[62]

When students cross the line into threatening speech it is easier for courts to assume that their conduct is materially disruptive to the school or invades the rights of others. For example, in *J.S. v. Bethlehem Area School District* (2000) a student's website with a teacher's severed head dripping blood and an animation of the teacher's face morphing into a picture of Adolf Hitler, combined with a request for funds to cover a hit man, was deemed to have been substantially disruptive.[63] In fact, the teacher took medical leave for the rest of the year. Concluding that the speech was not protected, the Pennsylvania Supreme Court upheld the student's permanent expulsion.

The Supreme Court has stated that the constitutional rights of public school students, while on campus, are not co-extensive with those of adults. Schools administrators may punish lewd, sexually explicit expression that interferes with a school's educational mission[64] and censor school-sponsored publications as long as their actions are reasonably related to legitimate pedagogical concerns.[65] Most recently, in *Morse v. Frederick* (2007), the Court held that schools could punish student speech that promotes illegal activities.[66] The student, Joseph Frederick, held a banner during an Olympic torch rally passing the school that proclaimed: "Bong hits 4 Jesus." Chief Justice Roberts, who wrote the opinion, cautioned that First Amendment protection is not lost because the speech is simply *offensive*, a term that might apply to much political or religious speech. In a concurring opinion, Justice Alito, joined by Justice Kennedy, also clarified that the decision "provides no support for any restriction of speech that can plausibly be interpreted as commenting on any political or social issue."[67] In a separate opinion, Justice Thomas opined that the Court should overturn *Tinker* and declare that students have no speech rights in public schools.

No Compelled Speech

Freedom of expression includes another element that receives less attention but is just as important – the right not to speak. The Supreme Court has said that "Since all speech inherently involves choices of what to say and what to leave unsaid, one important manifestation of the principle of free speech is that one who chooses to speak may also decide 'what not to say.'"[68] Government may not compel individuals to convey messages with which they disagree or associate individuals or groups with unwanted messages.[69]

First Amendment theories

The Constitution does not link protection of expression to any particular objective and the Supreme Court has not reached a consensus on a unified theory upon which to determine what should be protected. Various theories have emerged to explain the purpose of the First Amendment. Some focus on the collective process and the benefits to society as a whole. Others focus on individual rights.

One powerful theory suggests that freedom of expression is required for self-government.[70] The democratic process is dependant upon free expression, both for the purpose of participatory democracy and to ensure people have the information they need to vote intelligently. The Supreme Court has said that a fundamental principle of our constitutional system is "[t]he maintenance of the opportunity for free political discussion to the end that government may be responsive to the will of the people."[71] A related idea is that free expression is required as a check on the abuse of power. Vincent Blasi theorized that fear of public exposure deters government officials from going astray.[72]

Americans also believe that freedom of expression serves as a safety valve of sorts — a very important function in a period plagued by terrorism. Justice Louis Brandeis expressed this idea in the now-famous metaphor: "sunlight is the most powerful of all disinfectants."[73] He warned that

> it is hazardous to discourage thought, hope and imagination; that fear breeds repression; that repression breeds hate; that hate menaces stable government; that the path to safety lies in the opportunity to discuss freely supposed grievances and proposed remedies; and that the fitting remedy for evil counsels is good ones.[74]

In other words, although we may not like to hear what some people have to say, allowing people to express their views gets them out in the open where we can address them. Silencing people with whom we disagree does not make them change their views. It just increases their resentment.

Freedom of expression is also required for "individual self-fulfillment"[75] Through communication we relate to others, express our thoughts and emotions, and develop our personalities. Conversing with others is instrumental in developing our mental faculties.[76] It helps us form our own beliefs and opinions, promoting autonomous decision-making.[77] When others listen to what we have to say, we develop self respect. Limits placed on what we can say undermine our sense of dignity.[78]

The most common justification for freedom of expression is the search for truth. In *On Liberty*, John Stuart Mill argued that the particular danger of government suppression of speech is its potential to suppress ideas that are true. Moreover, even if a statement is clearly wrong, suppression denies the public the opportunity to re-examine and reaffirm what is true. Mill assumed that freedom of expression would result in the communication of good and bad information, but he also believed that if left unfettered society could, over time, sort out the truth. This theory of truth discovery is called the marketplace of ideas rationale. It was reiterated by Justice Oliver Wendell Holmes in his dissenting opinion in *Abrams v. United States* (1919).[79] Focusing on the collective search for truth, Holmes wrote:

> [W]hen men have realized that time has upset many fighting faiths, they may come to believe even more than they believe the very foundation of their own beliefs that the ultimate good desired is better reached by free trade of ideas — that the best test of truth is the power of the thought to get itself accepted in the competition of the market, and that truth is the only ground upon which their wishes safely can be carried out. That at any rate is the theory of our constitution. It is an experiment, as all life is an experiment.[80]

Aside from the existential question of whether truth exists, the primary criticism of the marketplace of ideas theory is that the marketplace is not equally open to everyone. The voices that dominate the marketplace are those that belong to people with enough power and money to demand access to the press, making it difficult for alternative views to be heard. To a certain extent, this criticism is valid. A man like Rupert Murdoch, who runs News Corporation with Fox Broadcasting, Twentieth Century Fox, and now MySpace, certainly has more power to be heard than the average person on the street. However, digital media have lowered the cost of entry into the marketplace of ideas. The online encyclopedia Wikipedia is an example of the marketplace theory in action. Anyone with Internet access can edit Wikipedia entries, which makes them vulnerable to bias and error. But, by the same token, biased or deceptive entries are usually corrected by other users. For example, the night before John McCain announced that Alaska Governor Sarah Palin would be his running mate in the 2008 presidential election, someone made 30 changes to Palin's Wikipedia entry, adding favorable references, including a description of her as a politician of "eye-popping integrity," while downplaying references that might be perceived as negative.[81] Within a day most of the changes had been reversed or toned down. Aside from Wikipedia, many blogs can boast audiences that are at least as big as those drawn by mainstream media. Celebrity gossip blog Perez Hilton attracts 100 million monthly readers – as many as *Forbes* magazine. Matt Drudge claims his Drudge Report gets 17 million hits a day.

Questions for Discussion

1. How is the Fourteenth Amendment used to make the First Amendment applicable to the states and why?
2. In what ways are First Amendment protections limited?
3. What is the difference between a content-neutral restriction and a content-based restriction? How do levels of judicial review differ for each?
4. How does First Amendment protection for student speech differ from First Amendment protection for adult speech?

3

Telecommunications Regulation

Although the First Amendment applies to all media, all media do not receive the same level of First Amendment protection. Electronic media, excluding the Internet, tend to be more heavily regulated by government in terms of ownership, the physical operation of their facilities, and the content transmitted through them. This intrusion is justified under the theory that wireless media, such as broadcast and satellite, benefit from the use of a scarce public resource – the electromagnetic spectrum. Wired media, such as cable and telephone systems, on the other hand, are subject to government regulation because their lines are strung along public rights of way.

This chapter discusses the varying levels of First Amendment protection allocated to broadcast, cable, satellite, and common carriers, as well as the regulatory limits and public service obligations imposed on them.

Regulating Telecommunications Media

The Federal Communications Commission regulates most telecommunications media in the United States. The Commission exerts control over broadcast media through its right to grant, renew, or revoke stations' licenses and over satellite media through its right to license construction and operation of direct broadcast satellite systems. Other forms of telecommunications, including cable, cellular, and telephone service, fall under its sphere of influence, although it does not have exclusive control of them. State and municipal governments grant cable companies franchises to operate in particular areas, and therefore play an important role in cable regulation. State public utility commissions regulate aspects of telephony.

The Communications Act

Congress established the FCC to implement and enforce provisions of the Communications Act of 1934. The law is divided into sections called titles. As new media have evolved, new titles have been added to bring them under the Act's regulatory umbrella.

- Title I outlines the purposes of the law, the FCC's jurisdiction, and its organizational structure.
- Title II authorizes the FCC to develop rules for the regulation of common carriers.
- Title III establishes the Commission's responsibility to license and regulate radio communications that use the electromagnetic spectrum.
- Title IV outlines the procedures for due process in FCC decision-making.
- Title V describes the range of civil and criminal penalties in force for violation of the Communications Act or rules developed by the Commission.
- Title VI sets out general provisions for ownership and operation of cable stations.
- Title VII contains miscellaneous provisions, such as requirements for communication services to establish reasonable access for the disabled.

The Telecommunications Act of 1996

Congress drastically overhauled the Communications Act with its passage of the Telecommunications Act of 1996.[1] The omnibus legislation, designed to prepare media for digital convergence, was arguably the first "digital media law." Through it, Congress eliminated ownership rules that prevented communication companies from offering services in more than one sector. The Act opened up new possibilities for digital communication by allowing phone companies to supply video and information services, cable companies to supply telecommunications services, broadcasters to own cable systems, regional telephone companies to offer long distance service and long distance companies to offer regional service. Congress also encouraged the FCC to eliminate other restrictions that might impede progress by requiring it to review its regulations every even-numbered year to determine whether any are no longer necessary to the public interest, and if not, to modify or repeal them.[2]

The Telecommunications Act also pushed electronic media in a digital direction. Congress allocated an additional six megahertz of spectrum to full-powered television stations so they could transition from analog to digital programming. By June of 2009, all full-powered stations were required to discontinue analog programming so their analog frequencies could be reclaimed for other uses. This provision brought the quality of broadcast programming up to that of satellite and cable, which were already transmitting digital as well as analog signals. Congress did not allocate additional spectrum for radio's transition to digital programming because it wasn't necessary. Radio stations can simulcast digital signals on either side of the frequency used for analog programming because they require less bandwidth than television.

FCC rulemaking

Although the FCC's primary role is to implement provisions of the Communications Act, it is also empowered to make rules of its own. The impetus for change may come from Congressional legislation that requires the FCC to fulfill its mandates by enacting specific rules, a judicial order that requires the agency to reconsider a course of action, or the agency's convictions that a change would improve telecommunications policy.

FCC organization

The Federal Communications Commission, first called the Federal Radio Commission, was established by the Radio Act of 1927 to control station interference. Congress expanded its powers to cover all telecommunications when it passed the Communications Act of 1934.[3] The Act authorizes the FCC to "make such regulations not inconsistent with law as it may deem necessary to prevent interference between stations and to carry out the provisions of [the] Act."[4]

The FCC is responsible for spectrum use. It allocates spectrum frequencies to nonprofit organizations, corporations, municipal governments and state governments and makes and enforces rules related to use of the spectrum by satellite, wi-fi, cellular, and broadcasting telecommunications media. The FCC is also concerned with wireline communications through telephones, digital subscriber lines (DSL), cable, or anything related to the development of broadband technology.

The FCC is directed by a five-member board of commissioners, appointed by the president and confirmed by the Senate. The commission must include two representatives from each of the major parties to ensure that it remains nonpartisan. But in reality, the president usually sways the balance by ensuring that the majority belongs to his party. Commissioners serve five-year terms that are staggered to ensure their terms expire in different years.

Commissioners have final decision-making authority on all FCC matters, but the day-to-day functions of the agency are divided among seven policy-making bureaus that handle the agency's workload:

- The *Media Bureau* develops and administers rules for cable television, broadcast television, radio, and satellite.
- The *Wireline Competition Bureau* develops policies and rules for phone companies.

- The *Wireless Telecommunications Bureau* oversees mobile phones, personal communications services, pagers, and two-way radios.
- The *International Bureau* oversees satellite and policy matters related to international telecommunications services.
- The *Consumer and Government Affairs Bureau* informs consumers about telecommunication products and services, coordinates telecommunications policy with other government agencies, and handles matters related to disability rights.
- The *Enforcement Bureau* enforces the Communications Act and the commission's rules.

- The *Public Safety and Homeland Security Bureau* recommends and administers telecommunications policy related to public safety and emergency management.[5]

The FCC's Office of Administrative Law Judges serves a judicial function within the agency. Administrative law judges conduct administrative hearings in cases involving alleged violations of FCC regulations. They act as fact finders and issue initial decisions that may be appealed to the Commission.

The agency acts through a notice and comment procedure. When an FCC bureau proposes to change or implement a rule, it publishes a *Notice of Proposed Rulemaking* in the Federal Register. The public is given a minimum of 30 days to comment on the proposed rule before the FCC acts. If the bureau wants feedback on an issue before proposing a specific rule, it may publish a *Notice of Inquiry* to solicit general comments instead. For example, in 2008 the FCC issued a Notice of Inquiry to solicit comments on whether broadcasters and cable operators should be required to identify sponsors of product placements and hidden advertisements embedded in programming to comply with its rules on sponsor identification.[6]

After assessing public comments, the agency may choose to revise and reissue its proposal as a *Further Notice of Proposed Rulemaking*. Alternatively, it may move forward to the next step by issuing a *Report and Order* containing its final decision. The Report and Order is generally accompanied by a detailed justification of the agency's policy to avoid accusations that the change was *arbitrary and capricious*. Because the Administrative Procedures Act requires federal agencies to articulate a rational basis for the choices they make, plaintiffs who challenge agency rules frequently do so on the principle that they are arbitrary and capricious.

Parties that object to the FCC's decision may file a *Petition for Reconsideration* within 30 days of the decision's publication in the Federal Register. After considering the petition, the Commission will respond with a *Memorandum and Order*. If the Commission denies the petition, the party may challenge the FCC order in a federal court of appeals.

Broadcast Regulation

Among electronic media, broadcast radio and television get the least First Amendment protection. Courts review content-based regulations affecting broadcast media under a standard of heightened scrutiny. Under this standard, the regulation may stand as long as it serves an important government interest and is no more restrictive of speech than necessary to accomplish its goal. In contrast, content-based restrictions affecting other media, including print, Internet, cable, and presumably satellite, are subject to strict scrutiny, which demands that the regulation be narrowly tailored to serve a compelling government interest. The Supreme Court has justified this disparity in treatment using two theories: *spectrum scarcity* and the *pervasiveness and accessibility of the medium.*

Broadcast station licensing

FCC power over broadcasters comes from the agency's ability to grant and take away station licenses, which literally means the difference between broadcasting life or death. A station cannot operate without a license.

Until 1993, the FCC allocated licenses through a competitive process – essentially evaluating two or more stations vying for the same license and basing its decision on which would be more likely to serve in the public interest, convenience, and necessity. The U.S. Court of Appeals for the D.C. Circuit effectively banned that process in *Bechtel v. FCC* (1993).[7] The FCC now issues licenses by auction. The FCC's auction of spectrum freed up by broadcasters' transition to digital programming netted $19.6 billion in 2008.[8]

The Commission will only award licenses to American applicants. It is barred by the Communications Act from granting a broadcast or common carrier license to a person who is not a citizen of the United States, a foreign company, any company of which more than one-fifth of the stock is owned by foreigners, or any company directed by another company of which one-fourth of the stock is foreign-owned.[9] The rule applies to radio and television stations and telephone companies that use a radio, satellite, or microwave link, but it does not apply to cable. In order to acquire the television stations in the Fox network, Rupert Murdoch, a native Australian, had to change his citizenship.

Stations are licensed for periods up to eight years and must apply for renewal before their terms expire. In their renewal applications they must show that they are in compliance with federal laws and FCC regulations and that they have operated in the public's interest.

Failure to comply with FCC regulations can result in sanctions. The Commission has the authority to (1) issue cease and desist orders, (2) impose monetary forfeitures (fines), (3) grant a short-term license renewal, (4) deny renewal, or (5) revoke a station's license. If a station's license is revoked, it may appeal the decision before an administrative law judge within the FCC. If the decision is upheld, it may appeal to the U.S. Court of Appeals for the D.C. Circuit and, eventually, the Supreme Court.

Aside from licensing, the FCC regulates technical aspects of operation, including station location, classification, call letters, frequencies, power, times of operation, and ownership restrictions.

Spectrum scarcity

The FCC imposes licensing and ownership restrictions, as well as some content requirements, on broadcast media under the theory that the electromagnetic spectrum is a scarce public resource. There are really two dimensions to this theory. The first reflects the fact that because the spectrum is a valuable public resource, the public, as its real owner, should be the beneficiary of its use. The second acknowledges that the medium is not open to all speakers. Therefore, those special few who do have access should be obligated to act in the public's interest. Public interest may be defined in a number of ways, but in general the FCC has attempted to foster three policy objectives: localism, competition, and diversity.

Electromagnetic spectrum

To understand government regulation of broadcast media based on their use of the public spectrum, it is helpful to understand what the electromagnetic spectrum is and how it works.

The electromagnetic spectrum is a band of radiation made up of oscillating electric and magnetic fields. The interaction of these two fields produces waves of energy of different lengths. These wavelengths correspond to unique frequencies assigned to electronic media. Frequency measures the number of times a wave moves up and down, or oscillates, per second. The unit of measurement employed to calculate frequency is the hertz (Hz). One hertz equals one oscillation per second. One hundred waves per second would be noted as 100 hertz (Hz). Kilohertz represents thousands of cycles per second, megahertz represents millions of cycles per second, and gigahertz represents billions.

We divide the electromagnetic spectrum into frequency bands that can be used for different purposes, such as radio, television, satellites, mobile phones, and personal communication devices.[10] The mid-range frequencies of the electromagnetic spectrum, those between 300 to 3,000 kHz, are used for radio broadcasts. The very high frequency (VHF) region, between 30 to 300 MHz, is used for television and FM radio broadcasts. The ultra-high-frequency (UHF) region, between 300 to 3,000 MHz, is also used for television, while satellites use bands near 4 and 6 GHz and between 11 and 13 GHz.

The 700 MHz band that analog television vacated was the last big corridor up for grabs. It is especially desirable because signals at this frequency penetrate walls so well.

Because transmissions cannot share the same frequency, the government manages spectrum use closely. While the Federal Communications Commission coordinates public, state, and municipal use of the electromagnetic spectrum, the National Telecommunications and Information Administration, a bureau of the Commerce Department, coordinates federal use of the spectrum. The NTIA develops policies for government use of the spectrum for public safety operations, government satellite networks, and federal agency radio communications.

Use of the electromagnetic spectrum is very competitive. Within the private sector, there has been an explosive growth in telecommunications – in satellite television, Wi-Fi, ultra wideband, cellular phones, third-generation advanced services (high-speed wireless for mobile phone devices or laptops, otherwise known as 3G), and global position satellite systems. Within the public sector, demand is also rising among public safety agencies and the armed forces for radio, radars, and defense systems.

Spectrum scarcity was upheld as a constitutional rationale for broadcast regulation in *National Broadcasting Company v. United States* (1943).[11] NBC and CBS challenged FCC limitations on contracts the networks could execute with their affiliates as a violation of the First Amendment. The FCC restrictions were meant to keep networks from shutting out local programming by replacing it with their own. The Supreme Court upheld the rules based on limited access to the spectrum. Writing for the Court, Justice Felix Frankfurter referred specifically to radio, but the theory expressed is applicable to all broadcast media:

> Freedom of utterance is abridged to many who wish to use the limited facilities of radio. Unlike other modes of expression, radio inherently is not available to all. That is its unique characteristic, and that is why, unlike other modes of expression, it is subject to governmental regulation.[12]

Ownership limitations imposed on broadcast media are also justified by spectrum scarcity. In the spirit of deregulation, the Telecommunications Act significantly reduced limits on the number of radio and television stations one company could own. The FCC has also lifted rules prohibiting cross-ownership of television stations and newspapers in some markets. Nevertheless, other ownership restrictions have been retained to preserve a diversity of media "voices," particularly in local markets.

The Supreme Court has upheld the FCC's right to impose content requirements on broadcasters, based on the scarcity rationale, to ensure the public gets sufficient access to information. The Fairness Doctrine, which the agency no longer enforces, required broadcasters to devote adequate time to the discussion of controversial issues of public importance in news and public affairs coverage. A Pennsylvania radio station challenged the constitutionality of the fairness doctrine in *Red Lion Broadcasting Co. v. FCC* (1969).[13] The station argued that the FCC rule violated the First Amendment because it treated broadcast media differently than print media. The FCC argued that the doctrine promoted the First Amendment rights of listeners because it ensured greater access to information.

The FCC's argument that the First Amendment protected listeners' right of access to information was founded on an expanded reading of First Amendment law. Nevertheless, the Supreme Court seemed to support the theory. In upholding the Fairness Doctrine, Justice White explained:

> Because of the scarcity of radio frequencies, the government is permitted to put restraints on licenses in favor of others whose views should be expressed in this unique medium. But the people as a whole retain their interest in free speech by radio and their collective right to have the medium function consistently with the ends and purposes of the First Amendment. It is the right of the viewers and listeners, not the right of the broadcasters, which is paramount ... It is the right of the public to receive suitable access to social, political, esthetic, moral and other ideas and experiences which is crucial here.[14]

This was a new idea – that the First Amendment protected not only the rights of speakers to convey information, but of listeners to receive information. However, it is not a theory that has thrived in Supreme Court doctrine. In later cases, the Supreme Court denied a right of access to print and broadcast media to petitioners who argued that access was necessary to preserve the public's right to information, preferencing instead the media's right to convey information without government interference.[15] Nevertheless, the enduring significance of the Supreme Court's *Red Lion* decision is its affirmation of the government's power to impose regulations on broadcast media that serve the public interest in exchange for exclusive licenses to use the public airwaves.

The FCC abandoned the Fairness Doctrine in 1987 under the theory that market forces reduced the need for such control. Thirteen years later, it rescinded related rules intended to promote fairness, which required broadcasters to give people criticized on air a right of reply.[16] In 1999, the U.S. Court of Appeals for the D.C. Circuit found that these "personal attack" rules "interfere[d] with editorial judgment of professional journalists and entangle[d] the government in day-to-day operations of the media."[17] The court held that it was incumbent upon the FCC to justify or repeal them. When the FCC did not act, an appeals court issued a writ of mandamus directing the Commission to repeal the rules the following year.[18]

The FCC still imposes some content requirements and restrictions on broadcasters, which are detailed later in the chapter. However, the scarcity rationale has fallen out of favor as a justification for broadcast content regulation as digital compression has opened the airwaves to more speakers. Broadcast media are no longer the only spectrum users. Satellite radio, satellite television, wireless broadband, and phone service providers all depend on spectrum use as well. Even cable is dependent on spectrum use to the extent that the company downloads programming sent via satellite. It is difficult to argue that use of the spectrum justifies content regulation in broadcast media while sparing other spectrum users from the same regulations.

Pervasiveness and accessibility

A more contemporary justification for content regulation in broadcast media is based on the pervasiveness of the medium and its unique accessibility to children. This theory, outlined in *Federal Communications Commission v. Pacifica Foundation* (1978), is used to justify limits on the broadcast of indecency, which unlike obscenity, is a protected form of speech.[19] In a segment about the cultural impact of language, one of Pacifica Foundation's radio stations ran a 12-minute monologue by satirist George Carlin titled "Filthy Words." In the monologue, Carlin repeated "the words you couldn't say on the public, ah, airwaves, um, the ones you definitely wouldn't say, ever" over and over in a variety of contexts. After receiving a complaint about the broadcast, the Commission reviewed it and characterized its language as "patently indecent."

The FCC issued a declaratory statement indicating that the station "could have been the subject of administrative sanctions" and would be if subsequent complaints were received.[20] Pacifica sued, arguing that because the recording was not obscene, prohibiting its broadcast was an abridgement of the First Amendment. The Supreme Court upheld the FCC's right to regulate broadcast indecency based on the medium's unique characteristics. Justice John Paul Stevens pointed out that of all media, broadcasting received the most limited form of First Amendment protection:

> The reasons for these distinctions are complex, but two have relevance in the present case. First, the broadcast media have established a uniquely pervasive presence in the lives of all Americans. Patently offensive, indecent material presented over the airwaves confronts the citizen, not only in public, but also in the privacy of the home where the individual's right to be let alone plainly outweighs the First Amendment rights of an intruder. Because the broadcast audience is constantly tuning in and out, prior warnings cannot completely protect the listener or viewer from unexpected program content. To say that one may avoid further offense by turning off the radio when he hears indecent language is like saying that the remedy for an assault is to run away after the first blow …
>
> Second, broadcasting is uniquely accessible to children, even those too young to read … The ease with which children may obtain access to broadcast material … amply justify special treatment of indecent broadcasting.[21]

The decision allowed the FCC to channel indecent broadcast speech into a period when children were less likely to be in the audience. This block of time, between 10 p.m. and 6 a.m., is known as the safe harbor period.

Broadcast content restrictions and requirements

The Communications Act explicitly prohibits the FCC from censoring broadcast content. Section 326 provides that:

> [n]othing in this chapter shall be understood or construed to give the Commission the power of censorship over the radio communications or signals transmitted by any radio [or television] station, and no regulation or condition shall be promulgated or fixed by the Commission which shall interfere with the right of free speech by means of radio communication.

However, the ban on censorship is really one against prior restraint. The FCC may not preview a program to determine whether it is suitable for broadcast, but it may impose penalties for content that violates its rules after the fact. In addition to channeling indecent content, the FCC restricts broadcasters from airing surreptitiously recorded phone conversations and on-air hoaxes. The government has also placed restrictions on certain advertisements carried over electronic media.

Indecency   The FCC will not give advisory opinions about content in advance of its broadcast lest they be interpreted as censorship. So finding a clear standard for what is and is not likely to violate FCC rules on indecency and profanity is crucial to broadcasters. The FCC defines indecency as material that "depicts or describes sexual or excretory organs or activities in terms patently offensive as measured by contemporary community standards for the broadcast medium." To determine whether the material is patently offensive, it considers three factors:

- whether the description or depiction is explicit or graphic;
- whether the material dwells on or repeats at length descriptions or depictions of sexual or excretory organs; and
- whether the material appears to pander or is used to titillate or shock.[22]

The Commission defines profanity as words that in context are highly offensive. The FCC judges profanity on a case-by-case basis, but has said that variations of the s-word and f-word are considered profane.

  The FCC is entitled to prohibit indecency and profanity under Title 18 of the United States Code, Section 1464, which bans the utterance of "any obscene, indecent or profane language by means of radio communication." Nevertheless, its policy following *FCC v. Pacifica* (1978) was to fine indecent or profane broadcast programming only when it was so "pervasive as to amount to 'shock treatment' for the audience."[23] In 2004, the FCC indicated that policy was "no longer good law." The Commission put broadcasters on notice that sustained use of profanity would no longer be required to find that material is patently offensive.[24] The Commission's about face came after NBC's broadcast of the 2003 Golden Globe Awards, when U2 singer Bono described his award as "f***ing brilliant." Fox was in the hot seat over two fleeting uses of profanity by Cher and Nicole Richie during the 2002 and 2003 Billboard Music Awards. In a 2004 Memorandum Opinion and Order, more commonly called the Golden Globe Awards Order, the Commission indicated that henceforth even isolated uses of profanity outside the safe harbor period could be considered a violation punishable by fines. Repeated violations could lead to the revocation of a station's license.

Several networks petitioned the FCC to withdraw the Golden Globe Awards order. When it did not, Fox, CBS, and NBC petitioned the U.S. Court of Appeals for the Second Circuit to review the order. In *Fox Television Stations, Inc. v. Federal Communications Commission* (2007), the Second Circuit struck down the new "fleeting expletive" policy as arbitrary and capricious under the Administrative Procedures Act.[25] The court concluded that the FCC had not presented a reasoned analysis for the change. It also seemed confused by the FCC's inconsistent application of the new rule. For example, although there is no specific news exception to FCC indecency rules, the Commission disregards the use of profanity in news stories or interviews.[26] Consequently, a clip of Bono's acceptance would not have been considered indecent as background material in a news story. The Commission also has allowed the repeated use of expletives in films, such as *Saving Private Ryan*, when raw language was central to the artistic integrity of a work. The court suggested that the FCC policy might violate the First Amendment as well, but did not decide the case on that basis.

By a narrow margin, the Supreme Court reversed the decision. Writing for the Court, Justice Scalia indicated that although an agency must show good reasons for a new policy, "it need not demonstrate to a court's satisfaction that the reasons for the new policy are better than the reasons for the old one."[27] It is sufficient "that the new policy is permissible under the statute, that there are good reasons for it, and that the agency believes it to be better …" The long-term significance of the Court's decision may have less to do with fleeting expletives than the expanded power it has granted administrative agencies to revise their policies.

The Court's decision only address the policy's legality under the Administrative Procedures Act. Acknowledging the possibility that the fleeting expletives policy might implicate the First Amendment, the Court remanded the case back to the Second Circuit for further analysis of the policy's potential impact on broadcasters' speech. Several justices expressed their concern about the FCC's stricter regulation of broadcast programming now that most people get it bundled with cable and satellite services that fall under a different regulatory structure.

The FCC's crackdown on indecency followed CBS's broadcast of the 2004 Super Bowl, when singer Justin Timberlake ripped Janet Jackson's bodice, exposing her left breast to 90 million viewers during the half-time show. Following the incident, Congress passed the Broadcast Decency Enforcement Act, raising the maximum fine for a single violation of indecency rules from $32,500 to $325,000 with a $3 million cap for continuing violation.[28] The FCC fined CBS $550,000 for the broadcast.[29] CBS appealed the fine in *CBS Corporation v. FCC* (2008).[30] The U.S. Court of Appeals for the Third Circuit concluded that the FCC "acted arbitrarily and capriciously" by fining CBS for a half-second of nudity because it deviated from a 30-year policy of exempting fleeting words and images. In light of its decision in *FCC v. Fox*, the Supreme Court ordered the Third Circuit to re-examine its ruling.

Broadcast of telephone conversations   Although it is legal in some states to record a conversation over the phone without obtaining permission from the other party, broadcasting a conversation recorded without permission is a violation of FCC rules.[31] The rule – put in place to protect individuals' expectation of privacy – applies equally to private individuals and public officials.[32] Some stations initiate prank calls and then ask the "victim's" permission to air the call, but this practice is technically a violation as well. The Commission has stated that the "recording of such [a] conversation with the intention of informing the other party later – whether during the conversation or after it is completed but before it is broadcast – does not comply with the Rule ..."[33] In 2004, the FCC fined a Miami radio station $3,500 for broadcasting a crank call made to Cuban President Fidel Castro.[34] DJs Joe Ferrero and Enrique Santos of WXDJ telephoned the Cuban Ministry of Foreign Relations and convinced several Cuban officials that President Hugo Chavez of Venezuela was waiting on the line to speak to President Castro about a matter of state business. When Castro answered the phone, the DJs admitted the call was a joke. The FCC said that it did not matter that Castro was informed before the actual broadcast that the conversation had been recorded.

The FCC rule does not apply to cable and satellite. The show Crank Yankers was built around the prank call concept. Comedians called their marks from Nevada, a state that allows phone conversations to be recorded without consent, and then persuaded the victims to let them air the program on Comedy Central.[35]

On-air hoaxes   FCC rules prohibit on-air hoaxes that include the broadcast of a false distress signal or the report of a crime or catastrophe. In 1990, Disc Jockey John Ulett of KSHE-FM in Crestwood, Missouri, interrupted regular programming with an announcement preceded by an air raid siren that stated "Attention, attention. This is an official civil defense warning. This is not a test. The United States is under nuclear attack." Although the station apologized repeatedly for the hoax, the FCC punished it with a $25,000 fine because Section 325(a) of the Communications Act prohibits broadcasters from issuing false distress signals.

The FCC revoked a station's license in 1980, largely due to its decision to stage the kidnapping of one of its disc jockeys. In 1974, the station manager of KIKX-FM in Tucson, Arizona, concocted a promotion centered around the disappearance of DJ Arthur Gropen. The station released details about the vehicle used in the abduction and the suspected kidnapper. It even incorporated a fake sound bite from the police. Worried listeners clogged police phone lines. Five days passed before the station admitted that the kidnapping was a hoax. When the FCC conducted a renewal hearing, the station was admonished for a number of violations, but the most serious charge was related to the hoax.

A station may be fined for broadcasting false information concerning a crime or catastrophe if the licensee knows the information is false, it is foreseeable that the broadcast of the information will cause substantial public harm, and broadcast of the information does in fact cause substantial public harm.[36] Harm is interpreted as damage to property or the health and safety of the public or a distraction of emergency workers from their duties.[37]

Limits on advertising   Congress and the FCC have imposed various limitations on broadcast advertising that have been extended to cable and satellite media. These include restrictions on the mode and length of advertisements intended for children and prohibitions against advertisements of certain tobacco products and types of lotteries. These are discussed in chapter 12 on commercial speech.

Broadcast content requirements

Despite a higher level of government regulation, broadcasters largely determine the content of their programming and who will have access to their facilities. There are, however, some narrow exceptions to this rule. For example, broadcasters are required to identify themselves regularly, provide quarterly reports of their programming, and offer programming specifically for children. Other requirements imposed on broadcasters – such as the obligation to provide equal time and access to candidates during an election and to identify sponsors – have been extended to cable and satellite providers.

Station identification   Broadcasters must identify themselves once every hour and at the beginning and end of each day. The identification must include the station's call letters and the community in which the station is located. Between those two bits of information, the broadcaster may also include the station's name and the channel or frequency.

Programming reports   In 2008, the FCC released "enhanced disclosure" rules. Stations are required to file quarterly reports, detailing all of their programming, including the amount and kind of local programming shown on their stations. The FCC also proposed new rules that would require broadcasters to supply a minimum amount of local programming.[38]

Children's programming   Television broadcasters are required to serve the educational and informational needs of children by offering at least three hours of core children's programming per channel per week. The FCC defines "educational and informational" programming as that which "in any respect furthers the educational and informational needs of children 16 years old and under (this includes their intellectual/cognitive or social/emotional needs)."[39] A program is specifically designed to serve children's educational and information needs if:

- it is designed to be informative;
- it is aired between 7 a.m. and 10 p.m.;
- it is a regularly scheduled weekly program; and
- it is at least 30 minutes in length.[40]

Equal opportunity (equal time) provision   In general, there is no First Amendment right of access to broadcast stations. The Supreme Court held that neither the Communications Act nor the First Amendment is violated when radio stations refuse to sell time to groups that want to air their editorial views in *CBS v. Democratic National Committee* (1973).[41] However, there is one exception. FCC rules mandate a certain amount of access to broadcast and satellite media for candidates in federal elections.[42]

Although cable programmers are not obligated under the Communications Act to sell airtime to state and local candidates, broadcast and direct broadcast satellite (DBS) providers are obligated to make time available for *federal* candidates at reasonable rates. The Communications Act does not define *reasonable*, but broadcasters and DBS providers are expected to provide candidates with equal opportunities to purchase time in popular timeslots at fair prices. They are not obligated to provide free airtime to competing candidates who cannot afford to advertise. But they are required to offer political advertisers the "lowest unit charge" or, the lowest rate charged to other advertisers for comparable time during the 45 days preceding a primary election and 60 days preceding a general election. The Communications Act provides that a broadcast station's license may be revoked for "willful or repeated failure to allow reasonable access to or to permit purchase of reasonable amounts of time for the use of a broadcasting station by a legally qualified candidate for Federal elective office."[43]

Broadcast, cable, and satellite programmers must give other political candidates equal opportunities to use their facilities if they decide to open their facilities to them.[44] A company that sells or gives away advertising space to one candidate must grant the same opportunity to the opposing candidate. This rule, now codified in Section 315 of the Communications Act, is intended to keep broadcasters from trying to manipulate elections by controlling the amount of media coverage candidates receive.

Concerned that news organizations might avoid covering political candidates because such coverage would obligate them to provide equal time to the candidate's opponent, Congress provided four exceptions to the rule: A candidate's appearance will not trigger the equal access rule if it occurs during:

- bona fide newscasts;
- news interviews;
- on-the-spot news events (including political conventions); and
- news documentaries (assuming they are not based on the candidate).

The FCC has since interpreted political debates to be on-the-spot news coverage, which allows stations to arrange debates involving some rather than all of the candidates in an election. The agency has also classified talk show appearances as news interviews. However, television appearances that have nothing to do with news will trigger the equal opportunity provision. During President Ronald Reagan's campaigns, television stations were careful to avoid showing movies from his earlier acting career.

The Communications Act also prohibits broadcast, cable, and satellite programmers from censoring candidates' on-air statements.[45] Consequently segregationists have been allowed to use racist terminology, while pro-life candidates have been allowed to show aborted fetuses in their ads. Daniel Becker, an anti-abortion congressional candidate from Georgia, submitted a videotape of a 30-minute political advertisement that included a graphic depiction of an abortion in progress to an Atlanta TV station. He wanted to run the ad immediately after a National Football League broadcast of a game between the Falcons and the Rams. The station considered the videotape indecent, but editing the footage was not an option, so it refused to run it outside of the safe harbor period between 10 p.m. and 6 a.m. The FCC issued a Memorandum Opinion and Order indicating that stations were entitled to make good faith editorial judgments in such matters. But the U.S. Court of Appeals for the District of Columbia Circuit reversed the decision on the theory that the ruling encouraged candidates to engage in self-censorship.[46] The court said the FCC rule put candidates in the position of sacrificing what they wanted to say to the audience they wanted to reach and allowed broadcasters to discriminate against them.

The Supreme Court has ruled that because broadcasters are not allowed to censor candidates' messages, they cannot be held responsible for them. In *Farmers Educational Cooperative Union v. WDAY*, Inc. (1943), it held that broadcasters cannot be liable for defamatory remarks made by candidates.[47]

Sponsor identification and underwriting   The Communications Act and FCC rules require all FCC licensees to identify the names of sponsors that have given them money or some other consideration for transmission of a program.[48] The rule is intended to protect the public's right to know the identity of program sponsors. Identification is not required "when it is clear that the mention of the name of the product constitutes a sponsorship identification."[49]

Multi-channel Video Program Distributors

More American households get television programming from multi-channel video programming distributors (MVPDs) than broadcasters. MVPDs, such as cable and direct broadcast satellite, sell programming for a price. Although some public service obligations have been imposed upon them, including a requirement to carry broadcast channels, cable and satellite get more First Amendment protection than broadcast media. Courts assume that consumers exercise a choice regarding subscription-based programming and therefore consider them less pervasive.

Cable television

Because cable does not use the public airwaves to distribute programming, and was not initially placed under the FCC's jurisdiction by Congress, the FCC was initially reluctant to regulate it. But the Commission reconsidered when it realized that, left unchecked, cable could undermine free broadcast television programming.

Approximately 60 percent of U.S. households rely on cable for their programming needs.[50] In comparison, fewer than 10 percent still rely on over-the-air broadcasting. This represents a dramatic audience gain since the 1940s when cable television was developed to import broadcast signals into rural and mountainous areas without local stations. As cable moved into areas with television stations, local broadcasters worried that viewers would prefer cable programming drawn from larger cities and pleaded with the FCC to regulate it.

In 1965, the FCC did just that by requiring cable systems to carry local channels and prohibiting them from importing signals that duplicated local programming. The cable industry challenged the FCC's authority to enact the regulations in *United States v. Southwestern Cable Co.* (1968). But the Supreme Court upheld them, concluding that the Communications Act empowered the FCC to regulate "all interstate and foreign communication by wire or radio," including cable.[51]

Must carry rules   Cable companies considered the "must carry" rule to be a form of compelled speech that infringed upon their First Amendment rights. When the rule was enacted most cable systems offered fewer than 20 channels. Carrying broadcast signals required them to give up channel capacity they would have preferred to use for something else. Congress agreed and repealed it in the Cable Act of 1984, when it deregulated the industry. With the must carry rule out of the way, cable systems began to drop independent local stations as the FCC had predicted.

In the early 1990s, 40 percent of American households still relied on over-the-air signals for programming. Congress began to realize that if local broadcasters lost more than half of their viewers as cable stations dropped them, they would also lose a significant percentage of their advertising revenue. The loss might make it impossible to continue to provide free programming to their remaining viewers. So it reinstated the must carry provision in the 1992 Cable Television Consumer Protection and Competition Act.[52] The law gives local broadcast stations the right to demand retransmission on local cable systems. It also requires cable providers to carry the stations' video and audio in full, without changes or deletions.

Cable mogul Ted Turner, who feared his networks would be dropped from cable systems forced to carry local broadcasters instead, challenged the must carry provision as a violation of the First and Fifth Amendments. The Supreme Court considered the case three times before narrowly upholding the provision. The Supreme Court acknowledged that the FCC's rule was a burden on cable programmers' speech, which is protected by the First Amendment. But because the provision did not distinguish between favored and disfavored speech on the basis of views

expressed, the Court classified it as a content-neutral regulation subject to intermediate scrutiny.[53] It concluded that the must carry provision serves an important
government interest (the preservation of free programming) without substantially
burdening more speech than necessary to further that interest.[54]

Cable systems with more than 12 channels must set aside one-third of their
capacity for local channels.[55] Inclusion is at the local broadcast station's discretion.
Some stations, like network affiliates with local news and weather, are valuable to
cable companies who might lose subscribers without them. The 1992 Cable Act
includes a *retransmission consent provision* that entitles local broadcast stations to
negotiate compensation for their retransmission over cable or additional channel
capacity on the cable system. Broadcasters are also protected by network non-
duplication, syndicated program exclusivity, and sports blackout rules that apply
to cable. The *network non-duplication rule* protects local affiliates' exclusive right to
distribute network programming on local cable systems. The *syndicated program
exclusivity rule* protects local stations' exclusive right to distribute syndicated programming on local cable systems. Broadcast stations may demand that the local
cable system black out duplicate networked or syndicated programs, even if the
local TV station's signal is not carried by the cable system in question. The *sports
blackout rule* protects the rights of entities that have negotiated the exclusive right
to disseminate a particular sports program. If a local station does not have permission to broadcast the sports program, a local cable system may not import another
broadcast signal carrying the game from another market.

The FCC required cable systems to continue to carry local broadcasters' signals
after the 2009 transition from an analog to digital format.[56] Many cable companies
continue to offer digital and analog programming. The FCC requires cable companies that offer both to "down-convert" broadcast stations' digital signals to analog
so subscribers with analog televisions can continue to view them. Cable companies
that transmit digital signals only are not expected to down-convert broadcasters'
signals. The rule has a three-year sunset provision.

Franchising authorities   The FCC does not issue licenses to cable companies as it
does broadcast stations. Cable companies must have a franchise to operate. These
are essentially contracts to build and operate a cable system in a particular area.
The local boards, commissions, and city councils that enter into contracts with cable
companies and regulate them locally are known as "local franchising authorities."

Franchising authorities are responsible for regulating rates for basic cable services. Rates for cable programming services beyond the basic tier and pay-per-view
channels are not regulated. Because cable is expensive, it is tempting to steal it.
Stealing cable TV is a crime. The 1984 Cable Act provides penalties of up to two
years in prison and/or $50,000 in fines for illegally intercepting cable or manufac-
turing or selling equipment used for interception.[57]

Access channels   Congress authorized franchising authorities to require cable
systems to set aside channels for public, educational, or government use as part of

their franchise contracts. These are known as PEG stations. To further its goal of encouraging local programming, the FCC also requires cable companies to set aside some channel capacity that organizations can lease in order to provide their own programming. A system with 36 to 54 channels must set aside 10 percent of its capacity for leased access, while a system with 55 channels or more must set aside 15 percent.

Cable companies may not alter the content of PEG stations, but they may impose minimum, content-neutral standards on production quality. The 1992 Cable Act gave cable operators the right to refuse to transmit sexually explicit programming on leased or public access channels. In 1996, the Supreme Court upheld cable operators' rights to control indecency on leased access stations, but not on public access stations.[58]

Content regulation   The one content area in which broadcast and cable rules differ significantly is indecency. Because cable viewers subscribe to the service, it is harder to argue that indecency sneaks up on them with no warning. In fact, some subscribers want channels that offer sexually oriented programming.

The Supreme Court held that cable is entitled to full First Amendment protection in *Turner Inc. v. FCC*.[59] It reasoned that cable unlike broadcast, is not limited to a select number of speakers licensed to use radio frequency, so it should not be subject to the same level of regulation. However, a very fractured court appeared to back down from that stance two years later in *Denver Area Educational Telecommunications Consortium, Inc. v. FCC.* (1996).[60] In the case, the Court considered whether the 1992 Cable Act provision that permitted cable operators to prohibit indecent material on access channels they lease to other programmers – a content-based restriction on speech – was constitutional. A plurality of the Court agreed that the need to protect children from indecent speech is compelling, but there was broad disagreement over whether the provision did this in the least restrictive way. Writing for the Court, Justice Breyer analogized indecency on leased access channels to the indecent radio broadcasts at issue in *FCC v. Pacifica Foundation*. He observed that cable television "is as 'accessible to children' as over-the-air broadcasting, if not more so … [Cable has] 'established a uniquely pervasive presence in the lives of all Americans,'" and can "'confron[t] the citizen' in the 'privacy of the home,'" with little or no prior warning."[61] Dissenting judges did not think strict scrutiny was applied to the content-based provision.

In *United States v. Playboy Entertainment Group* (2000), the Court held that strict scrutiny applies to content-based restrictions on cable television.[62] As originally written, Section 505 of the Telecommunications Act required cable companies to block all non-subscribers' access to video and audio on sexually explicit channels completely, whether requested to do so or not. Blocking a station that is digital is no problem; nothing shows. But analog signals are difficult to block without some seepage of audio or video. Consequently, while this provision was active, cable companies had to restrict sexually oriented channels to safe harbor hours. Playboy challenged the provision and the Supreme Court overturned it. Not only did the provision target particular types of speech, but also particular types of speakers. Applying strict scrutiny, which demands that a government regulation be narrowly tailored to serve a compelling government interest, it found the provision unconstitutional. The provision failed because a less restrictive option was available. Section 504 of the Act requires cable companies to provide blocking devices to subscribers who request them.

Direct broadcast satellite service

Direct broadcast satellite service is the second most popular paid programming option, capturing approximately 30 percent of U.S. households. Congress vested the FCC with regulatory authority over direct broadcast satellite service through the Communications Satellite Act of 1962. But classification of DBS for regulatory purposes has been a little tricky. Communication satellites, like broadcasters, require the use of the electromagnetic spectrum to disseminate video programming. On the other hand, they are also subscription-based services like cable that transmit data like common carriers.

Sensing the potential impact that DBS providers, like DIRECTV and Echostar, might have on local advertising revenue if satellite operators imported signals that would lure viewers away from local stations, broadcasters asked the FCC to impose the same regulations on DBS they face. But the FCC refused.

The Commission justified its decision by concluding that DBS is not a broadcaster in the classic sense, but a hybrid between broadcasters and common carriers. Broadcasters challenged the decision in federal court. The U.S. Court of Appeals for the D.C. Circuit upheld the FCC's decision that DBS operators could be excused from broadcast obligations. But it remanded the case back to the FCC with instructions to clarify the distinction between DBS operators and broadcasters.[63] On remand, the FCC focused its definition of broadcasting on whether or not a programmer scrambled its signals. Broadcasting is made available "to the general public."[64] A programming provider's decision to scramble a signal that would be sold by subscription indicated a lack of intent to send a signal "to all alike, without charge or restriction to any listener." The appellate court upheld the FCC's categorization.[65]

Satellite content regulation   The Supreme Court has not yet considered whether direct broadcast satellite programmers are entitled to the same First Amendment protection as cable television. Two federal circuit courts have come to opposite conclusions on the issue. The U.S. Court of Appeals for the District of Columbia Circuit concluded that DBS providers, like broadcasters, are afforded lesser First Amendment protections because they are both beneficiaries of limited spectrum. In contrast, the Fourth Circuit concluded that "both satellite carriers and cable operators engage in speech protected by the First Amendment when they exercise editorial discretion over the menu of channels they offer to their subscribers."[66]

But the FCC has made it clear that it has no plans to regulate satellite content like broadcast content. In 2008, former FCC Chairman Kevin Martin said the Commission strived for regulatory parity between satellite and cable.[67] Satellite programmers are also required to meet some of the same public interest obligations that cable providers do. For example, DBS providers must set aside some channel capacity for public use and carry local broadcast channels equally.

Channel set-asides   In 1992, the FCC adopted a proposal that required DBS providers to set aside 4 percent of their channel capacity for noncommercial educational or informational programming.[68] Time Warner challenged the provision as a violation of the First Amendment. The D.C. Circuit, which upheld the provision, refused to analyze it under strict scrutiny, concluding that it "should be analyzed under the same relaxed standard of scrutiny that the court has applied to the traditional broadcast media."[69]

Although DBS services may apply minimal technical standards, they have no editorial control over program content on channels set aside for public interest use. They may not pre-screen or refuse to air programming unless they believe, in good faith, that the programming does not meet the noncommercial educational or informational requirement. However, if DBS providers have more demand from potential educational programmers than channel capacity to offer, they may select programmers from the overall pool based on factors such as the programmer's experience, reliability, and reputation for quality programming. They also may charge noncommercial programmers no more than 50 percent of the cost of making the set-aside channel available.

Carry one, carry all provision   The must carry provision cable companies fought against initially put them in a stronger position than DBS providers because they were able to supply local programming to their customers while satellite subscribers had to pay an additional fee for local programs. In 1999, Congress passed the Satellite Home Viewer Improvement Act, which created a statutory license that allowed satellite carriers to transmit local broadcast signals without getting special permission from the copyright holders. A "carry one, carry all" provision in the Act obligated satellite carriers that wanted to take advantage of the license to carry one station, to carry all requesting stations within the same market in order to preserve free broadcast programming. The Act also instructed the FCC to develop rules for mandatory carriage of broadcast signals, retransmission consent, network non-duplication, syndicated exclusivity, and sports blackout to put satellite television carriers on a level playing field with cable.[70] Satellite providers challenged the carry one, carry all provision as a violation of the First Amendment in *Satellite Broadcasting and Communications Ass'n. v. FCC* (2001). Citing *Turner v. FCC*, the Fourth Circuit upheld the provision as a content-neutral regulation that served an important government purpose.[71]

Common Carriers

The FCC also has regulatory authority over common carriers, which act as a nondiscriminatory conduit for others' communications rather than their own. Traditional local exchange carriers (local phone companies) fall under the supervision of the FCC's Wireline Bureau, while its Wireless Telecommunications Bureau regulates commercial mobile services.

A mobile phone works by converting a user's voice into radio waves carried through the electromagnetic spectrum. In 2008, cellular service licensees were allowed to drop analog service. Providers of broadband personal communications service used for voice and two-way data capabilities through Blackberry-ish devices were never obligated to use analog signals.

In Europe, mobile devices work with all carriers, creating more content options for wireless consumers. For the first time, the FCC moved in that direction by requiring that the auction winner for the 700 MHz spectrum vacated by analog TV stations open its service to all devices. As the winner, Verizon will have to provide service to any wireless phone or personal communication device. The new rule, which applies only to the 700 MHz spectrum, will take effect in 2010. The FCC has not mandated that other wireless services open their handsets for universal use.

However, the FCC has mandated number portability. Wireless phone services must allow their customers who change service providers in the same local area to keep their local numbers. Customers may also move a wired telephone number to a mobile phone in some cases.

Mobile phones will likely be a driving force behind the continued growth of the Internet, particularly at the international level, because more people can afford cell phones than personal computers. The FCC classifies phone service used for data transmission as an "information service" rather than a telecommunications service subject to common carrier rules. Consequently digital subscriber line (DSL) providers are not required to provide broadband access to competing Internet service providers, like Earthlink, under the same terms and conditions as their own. This decision effectively limited consumers' DSL options to companies that own the phone lines into their homes.

The FCC is in the process of determining whether mobile phone text messages and short codes are covered by the Telecommunications Act's non-discrimination provisions. As common carriers, cell phone companies may not censor their customers' calls. But Verizon refused to issue a short phone code to the National Abortion Rights League that people could use to sign in and receive alerts. Several public interest groups filed a petition with the FCC to protest Verizon's censorship of pro-choice messages and to request a ruling that cell phone carriers not be allowed to discriminate against particular types of speech.[72] Verizon reversed its decision as soon as it was reported in the media.

Media ownership rules

Government limits on the number and kind of media outlets that one person or company could own were put in place to encourage a healthy marketplace of ideas. Over the years they have been reduced significantly by Congress through the Telecommunications Act, FCC rule-making, and courts in challenges based on the First Amendment. However, the following rules remain in place regarding:

- **National television ownership:** There is no particular limit on the number of television broadcast stations that one person or company can own, but the aggregate national reach of stations owned cannot exceed 39 percent of the national population. UHF stations are factored into the equation at only 50 percent of their audience reach. An FCC rule limiting the aggregate national reach of cable stations owned by one party to 30 percent was struck down in 2009 by the U.S. Court of Appeals of the D.C. Circuit. No limits are imposed on satellite or fiber optic providers.
- **Duopolies:** One party may own two television stations in the same market if eight full-power independent television stations (commercial and noncommercial) will remain after the merger and one of them is not among the top-four ranked stations based on its audience share. This has come to be known as the "voices test" because it is supposed to guarantee that adequate voices remain in the market to ensure a diversity of views and news. Co-ownership is also allowed in markets in which the licensee is the only reasonably available buyer and the station purchased is failing.

The FCC also may waive the rule for a licensee that plans to build a new station.

- **Broadcast/cable cross ownership:** One party may own a television station and a cable television service in the same market, as long as the cable operator faces effective competition in the market.
- **Dual network ownership:** One party may own a major VHF network like ABC, CBS, Fox, or NBC and a UHF network like UPN or WB. Viacom, for example, owns CBS and a large portion of UPN. However, major networks may not combine with each other.
- **Broadcast/newspaper cross ownership:** In December of 2007, the FCC relaxed the broadcast/newspaper cross ownership ban it established in 1975. One party may now own a television or radio station and a newspaper in the top 20 media markets in the United States. Co-ownership is only allowed if at least eight independently owned and operating major media voices (including major newspapers and full-power TV stations) would remain. Additionally, a newspaper cannot be co-owned with a station that is among the top four ranked by market share.

The cross-ownership ban remains in place in smaller markets to preserve diversity in local news by preventing one person or entity from becoming the sole suppler of news. However, the FCC has the right to override it under certain circumstances. Criteria that would factor into such a decision include: the level of media concentration in the market, whether lifting the ban would increase available news, and whether allowing mergers would preserve newspapers in financial trouble. Newspapers are struggling to hold on to their readership, however preservation of the newspaper industry is not the FCC's responsibility. It is likely that newspapers will begin to buy up smaller stations in hope of launching convergence projects.

The move was swiftly opposed by media interests groups. The FCC reported in a letter to the Judicial Panel on Multidistrict Litigation of Multicircuit Petitions for Review that more than a dozen lawsuits were filed against the rules by activists who complained that they either went too far or not far enough.[73]

- ***Television/radio co-ownership:*** One party that owns a television station (or two under the duopoly rule) may own:
  - up to four radio stations in any market where at least 10 independent voices would remain post-merger; and
  - up to six radio stations in any market where at least 20 independent voices would remain post-merger; or
  - one radio station (AM or FM) regardless of the number of other stations in the market.
- ***National radio ownership:*** There is no national cap on the number of radio stations one party can own. But there are restrictions on the number of stations owned in one market. One party may own, operate, or control:
  - up to 8 commercial radio stations in a market with 45 or more commercial radio stations, provided that no more than 5 of the stations are in the same service (AM or FM);
  - up to 7 commercial radio stations in a market with between 30 and 44 commercial radio stations, provided that no more than 4 are in the same service (AM or FM);
  - up to 6 commercial radio stations in a market with between 15 and 29 commercial radio stations, provided that no more than 4 are in the same service (AM or FM); and
  - up to 5 commercial radio stations in a market with 14 or fewer commercial radio stations, provided that no more than 3 are in the same service (AM or FM), with the exception that one party may not own more than 50 percent of the stations in a market.

The Telecommunications Act has been particularly criticized for its drastic deregulation of radio ownership. Before the Act was passed, one party could own no more than 20 AM stations and 20 FM stations. After it was passed, Clear Channel purchased nearly 1,200 stations.

Questions for Discussion

1. What are the two theories used to justify content and ownership restrictions on broadcast media?

2. Why are multi-channel program distributors regulated more leniently than broadcast, even though they provide more than 86 percent of television programming?
3. How have media ownership restrictions changed since the Telecommunications Act of 1996 was passed and what impact has that had on the media industry?
4. What content requirements do broadcast and multi-channel program distributors have in common?

4

Internet Regulation

In contrast to the telecommunications discussed in chapter 3, the Internet is more informally regulated. There is no broad political oversight of the Internet – no agency like the FCC in charge of licensing service providers, ensuring universal access, regulating prices, or controlling content. The Internet's global reach and distributed architecture makes it impossible for one agency to control it effectively.

That does not mean, however, that the Internet is beyond regulation. It receives narrow political oversight through the Internet Corporation for Assigned Names and Numbers (ICANN), a non-profit corporation in charge of the Internet's key traffic-management technologies.

This chapter discusses the managerial role that ICANN plays in the Internet's functionality, the political influence the United States wields through ICANN, and the larger participatory role other nations desire in the Internet's governance. It explains the difference between global and domestic concepts of net neutrality. It also provides an overview of legislative efforts to control cybercrime and introduces the concept of virtual law.

ICANN, the Internet's Manager

The Internet Corporation for Assigned Names and Numbers (ICANN) coordinates the Internet's technical function, essentially serving as its manager. The non-profit corporation was created in 1998, under the auspices of the U.S. Department of Commerce, to assume control of the Internet domain name system (DNS). The DNS is a global, distributed database that translates easy-to-remember mnemonic addresses, like www.digitalmedialaw.us, into numerical identifiers, like 213.86.83.116, that computers can use to locate websites and deliver e-mail.[1] Each numerical identifier – called an Internet Protocol address – leads to one computer, the way a telephone number points to one phone. ICANN ensures that domain names and their corresponding IP addresses are globally unique, so the same address always leads to the same location.

ICANN is also responsible for the delegation of top-level domain (TLD) names, like .com, .net, and .org, and country codes, like .us or .uk. It accredits both the registries assigned to manage particular top-level domains (like Verisign, which is responsible for housing all of the domains ending in .com, .net, and .tv in its databases) and the companies that register individual domain names.

The Commerce Department has consistently maintained that its eventual goal was to release ICANN from government supervision as soon as it is ready to stand on its own. The original target date for independence was 2000. In Sept. 30, 2009, the U.S. government signed a new agreement with ICANN giving up unilateral control of the organization.[2] The new agreement will transition the organization from U.S. control to a multinational oversight. In place of an annual review conducted by the Commerce Department, the nonprofit organization that manages the Internet's domain name system will be subject to three-year multi-national reviews. The U.S. will now participate as one of the nations in ICANN's Governmental Advisory Committee.

Internet Assigned Numbers Authority

However, the U.S. government also asserts political oversight over ICANN through a separate mechanism. It has awarded the corporation a government contract to perform Internet traffic management functions allocated to the Internet Assigned Numbers Authority (IANA). The IANA is the original organization founded by Internet pioneer Jon Postal to perform technical functions needed to keep the Internet running smoothly. When Postal died in 1998, its contract with University of Southern California, where he taught, was transferred to ICANN. IANA responsibilities include:

*   coordinating the assignment of technical parameters used in Internet protocols;
*   allocating blocks of addresses to regional registries that, in turn, allocate them through Internet service providers to Internet end users; and
*   administering functions related to the management of the root zone of the domain name system.[3]

The third responsibility is, perhaps, ICANN's most important function, at least from the perspective of other countries. ICANN edits the root zone file, which lists the names and numeric IP addresses of the authoritative DNS servers for all top-level domains (TLDs) such as .org, .com, and .us. The root zone file is stored on thirteen distributed root server networks. ICANN does not control the root servers; various corporations, professional associations, and government organizations do.

But ICANN has the power to change the file stored on the root servers, which contains the information the servers need to direct queries to the TLD registries that can supply the location of all other web addresses.

Here's how it works. TLD registry locations are stored on the root servers, but all Internet traffic does not travel through them because the volume would be overwhelming. So other DNS servers cache the information on root servers, querying them periodically for updates. When you search for a domain like www. digitalmedialaw.us for the first time, your computer works on the address from right to left. It consults one of the DNS servers with cached root server information to locate the registry that manages the top-level domain in your address. Once it finds the right TLD registry, in this case NeuStar, Inc., it queries the registry for the IP address corresponding to the rest of the website.

From its inception, ICANN has asserted control over the root zone file through the IANA contract in connection with its overall management of the domain name system. It was assumed that the United States would relinquish control over the root zone file when it freed ICANN. However, in 2005, the National Telecommunications and Information Administration, the Commerce Department branch that works with ICANN, asserted permanent control over the root zone file.[4] In 2006, the Commerce Department made it clear that the IANA contract is not inextricably tied to ICANN and could be given to another operator. The implication was that regardless of ICANN's independence, the U.S. would hold onto control of that aspect of Internet function.

Alternatives to ICANN

Although the United States developed the Internet, it is no longer the Internet's majority user. The Commerce Department's decision to transition ICANN to international oversight was a political one. Other countries have not been particularly comfortable with unilateral U.S. control of the Internet and have expressed preference for ICANN's independence or an alternative governing body that would be more inclusive. In fact, the United Nations has twice sponsored international summits in which developing a new structure for Internet governance was a key issue.

The United Nations expressed an interest in exploring alternatives to ICANN in reaction to its member countries' concerns about the network's operation. These include network security, protection of information, the proliferation of spam, and a desire for greater openness. Developing countries, in particular, want decision-making regarding the Internet to be more inclusive. The Internet has one billion users and is expected to gain another billion in the next decade.[5] Most of that growth will come from developing countries. Even in places where computers are in short supply, Web-enabled cell phones will bring millions of new users to the Internet. India, for example, expects half a billion people to have mobile phones by 2011.[6]

One issue of particular concern has been the dominance of English language domains, even though 70 percent of the world does not use English. The technology for creating multilinguistic domains has been available for more than 10 years, but until 2008, ICANN was reluctant to veer from the Roman alphabet, fearing that it might destabilize the Internet. It only allows domains that are half-written in foreign characters, e.g. [Arabic text].com. Internet users in other countries still must use English characters for the top-level domains like .com or .net in websites and e-mail addresses. This has been a problem for Internet users whose keyboards do not include the Roman letters of Ascii code.[7]

Some countries, such as China, have reacted by creating their own domains and versions of the Internet, and are using Chinese characters for three top-level domains: .net, .com, and .cn. Russia is planning to create a network that operates entirely in Cyrillic. This practice raises questions about the Internet's continued global interoperability. For example, will such networks use their own root servers or the ones already in place? Likewise, will they create a bridge that would coordinate their own national Internet with the Ascii code used on the worldwide network?[8] Without coordination, Russians, for example, would be isolated from the rest of the Internet – at least until their own hackers could resolve the problem.

Internet Governance Forum

The United Nations sponsored World Summit on the Information Society meetings in 2003 and 2005, in which delegates considered what a new structure for Internet governance might look like. They were not able to agree on a particular model. As a compromise, they settled on the implementation of a nonbinding organization called the Internet Governance Forum. The role of the IGF is to make policy recommendations on Internet governance drawn from a range of stakeholders, including governments, civil society, and businesses, to the international community.[9] The organization has the mandate to operate until 2010. The IGF's future after that is murky. Although dissatisfaction with ICANN prompted its implementation, Washington's release of ICANN and moves within ICANN to be more inclusive and to test domain names in other alphabets have tempered its steam.

Whois

Internationally, ICANN has been criticized for the way it handles private data. ICANN requires registrars of domain names to log information about domain name registrants in the publicly available database Whois (pronounced "who is"). Information collected includes the domain name, the date the domain was created, the date it will expire, the registrar, the name of the domain owner, and the domain owner's contact information. If the registrar offers private registration, contact information is supplied for the registrar instead. Privacy advocates complain that anyone can search through Whois to find the source of information of Internet speech, interfering with anonymity.

It is not illegal to supply false registration information when registering a domain name, and many people do who want to retain their privacy. But it is a violation of law if the domain is used to carry out illegal activity. The Fraudulent Online Identity Sanctions Act amended the Trademark Act and federal copyright law to classify trademark or copyright infringements as "willful," and therefore punishable by an increased fine, if the infringer provided false of misleading contact information when registering, maintaining, or renewing an Internet domain connected with the offense.[10] It also amended the federal penal code to enhance sentences for criminal violations committed through a domain registered with false contact information.

Cybersquatting

One of the offenses that can trigger the Fraudulent Online Identity Sanctions Act is cybersquatting, which involves the registration of a domain name in bad faith with the intent to profit from it. This usually involves trying to sell the domain name back to the person or company that rightfully owns the trademarked name in the domain address. Although most domain registrants don't realize it when they sign up for their domains, ICANN requires people and companies that own a domain ending in .com, .net and .org to submit to an arbitration proceeding if a trademark owner files a complaint against them for cybersquatting. It has also developed a Uniform Domain Name Resolution Policy that is used in arbitration proceedings to settle these disputes. Cybersquatting is discussed in greater detail in chapter 8 along with trademark law.

Network Neutrality

The Internet governance movement describes freedom of expression as one of its primary goals but conceptualizes the issue in terms of network neutrality. Network neutrality is the principle that all content flowing through the Internet should be treated equally. Applied as policy, however, the term can be confusing because it actually has two meanings. Internationally, network neutrality refers to the idea that end-to-end Internet use should be unimpeded, regardless of content, application, or sender. International advocates of net neutrality want to eliminate barriers to Internet access. Domestically, the term network neutrality refers to the notion that high-speed Internet, or broadband, access providers should not be allowed to show preference to certain providers of content or types of content by supplying them with faster service. Advocates of net neutrality as end-to-end access would prefer that Americans not use the term network neutrality in relation to bandwidth management. From their perspective, it trivializes a much larger issue – universal access to the Internet generally and more specifically to its content. Both ideas are discussed in the next section.

Net neutrality as end-to-end access

Although it has grown exponentially, the Internet is still used by a minority of the world's population. Many developing countries provide their citizens with Internet access that is slow or expensive, or worse, no access at all. Consequently, populations in underdeveloped countries are deprived of informational and economic resources that could improve their standard of living. Barriers to overcome include inadequate communications infrastructure, unreliable electrical power, limited access to equipment, and substandard educational systems that cannot produce the human capital needed to build and operate a national network. In some countries, unstable governments compound the problem. Africa is, by far, the least connected part of the world. According to the International Telecommunications Union, only 4.8 percent of Africans have Internet access.[11]

In other places around the world, cultural barriers deprive individuals of full access to the Internet. Countries such as China and Iran, for example, provide their citizens with access to the latest technology, but censor the content that comes through it. Iran's Directorate of Management and Support of the Information Technology Network, for example, boasts that various government agencies in his country have blocked up to 10 million Internet sites using filtering techniques.

The Open Net Initiative has monitored government censorship of the Internet since 2001. The organization has found that filtering is most prevalent in Central Asia, East Asia, Northern Africa, and the Middle East. Governments use it to block websites with content they consider controversial, such as pornography, gambling, political or religious information, or popular culture deemed offensive. Occasionally, Internet applications, such as Voice over Internet Protocol, are targeted. But censorship is more commonly carried out by Internet Service Providers who are either licensed to operate on the condition that they filter objectionable content or made legally liable for it. Some filter URLs or websites that contain key words. Others filter specific sites known to contain particular kinds of content.

A particular irony is that American companies have participated directly in censorship efforts, particularly in China. Google launched a censored search engine in China, www.google.cn, in 2006. Yahoo!, Microsoft, and Skype have censored sites for China as well, either at its direct request or as a self-protective measure to avoid being filtered by the government.[12] Cisco supplied equipment Chinese authorities used for censorship. Yahoo, in particular, has been criticized for turning over the e-mail records of four Chinese dissidents to the Chinese government in 2004, which resulted in their imprisonment.[13]

Internet censorship is not limited to non-democratic countries. Worldwide, it is common to prohibit content that is considered obscene. European countries prohibit hate speech. Germany, in particular, prohibits "propaganda against the democratic constitutional order," incitement to hatred, denial of the holocaust, glorified depictions of human violence, depictions that instigate or incite the commission of certain crimes or violation of human dignity through the depiction of human death or mortal suffering.[14] The United States prohibits online gambling, discussed later in the chapter.

Net neutrality as broadband management

In the United States, network neutrality is more commonly seen as a domestic regulatory issue. The FCC has freed broadband service providers of common carrier obligations, giving them the prerogative to deny competing Internet service providers access to their conduits into consumer homes. The decision also gives broadband providers greater control over the use of their bandwidth by opening the door for providers to offer different levels of service. Consumers willing to pay more will get speedier delivery of data. Broadband service providers could also favor their own content and applications.

The FCC's decision to deregulate broadband was precipitated by a change in the Telecommunications Act of 1996. In it, Congress distinguished between "telecommunications services" and "information services." A *telecommunications service* provides for "the transmission, between or among points specified by the user, of information of the user's choosing, without change in the form or content of the information as sent and received."[15] In contrast, an *information service* provides users with the "capability for generating, acquiring, storing, transforming, processing, retrieving, utilizing, or making available information via telecommunications ..." but does not include any use of any such capability "for the management, control, or operation of a telecommunications system or the management of a telecommunications service."[16]

In 2002, the FCC issued a declaratory ruling that broadband service provided through cable qualifies as an information service. In earlier precedents, the FCC had classified companies that provided data over other carriers' lines as information services and companies that carried data over their own lines as telecommunications services subject to common carrier regulations. Under this classification, broadband supplied by cable companies would be considered a telecommunications service because it was transmitted over cable lines. Upon reconsideration, the FCC determined that cable's broadband service, examined in isolation from its other services, was essentially no different than that offered by Internet service providers that do not transmit data over their own lines. Freed of common carrier burdens, cable could deny use of its lines to other Internet service providers.

Rival Internet service providers challenged the FCC's new interpretation. The Ninth Circuit held that the FCC had misinterpreted definitions in the Telecommunications Act of 1996 and vacated the agency's ruling.[17] The Supreme Court reversed the decision. In *National Cable & Telecommunications Association v. Brand X* (2005), the Court upheld the FCC's regulatory scheme to spare cable from common carrier rules.[18]

One month after the Supreme Court's *Brand X* ruling, the FCC issued another declaratory ruling categorizing digital subscriber line (DSL) suppliers as information service providers, outside the boundaries of common carrier regulation as well. While creating a uniform regulatory scheme for broadband access, the decision represented another policy reversal. The FCC had previously characterized wireline broadband as a telecommunications service subject to common-carrier provisions. The FCC's about-face gave phone companies the right to deny competing Internet service providers access to their DSL lines. Dial-up service, however, still falls under common carrier regulations.

Broadband management and censorship

The notion that telecom companies will be deciding what will and will not go through their networks and at what rate of speed is unsettling to the Internet community. Critics have questioned whether the *Brand X* decision will interfere with Internet users' rights to send and receive information, now that access to the architecture is subject to restriction.

In August of 2008, the FCC sanctioned Comcast for secretly blocking the peer-to-peer (P2P) application BitTorrent.[19] With 160 million registered users, BitTorrent is the largest P2P and is widely used to distribute large data files, like video, that take up a lot of bandwidth. Comcast denied blocking BitTorrent until it couldn't anymore. The Associated Press conducted nationwide tests using the King James Bible that demonstrated that Comcast was preventing users from uploading even relatively small files on BitTorrent by sending messages to their computers that ended the connection. The FCC did not fine Comcast, but demanded that it stop discriminating against particular applications, disclose the extent and manner in which it engaged in blocking, and publicly disclose its broadband management policies. The FCC's policy on broadband management is vague. A statement issued in 2005 said "consumers are entitled to run applications and services of their choice … subject to reasonable network management." Congress considered measures to regulate bandwidth management in 2006, but never acted on them. Without congressional authority, it is not clear whether the FCC really has the authority to act against Comcast.

Broadband companies also use another technology to manage bandwidth called deep packet inspection. DPI is a computer network packet filtering technique that can be used to detect the type of material transmitted in Internet packets, e.g. an e-mail, VoIP, or peer-to-peer download, and prioritize or delay its transmission. It is already commonly used to manage bandwidth in Europe and Asia. Time Warner and AT&T are using DPI to meter usage in some U.S. markets. Customers who go over a set gigabyte allowance have to pay overage fees like customers who use too many cell phone minutes.

Opening a third pipe

Some communities have responded to the telecom/cable lock on broadband by offering to provide wireless broadband service. Meanwhile, private broadband providers have lobbied for legislation to stop municipalities from offering competing services. State governments that restrict municipalities from offering telecommunications services usually do so on the theory that government ownership is likely to impede progress that market competition would encourage. Missouri enacted a statute that barred political subdivisions within the state from offering telecommunications services. Municipal utilities within the state countered that the Telecommunications Act bars state or local laws that "prohibit or have the effect of prohibiting the ability of *any entity* to provide any interstate or intrastate telecommunications service," and authorizes the FCC to prohibit the enforcement of any such attempt.[20] When the FCC refused to step in, they sued. In *Nixon v. Municipal Missouri League et al.* (2004), the Supreme Court ruled that Congress did not mean to include in the words "any entity" a state's own political subdivisions.[21] The Court asserted that "any entity" refers only to private entities. Under that conclusion, states have the power to prevent municipalities from offering such services. At least 15 states – Arkansas, Florida, Iowa, Minnesota, Missouri, Nebraska, Nevada, Pennsylvania, South Carolina, Tennessee, Texas, Utah, Virginia, Washington, and Wisconsin – have passed bills restricting the implementation of new publicly funded broadband projects, although existing initiatives are allowed to operate.[22] Other states, like Vermont and New Jersey, have passed bills that authorize communities to provide broadband infrastructure and service.[23]

Voice over Internet Protocol

One of the most popular uses for broadband technology is Voice over Internet Protocol. VoIP allows computer users to make phone calls over the Internet rather than through traditional telephone systems. VoIP converts analog voice or facsimile transmissions into digital signals. These signals can then be carried in data packets over the Internet, like any other file, as long as subscribers have a broadband connection and an analog telephone adapter to take advantage of the service.

In 2005, the Federal Communications Commission required VoIP providers that offer interconnected service to all other phones on switched networks to support 911 calls.[24] It also required VoIP operators to comply with the Communications Assistance for Law Enforcement Act of 1994, which compels telecommunications carriers to assist law enforcement in electronic surveillance pursuant to a court order or other lawful authorization, and to contribute to the Universal Service Fund, as other telecommunications companies do, to support telecommunications access in high-cost areas. Beyond that, VoIP is not regulated as other telecommunications carriers.[25] In fact, the FCC has yet to classify them as either an information or telecommunications service.

Individual states do not regulate VoIP either, because Internet-based phone companies offer an interstate service. Unlike other phone services, VoIP services allow their subscribers to travel with their numbers and route calls to different states. The numbers are not tied to a particular location. In fact, subscribers may even choose their own area code. The FCC barred states from regulating VoIP in 2004 when Minnesota attempted to apply its telephone company regulations, including state tariffs and rate regulations, to Vonage. A federal court upheld the FCC order.[26]

Cybercrime

As the Internet has opened up new avenues for communication, it has also opened up new avenues for illegal behavior. Some crimes and torts – like dissemination of pornography, copyright infringement, and defamation – are simply made more expedient by virtue of the Internet, and therefore not an issue for this chapter. But other activities – like computer hacking and misuse – are practically defined by Internet use. Meanwhile activities like gambling and hate speech are complicated by the Internet because they are illegal in some countries but not in others. Regulating any illegal behavior on the Internet is always a challenge because, while the effects of the activity may be felt locally, the actual crime may be initiated halfway across the world.

Computer misuse – viruses, worms, and Trojan horses

In 2008, the Computer Security Institute found that almost half of the 522 respondents to its annual Computer Crime and Security Survey experienced a computer crime in the previous year.[27] Most frequently, organizations were the victims of malware – software maliciously designed to harm other computers. The most common forms of malware are worms and viruses. A *computer virus* is a parasitic program that attaches itself to another application. When it is activated, it self replicates and spreads throughout a computer system and then, via shared files, to other computers. Some viruses are simply pranks that spread strange messages or pictures. Others do serious damage by erasing data and corrupting hard drives. *Computer worms* engage in the same malicious behavior, but do so independently. The essential difference between them is that worms do not need a host application. Viruses and worms are most commonly spread through e-mail attachments, links to infected websites, P2P file sharing, and free software downloads from the Internet.

Another form of malware is the Trojan horse. A *Trojan horse* is a software program that appears friendly, but actually may be a carrier for a virus, worm, or spyware that gathers information about the computer user. Spyware can record the names, passwords, financial information, and browsing histories of computer users. Hackers also use Trojan horses to gain remote access to a victim's computer. Trojan "back doors" allow hackers to manipulate another computer, store data, trade files, and even send e-mails on behalf of its owner.

Hackers sometimes trick Internet users into downloading Trojan programs by associating them with websites tied to current events. Following the death of actor Heath Ledger, Google's search index was poisoned.[28] Hackers deployed search optimization tricks that prioritized malicious sites linked to Ledger's name. Google users who followed the links encountered a "Video ActiveX Object Error" message that prompted them to download a new version of the video codec to view video on the site. Those who downloaded the software installed a Trojan horse on their computers.

In an effort to short circuit malware on government computers, the White House (through the Office of Management and Budget) implemented a directive in 2008 that eliminates administrative privileges on government desktops and laptops that use Windows XP or Vista.[29] The Federal Desktop Core Configuration directive is intended to prevent users of government computers from downloading malware. The directive not only disables administrative privileges, but wireless access and Internet Explorer 7. It also applies to contractors' Windows-based computers that run on federal networks.

Phishing and pharming

Internet identity theft, called *phishing*, involves schemes to trick people into revealing their personal identifying information or financial data, which is then sold or used for fraudulent purposes. In 2006, 109 million Americans received phishing e-mails. Among those hooked, the aggregate loss was $2.8 billion.[30] In 2007, there were more than 25,000 phishing websites.[31] Most phishing attacks come from the United States or China.[32]

Phishers use two primary methods. The dragnet technique involves indiscriminately sending phony e-mails with corporate identifying information to Internet users to bait them into giving up their personal information. The "rod and reel" method targets specific victims. Information sent to them is designed to look like documents they would be likely to receive from their own financial institutions. Phishing is a two-for-one crime because it almost always involves two forms of fraud.[33] The phisher first steals the identity of the business it is impersonating and then steals the personal information of the unwitting customers who fall for the ruse. According to the domain name service OpenDNS, a unique phishing scam is launched every two minutes.[34]

Pharming is a related scam that involves domain spoofing. Pharmers redirect users from legitimate commercial websites to malicious ones that look identical. The cloned sites are used to steal social security numbers, bank account numbers, credit card numbers, debit card pins, mothers' maiden names, and passwords.[35] When users enter their identifying information, the hackers who run the site capture it for their own use.[36] eBay and PayPal are the companies most often spoofed.[37]

Pharmers also plant spyware on computers to steal private information, frequently through the use of Trojan horses.[38]

Pharmers may use Trojan horses to attack a computer user's browser, redirecting it to a spoofed site, or a more sophisticated technique, known as domain name system (DNS) poisoning, that manipulates the Internet server. DNS poisoning, also known as cache poisoning, corrupts the server's domain name system table by substituting a legitimate site's Internet protocol address with the IP address for a phony site. When users type in the correct URL for the site they are trying to reach, they are redirected to another site designed to look like the original.[39] If the spoof is done well, they won't be able to tell the difference.

Statutes to combat computer misuse

At least seven states have enacted anti-phishing legislation. These include California, Florida, New Mexico, New York, Vermont, Virginia, and Washington. Anti-phishing bills have also been proposed in Congress to combat electronic identity theft at the federal level. But they aren't really necessary. Protection from computer misuse exists through several statutes already in place, including statues that prohibit computer fraud and abuse, computer-related identity theft, wire fraud, and e-mail fraud.

Computer fraud   Computer fraud is prohibited by 18 U.S.C. 1030. The statute makes it a felony offense to hack into a protected computer, transmit a virus, or traffic in computer passwords. A protected computer is one used in interstate or foreign commerce, located in or outside the United States, or one used by the U.S. government or a financial institution. Specifically, the statute prohibits intentionally accessing a computer without authorization or exceeding authorized access to obtain information from any protected computer if the conduct involves an interstate or foreign communication. The Act also criminalizes knowingly causing "the transmission of a program, information, code, or command" that intentionally causes damage to a protected computer or "trafficking in any password or similar information through which a computer may be accessed without authorization."

The punishment for unauthorized access is normally a fine or up to one year in prison. It increases to five years if the unauthorized access is for commercial advantage, furthers another tortious act, or the value of the information obtained exceeds $5,000. The statue also entitles those who suffer damage or loss due to behavior prohibited by the Act to file a civil suit against the violator.

Computer-related identify theft   Fraud related to identity theft and falsification of documents is addressed in 18 U.S.C. 1028(a)(7). The statute prohibits the knowing transfer, possession, or use of another person's means of identification without authorization to commit a crime. The term "means of identification" can include: name, social security number, date of birth, driver's license or identification number, alien registration number, government passport number, or employer or taxpayer identification number. It also apples to electronic identification numbers, addresses, or routing codes and to telecommunication identifying information or access devices.

The law criminalizes falsification of identifying documents, particularly those that would be issued by the federal government, such as birth certificates; driver's licenses; personal identification cards; or authentication features like holograms, watermarks, certifications, symbols, codes, images, or sequences of numbers or letters. The statute also prohibits the production, transfer, or possession of document-making implements, such as templates, computer files, computer discs, electronic devices, or computer hardware or software, specifically configured or primarily used for making identification documents.

An offense related to identification theft or the production of fraudulent documents is punishable by a fine or up to five years imprisonment, or both. The punishment may increase to 15 years if, as a result of the offense, any individual involved obtains something of value worth $1,000 or the fraudulent identification appears to be issued by the United States. Penalties can reach between 20 and 30 years if the fraud is committed in conjunction with another crime that involves drug trafficking, violence, or domestic terrorism.

Wire fraud   Wire fraud is prohibited by 18 U.S.C. 1343, which applies to any scheme to defraud or obtain money or property under false pretenses by a means of wire, radio, or television communication in interstate or foreign commerce. The offense is punishable by fines of up to $250,000 or 20 years in prison. Maximum penalties include fines up to $1 million or 30 years imprisonment if the wire fraud affects a financial institution or disbursement paid in connection with a national disaster or emergency.

E-mail fraud   E-mail fraud is prohibited by 18 U.S.C. 1037. The Act criminalizes both the transmission of multiple commercial e-mail messages through a protected computer with the intent to deceive recipients and the use of false header information on multiple commercial e-mails. Maximum penalties can reach five years if the offense is conducted in conjunction with a felony or the offender has been previously convicted of sending spam. This provision is discussed in greater depth in chapter 12 in conjunction with the CAN-SPAM Act's restrictions on commercial speech.

"I love you," not really

Computer misuse laws vary considerably at the international level. Some countries have yet to enact them. A virus dubbed the "Love Bug" traveled through 45 million computers in 2000, destroying data as it went. It got its name from the "I love you" subject line of the e-mails that carried it. When a victim opened one of the infected

e-mails, the virus replicated by sending itself to everyone listed in the victim's contacts file. All told, it is estimated that it caused $10 billion in damages. Filipino
hacker Onel de Guzman admitted responsibility for the attack but was never punished because the Philippines had no law criminalizing misuse of computers.

The following year, the Council of Europe drafted the Convention on
Cybercrime.[40] The treaty stipulates that all signatories will adopt legislation that
criminalizes illegal access to a computer system, illegal interception of nonpublic
data transmissions, data interference, system interference, misuse of devices for
transmission of malware, computer-related forgery, and computer-related fraud.
The convention also applies to traditional crimes committed via a computer, such
as offenses related to child pornography, copyright infringement, or aiding and
abetting another's criminal activities. Only 23 nations, including the United States,
have ratified the treaty.[41]

Although it was a signatory to the cybercrime convention, Japan failed to implement the legislation needed to ratify it. With no computer misuse law in place,
Japanese officials were forced to use copyright law to arrest a man for disseminating
a computer virus in Japan. The hacker used still images and video clips from a
popular anime series to spread the virus. Because the anime clips were copyrighted,
the authorities could arrest the 24-year-old hacker, whose virus, which was carried
through a file sharing network, taunted its recipients with messages like: "This is a
visit from the prevalent Piro virus! Stop P2P! If you don't I'll tell the police!" and
"Ah, I see you are using P2P again … if you don't stop within 0.5 seconds, I'm
going to kill you!"[42]

All countries are not in agreement on all laws related to the Internet. After the
Council of Europe's Convention on Cybercrime went into effect, an additional
protocol was added to prevent the dissemination of hate speech. The protocol
entered into force in January of 2006.[43] The 20 nations that signed the protocol
agreed to "establish as criminal offences under its domestic law, when committed
intentionally and without right," the act of "distributing, or otherwise making available, racist and xenophobic material to the public through a computer system"
(Additional Protocol, 2002, p. 14). Although the United States signed the larger
Cybercrime convention, it did not sign the protocol because it conflicted with the
First Amendment.

"Trespassing" on Websites

Spiders, robots, and web crawlers are all names for the same idea – an automated
program that visits websites to gather information from them. Without them,
search engines like Google or Yahoo would never be able to keep track of the
growing and changing content offered online. Some companies also use web crawlers to monitor their competition. When a web crawler's visits become excessive,
however, its search queries can tie up valuable server time.

Companies have sued competitors for web crawler invasions under the common
law tort of trespass to chattels. Unlike trespass, which involves unauthorized access

to real property (land), trespass to chattels refers to interference with possession of personal property (things) that causes damage or prevents the owner from using it. This theory was applied to web crawlers by a federal district court in *eBay, Inc. v. Bidder's Edge* (2000). The defendant, Bidder's Edge, ran AuctionWatch.com, which aggregated data from auction sites so its users could keep track of multiple auctions of a particular product on the same screen. eBay sued Bidder's Edge because its web crawlers were accessing eBay's server more than 100,000 times a day. To prevail on a claim for trespass to chattels, involving unauthorized access to a computer system, the plaintiff must show that the defendant (1) intentionally and without authorization interfered with plaintiff's computer system and that (2) the use directly resulted in damage to the plaintiff.[44]

Although no particular damage resulted to eBay's system, the court enjoined Bidder's Edge from using its web crawler on eBay's server. It did so on the slippery slope theory that if Bidder's Edge were allowed to continue to use eBay's system in such a way, other web crawlers would do so as well, and eBay's system eventually would be overwhelmed.

A New York district court similarly held in *Register.com v. Verio* (2000), that a competing Web hosting company's repeated use of a web crawler to query Register.com's Whois database to look for potential customers amounted to trespass to chattels.[45] The court concluded that Register.com had a legitimate fear that its servers would be "flooded by search robots."[46]

Some legal scholars have argued that the application of a trespass theory to websites suggests that, for legal purposes, courts really do think of them spaces to be protected.[47] Neither Verio nor Bidder's Edge harmed the plaintiffs' property with their queries. Traditionally, the trespass to chattels tort has required significant harm, while trespass to real property has not. Moreover, courts have defined chattel as the computer, bandwidth, capacity, processing power, or network. With the exception of the computer, none of these are chattels because there is no private property right in bandwidth, processing power, or network.[48]

The California Supreme Court rejected the notion of extending trespass law to websites and servers in *Intel v. Hamidi* (2003), reasoning that

[c]reating an absolute property right to exclude undesired communications from one's e-mail and Web servers might help force spammers to internalize the costs they impose on ISP's and their customers. But such a property rule might also create substantial new costs, to e-mail and e-commerce users and to society generally, in lost ease and openness of communication and in lost network benefits.[49]

The court clarified that under California law, the trespass to chattels tort "does not encompass, and should not be extended to encompass, an electronic communication that neither damages the recipient computer system nor impairs its functioning."[50] It reversed an injunction against the defendant, a disgruntled employee who used Intel's e-mail system to send critical messages to employees about the company's employment practices, because Intel's e-mail system was never impaired. It added that while a private entity's refusal to transmit another's electronic mail messages does not implicate the First Amendment, because no governmental action is involved, the issuance of an injunction in a private lawsuit is an application of state power that must comply with First Amendment limits.[51]

Internet Gambling

While at least 50 countries consider gambling on the Internet to be a legal activity, the United States does not.[52] In the past decade, the industry has grown considerably. There are now approximately 2,000 online gambling sites, operating oversees, particularly in Europe, the Caribbean, and the Asian/Pacific rim. Ironically, their customer base is largely drawn from the United States. In 2005, online gaming generated $12 billion in revenue, half of which came from U.S. customers, according to a report conducted by Peter D. Hart Research Associates for the American Gaming Association (AGA).[53] That figure is projected to double by 2010.[54]

Although federal law does not directly prohibit U.S. citizens from gambling online, Congress has attempted to curtail the practice by passing legislation that prohibits businesses from taking bets online and banks from accepting payments from online gambling operations. State law generally determines whether a state's residents can legally engage in gambling activities. A person who lives in a state that makes gambling illegal would be violating the law by betting online even if the online casino is located outside the state. At least six states specifically address Internet gambling (Illinois, Louisiana, Nevada, Oregon, South Dakota, Washington).[55] Other states simply apply existing gambling laws to the Internet. But because most gambling crosses state and foreign borders, federal laws are more applicable.

In 2006, Congress passed the Unlawful Internet Gambling Enforcement Act, which applied to Internet wagers on sporting events as well as bets through online casinos. The statute prohibits gambling businesses from accepting credit cards, electronic fund transfers, checks, or drafts from Internet customers. It also directs the Federal Reserve, in consultation with the Attorney General, to prescribe regulations to require banks to identify and block financial transactions associated with Internet gambling.[56]

The Wire Communications Act is also used to control Internet gambling. It prohibits gambling businesses from "knowingly us[ing] a wire communication facility for the transmission in interstate or foreign commerce of bets or wagers or information assisting in the placing of bets or wagers on any sporting event or contest."[57] It also prohibits wire communications that entitle the recipient to receive money or credit as a result of bets or wagers or provide information to assist in the placing of bets or wagers. Because the statute bars "information assisting in the placing of bets or wagers on any sporting event or contest," the statute has been interpreted by some courts as applying only to sporting events and not to online casinos. But the Department of Justice disagrees with this interpretation.

Two other statutes used to curtail gambling are the Travel Act and the Illegal Gambling Business Act. The Travel Act prohibits the distribution of proceeds from any unlawful activity, including any enterprise involving gambling, in interstate or foreign commerce.[58] The Illegal Gambling Business Act makes it a crime to operate a gambling business prohibited by state law, involving five or more people, in operation more than 30 days or grossing more than $2,000 in one day. Congress passed the law in 1970 to target illegal gambling used to finance organized crime, an activity that affected interstate commerce.[59]

There is a domestic exception to Internet gambling, however. Congress included a specific exemption for horse racing in the Unlawful Internet Gambling Enforcement Act because a number of states allow pari-mutuel wagering on horse races.[60] In pari-mutuel wagers, gamblers bet against one another rather than against the house. Their money is pooled and most is distributed to the winner. A percentage is reserved for the racetrack, jockeys, and government.

Another exemption, for all practical purposes, is fantasy sports, which have become a $1.5 billion Internet industry. Participants in fantasy sports leagues manage virtual teams in a competition to get the best statistical outcome. Colorado attorney Charles Humphrey challenged the legality of fantasy sports in a suit against Viacom, CBS, ESPN, Inc., Sportsline.com Inc., and Vulcan Sports Media filed under anti-gambling and gambling loss recovery laws in New Jersey and several other states. The federal district court dismissed the suit, holding that the activities did not constitute online gambling because: "(1) the entry fees are paid unconditionally, (2) the prizes offered to fantasy sports contestants are for amounts certain and are guaranteed to be awarded and (3) defendants do not compete for the prizes."[61]

The United States imposes its gambling laws outside its borders. A foreign site that accepts a bet from an American citizen through the Internet violates the Wire Act. One that accepts payment from an American citizen via credit, bank transfer, or check violates the Unlawful Internet Gambling Enforcement Act. Sites that accept bets from residents of states in which gambling is illegal also violate the Travel Act and the Illegal Gambling Business Act.

The World Trade Organization (WTO) censured the United States for violating its General Agreement on Trade in Services obligations by preventing other nations from offering Internet gambling services to U.S. citizens. Antigua, a Caribbean nation that earns substantial profits from online gambling, filed a complaint with the WTO, claiming that a combination of the Wire Act, the Travel Act, and the Illegal Gambling Business Act blocked all gambling exchanges between the United States and Antigua. The WTO sided with Antigua in 2004 and the decision was upheld on appeal in 2005.[62] The WTO focused on the disconnect between banning international gambling sites from serving Americans while allowing domestic Internet gambling on horse races. The WTO ruled that the United States could either ban all forms of gambling or allow Americans to do business with offshore sites. When the U.S. ignored the ruling, the WTO awarded Antigua a $21 million credit on trade sanctions to be taken out in intellectual property.[63] In other words, the WTO will allow the island nation to violate the copyrights of American copyright holders up to the value of $21 million.

Virtual law

One area of digital law with growth potential concerns property and relationships that take place in virtual worlds but are litigated in the real world. Virtual worlds, like Second Life and other simulations (commonly known as sims), are used for gaming, social networking, business, education, and entertainment. Computer users inhabit these worlds through graphic representations of themselves called avatars. In many sims, users exchange virtual currency to buy and sell "property" online. Some games also allow users to convert virtual currency into real currency.

In the United States suits inspired by virtual relationships haven't gone far. For example, in 2007, Marc Bragg sued Linden Lab, the company behind Second Life, for suspending his account and confiscating online property that he used for business purposes "in world." Although Linden was convinced that Bragg had violated its terms of service, no decision came from the case because the parties settled out of court.[64]

World of Warcraft player Antonio Hernandez sued Internet Gaming Entertainment for diminishing the entertainment value of the game through a process called "gold mining."[65] IGE is a Massive Multiplayer Online Role Playing Game (MMORPG) Services Company that sold its players virtual currency they could use to advance in World of Warcraft without "earning" their status by overcoming challenges that more experienced gamers had conquered. The case was settled in 2008 when IGE promised to discontinue the practice.

However, outside the United States, virtual crime is taken more seriously. In Holland, for example, two 14-year-old boys were convicted of virtual property theft after they forced another boy to transfer virtual items from his account to theirs. Although the teens coerced their victim to transfer virtual items and currency he had won in the game by threatening him with a knife, the court focused on the property theft rather than the assault. Finding that "virtual goods are goods" under Dutch law, the court sentenced the boys to community service and probation for the theft.[66] In a second case, a Dutch teenager was arrested for theft and computer hacking because he hacked into other users' accounts to steal the equivalent of $6,000 in virtual furniture in the online game Habbo Hotel.[67]

A Japanese woman was arrested for computer hacking in 2008 after she "killed" another player's avatar.[68] When her virtual husband divorced her in the anime-style game Maple Story, she logged into his account and terminated his license, effectively terminating him as well.

In China Li Hongchen successfully sued the manufacturer of the game Red Moon after another avatar exploited a programming weakness to steal his online treasure and weapons. The Beijing Chaoyang District People's Court recognized the value of Hongchen's labor and awarded him a sum equal to the real-world value of the items.[69] China has also become the first country to tax profits made through virtual currency.[70]

Questions for Discussion

1. What role does ICANN play in the Internet's management? Why do other countries in the world prefer ICANN to function independently from the United States or to have some other system of Internet governance?
2. What is the difference between the domestic and international concepts of network neutrality?
3. What federal statutes are in place to combat computer misuse? What is the challenge that lawmakers face regarding international computer crimes?
4. What is virtual law? Should it be litigated in "real world" courts?

5

Conflict of Laws

From a technology perspective, we've never been closer to Marshall McLuhan's vision of a global village. Internet content can be accessed anywhere. Mobile phones and VoIP numbers cross borders as easily as the people who carry them. The footprint of a geostationary satellite can span multiple continents at once, and broadcast signals cross all borders within their area of reception. But from a legal perspective, our villages are still quite distinct. The world is made up of sovereign territories that do not always agree about the suitability of content that crosses their borders. Although they may praise digital media's power to extend science, art, and commerce, they also worry about its ability to exacerbate defamation, obscenity, hate speech, and fraud.

One might assume that nations and states have no recourse to battle content that is published elsewhere in the world – particularly through a medium like the Internet that goes everywhere. But it does occur and with greater frequency. States will prosecute publishers in other countries who disseminate content they consider illegal. They will allow their citizens to sue content producers in other countries for material perceived to cause harm. In some cases, they will even allow nonresidents to sue other nonresidents in their courts for online content received within their borders.

Internet publishers have been summoned to courts all over the world for content posted online that was legal in their home countries, but which was alleged to violate the law somewhere else. For example, Dow Jones was sued in Australia and England for material accessible through its *Barron's* magazine and *Wall Street Journal* websites. *The Washington Post* was sued in Canada for a story about an African UN worker. *Forbes* was sued by two Russian citizens in England. A French court found Yahoo! guilty of listing Nazi paraphernalia on its website. Germany tried and convicted an Australian for operating an English-language holocaust denial website.

These controversies highlight the increasing importance of an area of procedural law called *conflict of laws*, which is used to determine where conflicts between litigants from different places will be resolved and which nation or state's laws will apply. *Procedural law* is the body of legal rules that control access to the legal system. It is generally given less attention than *substantive law*, which defines a person's rights and limitations in a civil society. But it is an area of law that no one in digital media can afford to ignore.

This chapter explains how jurisdiction is determined in transborder conflicts, particularly in cases involving material published on the Internet. It also discusses the related concepts of choice of law and enforcement of foreign judgments, as well as alternative solutions to transborder conflicts, such as online dispute resolution and geolocation filtering.

Jurisdiction, Choice of Law, and Enforcement of Judgments

In the United States, conflicts law has three distinct branches: jurisdiction, choice of law, and enforcement of judgments. *Jurisdiction* refers to a court's prerogative to hear and adjudicate a case. A court with jurisdiction to decide a case is known as the forum court. *Choice of law* refers to the law that will apply in the case. In criminal cases, the applicable law will always be the law of the forum, *lex fori*. But in civil cases involving parties from different states, the applicable law is normally that of the state with the closest connection to the conflict. If the case involves a tortious act committed elsewhere, the law of the place of the harm, *lex loci*, usually applies. *Enforcement of judgments* refers to the state's power to put a court's judgment into effect. A state is powerless to enforce a judgment outside of its own jurisdiction. A plaintiff who wins a judgment in a forum court against a defendant who resides in another state will be forced to petition a court within the defendant's jurisdiction to enforce the foreign judgment.

Jurisdiction

A sovereign's power to legislate, interpret, and impose law is limited by its jurisdiction. The term jurisdiction refers to the territory in which a sovereign may exercise its authority. *Territory* can be taken literally to mean "geographic region," but it should also be taken metaphorically to mean "purview," referring to the people and subject matter over which it may impose its authority. There are two kinds of jurisdiction: personal jurisdiction and subject matter jurisdiction.

Personal jurisdiction

A state may claim jurisdiction over its own residents and businesses that operate within its territory. Under certain circumstances, it also may exercise jurisdiction over a nonresident defendant if doing so would not violate the defendant's right to due process. Due process refers to the fair application of legal procedures. The concept can be traced to thirteenth-century England. After years of enduring King John's abuse, English barons turned on him and extracted a promise that from then forward he would act only in accordance with the "law of the land." His promises were incorporated into the Magna Carta, the forerunner of modern constitutions. Due process rights are guaranteed in the U.S. Constitution's Fifth and Fourteenth Amendments, which stipulate that no person may be deprived of "life, liberty, or property, without due process of law."

A court may exercise *specific jurisdiction* over a nonresident defendant without violating due process if the controversy before it is related to or "arises out of" the defendant's contacts with the forum state.[1] The landmark case on personal jurisdiction in the United States is *International Shoe Co. v. Washington* (1945). In it the Supreme Court held that a state may assert jurisdiction over a defendant that is not present within a state if the defendant has established "minimum contacts with [the forum] such that the maintenance of the suit does not offend traditional notions of fair play and substantial justice."[2] A court will not assert jurisdiction over an out-of-state defendant based on the court's connection to the plaintiff. The court must have a connection to the defendant. The critical question in assessing the strength of that relationship is whether the defendant "purposely avail[ed] ... of the privilege of conducting activities within the forum State, thus invoking the benefits and protections of its laws," and consequently "should reasonably anticipate being haled into court there."[3]

On occasion, states do claim jurisdiction over defendants who have had little to no contact with the forum, but whose actions have nonetheless caused injury there. In order to satisfy due process in such situations, courts look for indicators of the defendant's intent to harm. In *Calder v. Jones* (1984), actress Shirley Jones, a resident of California, sued the *National Enquirer* and members of its staff for defamation.[4] The *Enquirer* is a weekly magazine published in Florida and Calder, its editor, was a Florida resident who had been to California on only two occasions unrelated to the article. The Supreme Court concluded that California's jurisdiction over the defendants was reasonable under the circumstances because the defendants *purposely aimed their actions toward a resident of the state, knowing that the brunt of the injury would be felt there.* Evidence that the defendant targeted the state, knowing harm could occur there is required to meet the *Calder* test. It is not satisfied merely because the plaintiff, who resides in the forum, feels the effects of the defendant's actions there.

If the plaintiff's cause of action does not arise from the defendant's contacts with the state, a court may still exercise *general jurisdiction* over the defendant if the defendant's general contacts with the state have been continuous and systematic[5]. In *Keeton v. Hustler Magazine* (1984), a New York resident sued an Ohio publisher in New Hampshire because it was the only state left in which the statute of limitations for a defamation action had not expired.[6] The Supreme Court held that the defendant's regular circulation of the magazine in the state was sufficient to justify

New Hampshire's exercise of personal jurisdiction over it. Furthermore, it did not matter that the petitioner was not a resident of New Hampshire. The Court concluded that "lack of residence will not defeat jurisdiction established on the basis of the defendant's contacts."[7]

Criteria for specific jurisdiction

(1) The defendant must have purposely availed of the forum state's benefits.
(2) The claim must arise out of the defendant's contacts with the forum.
(3) The exercise of jurisdiction must be consistent with due process notions of "fair play" and "substantial justice."

Criteria for general jurisdiction

(1) the defendant's contacts with the state, if unrelated to the cause of action, must be continuous and systematic.

Long-arm statutes

Following the Supreme Court's decision in *International Shoe* to allow states to assert jurisdiction over nonresidents, states began to pass *long-arm statutes* specifying the conditions under which courts could serve process to out-of-state defendants. Many modeled their statutes on the Uniform Interstate and International Procedures Act, which suggests jurisdiction over out-of-state defendants is appropriate when they:

• transact business within the state;
• perform a tortious act within the state;
• own or possess real estate within the state;
• insure a person or property within the state; or
• engage in an activity outside the state that causes injury within the state.

Most long-arm statutes permit personal jurisdiction to the full extent allowed by the Constitution. Consequently, a court's consideration of whether it may lawfully claim jurisdiction over a nonresident defendant is a two-part process. It must first examine its state's long-arm statute to determine whether its assertion of jurisdiction would be consistent with state law. If so, it moves to the second phase of analysis, determining whether personal jurisdiction would be consistent with the defendant's right to due process.

Subject matter jurisdiction

In addition to personal jurisdiction, courts must have subject matter jurisdiction to hear a particular kind of controversy. State courts of limited jurisdiction may hear only certain types of controversies involving traffic, juveniles, or probate cases. State courts of general jurisdiction may hear any case that is not prohibited by state law. States generally prohibit their courts from hearing controversies that do not involve their residents or issues related to the state. A Florida court could not, for example, hear a case involving two residents of Mississippi about a matter that had nothing to do with Florida.

The subject matter jurisdiction of federal courts is limited to actions described in Article III, Section II of the Constitution and federal statutes passed by Congress. Federal courts may consider:

*   controversies arising under the Constitution, laws of the United States, and treaties;
*   cases in which the United States is a party;
*   cases between a state or its citizens and foreign states or their citizens;
*   cases involving ambassadors and representatives from foreign states as parties;
*   cases based on admiralty law (the law of the seas);
*   copyright and patent cases;
*   bankruptcy proceedings;
*   lawsuits involving the military;
*   diversity cases involving claims in excess of $75,000.[8]

Diversity cases are civil actions that involve plaintiffs and defendants who are residents of different states or nations.

A federal court may assume jurisdiction over a case that began in a state court if a constitutional or federal right is threatened during the course of litigation. For example, a federal court may accept a case in which the defendant claims that his right to due process was violated by a state's unreasonable exercise of jurisdiction over him.

The Constitution limits the Supreme Court's original jurisdiction – its right to be the first court to hear a case – to controversies between two or more states, between the United States and a state, or in which foreign officials are involved.[9] In every other case, the Supreme Court has appellate jurisdiction, meaning that it reviews cases that have already been through lower courts.

Forum non conveniens

Once a court has determined that it has the right to exercise jurisdiction over an out-of-state defendant, it must decide whether it should. In common law systems, defendants may petition a court to stay (suspend) an action under the doctrine *of forum non conveniens* (a Latin term that means inconvenient forum) if litigating the case in the plaintiff's chosen jurisdiction would pose a particular hardship to other parties in the case and a competent alternative forum exists. The court may oblige if it believes that the interests of justice and the parties involved would be better served elsewhere.[10]

In a trial involving foreign citizens and residents of the United States, the Supreme Court has made it clear that one factor that would not apply to a decision of forum non conveniens is "whether the substantive law that would be applied in the alternative forum is less favorable to the plaintiffs than that of the present forum."[11] The Court reiterated that the central issue in a forum non conveniens decision is convenience. It recognized that there would be exceptions, however, adding that "if the remedy provided by the alternative forum is so clearly inadequate or unsatisfactory that it is no remedy at all, the unfavorable change in law may be given substantial weight ..."[12]

The Supreme Court also noted that although courts normally defer to the plaintiff in choice of forum, less deference would be granted when the plaintiff is foreign. It justified the distinction by pointing out that "[A] plaintiff's choice of forum is entitled to greater deference when the plaintiff has chosen the home forum. When the home forum has been chosen, it is reasonable to assume that this choice is convenient. When the plaintiff is foreign, however, this assumption is much less reasonable."[13]

Evolution of jurisdiction in light of the Internet

The United States – with 50 separate jurisdictions – has more experience with Internet jurisdiction than any other country in the world. Over the last two decades, its philosophy has evolved considerably. Originally, courts based jurisdiction on whether or not the site was accessible within the forum. In 1996, for example, a Connecticut federal court claimed jurisdiction over a Massachusetts defendant in a trademark infringement case. The court concluded the defendant could reasonably anticipate being haled into Connecticut because its Internet advertisements were directed toward all states, including Connecticut.[14]

As courts' understanding of the Internet became more sophisticated, they began to reject the proposition that jurisdiction could be based on Internet access alone. An alternative test was developed by a Pennsylvania district court in *Zippo Manufacturing Company v. Zippo Dot Com, Inc.* (1997). The court concluded that a website operator's contacts with a forum should be assessed on a sliding scale, based on the website's level of commercial activity and interactive ability. At one end of the spectrum are websites that do business over the Internet. If the defendant regularly exchanges files and enters into contracts with customers, personal jurisdiction is appropriate. At the other end are passive websites. If the defendant simply posts information for anyone to read, jurisdiction is not appropriate. In between are interactive websites. In these cases, courts must consider "the level of inter-activity and commercial nature of the exchange of information that occurs on the Web site."[15]

The *Zippo* test is widely used among federal and state courts to establish a defendant's personal availment of a forum's benefits in an Internet context.[16] Its application is particularly appropriate in commercial cases. For example, the California Supreme Court used the *Zippo* test to establish personal availment in *Snowney v. Harrah's Entertainment, Inc.* (2005).[17] A California resident sued Harrah's hotel in Las Vegas for overcharging him. When the defendant moved to have the summons quashed for lack of personal jurisdiction, the trial court granted the motion. But a California appellate court reversed, and the California Supreme Court upheld the decision. The California Supreme Court observed that the defendant's website, which quoted rates and accepted reservations, was interactive, putting it in the middle of the *Zippo* sliding scale. Also, by advertising in California and supplying directions to the hotel from California, the defendant targeted the state. Many of the hotel's guests were from California, so the defendant benefited from the state – personally availing itself of conducting business there.

Zippo's emphasis on commercial activity is appropriate for Internet cases related to e-commerce, such as trademark infringement or dilution, unfair competition, or false advertising. It has been applied in other contexts, such as defamation, but the conceptual connection is less apparent. The *Zippo* test focuses on the character of the website rather than the character of the statement. However, a libelous statement posted on a passive, noncommercial website may be just as harmful as one made on an interactive, commercial site.

The *Calder* effects test is more commonly used to assess jurisdiction in Internet defamation cases. Courts use it to look for evidence that the defendant targeted its actions at a particular state knowing that harm was likely to occur there. The U.S. Court of Appeals for the Fourth Circuit applied the *Calder* test in *Young v. New Haven Advocate* (2002).[18] The case involved a Virginia prison warden who sued two Connecticut newspapers in Virginia for libel in response to newspaper articles published on their websites. He believed the articles, which concerned Connecticut prisoners housed in a Virginia prison under his care, suggested that the prisoners were being mistreated. Applying the *Calder* test, the Fourth Circuit reached the conclusion that jurisdiction in Virginia would not be reasonable. Although the articles were accessible in Virginia via the Internet, they were targeted at Connecticut readers. The court took into account that the newspapers had no offices in Virginia or personnel who worked there, and that most of their subscribers lived in Connecticut.

However, a New Jersey appellate court found that targeting was apparent in the Internet libel case *Goldhaber v. Kohlenberg* (2007).[19] The defendant in the case, a resident of California, was alleged to have made disparaging remarks on an Internet forum about two residents of New Jersey. It was clear that the author of the remarks, which involved accusations of incest and bestiality, knew where the plaintiff resided, because his references extended beyond the plaintiffs to their town, its police department, and the plaintiffs' neighbors. Applying *Calder*, the court concluded that the defendant had in fact targeted the plaintiff in New Jersey and that his conduct was such that he should have reasonably anticipated being haled into court there.

It is not particularly difficult to find contradictory decisions regarding jurisdiction in Internet cases, but there is a definite trend in the United States toward demanding more than harm felt by the plaintiff. Where speech is at issue, courts generally have concluded that defendants who post messages on websites, listservs, and newsgroups accessible in another state do not establish minimum contacts with the state sufficient to justify personal jurisdiction, unless they avail themselves of the state's benefits in some way or engage in a specific action to target the state, knowing harm will result there.[20]

Choice of law

Intuitively one would assume that the court that handles a case would apply its own law, but this is not always true. In conflicts law, jurisdiction and choice of law are two separate issues. It is standard practice for courts to apply their own procedural law to determine jurisdiction and how process will be served. But in cases involving litigants from different places, the forum court may decide that justice would be better served by applying another state or nation's substantive law to the matter at issue in the case. Criminal cases are an exception. The law of the forum always applies in criminal trials, for procedural and substantive decisions.

Until the mid-20th century, U.S. courts primarily based choice-of-law decisions on territorial considerations. In tort cases, in which plaintiffs claimed that a foreign defendant had injured them in some way (physically, emotionally, or financially), U.S. courts applied the substantive law of the place where the injury occurred (*lex loci delicti commissi*). In this respect, American conflicts law was aligned with the practices of other common law and civil law systems, which also favored lex loci.

But in the latter half of the 20th century, a philosophical movement called legal realism took hold in the United States. Legal realists questioned the practice of applying other states' or nations' laws rather than applying the law of the forum, which would further its social policies. As an alternative to basing choice of law on the place of the wrong, they suggested basing choice of law on government interests, functional analysis, or the better law for the particular case. Their theories had the effect of promoting forum law. Other areas of the world considered the approach more parochial than revolutionary. This period of change in the United States has come to be known as the "conflicts revolution."

Seeking a compromise between the two perspectives on choice of law, the American Law Institute published the Restatement (Second) of the Conflict of Laws, which applies the laws of the state with "the most significant relationship to the occurrence and the parties."[21] To determine which state has the most significant relationship, the forum court must consider a range of factors, including:

- the needs of the interstate or international system;
- policies of the forum and interested states;
- protection of the parties' expectations;
- general policies underlying the particular area of law;
- the need for certainty, predictability, and uniformity of result;
- ease in determining and applying the law;
- the place where the harm occurred and the conduct causing the injury;
- nationalities of the parties, their residence or place of incorporation; and
- where the relationship between the parties, if any, exists.[22]

The process of balancing these factors is often referred to as interest analysis. American courts like the approach because it gives them flexibility. Consequently, most jurisdictions in the United States have adopted it. But the sacrifice for flexibility has been the consistency and predictability that other nations prize.

Enforcement of judgments

In general, states are obligated to enforce one another's judgments, even if they would not be able to render the same judgment under their own laws. Article 4, Section 1 of the Constitution stipulates that states must give "full faith and credit" to the laws and proceedings of other states in the nation.

However, if the court asked to enforce the out-of-state judgment is not convinced that the original court had jurisdiction over the defendant when the judgment was rendered, it may refuse. The Supreme Court of Minnesota rejected an Alabama judgment based on lack of jurisdiction in *Griffis v. Luban* (2002). A University of Alabama professor of Egyptology brought a libel action against a Minnesota resident who disparaged her academic credentials on an Internet archaeology newsgroup. When the defendant did not answer the suit, the Alabama court entered a default judgment against her. The defendant fought the plaintiff's attempts to enforce the judgment up to Minnesota's Supreme Court. It concluded that Alabama's jurisdiction was not proper because the defendant had not "expressly aimed the allegedly tortious conduct" at Alabama.[23]

Private International Law

Beyond U.S. borders, conflicts law is more commonly called *private international law*. The term private international law can be somewhat misleading because it suggests there is an international body of law that applies to transborder conflicts when, in fact, there is not. The word *private* characterizes the type of litigants involved in civil cases – individuals, corporations, or organizations, while the word *international* reflects the fact that they come from different countries. Private international law is, in fact, a domestic branch of law. Each country (or state, in the case of federations like the United States) establishes its own conflicts rules. There are, however, many similarities among the approaches taken by sovereign nations that share common legal systems.

International law, the body of law governing the legal relationships between nations rather than individuals, is distinguished from private international law by most countries as *public international law*. Public international law includes treaties, decisions of the International Court of Justice, United Nations resolutions, and criminal law.

International jurisdiction takes three forms: (a) jurisdiction to adjudicate, (b) jurisdiction to prescribe, and (c) jurisdiction to enforce, which correspond to personal jurisdiction, choice of law, and enforcement of foreign judgments.[24]

Jurisdiction to adjudicate

Jurisdiction to adjudicate, also called adjudicatory or judicial jurisdiction, refers to a nation's authority to subject persons or things to the process of its courts or administrative tribunals.[25] Before a court may adjudicate a case, it must have jurisdiction over the parties and the subject matter involved. Although nations address due process concerns differently, most follow procedural standards to ensure that jurisdiction is reasonable, based on factors such as whether

- there is a link between one of the parties and the state;
- the party has consented to exercise of jurisdiction;
- the party regularly does business in the state; or
- the party engaged in an activity outside the state that had a substantial and foreseeable effect within the state.[26]

Transnational conflicts involving the Internet are often based on the last factor.

Foreseeable effects The international approach to personal jurisdiction based on the effects of Internet content differs from that of the United States with respect to what is required to satisfy due process concerns. Before asserting jurisdiction over a foreign defendant, an American court would have to be satisfied that the defendant had established a connection to the forum. If the defendant's contacts were not continuous and systematic, but rather minimum in scope, he or she must have targeted the forum or at least personally availed of its benefits before jurisdiction would be considered reasonable. In contrast, most nations do not demand a specific connection between the forum and the defendant to satisfy due process. It is sufficient that the defendant could have reasonably foreseen that his actions would cause harm in the forum and that his actions did, in fact, cause harm there.[27]

Dow Jones v. Gutnick (2001) Internationally, the most significant transnational case to consider jurisdiction in a conflict involving Internet material is *Dow Jones v. Gutnick* (2001).[28] As the first of such cases to reach a nation's highest court, it has been widely cited as an influential precedent by other courts around the world. The case involved a libel suit filed by Joseph Gutnick, an Australian entrepreneur, against Dow Jones, the American publisher of *Barron's* magazine, in response to a *Barron's* article that implied he was involved in money laundering. Although the article was published in New Jersey, it could be accessed via an online subscription in Victoria, Australia, where Gutnick resided and filed the suit.

Dow Jones filed a motion for forum non conveniens, arguing that Victoria was an inconvenient forum because its editorial offices and servers were located in the United States, along with 95 percent of its subscribers. But the company conceded that it had 1,700 subscribers in Australia and that several hundred of them resided in Victoria. The trial court concluded that Victoria was the more appropriate forum for the suit because any harm to Gutnick's reputation was likely to have occurred there.

Dow Jones appealed to Australia's High Court, which upheld the lower court's decision. In its appeal, Dow Jones argued that the action should be litigated in New Jersey, where the article was published. But the High Court distinguished between publication as an *act* and publication as a *fact*. While acknowledging that the article was uploaded to a server in New Jersey, the Court contended that publication actually takes place when the material is downloaded. It reasoned that "[h]arm to reputation is done when a defamatory publication is comprehended by the reader, the listener, or the observer ... This being so it would be wrong to treat publication as if it were a unilateral act on the part of the publisher alone."[29]

In fact, the Court explained, it is "the bilateral nature of publication [that] underpins the long-established common law rule that every communication of defamatory matter founds a separate cause of action."[30] Australia, like many other countries around the world, allows plaintiffs to sue for multiple causes of action, meaning they can file suit in every jurisdiction in which they experience injury. For example, a plaintiff libeled in a book published in Australia and Canada could sue the defendant in both places.

Dow Jones contended that the court's theory that publication takes place at the point of reception, combined with its policy of allowing multiple causes of action, would expose a publisher to litigation wherever the material is accessible. However, the High Court considered this unlikely. It reasoned that plaintiffs would only be likely to sue in places where they had a reputation to protect and a judgment would be of value to them, and that a judgment's value would depend on whether the defendant had assets there. Nevertheless, the court clearly considered it "foreseeable" to defendants who publish on the Internet that harm could occur anywhere. It said "However broad may be the reach of any particular means of communication, those who post information on the World Wide Web do so knowing that the information they make available is available to all and sundry without any geographic restriction."[31]

The Supreme Court of Judicature in England cited this passage from *Gutnick* when it upheld a lower court's assertion of jurisdiction over an Internet libel case in which both the plaintiff and defendants were U.S. residents and the websites carrying the disputed material were based in California. This practice of filing libel suits in countries that are especially plaintiff friendly is known as "libel tourism." American boxing promoter Don King filed suit against boxer Lennox Lewis (who is an English citizen, but a resident of New York), his promoter, and his attorney, in England where libel laws are much more favorable to plaintiffs than those in the United States. When the suit was filed, all parties resided in the United States and were involved in a separate suit that had generated heated public comments. By the time it reached trial, the defendants in *Lewis and others v. King* had dwindled down to one, Lewis's attorney, Judd Burstein, who had described King as anti-Semitic in interviews published on two California websites for boxing aficionados. The case seemingly had no connection to England other than the fact that the websites were accessible there. But the English court that claimed jurisdiction observed that King was well known in England (and therefore considered to have had a reputation there to protect). King also provided evidence that English boxing fans had read the websites and were aware of the accusation. The justices dismissed Burstein's argument that the appropriate forum should be the one targeted by the publisher. The court said "it makes little sense to distinguish between one jurisdiction and another in order to decide which the defendant has 'targeted,' when in truth he has 'targeted' every jurisdiction where his text may be downloaded."[32]

The English House of Lords affirmed a lower court's decision to allow two Russian citizens to sue *Forbes* magazine in the United Kingdom in *Berezovsky v. Michaels* (2000).[33] The plaintiffs sued the magazine after it published an exposé, in print and on its website, suggesting that they were involved in organized crime. The article, titled "Godfather of the Kremlin?" described the plaintiffs as "criminals on an outrageous scale" and suggested Berezovsky was involved in the murder of a Russian television personality. The article was based on police reports and interviews with dozens of witnesses, but Berezovsky was never charged with the crime. *Forbes* motioned for forum non conveniens, arguing that the case would be better tried in the United States, where the magazine is published, or in Russia, where the plaintiffs resided. But the court refused. The plaintiffs engaged in business in London, so the court considered England an appropriate forum for the suit despite *Forbes*'s limited circulation there. *Forbes* was forced to issue an apology and a retraction. Four years later the *Forbes* reporter who wrote the article was murdered in Russia.[34] The case remains unsolved.

Canada also bases jurisdiction on foreseeability. In *Burke v. NYP Holdings, Inc.* (2005), a British Columbia court asserted jurisdiction over the *New York Post* in an Internet defamation case.[35] The plaintiff, Vancouver Canucks' ex-manager Brian Burke, sued the newspaper for publishing a column that suggested he had challenged his players to harm a member of an opposing team in a hockey game. The *Post* did not deliver the paper to British Columbia, but the column was accessible there via the Web. The newspaper could not tell how many people had accessed the site in British Columbia, but it was clear that at least one person had.

A Canadian radio host read the article on his show. The court asserted that the defendant should have reasonably foreseen that the article would be republished in Canada.

But foreseeability has its limits. The Ontario Court of Appeals reversed a lower court's decision to claim jurisdiction over the *Washington Post* in a libel suit based on articles it had published about the plaintiff while he lived in Africa.[36] Cheickh Bangoura worked for the United Nations as a regional director for its U.N. Drug Control Program. While he was working in Kenya, the *Washington Post* reported that his colleagues had accused him of "sexual harassment, financial improprieties and nepotism."[37] Bangoura subsequently lost his job and moved to Montreal, then three years later to Ontario, where he filed the suit after three more years. The articles were accessible in Ontario through the newspaper's Internet archive, but only one person had accessed them – Bangoura's attorney. The court said the *Washington Post* could not have foreseen that Bangoura would move to Canada. "To hold otherwise would mean that a defendant could be sued almost anywhere in the world based upon where a plaintiff may decide to establish his or her residence long after the publication of the defamation." (¶ 25)

The basic principle of assuming jurisdiction where the harm occurs applies to all media, including broadcast. In *Jenner v. Sun Oil Company Limited et al.* (1952), an Ontario court claimed jurisdiction over two American broadcasters and a New York radio station because their New York broadcast about the plaintiff could be heard in Ontario.[38]

Jurisdiction to prescribe

Jurisdiction to prescribe, also called prescriptive or legislative jurisdiction, is the international analog to choice of law. It refers to a nation's authority to apply its substantive law to particular individuals and circumstances.[39] A nation or state may apply its laws to a conflict or controversy as long as there is a sufficient nexus between it and the conduct at issue to justify state action.[40] Prescriptive jurisdiction may be based on four principles: territoriality, nationality, effects, and protection. Section 402 of the Restatement (Third) of the Foreign Relations Law of the United States indicates that a state may prescribe its laws to:

1. (a) conduct that, wholly or in substantial part, takes place within its territory;
    (b) the status of persons, or interests in things, present within its territory;
    (c) conduct outside its territory that has or is intended to have substantial effect within its territory;
2. the activities, interests, status, or relations of its nationals outside as well as within its territory; and
3. certain conduct outside its territory by persons not its nationals that is directed against the security of the state or against a limited class of other state interests.[41]

There is one other principle upon which prescriptive jurisdiction may be based – universality.[42] States may prescribe punishment for certain offenses that are recognized among nations as of universal concern, even when none of the bases of jurisdiction indicated in Section 402 is present. These include piracy, slave trade, attacks on or hijacking of aircraft, genocide, war crimes, and certain acts of terrorism.

Comity   A state exercising prescriptive jurisdiction is obligated to consider the interests of other states that might have a connection to the controversy. This practice is known as *comity*. "The doctrine of comity asserts that the courts of each country should exercise their judicial powers in a manner that takes into consideration the aims and interests of other states in order to further cooperation, reciprocity and international courtesy."[43] Most courts equate comity with reasonableness.[44]

Jurisdiction to enforce

Jurisdiction to enforce, or executive jurisdiction, refers to a state's abilities to enforce judgments rendered against a defendant. Although a court that claims jurisdiction over a defendant may render a judgment against the party, the court is powerless to enforce the judgment outside of its own jurisdiction. Consequently, if the defendant has no assets in the jurisdiction and resides elsewhere, the plaintiff is forced to take the judgment to a court within the defendant's jurisdiction to request that it enforce the foreign judgment.

The doctrine of comity suggests that unless there is an overwhelming reason not to honor the foreign judgment, a court should do so. However, there are occasions when enforcing a foreign judgment may be seen as inappropriate. For example, a court may refuse to enforce a foreign judgment if it believes (1) the judicial system that rendered it does not provide impartial tribunals; (2) the judgment was obtained fraudulently; (3) a valid, earlier judgment is in effect that contradicts it; or (4) that the forum court exercised exorbitant jurisdiction by accepting a case when it had no real connection to the claim.[45]

The public policy exception   Courts are also within their rights to refuse judgments that contradict their deeply rooted public policies. American courts have used the public policy exception to reject judgments that would undermine First Amendment protections.[46] This was the issue in the now famous case *Yahoo! Inc. v. La Ligue Contre Le Racisme et L'Antisemitisme.*[47]

A French court issued a judgment against Yahoo! for selling Nazi memorabilia on its American auction site, accessible through the Internet in France where the sale or display of racist material is a crime.[48] Yahoo! subsequently sought a declaratory judgment to confirm that an American court's enforcement of the order would violate the First Amendment.[49] Courts may issue declaratory judgments to establish the rights and obligations of parties in cases that present an actual controversy.[50] A California federal district court granted the declaratory judgment, but the Ninth Circuit reversed. The court of appeals concluded that the case was not ripe for adjudication because the French plaintiffs had not moved to enforce the judgment.[51] In the United States, courts prefer to wait until a controversy is "ripe" before adjudicating the matter, not only to conserve judicial resources, but also to avoid setting a bad precedent in a situation that is too abstract.

Several states, including New York, Illinois, and Florida, now require their courts to refuse to enforce libel judgments against their residents if the judgments were rendered by foreign courts that lack the same speech protections guaranteed by the U.S. Constitution and their state constitutions. In 2008, the New York Assembly and Senate unanimously passed the Libel Terrorism Protection Act, inspired by New York author Rachel Ehrenfeld.[52] Dr. Ehrenfeld is a recognized authority on financing international terrorism who was sued for libel in England by Saudi banker Khalid bin Mahfouz after she accused him of funding Osama bin Laden in her book *Funding Evil: How Terrorism Is Financed and How to Stop It.* Only 23 copies of the book found their way to England – all through Internet orders. Nevertheless an English court issued a default judgment against her for $225,000 and demanded that she destroy all remaining copies of her book.

Rachel Ehrenfeld, a expert on terrorism finance, was sued in England by a Saudi businessman who claimed to have been libeled in her book, *Funding Evil*. Her case inspired passage of a New York law to combat libel tourism.

A New York Congressman introduced similar legislation in the U.S. House of Representatives called the Freedom of Speech Protection Act.[53] The bill passed the House but stalled in the Senate during the 2008 election cycle. It was reintroduced in the 111th Congressional session.[54] If voted into law, it will prevent U.S. courts from enforcing libel judgments that would be unconstitutional in the United States, but would not apply to other kinds of judgments.

Criminal judgments   Comity does not extend to the enforcement of foreign criminal judgments. However, to assist a foreign court that has rendered a penal judgment against a defendant, another country may agree to cooperate in extradition proceedings, by surrendering the defendant to the state with jurisdiction.

Alternatively, the court that rendered the judgment will have to wait to enforce it until the defendant enters the country. This is what happened to Fredrick Tobin, an Australian citizen, prosecuted in absentia in Germany, for dissemination of hate speech. Tobin, who was born in Germany, operated a website in Australia that he used to question Holocaust history. Although the documents were printed in English and posted on an Australian server, the court observed that the website was accessible in Germany where people might read the text and re-circulate it. When Tobin visited Germany, he was arrested and jailed for seven months.[55] Germany is the first country to prosecute someone from another country for disseminating hate speech on the Internet.

Choice of Forum / Choice of Law Agreements

It has now common among companies engaged in business to include clauses within their contracts specifying the jurisdiction and law that would apply should a legal dispute occur. Usually the two clauses are side by side. If the parties to a contract have not made a specific choice regarding the law to be applied in the event of a legal clash, the court will infer a choice based on the law of the place with the closest connection to the contract. This is usually either where the contract was signed or executed.

Most Internet users are parties to choice of forum and choice of court agreements whether they realize it or not. These clauses are buried in the terms of use agreements that users must accept by clicking "OK" or "I accept" before registering to use a commercial site like Amazon or eBay. American courts enforce these contracts, regardless of whether the party who clicks assent actually reads the terms. They are not, however, enforceable in all countries. The European Union, for example, will not enforce choice of forum clauses. Its refusal to do so is intended to protect online consumers, so they can litigate conflicts at home rather than traveling to a retailer's jurisdiction. The policy is balanced, however, by the EU's E-Commerce Directive, which dictates that choice of law in e-commerce cases is

that of the country of origination rather than the country of reception.[56] So while
an EU plaintiff from France might be able to sue an online retailer from Germany
in France, German law would apply. The directive only applies to commercial messages. It is not applicable to personal torts like defamation or invasion of privacy.
The directive also preferences EU states. If a defendant like Yahoo! operates a
website outside the EU, choice of law reverts back to the member state. Consequently,
a French plaintiff could sue in France under French law.

Audiovisual Media Services Directive

The European Union's Audiovisual Media Services Directive, which applies to
video on demand, mobile TV, and audiovisual services on digital TV, assigns jurisdiction in cases involving programming to the country of origin. The directive
applies only to commercial "television-like" mass media services. Its application to
the Internet is limited. It is not intended to apply to text-based online communications or audio programming, but it does apply to video programs that are streamed,
webcast, or downloaded from the Internet. It does not mention privacy or defamation explicitly for jurisdictional purposes, but it includes a provision for a right of
reply in cases in which someone's reputation is harmed by a television program
that uses incorrect information.[57]

Treaties on Jurisdiction and Choice of Law

Various courts have suggested that the conflict of laws problem is intransigent and
that the only real solution will have to come through diplomatic negotiations at the
international level. The Hague Conference on Private International Law took up
the challenge of developing an international treaty on recognition of jurisdiction
and foreign judgments in the late 1990s, but did not succeed.[58] The treaty finally
negotiated was a dramatically scaled-down version of the original goal that addressed
business-to-business choice of court agreements.

   In contrast, the European Union has successfully negotiated treaties on jurisdiction and choice of law with its member states. The EU's treaty governing jurisdiction is called the Brussels Regulation.[59] In general, it establishes jurisdiction in the
state where the defendant resides. But in cases involving torts like defamation or
invasion of privacy, it assigns jurisdiction to the place where the harmful event
occurred or may occur.

   The world's largest treaty on choice of law agreements is the European Union's
Rome Convention.[60] The treaty, signed in Rome in 1980, indicates that choice of
law in cases arising from contract disputes will be the law of the state specified
in the terms of the contract. In 2007, members of the European Union also

finalized a treaty on choice of law in noncontractual obligations – including torts – called Rome II. Although member nations seemed to be in agreement on jurisdiction, choice of law was another issue. Negotiating the treaty took four years and the members were never able to reach a consensus on the applicable law in defamation and privacy actions, particularly where the Internet is concerned.

"The problem is clear," said EU Vice President of Parliament Diana Wallis. "They don't want to be subject to each other's laws. The UK media will tell you that they don't want to be subject to French privacy laws. Look at it from the French side; they are scared silly about damage awards in the UK."[61]

Alternative Dispute Resolution

In the absence of a multinational agreement, parties in transborder conflicts may have to seek out their own diplomacy through private dispute resolution specialists. As an alternative to litigation through the traditional legal system, more digital content providers are turning to arbitration and mediation.

Arbitration is a dispute resolution process in which a legally trained, neutral third person or panel of experts hears a dispute between two or more parties in conflict and, after considering the evidence, renders a verdict based on law in favor of one party. In essence, the arbitrator takes the place of judge and jury. Arbitration offers the same range of legal remedies that courts offer, but opportunities for appeal are limited. If the parties opt for binding arbitration, the arbitrator's decision will be legally enforceable. If the disputing parties opt for nonbinding arbitration, they will still have the opportunity to pursue litigation following the arbitration if they are not satisfied with its outcome. Many of the click-through contracts that commercial websites employ now require consumers to submit to binding arbitration.

Mediation is an alternative dispute resolution process in which disputing parties volunteer to work together with a neutral mediator to find a mutually agreeable solution. The resulting solution is negotiated rather than imposed on the parties involved. It may be legally enforced if the parties agree to turn it into a binding settlement agreement.

Alternative dispute resolution has gained popularity because disputes are generally settled faster and less expensively than they would be in a traditional court system. Dispute resolution services are also available online, using web-based technology such as VoIP, e-mail, chat rooms, instant messaging, video conferencing, and wikis, which is much more convenient for people who cannot afford the cost of travel or the time that goes into traditional litigation.[62] In an international dispute, online dispute resolution also bypasses the issue of whether a particular court has jurisdiction over a dispute.

Geolocation filtering: code v. law

Computer code is also used as an alternative to litigation with mixed results. Because publishers are not sure where they may be liable for the content they publish, some are experimenting with geolocation software that restricts access to readers from particular countries.

The *New York Times*, for example, prevented British readers from accessing an article it published about a foiled terrorism plot in London. In 2006, London police arrested more than 20 people for plotting to detonate explosives on trans-Atlantic flights between England and the United States. One week later, the *New York Times* published a front-page article titled "In Tapes, Receipts and a Diary, Details of the British Terror Case Emerge," which detailed all that had been learned since the arrest. The story posed no problems under U.S. laws. However, the *New York Times* editorial staff was concerned that it might violate England's Contempt of Court Act, which prohibits media organizations from publishing anything about a suspect arrested for a criminal act that might bias a jury pool. Editors who violate the Act risk jail. England has demonstrated its willingness to assert jurisdiction in other circumstances involving Internet material published in the United States. With this in mind, editors at the *Times* blocked English readers' access with the same software it uses to direct advertisements to readers in particular geographic locations.

The *New York Times* hasn't attempted to block a story since and doesn't have an official policy on it. "Whether we would do something similar again would depend on the circumstances," said George Freeman, vice president and assistant general counsel of the *New York Times*.[63] "The law is, from our perspective, very strict. There were some who argued that we ought to oppose it. But it is tough to fight a battle like that not on your home turf. It would also put us in the position of telling another country what's appropriate, and that's not a good position to be in."

Geolocation technology works by blocking Internet Protocol addresses – the unique numerical identifiers that allow computers to communicate with one another on the Internet. When a computer user requests access to a file online, like a particular article in an online publication for example, the user's browser supplies the file server with an IP address that tells it where to send the information. A server programmed to consider the user's location before granting access to a file will forward the request to a geolocation service first to see if it should grant access to the information.

Other online content providers, like the popular photo-sharing site Flickr, also use geolocation filtering. Flickr blocks Internet users in Germany, Singapore, Hong Kong, and Korea from accessing particular types of imagery to avoid litigation. The photo site, which carries millions of images that range from innocent to indecent, categorizes its content as safe, moderate, and restricted based on its suitability for varying types of audiences. The site's SafeSearch filter restricts access to safe images, unless web users register for a membership. Members who are 18 or older can adjust the filter for access to all content if they like, unless they reside in one of these four countries.

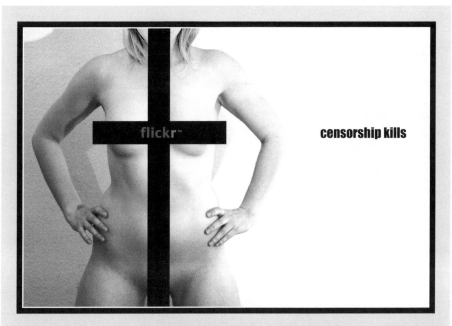

© Hannes.Trapp, http://everystockphoto.com/photo.php?imageId=2758333

Flickr's decision to use geolocation filtering to limit access to controversial images in Germany and other countries angered many of its users who posted a series of provocative images on the Internet in protest.

As geolocation technology becomes more prevalent, courts are more likely to expect websites to use it. In *Yahoo! v. LICRA*, Yahoo! was ordered to block French users' access to its American website with Nazi paraphernalia. In *Dow Jones v. Gutnick*, the publishing company's attorney threatened that if Australia claimed jurisdiction over American publishing companies, they might just find it cheaper to deny Australians access to U.S. content than contend with potential legal fees. To his surprise, one of the justices replied "It is inconceivable to me that that has not been done."[64]

Geolocation technology is not that precise; users with the incentive and know-how to get around geolocation filtering usually can. Even if it were completely accurate, it would still be time consuming and difficult to filter content for particular audiences. There are at least 190 libel laws to consider, apart from other national laws regarding trademark, copyright, obscenity, and privacy that vary by jurisdiction.[65] Realistically, it would be simpler to block everyone but domestic readers. Kurt Wimmer, senior vice president and general counsel for Gannett Co., says the company would be hesitant to use geolocation technology for editorial purposes. "The true value of the Internet as a means of fostering free expression beyond borders is the ability of people in potentially restrictive countries to have full access to information. Once we start erecting border-crossings on the Internet and block access for countries where content might be seen as inappropriate, we've lost that potential value."[66]

© Gerriet, http://everystockphoto.com/photo.php?imageId=3666681
Example of user protest against Flickr's use of geolocation filtering in Germany.

Questions for Discussion

1. What is due process? How does the American concept of due process lead it to treat jurisdiction differently than other parts of the world?
2. What is personal jurisdiction? How do the criteria for special and general jurisdiction differ?
3. How has the treatment of jurisdiction evolved due to the Internet?
4. Is geolocation filtering a suitable substitute for a treaty on conflict of laws?

6

Information Access and Protection

Digital media have expanded the concept of freedom of expression by making information and the means to share it more accessible. Easier access to information has not only benefited traditional media, but precipitated new levels of citizen reporting in the form of blogs, podcasts, and webcasts. In fact, some blogs get more than 1 million visitors a month, attracting larger audiences than many traditional media sources.[1] Companies, professional associations, and special interest groups also supply news related to particular industries and causes through e-publications that serve a quasi-journalistic role. This democratization of information raises legal questions addressed in this chapter about what it means to be a journalist and who should qualify for the privileges and protections traditionally extended to journalists regarding access to information and protection for their sources.

Access to Information

Access to information is a basic human right recognized by more than 80 countries in two international treaties – the American Convention on Human Rights (1978) and the International Covenant on Civil and Political Rights (1966). At least 40 nations, including the United States, have also enacted laws to protect the right to receive information. The U.S. Supreme Court has also stated that the "right to receive information and ideas" is encompassed in the First Amendment.[2]

At the most basic level, access to information is necessary for self-preservation. Harvard economist and Nobel Prize winner Amartya Sen has observed, for example, that there has never been a famine in country with a free press.[3] Information is also the means by which people govern themselves in a democracy. Digital media have not only armed people with information, according to researcher Christopher Kedzie; they have been instrumental in the spread of democracy. Kedzie found that computer network connectivity proved to be the "single predictor, dominant over economic development, schooling, ethnic homogeneity, life expectancy and population size" in the spread of democracy.[4]

The Freedom of Information Act

In the United States, the Freedom of Information Act (FOIA) facilitates access to government information.[5] Congress passed the law in 1966 to open records in the executive branch to public inspection. Although it does not extend to the legislative or judicial branches, its reach is significant. It provides access to every federal department, military branch, independent regulatory agency, government-controlled corporation, and the Executive Office of the President.[6] Together, 90 "agencies" fall within its purview.

The FOIA does not require agencies to answer specific questions or to create documents. It requires them to produce records they already have in their possession. These include rules, opinions, orders, files, and proceedings they have created or control that exist in any format – as paper, photographs, film, digital bits, or even three-dimensional objects. In contrast, personal notes, papers, and calendars are not public documents. To distinguish between public and personal records for purposes of the Act, the U.S. Court of Appeals for the District of Columbia developed a four-part test. A court will consider:

1. the intent of the document's creator to retain or relinquish control over the records;
2. the ability of the agency to use and dispose of the record as it sees fit;
3. the extent to which agency personnel have read or relied upon the document; and
4. the degree to which the document was integrated into agency's record system or files.[7]

According to a report by OpenTheGovernment.org, which is based on data gathered by the National Archives, almost 22 million FOIA requests were filed in 2007.[8]

Requesting information   Anyone can request information from the government using the Freedom of Information Act. The requester's identity and purpose are irrelevant.[9] The Supreme Court has said that "when documents are within FOIA's disclosure provisions, citizens should not be required to explain why they seek the information. A person requesting the information needs no preconceived idea of the uses the data might serve. The information belongs to citizens to do with as they choose."[10]

All requests for information must be submitted in writing. Each agency now offers a link on its website with instructions for filing an FOIA request.[11] The more detailed the request, the more likely the information officer will be able to fulfill it.

But the request does not need to precisely name the document. A description that enables an agency employee familiar with the subject area of the request to locate the information with a reasonable amount of effort is sufficient.[12] Agencies are entitled to charge reasonable fees for search time and duplication costs, but favored requesters – from educational and noncommercial scientific institutions and representatives of the media – receive two hours of free search time and their first 100 pages free.

The Act defines "a representative of the news media" as "any person or entity that gathers information of potential interest to a segment of the public, uses its editorial skills to turn the raw materials into a distinct work, and distributes that work to an audience."[13] It defines "news" as "information that is about current events or that would be of current interest to the public."[14] Nonexclusive examples of news media entities included "television or radio stations broadcasting to the public at large and publishers of periodicals (but only if such entities qualify as disseminators of "news") who make their products available for purchase by or subscriptions by or free distribution to the general public."[15] The Act recognizes that news delivery has evolved and includes electronic media delivered via telecommunications services. It also recognizes that the definition of journalist has evolved and includes freelance journalists. But it doesn't leave the door wide open for anyone to claim to be a freelance journalist. It says a freelancer "shall be regarded as working for a news media entity if the journalist can demonstrate a solid basis for expecting publication through that entity, whether or not the journalist is actually employed by that entity."[16] It suggests that a publication contract or record of past publication could be used to establish that basis. It is not clear whether the expanded definition would include bloggers who are not working for a particular organization either on a full or freelance basis. Bloggers should request the exemption, though, because agencies have the discretion to waive fees entirely if the information sought is likely to "contribute significantly to public understanding of the operations or activities of the government and is not primarily in the commercial interest of the requester."[17]

An agency has 20 business days to fulfill the request. The clock starts ticking when the request is first received by the appropriate component of the agency (and no later than 10 days after the request is received by any component of the agency). If the agency must ask for clarification on some point regarding the request, for example its proposed fee assessment, the clock may stop while it is waiting for an answer.

Individuals who demonstrate a compelling need for rapid access to the information may request expedited processing. A compelling need includes imminent threat to life or safety or, in the case of media representatives, urgency to inform the public about an actual or alleged government activity.[18] The agency must provide notice of its determination regarding requests for expedited processing within 10 days.

If the agency fails to comply with the time limit on the request, and there are no unusual or exceptional circumstances to justify the delay, it may not assess search fees or in the case of a favored requester (e.g. a representative of the news media or someone from an educational institution) duplication fees. *Unusual circumstances* refer to delays caused when records are stored off-site, when the number of records that must be searched is voluminous, or the agency is required to consult with another agency that also may have an interest in the request. If the agency encounters any of the three unusual circumstances, it is obligated to contact the requester to inform him or her of the expected delay and to offer the requester an opportunity to limit the scope of the request so it can be processed in time or arrange an alternative time frame. A person's refusal to do either would be considered a factor in determining whether an *exceptional circumstance* existed. An exceptional circumstance does not, however, include "a delay that results from a predictable agency workload of requests … unless the agency demonstrates reasonable progress in reducing its backlog of pending requests."[19]

Electronic Freedom of Information Act   Congress amended the FOIA in 1996 to apply to electronic records. The Electronic Freedom of Information Act requires agencies to publish online indexes of the documents they possess. Many of these indexes include full-text documents for download. The amendment also required agencies to provide records in electronic form to requesters who prefer that format if the records are computerized. This makes it easier for media operations to do database comparisons that would be too expensive to manage with paper records. For example, the *St. Louis Post Dispatch* used electronic records to uncover voter fraud in East St. Louis, Illinois. By merging voter and death records, its reporters discovered that deceased residents of East St. Louis were still voting.[20]

The OPEN Government Act

Although the Supreme Court has clearly stated that the Freedom of Information Act establishes a "strong presumption in favor of disclosure" and that its dominant objective is "disclosure, not secrecy," federal agencies have not always been that forthcoming.[21] In fact, following the terrorist attacks on Sept. 11, 2001, there appeared to be a presumption in favor of withholding information. In 2001, Attorney General John Ashcroft authorized federal agencies "to disclose information protected under the FOIA … only after full and deliberate consideration of the institutional, commercial, and personal privacy interests that could be implicated by disclosure of the information."[22] He promised that the Justice Department would defend decisions "to withhold records, in whole or in part … unless they lack[ed] a sound legal basis or present[ed] an unwarranted risk of adverse impact on the ability of other agencies to protect other important records."[23] In 2006, federal agencies spent $8.2 billion keeping documents classified, according to OpenTheGovernment.org.[24]

Congress addressed the problem in 2007 by passing the Openness Promotes Effectiveness in our National (OPEN) Government Act, otherwise known as the

Open Government Act.[25] The amendment makes federal agencies more accountable to FOIA requesters. It requires agencies to assign individual tracking numbers to requests that take more than 10 days to process and establish a phone or Internet system that requesters can use to check on the status of their requests. Agencies must provide a public liaison to assist in the resolution of disputes between the agency and the FOIA requester. The Act established an office in the National Archives and Records Administration to review agency compliance with FOIA policies and procedures, and to offer mediation services to resolve disputes between requesters and agencies as a nonexclusive alternative to litigation. Federal agencies are also required to submit annual reports to Congress detailing their FOIA activities.

FOIA exemptions

Agencies have the discretion, although not the duty, to deny a request for information if it falls within the boundaries of nine exemptions provided by the Act.[26] These include:

1. *National security*
    Agencies may protect matters "specifically authorized under criteria established by an Executive order to be kept secret in the interest of national defense or foreign policy and … properly classified pursuant to such Executive order."
2. *Internal agency personnel rules and practices*
    The exemption protects "routine housekeeping matters" and internal agency management, involving policies such as pay, sick-leave, vacation time, and parking, in which it can be presumed the public lacks any substantial interest.[27]
3. *Information exempted from disclosure by other statutes*
    Agencies may shield information that is protected by other statutes. For example, the Privacy Act of 1974 (discussed in chapter 10) prevents agencies from releasing certain information.[28] Personal information accumulated for tax and census purposes is also protected from public disclosure.
4. *Trade secrets and commercial or financial information that is privileged or confidential*
    The only way to protect a trade secret is to keep it secret, so government agencies, like the Food and Drug Administration for example, are careful not to release secret processes and formulas that could give an unfair advantage to a business's competitors.
5. *Inter-agency or intra-agency memos or letters that would not be available by law to a party other than an agency in litigation with the agency*
    As explained by the Court of Appeals for the District of Columbia Circuit, the "exemption was intended to encourage the free exchange of ideas during the process of deliberation and policymaking; accordingly, it has been held to

protect internal communications consisting of advice, recommendations, opinions, and other material reflecting deliberative or policy-making processes, but not purely factual or investigatory reports."[29] It is also used to protect the attorney-client privilege.

6. *Personnel and medical files or similar files that would involve an unwarranted invasion of privacy*

   Congress explained in the legislative history of the Act that the phrase "unwarranted invasion of personal privacy" demands a "balancing of interests between the protection of an individual's private affairs from unnecessary public scrutiny, and the preservation of the public's right to governmental information."[30]

7. *Investigatory records of law enforcement*

   Agency protection is warranted if the information might be expected to interfere in law enforcement proceedings or provide information about law enforcement techniques that would enable someone to circumvent the law. Information is also protected if its release could endanger the life or safety of any individual, deprive a person of the right to a fair trial, disclose a confidential source, or violate someone's right of privacy.

8. *Reports prepared on behalf of agencies that regulate or supervise financial institutions*

   The exemption is intended to promote the candor of bank officials regarding conditions that affect their institution's condition and lending policies. Financial institutions are given extra consideration because of their unique role in the economy, their vulnerability to rumors and speculation, and the government's obligation to protect the federal deposit insurance fund.[31]

9. *Geological and geophysical information*

   Agencies protect information, such as geological maps concerning wells, which would lead to prospecting.

Redaction   Information covered by one of the exemptions may be deleted or blacked out through redaction so that the remaining parts of a record may be released to the requester. An agency may only withhold an entire record if its exempt and nonexempt parts are "'inextricably intertwined,' such that the excision of exempt information would impose significant costs on the agency and produce an edited document with little informational value."[32] When releasing documents that have been redacted, the agency should specify the amount of the information that has been deleted and where, along with the exemption under which the deletion is made.

In some cases involving national security or privacy, agencies refuse to acknowledge whether or not the requested information exists. This is known as the "Glomar response." The name comes from a case challenging the CIA's refusal to confirm or deny records in an FOIA request regarding its ties to Howard Hughes's experimental ship, the *Glomar Explorer*.[33] The ship was supposedly designed for undersea mining, but alleged to have been a CIA project to recover sunken Soviet submarines. Courts allow agencies to use the Glomar response in national security exemption cases.[34] The Justice Department also applies it in privacy exemption cases. Its policy is that the "'Glomar' response can be justified only when the confirmation or denial of the existence of responsive records would, in and of itself, reveal exempt information."[35]

FOIA appeals　An agency that denies a FOIA request must cite the appropriate exemption within 20 days and provide information regarding its procedure to appeal the decision. Requesters who appeal a decision and are denied at the administrative level may ask a federal court to review the decision – either in the federal district in which they reside or operate a place of business, in the federal district in which the records are located, or in the District of Columbia.

FOIA appeals are not easy to win. Technically, the agency bears the burden of proving that the documents should be withheld, but courts are under obligation to afford "substantial weight" to agency affidavits explaining their justification for withholding the information. Because plaintiffs have not seen the documents, it may be impossible to rebut the agency's argument. Courts have the authority to examine the documents in camera, meaning in the judge's chambers, to determine whether they were properly withheld, but they rarely do so.

However, if the court finds evidence that agency personnel arbitrarily or capriciously withheld documents from the requester, it will direct a special counsel to initiate an investigation to determine whether disciplinary action is warranted against the individual or individuals responsible for the decision. If disciplinary action is warranted, the special prosecutor will inform the head of the agency responsible for administering it. If the agency reverses its position after the suit commences, the court may assess the agency fees and court costs. If a court grants relief to a requester and the agency continues to withhold the information sought, the court may order agency personnel in contempt.

The National Security Archive

The National Security Archive is an independent repository for documents obtained under the Freedom of Information Act. The archive, housed at George Washington University in Washington, D.C., has won access to thousands of classified documents containing intelligence from major national events ranging from the Cuban Missile Crisis in 1962 to the terrorist attacks of 2001.

It is accustomed to refusals and doggedly tracks the records of agencies that do not comply with the law. Each year it gives the Rosemary Award to the agency with the worst FOIA record. The award is named after President Nixon's secretary, Rosemary Woods, who testified to erasing 18.5 minutes of the White House tapes containing conversations about Watergate. The 2008 award went to the U.S. Treasury Department.

Executive privilege

The FOIA applies to the Executive Office of the president, but not to the president or his immediate staff. The Conference Report for the 1974 FOIA Amendments indicates that "the President's immediate personal staff or units in the Executive Office whose sole function is to advise and assist the President" are not included within the term "agency" under the FOIA.[36] Offices of the Chief of Staff or the President's Counsel are considered to serve an advisory role.

The law is less clear concerning the White House's executive privilege to withhold documents or refuse to testify before a court or Congress. In 2007, Congress subpoenaed former White House counsel Harriet Miers to testify about her role in the firing of nine U.S. attorneys. When it became clear that seven attorneys were fired on the same day, the Senate Judiciary and House Judiciary Committees launched investigations into allegations that the decisions were politically motivated. Ultimately, Attorney General Alberto Gonzales resigned over the affair. Congress also subpoenaed White House documents and e-mails related to the investigation. The Bush administration invoked executive privilege, submitting neither Miers nor the documents. The law is gray in this area. There are precedents from earlier administrations in which presidential aides – from the Nixon, Carter, Reagan, and Clinton administrations – testified before Congress, some under threat of subpoena.[37] In 1974, the Supreme Court prohibited the Nixon administration from withholding Watergate tapes from federal prosecutors. But the Court would not address the larger issue of whether presidents may refuse Congressional demands for testimony from White House staff. In 2008, the House of Representatives cited Miers and White House Chief of Staff Joshua Bolton for contempt of Congress.[38] It was the first time that a White House official had been cited for contempt. However the Justice Department refused to act on the contempt order because the White House refused to cooperate based on the Justice Department's ruling that executive privilege applied in the case. Having no other recourse, the House Judiciary Committee filed a civil lawsuit in federal court to compel Miers and Bolton to submit to its requests. The federal district court denied Miers's claim to absolute immunity from compelled compliance with the subpoena. It concluded that she must appear before the committee where she might invoke executive privilege to specific questions, which could be analyzed later.[39]

Presidential Records Act of 1978

Documents concerning particular presidential administrations can be accessed through the Presidential Records Act. The Act gives the United States ownership and control of presidential and vice presidential records and requires the president to take the necessary steps to assure "that the activities, deliberations, decisions, and policies that reflect the performance of his constitutional, statutory, or other official or ceremonial duties are adequately documented" and maintained as Presidential records.[40]

The Presidential Records Act applies to documentary materials created by the president and his immediate staff. The term documentary materials includes "books, correspondence, memorandums, documents, papers, pamphlets, works of art, models, pictures, photographs, plats, maps, films, and motion pictures, including, but not limited to, audio, audiovisual, or other electronic or mechanical recordations" created in the course of activities that relate to the president's responsibilities.[41] The Act does not apply to personal records, such as notes or diaries, that have nothing to do with presidential duties or to information strictly related to the president's election campaign.

At the end of a president's term in office, the National Archivist assumes custody of the presidential records. The president may claim executive privilege to withhold the information, but his power to do so is not absolute. President Barack Obama passed a resolution on his first day in office giving the Attorney General and White House Counsel discretion to determine that invocation of executive privilege is not justified.[42] The order also revokes the right of former presidents to withhold their records. The president may dispose of records that have no more administrative, historical, informational, or evidentiary value after first consulting with the National Archivist.

The National Security Archive filed suit against the White House in 2007 when it learned that the White House was missing key e-mails from the Bush administration.[43] The loss of documents was first noticed on January 23, 2006, during a trial against Lewis "Scooter" Libby, the chief of staff for former Vice President Dick Cheney, for perjury and obstruction of justice. Prosecutors informed Libby's counsel that they were unable to find e-mails the defense requested. In 2007, Citizens for Responsibility and Ethics in Washington issued a report indicating that as many as 5 million e-mails were missing from the Executive Office of the President from 2003–5. President Bush's staff also recycled its backup e-mail tapes until October 2003. The period of lost e-mail would encompass communications involving decision to go to war, invasions of Afghanistan and Iraq and pursuit of Saddam Hussein.

Access to Legislative Information

The Freedom of Information Act does not apply to the legislative branch, but it is possible to track federal legislative information through various digital sources. The primary access point for citizens who want to follow legislation is the Thomas database.[44] The database includes the text of all bills currently under consideration in Congress and their status. The information includes sponsors, cosponsors, short and official titles, floor and executive actions, legislative history, Congressional Record references, and committee and subcommittee referrals. The full text of bills going back to the 101st Congress is also available. The site also includes committee reports, treaties, information about activities taking place on the floor of Congress, and a daily digest from the Congressional Record.

The Government Printing Office also disseminates legislative information, along with information from the executive and judicial branches of government. Its website includes conference reports, congressional hearing transcripts, congressional bills, the Congressional Record, public and private laws, and the U.S. Code.

Access to Judicial Information

The Freedom of Information Act does not apply to the judicial branch of government either, but judicial information is accessible though a variety of sources. The U.S. Judiciary supplies case information in real time from the federal appellate, district, and bankruptcy courts through the Public Access to Court Electronic Records (PACER) database.[45] Through an Internet connection, anyone can access civil and bankruptcy case information, including the names of case litigants, judges, attorneys, and trustees; the nature of a suit or cause of action; a chronology of case events; a listing of daily cases; appellate court opinions; judgments; and copies of documents filed for certain cases. In addition, most federal courts post selected published and unpublished decisions and dockets on their websites.

The Judicial Conference of the United States, the principal policy-making body for the U.S. Federal Courts, adopted privacy policies to protect some personal information in court documents. Upon the request of the litigants, personal data identifiers, such as Social Security numbers, dates of birth, financial account numbers, and names of minor children, which might appear in civil or bankruptcy files, will be modified or partially redacted.

The Judicial Conference has not approved unfettered public remote electronic access to criminal case files. It has justified its decision by pointing out that routine access to criminal files would expose defendants' cooperation with law enforcement in some government cases, which might subject them or their families to greater risk of intimidation or harm. The judiciary was also concerned that electronic public access to criminal files might "inadvertently increase the risk of unauthorized public access to pre-indictment information, such as unexecuted arrest and search warrants," which might put law enforcement personnel in danger. The policy gives judges the discretion to disseminate criminal documents through PACER and court websites, but does not require them to do so.

State Freedom of Information Laws

All states have statutes giving the public access to state records.[46] Ten states also provide access to government records in their state constitutions.[47] Like the federal

Freedom of Information Act, state public information acts apply to the executive branch of government. However, some states, like Texas for example, provide access to records from the legislative branch as well.

Public information acts vary from state to state in their comprehensiveness. More than half of the states list computer records in their definition of public documents or provide that a public record can be any recorded information, regardless of form. Some also specifically mention e-mail in their definitions. At least 22 states direct public bodies to make records available to the public in an electronic format or through a database if the record is already available in a digitized form.[48]

Most states open public records to anyone who requests them. Six states – Virginia, Arkansas, Tennessee, Georgia, South Dakota, and Alabama – specify that records are open to the citizens of their states. In general the purpose of the request is irrelevant, although some states do require requesters to provide identification.

Most states also provide civil penalties for public records officers who violate the law. Fines normally reach $1,000, or may include monetary damages to individuals who incurred a loss due to the inaccessibility of the records.

Access to Public Officials

Although individuals have every right to use their state open records acts to gather information from public officials, they do not have a right to interview them. Courts have distinguished between access to public records, events, and facilities and access to individuals for interviews. In general, journalists are not entitled to information that is not ordinarily available to the public. In a series of cases, courts have sided with government officials who issued "no comment" directives after being offended by press coverage, concluding that journalists are not entitled to one-on-one interviews "not otherwise available to the public."[49]

A local newspaper sued the mayor of Youngtown, Ohio, for example, after he prohibited city employees from speaking to its reporters about any topic related to city business. The newspaper published a series of articles criticizing the mayor and his administration for their work regarding the planning and construction of a convocation center. The paper claimed that the mayor had retaliated against it for exercising its First Amendment rights and asked for an injunction to prevent the mayor from enforcing the "no comment" policy.

A federal district court observed that the city had not opened a forum for all members of the press and public to solicit comments from city employees and concluded that the paper was seeking special treatment unavailable to the rest of the public. It clarified that "A reporter may achieve privileged access to government information, but a reporter does not have a constitutional right to maintain privileged access."[50] The court also pointed out that government officials have a First Amendment right not to speak with members of the press.

Protection of Information

In addition to the many publicly available sources of information, it is inevitable that those who do reporting will gain access to information that is proprietary, confidential, or illegally obtained. From a legal perspective, access to such information raises two questions: (1) whether the information can be reported and (2) whether the source of the information can be protected.

Reporting on illegally obtained information

The Supreme Court has determined that media disclosure of illegally intercepted information about a public issue is protected by the First Amendment, if the media do not participate in the illegal interception. But it is not clear whether the same protection would apply to nontraditional media sources or to the publication of classified documents.

In *Bartnicki v. Vopper* (2001), the Supreme Court considered whether the broadcast of an illegally intercepted cellular telephone conversation violated federal and state wiretapping laws.[51] Gloria Bartnicki, the petitioner in the case, was the chief negotiator in a looming teacher strike in Pennsylvania, whose cell phone call to the president of the teacher's union was intercepted and later broadcast on a local radio station. Frederick Vopper, the respondent, was a radio commentator who received a tape of the conversation from a man who claimed to have found it in his mailbox. Vopper played the tape on the radio in conjunction with news coverage regarding the strike.

The Court acknowledged that the respondents in the case violated the Wiretapping and Electronic Surveillance statute, which not only prohibits the interception but also the disclosure of wire, electronic, and oral communications.[52] But under the circumstances, it decided that application of the statute violated the First Amendment. Three factors weighed in the decision: the respondents played no part in the illegal interception of the material, their access to it was lawfully obtained, and it concerned a matter of public interest.

The government, which stepped in to protect the statute from the constitutional challenge, raised two issues: that it served as a deterrent against illegal wiretapping and that it protected the privacy interests of others. The Court dismissed the deterrent argument since Vopper had nothing to do with the actual interception. But it took the privacy argument seriously. Writing for the Court, Justice Stevens noted that "some intrusions on privacy are more offensive than others, and that the disclosure of the contents of a private conversation can be an even greater intrusion on privacy than the interception itself."[53] Nevertheless, the Court chose to balance the interests of privacy and speech, and in this case found that "privacy concerns give way when balanced against the interest in publishing matters of public importance."[54]

Emphasizing the narrowness of the holding, Justice Stevens would not consider how privacy interests might balance against other illegally intercepted information, such as trade secrets, domestic gossip, or purely private information. The Court has refused to state categorically that there can be no restrictions on the publication of truthful information, out of concern that the future may bring a situation that they have not anticipated, but statutes that punish truthful speech rarely withstand constitutional scrutiny. In the famous Pentagon Papers case, *New York Times Co. v. United States* (1971), the Court upheld the right of the press to publish information from stolen government documents because the information was of public concern.[55] The Court focused on the character of the information, weighing the risk of publication to national security first. It did not, however, resolve the question of whether the newspaper could be punished for publishing information it received from someone who illegally acquired it until *Bartnicki*.

Journalist's privilege

When a journalist has access to information that is either gained illegally or considered potentially useful in a civil or criminal case, the information may be subpoenaed by law enforcement. Rules of evidence afford protections for information communicated in certain types of relationships. Collectively, these rules comprise the law of privilege.[56] A privilege exists between attorneys and their clients, doctors and their patients, clergy and penitents, and husbands and wives. Courts and legislatures have implemented these privileges because they think that other policy considerations outweigh the interests that may be served by the evidence the person could provide. Most jurisdictions recognize a journalist's privilege to protect confidential sources of information and even nonconfidential sources in some instances. However, the privilege is generally qualified, meaning that it can be overcome if a court sees the need.

For a variety of reasons, journalists do not like to share the names of sources or documentary materials with law enforcement. Journalists worry that if they are perceived to be tools of law enforcement, sources will be less likely to share information. They argue that the First Amendment should provide the privilege to keep sources of information confidential in order to preserve channels of information that ultimately benefit the public. Journalists also want to protect their sources from retribution. Sources who share information about criminal activities may be harassed or harmed by criminals who want to keep their activities secret. Sources who blow the whistle on their employers for engaging in illegal or unethical actions may be punished or fired by their employers for sharing information with the media.

Of course, sources themselves want journalists to protect their identities, not only for the aforementioned reasons, but also because they may be involved in illegal activities or simply want to protect their privacy. On several occasions sources have sued media organizations for revealing their identities. Sources who were promised confidentiality and later betrayed have earned courts' sympathy. The Supreme Court held that a source may sue a reporter who violates a promise of confidentiality for promissory estoppel (a tort analogous to violating an oral contract) without violating the First Amendment.[57] Sources who are guilty of crimes do not receive the same sympathy. The Sixth Circuit dismissed a lawsuit against a *Cincinnati Enquirer* reporter who identified his source to a grand jury investigating the reporter's illegal access to a company's phone mail system. The Sixth Circuit found no breach of contract because the source aided the reporter by supplying him with access codes, and public policy "precludes enforcements of agreements to conceal a crime."[58]

Finally, journalists know that if they are perceived as tools of law enforcement, they are more likely to be harmed as they search for information. Wall Street Journal Asia bureau chief Daniel Pearl was murdered in 2002 by terrorists in Pakistan who assumed he was connected with the CIA. The CIA purported to ban the use of journalists as spies in 1977, but a 1996 Council on Foreign Relations task force report showed that the agency continued to cloak agents as journalists.[59] In 1996, Congress passed an Intelligence Authorization Act that supposedly prohibited the use of journalists for intelligence gathering, but in effect through its exemptions, authorized the president or the CIA director to waive the restriction by notifying the House and Senate Intelligence oversight committees. It also exempted the use of willing participants as spies.

The media are not alone in believing that journalist's privilege is important. Most Americans support the idea as well. A poll conducted by the First Amendment Center in 2008 found that 70 percent of Americans agree with the statement: "Journalists should be allowed to keep a news source confidential."[60] States also support the privilege. Forty-nine states and the District of Columbia offer some level of protection for a journalist's sources.[61] (Wyoming is the exception.) There is very little uniformity among them, however.

Contempt of court   If a journalist ignores a subpoena to testify in a judicial proceeding, he or she may be held in contempt of court. A court may attempt to compel compliance by fining or incarcerating the journalist until he or she cooperates. A court may jail an individual for civil contempt up to 18 months or until the subpoenaed materials are relinquished.[62] If the court finds that the journalist has interfered with its ability to function, it may issue a finding of criminal contempt, which may also result in a fine or incarceration. However, in this case, the journalist no longer holds the key to the door. Revocation of the penalty is not tied to the journalist's decision to cooperate.

Shield laws   Thirty-seven states have passed "shield laws" that entitle journalists to protect the identities of their sources or other aspects of information collected under certain circumstances. These include Alabama, Alaska, Arizona, Arkansas, California, Colorado, Connecticut, Delaware, Florida, Georgia, Hawaii, Illinois, Indiana, Kentucky, Louisiana, Maine, Maryland, Michigan, Minnesota, Montana,

Nebraska, Nevada, New Jersey, New Mexico, New York, North Carolina, North Dakota, Ohio, Oklahoma, Oregon, Pennsylvania, Rhode Island, South Carolina, Tennessee, Texas, Utah, Washington, and the District of Columbia.

Shield laws vary considerably by jurisdiction. Protection depends on the type of case (criminal or civil), the role of the journalist in the case (defendant, witness, or third party), and the kind of information sought in the case (the name of a confidential source, documentary materials, or work products.) There is no national shield law. A bill to provide one passed the House of Representatives in 2007, but never made it through the Senate.[63]

State constitutions   Some states have added journalist privilege provisions to their constitutions. California's constitution, for example, protects a "publisher, editor, reporter, or other person connected with or employed upon a newspaper, magazine, or other periodical publication, or by a press association or wire service, or any person who has been so connected or employed" from being held in contempt for failing to reveal the name of a source. New York's highest court has also recognized a journalist's privilege based on New York's constitution.[64]

State courts and journalist's privilege   Where legislatures have not acted, courts have – by finding the privilege within common law or adopting it within their own rules of procedure. Courts in 18 states offer varying protections for journalists' sources. These are Hawaii, Idaho, Iowa, Kansas, Maine, Massachusetts, Mississippi, Missouri, New Hampshire, New Mexico, South Dakota, Texas, Utah, Vermont, Virginia, West Virginia, Washington, and Wisconsin.

Most courts employ a balancing test. In order to compel a journalist to disclose sources of information, the other party must establish that the public benefit brought by disclosure of the information outweighs the inhibiting effect of forced disclosure on the free flow of information.

Journalist's privilege and the First Amendment   Although journalists argue that the First Amendment protects journalist's privilege, courts are not unanimously convinced that it does. The Supreme Court rejected the notion that the First Amendment protects journalists from having to testify before a grand jury in *Branzburg v. Hayes* (1972).[65] Nevertheless, many lower courts believe it can be applied in other circumstances.

The Supreme Court's landmark ruling in *Branzburg v. Hayes* has confused journalists and lower courts. In it, the Court consolidated three cases, each involving the question of whether a reporter could choose to ignore a grand jury summons. Lower courts that had examined the cases were split on the issue.

The Supreme Court rejected a First Amendment privilege to refuse to testify before a grand jury hearing. It clarified that grand juries serve an essential role in the carriage of justice and, like all citizens, the petitioners had a duty to cooperate with grand jury investigations. The Court observed that media have the right not to publish information, but "the right to withhold news is not equivalent to a First

Amendment exemption from an ordinary duty of all other citizens to furnish relevant information to a grand jury performing an important public function."[66]

Writing for the Court, Justice White pointed out that "the only testimonial privilege for unofficial witnesses that is rooted in the Federal Constitution is the Fifth Amendment privilege against compelled self-incrimination."[67] The Court had no intention of creating a new one, even to secure channels of information regarding criminal activity. Justice White reasoned that when a confidential source has committed a crime, the Court could not "seriously entertain the notion that the First Amendment protects a newsman's agreement to conceal the criminal conduct of his source, or evidence thereof, on the theory that it is better to write about a crime than to do something about it."[68] When a confidential source has not committed a crime, but may be aware of criminal activity, the Court could not "accept the argument that the public interest in possible future news about crime from undisclosed, unverified sources must take precedence over the public interest in pursuing and prosecuting those crimes reported to the press by informants and in thus deterring the commission of such crimes in the future."[69] The majority determined that no privilege existed unless the recipient could demonstrate that the subpoena was issued by the grand jury in bad faith or as a means of harassment – the same exception that would apply to anyone summoned to testify.

Four justices dissented from the majority opinion. Justice Douglas argued that journalist's privilege not only existed but should be absolute unless the journalist was the one being investigated for the criminal act. Justice Stewart, joined by Justices Brennan and Marshall, took a more measured approach. Justice Stewart suggested that journalist's privilege should be evaluated objectively based on its relevance to the outcome of the trial and the potential availability of the information from other sources.[70]

In a Court divided on the issue, Justice Powell broke the tie by agreeing with the majority's decision, but submitted a concurring opinion with his own reasoning. In it he suggested that while no constitutional protection existed to refuse to testify before grand juries, reporters may be entitled to a qualified protection in other areas. He wrote "The asserted claim to privilege should be judged on its facts by the striking of a proper balance between freedom of the press and the obligation of all citizens to give relevant testimony with respect to criminal conduct."[71] He added if the journalist "is called upon to give information bearing only on a remote and tenuous relationship to the subject of the investigation, or if he has some other reason to believe that his testimony implicates confidential source relationships without a legitimate need of law enforcement, he will have access to the court on a motion to quash and an appropriate protective order may be entered."[72] A concurring opinion, like Justice Powell's, is not part of the authoritative precedent set by the majority. Nevertheless, many lower courts have assumed that some kind of qualified privilege based on the First Amendment must exist for journalists in cases that do *not* involve grand jury testimony, the specific circumstance addressed in *Branzburg*.

Federal common law and journalist's privilege   Among the 13 U.S. Courts of Appeals, eleven recognize a qualified privilege for journalists against forced disclosure of their sources. The Sixth Circuit has refused to recognize the privilege until it is forced to by the Supreme Court. The Seventh Circuit has not ruled on the issue directly, but its opinions suggest that it is skeptical of the privilege.[73] The Eighth Circuit considers the question "open," but the privilege is extended in some of its districts.[74]

Although circuits may disagree over whether and in what context the First Amendment protects journalistic privilege, most agree that a qualified privilege has developed through federal common law. Three years after *Branzburg* was decided, Congress delegated power to federal courts to develop rules on evidentiary privileges. In Rule 501 of the Federal Rules of Evidence, Congress provided that the privilege of witnesses "shall be governed by the principles of the common law as they may be interpreted by the courts of the United States in the light of reason and experience."[75]

Congressman William Hungate, who drafted the rule, explained Congress's intentions in passing the Act:

> The phrase "governed by the principles of the common law as they may be interpreted by the courts of the United States in light of reason and experience," is intended to provide the courts with the flexibility to develop rules of privileges on a case-by-case basis. For example, the Supreme Court's rule of evidence contained no rule of privilege for a newspaperperson. The language of Rule 501 permits the courts to develop a privilege for newspaperpeople on a case-by-case basis. The language cannot be interpreted as a congressional expression in favor of having no such privilege, nor can the conference action be interpreted as denying to newspaperpeople any protection they may have from State newsperson's laws.[76]

Federal courts are also required to apply state rules on journalist's privilege in civil cases that arise under state law but which are brought into the federal court system.

Justice Department guidelines   The Justice Department has created guidelines to use in the event that it is considering subpoenaing a member of the media. In summary, they specify that before issuing a subpoena to the media, the department should believe that "information sought is essential to a successful investigation – particularly with reference to establishing guilt or innocence" and that "all reasonable efforts should be made to obtain the desired information from alternative sources."[77] They also assert that whenever possible subpoenas should be targeted toward a narrow topic and period of time and that the Justice Department should be willing to negotiate with the media to find a solution that accommodates both of their interests. However, ultimately observation of the guidelines is at the Justice Department's discretion. Legally, they are unenforceable.

Journalist's privilege in criminal cases

Courts are least likely to recognize journalist's privilege when sources could provide information relevant to a criminal case. Individuals facing prosecution have a Sixth Amendment right to compel testimony from witnesses that may be used to prove their innocence. Courts often make this determination by following the balancing approach suggested by Justice Powell in his concurring opinion in *Branzburg.* Using Justice Powell's approach, courts balance the defendant's Sixth Amendment right to a fair trial against the public's interest in preserving the free flow of information. In some cases, the court may also determine that the public's greater interest is better served by compelling disclosure of evidence that can resolve a crime.

Alternatively, courts may resolve the issue by applying a three-pronged approach suggested by Justice Stewart in his dissenting opinion in *Branzburg v. Hayes.* Justice Stewart suggested that in order to compel a journalist to testify in a criminal proceeding, the prosecution must establish that:

(1)   the information is clearly relevant to the specific violation of law;
(2)   the information cannot be obtained by alternative means less destructive of First Amendment rights; and
(3)   there is compelling and overriding need for the information.[78]

A need for information is compelling if it is likely to affect the outcome of the case.

Perhaps the most famous confidential source in the United States is Deep Throat, later identified as Mark Felt, the FBI's second in command during the Nixon administration. Felt's revelations were instrumental in bringing down the Nixon presidency during the Watergate scandal. For 33 years the *Washington Post* and its reporters, Bob Woodward and Carl Bernstein, protected Felt's secret until 2005 when he and his family chose to reveal it.[79] It is highly unlikely that, under the same circumstances, the journalists would be allowed to protect the secret today.

Although protections for journalists' sources have expanded, the quality of the protection seems to have declined. Within the last six years, four U.S. Courts of Appeals have affirmed contempt citations resulting in harsher sentences than any previously experienced in American history against reporters who refused to reveal their sources.[80]

Government leaks   One of the most prominent recent cases involved a journalist from the *New York Times* who was held in jail for 12 weeks until she revealed her source with his permission. In the 2003 State of the Union address, leading up to the invasion of Iraq, President George Bush stated that "The British government has learned that Saddam Hussein recently sought significant quantities of uranium from Africa." The statement implied that the Iraqi leader was searching for a key ingredient for nuclear weapons. Former U.S. Ambassador Joseph Wilson wrote an op-ed article published by the *New York Times* six months later that cast doubt on the president's statement.[81] Wilson claimed to have been sent by the CIA to Niger in 2002 to answer Vice President Cheney's inquiry regarding whether Saddam Hussein had tried to purchase uranium from the country. Wilson said he conducted an investigation and found no evidence that Iraq had approached Niger for uranium. A week after Wilson's op-ed appeared, Robert Novak, a *Chicago Sun-Times* columnist, wrote that two senior administration officials had told him that Wilson was not sent to Niger at the behest of CIA Director George Tenet, but on the recommendation of Wilson's wife, Valerie Plame, a CIA "operative on weapons of mass destruction."[82] Wilson accused Novak's sources of divulging his wife's secret identity as payback for embarrassing the president. Following his assertion, other reporters claimed to have been contacted by administration officials who offered the same information. The unauthorized disclosure of the identity of a CIA agent is a federal crime.[83] The Justice Department launched an investigation to determine whether someone in the White House had violated the law and appointed Special Counsel Patrick Fitzgerald to lead the investigation.

Two of the reporters subpoenaed to testify in a grand jury investigation of the leak were Matthew Cooper of *Time* magazine and Judith Miller of the *New York Times*. The journalists moved to quash the subpoenas based on a First Amendment privilege to protect media sources. When their motions were denied and they failed to comply, the district court held them in civil contempt. The U.S. Court of Appeals for the D.C. Circuit upheld the decision based on *Branzburg* and the Supreme Court denied certiorari.[84] It is instructive, however, that attorneys general from 34 states and the District of Columbia encouraged the Court to reverse the opinion stating: "A federal policy that allows journalists to be imprisoned for engaging in the same conduct that these State privileges encourage and protect 'buck(s) that clear policy of virtually all states,' and undermines both the purpose of the shield laws, and the policy determinations of the State courts and legislatures that adopted them."[85]

The night before Cooper was to go to jail, the president's deputy chief of staff released him from his promise of confidentiality. Twelve weeks into her confinement, Miller claimed that the vice president's chief of staff, Scooter Libby, absolved her of her promise, although he claimed to have done it a year earlier. However, the decision to waive the promise of anonymity belongs to the journalist, not the source. Judge Tatel explained in his concurring opinion that "a source's waiver is irrelevant to the reasons for the privilege. Because the government could demand waivers – perhaps even before any leak occurs – as a condition of employment, a privilege subject to waiver may, again, amount to no privilege at all, even in those leak cases where protecting the confidential source is most compelling."[86] He also pointed out that while a source's interest "is limited to the particular case, the reporter's interest aligns with the public, for journalists must cultivate relationships with other sources who might keep mum if waiving confidentiality at the government's behest could lead to their exposure."[87]

Journalist's privilege in civil cases

Courts are more willing to recognize journalist's privilege in the context of civil cases, where the Supreme Court's *Branzburg* decision is not considered controlling. In fact, the Fifth and Tenth Circuits recognize journalist's privilege exclusively in civil cases. In criminal cases, courts have to balance the public benefit of First Amendment protection of information against the public benefit of justice served through compelled disclosure. Although justice is still the issue in civil cases, the balance shifts. Courts weigh the public interest in protecting the journalist's sources against the plaintiff's private interest in compelling the journalist's testimony.

Tests used for journalist's privilege in civil trials are similar to those used in criminal trials. Some courts apply a version of Justice Powell's balancing test. Others apply a version of Justice Stewart's three-part test that looks for relevance, a compelling interest in the information, and evidence that the information cannot be obtained by other means.[88]

A court's willingness to extend the qualified privilege depends on the position of the journalist and the type of information sought. Journalist's privilege is strongest when the reporter is not a party to the suit and when the source protected has been promised confidentiality.

Who is a journalist?

When *Branzburg* was decided, the Supreme Court was reluctant to create a special privilege for journalists, because it would require courts to determine who would qualify for it. Justice White pointed out that this would be a questionable procedure in light of the traditional doctrine that "liberty of the press is the right of the lonely pamphleteer who uses carbon paper or a mimeograph just as much as of the large metropolitan publisher who utilizes the latest photocomposition methods."[89] In the 1970s it was still relatively easy to distinguish journalists. Still the court acknowledged "freedom of the press is a 'fundamental personal right … not confined to newspapers and periodicals. It necessarily embraces pamphlets and leaflets … The press in its historic connotation comprehends every sort of publication which affords a vehicle of information and opinion.'"[90] Today, the definition of "journalist" is much more complicated.

Changes in technology have redefined news organizations and the people who disseminate news. In addition to traditional journalism, which appears in a broader array of forms, companies and associations are now using the Internet to report stories to their constituents. More individuals are also taking advantage of digital technology by circulating information through blogs and podcasts. According to a 2006 Pew Internet & American Life Project, of 147 million adult Internet users, 57 million read blogs and 12 million keep blogs.[91] Judge Sentelle of the D.C. Circuit Court mulled the distinction between blogger and journalist in his concurring opinion in the Judith Miller case, asking:

Are we then to create a privilege that protects only those reporters employed by *Time* magazine, the *New York Times*, and other media giants, or do we extend that protection as well to the owner of a desktop printer producing a weekly newsletter to inform his neighbors, lodge brothers, co-religionists, or co-conspirators? Perhaps more to the point today, does the privilege also protect the proprietor of a web log: the stereotypical "blogger" sitting in his pajamas at his personal computer posting on the World Wide Web his best product to inform whoever happens to browse his way? If not, why not? How could one draw a distinction consistent with the court's vision of a broadly granted personal right?[92]

The U.S. Court of Appeals for the Third Circuit did attempt to define a journalist in the case *In re Madden, Titan Sports v. Turner Broadcasting Systems* (1998).[93] The court considered whether Mark Madden, a wrestling commentator for a 900 number, qualified as a journalist entitled to claim journalist's privilege. It concluded that to be a journalist, someone must be

1. engaged in investigative reporting;
2. gathering news; and
3. possessing the intent at the beginning of the news-gathering process to disseminate the information to the public.

Based on these criteria, the court found that Madden was not a journalist because much of his work was "creative fiction." As such, his primary goal at the inception of his work was to provide entertainment rather than news to the public.

Privileges for bloggers

A California appellate court recently concluded that online journalists enjoy the same rights to protect sources that offline journalists do.[94] In December of 2004, Apple realized that two websites were carrying information about a new product it had not yet disclosed. The company attempted to identify the source of the leaks by subpoenaing e-mail records from NFox.com, the Internet service provider for one of the websites.[95] A lower court refused the website publisher's motion for a protective order to prevent Apple's discovery. But a state appellate court reversed the decision in *O'Grady v. Superior Court of Santa Clara County* (2006).

Jason O'Grady, the lead petitioner in the case, operates a news site called O'Grady's Powerpage that has reported on Apple developments since 1995. The online magazine, or blog, has a staff of nine editors and reporters and an average circulation of 300,000 visitors per month. O'Grady's site and another called AppleInsider.com announced that Apple had developed a firewire interface that would allow users of its digital recording and editing program Garageband to record analog audio.

The California Court of Appeals quashed the subpoenas against O'Grady's ISP for two reasons. First, it concluded that enforcing the subpoenas would require the

ISP to violate the Stored Communications Act (discussed in greater depth in chapter 10), which provides that subject to some exceptions "a person or entity providing an electronic communication service to the public shall not knowingly divulge to any person or entity the contents of a communication while in electronic storage by that service ..."[96] A subpoena for civil discovery is not enumerated among the exceptions. Forcing the ISP to release O'Grady's e-mails in contradiction of the Act would violate the principle of federal supremacy, which dictates that a state court may not enforce a state law that runs contrary to federal law.[97]

Second, the court rejected Apple's argument that the websites were not published by legitimate journalists entitled to protect their sources. California's constitution states "A publisher, editor, reporter, or other person connected with or employed upon a newspaper, magazine, or other periodical publication ... shall not be adjudged in contempt ... for refusing to disclose the source of any information procured while so connected or employed for publication in a newspaper, magazine or other periodical publication, or for refusing to disclose any unpublished information obtained or prepared in gathering, receiving or processing of information for communication to the public."[98]

The court considered whether journalist's privilege applied to the petitioners on the basis of First Amendment protection and concluded that it must. It stated "we can see no sustainable basis to distinguish petitioners from the reporters, editors, and publishers who provide news to the public through traditional print and broadcast media. It is established without contradiction that they gather, select, and prepare, for purposes of publication to a mass audience, information about current events of interest and concern to that audience."[99]

It is more likely, however, that these protections will apply to professional bloggers. For example, Texas' shield law applies only to online journalists, but only those whose journalistic activities amount to "a substantial portion" of their livelihoods or "substantial financial gain."[100]

In some states, "commenters" on media-sponsored blogs have been protected from attempts to unmask their identity in libel cases.[101] The *Billings Gazette* successfully fought a libel plaintiff's attempt to subpoena the name of an anonymous commenter on its blog who criticized a political candidate.[102] A Montana judge ruled that the state's shield law, normally used to protect confidential sources, also protected the newspaper from revealing the names of commentators. An Oregon state court followed suit, concluding that Oregon's shield law protects "not only news, but also "data" and what is commonly understood as information," which it interpreted to include the e-mail and IP addresses of the commentators on the *Portland Mercury* blog.[103]

Bloggers in federal courts have not fared as well. Blogger and videographer Josh Wolf served eight months in jail in 2006 for refusing to turn over video footage that he shot during a San Francisco protest of a Group of Eight (G8) summit in Scotland. The FBI subpoenaed the tape because it suspected that Wolf might have documented an attack on a police officer during the protest and an attempt to set fire to a police car. The federal agency claimed jurisdiction over the case because part of the car was purchased with federal funds.

Because the matter took place in a federal court, California's shield law did not protect Wolf as it had the bloggers in the Apple case. When Wolf refused to give up the video, a federal district court held him in civil contempt. Not only was Wolf the first blogger to go to jail for refusing to share information with the government, he served the longest sentence ever given a journalist. He was released when he finally agreed to give up the tape but did not have to testify before the grand jury.

Wolf's incarceration was only slightly longer than Vanessa Leggett's. Another "questionable journalist," Leggett was a part-time lecturer at a Houston university, who spent five and a half months in jail for contempt of court because she refused to give a federal grand jury her notes and tapes of interviews with confidential sources for a book she said she planned to write about the 1997 murder of a Houston socialite. A federal grand jury was considering whether there was enough evidence to indict the victim's husband, who had been acquitted of the murder charge in state court. The Fifth Circuit, which recognizes no journalist's privilege in criminal cases, upheld Leggett's contempt citation. It stated, "Even assuming that Leggett, a virtually unpublished free-lance writer operating without an employer or a contract for publication, qualifies as a journalist under the law, the journalist's privilege is ineffectual against a grand jury subpoena absent evidence of government harassment or oppression."[104]

Leggett never revealed the information. She was released after 168 days because the grand jury's term expired. The next grand jury empanelled returned an indictment without her notes or testimony.

Privacy Protection Act of 1980

Another point to be debated in relation to bloggers is whether the Privacy Protection Act of 1980 applies to them. Congress passed the Act in 1980 in reaction to the Supreme Court decision in *Zurcher v. Stanford Daily* (1978), finding that the Fourth Amendment did not prohibit police searches of documentary evidence held by third parties like journalists.[105] The Act was meant to shield journalists' work products and documentary materials from newsroom searches used to skirt delays normally associated with a subpoena.[106] But the law's wording does not specifically refer to newsrooms, and if interpreted plainly should apply to bloggers. It says:

> Notwithstanding any other law, it shall be unlawful for a government officer or employee, in connection with the investigation or prosecution of a criminal offense, to search for or seize any work product materials *possessed by a person reasonably believed to have a purpose to disseminate to the public a newspaper, book, broadcast, or other similar form of public communication, in or affecting interstate or foreign commerce* ...[107]

The same standards and exceptions apply to documentary materials (like notes, photographs, or tapes) used in connection with the dissemination of information to the public. Exceptions would apply if

- there is probable cause to believe the person possessing the materials is committing the criminal offense under investigation;
- immediate seizure of the materials is necessary to prevent bodily harm to someone;
- there is reason to believe that issuing a subpoena first would result in the destruction, alteration, or concealment of the materials; or
- the materials have not been produced in response to a court order directing compliance with a subpoena, all appellate remedies have been exhausted, and there is reason to believe that further delay would threaten justice.

A federal district court in Texas concluded that the U.S. Secret Service violated the Privacy Protection Act by raiding the office of Steve Jackson Games and confiscating its computing equipment. The Austin-based company publishes fantasy books and computer games and formerly operated a bulletin board service for gamers called Illuminati. In 1990, the Secret Service incorrectly believed that one of Jackson's employees possessed information about a hacker who had broken into Bell South's computer system. It not only raided the employee's home, but confiscated Jackson's equipment for four months. During that period, Jackson's company nearly went out of business. It closed the Illuminati BBS, missed publishing deadlines, and laid off half the workers. When the computers were returned, data was missing. The court awarded Jackson $51,000 for damages under the Privacy Protection Act.[108]

Questions for Discussion

1. What does the Freedom of Information Act do? What is an "agency" under the Freedom of Information Act?
2. How can people get information about the legislative and judicial branches?
3. Does the First Amendment protect journalist's privilege?
4. Are bloggers protected by journalist's privilege? Does the Privacy Protection Act of 1980 apply to them?

7

Intellectual Property: Copyright

No area of law has been more affected by digital media than intellectual property. The ease with which digital works can be reproduced, manipulated, and shared has transformed copyright law, in particular, from the realm of the obscure into a subject that lay people genuinely want to understand. And if they have difficulty understanding, it is no wonder. The law is very much still in transition as lawmakers struggle to adapt copyright protection to a fluid medium while maintaining a balance between the rights of copyright holders and copyright users.

The struggle has met with mixed success. Efforts to protect copyright holders against digital piracy have changed assumptions about fair use and criminalized some forms of conduct that were formerly protected. Changes in the law to make it more consistent with copyright in other countries have provided better international protection for U.S. works, but also kept millions of works out of the public domain. Meanwhile, although courts are reaching a greater consensus on how copyright protection applies online, there are still areas of litigation, particularly regarding file sharing, that have produced contradictory opinions.

This chapter will discuss what can and cannot be copyrighted, what constitutes infringement and how to avoid it, fair use, file trading, sampling, and the First Amendment implications of copyright law.

Source and Purpose of Intellectual Property Protection

The Constitution's copyright and patent clause empowers Congress "To promote the Progress of Science and useful Arts, by securing for limited Times to Authors and Inventors the exclusive Right to their respective Writings and Discoveries." Implicit is the assumption that people will produce more creative work if they are guaranteed protection for the fruits of their labors. If others can exploit their work for personal benefit without contributing to its production, creators have less of an incentive to produce.

Intellectual property protection is not unlimited, however. It is counterbalanced by the notion that after a certain period of time the work should move into the public domain, where it will be accessible to others who also may use it to contribute to the body of knowledge. Although we may speak of intellectual property *owners*, copyrights and patents are not permanent property rights in the traditional sense. They are actually limited monopoly rights.

What Can Be Copyrighted?

Of all forms of intellectual property protection, copyright is the most directly applicable to digital media products. It protects all forms of art, literature, music, video, imagery, and software that a digital artist or producer is likely to create. Specifically, copyright law protects "original works of authorship fixed in any tangible medium of expression."[1] The Supreme Court has clarified that "[o]riginality does not signify novelty."[2] In fact, should two artists miraculously create the same piece, each without knowing of the work of the other, both works would be copyrightable. Instead, it means that the work must be a product of the author's labor, rather than borrowed from some other source.

For purposes of copyright, a work is considered fixed in a tangible medium if it is "sufficiently permanent or stable to permit it to be perceived, reproduced, or otherwise communicated for a period of more than transitory duration."[3] The fixation requirement is technologically neutral. In 1976, Congress amended copyright law to apply to works in any medium of expression "now known or later developed, from which they can be perceived, reproduced, or otherwise communicated, either directly or with the aid of a machine or device."[4] Fixation has been interpreted to include paper, film, video, CDs, ROM, and RAM – essentially anything that can retain information. It is the difference between a speech saved in a file on a computer, for example, and a speaker's impromptu remarks that evaporate when spoken.

To qualify for protection, a work also must display "some minimal level of *creativity*."[5] Creativity is not judged by the caliber of the work. In fact, the Supreme Court has acknowledged that the level of creativity required is "extremely low." Most works qualify for copyright "no matter how crude, humble or obvious" they might be as long as there is some sign of "intellectual production, of thought, and conception."[6] To earn copyright protection, a work must be:

(1) original;
(2) fixed in a tangible medium of expression; and
(3) moderately creative.

The Copyright Act places "original works of authorship" eligible for protection into the following categories:

- literary works, including computer programs;
- musical works;
- dramatic works;
- pantomimes and choreographic works;
- pictorial, graphic, and sculptural works;
- motion pictures and other audiovisual works;
- sound recordings; and
- architectural works.

Copyright protection for architectural works is intended to prohibit the unauthorized duplication of a building or its architectural blueprints. It does not prevent others from making, distributing, or publicly displaying paintings, photographs, or other pictorial representations of a building that is easily viewed by the public.[7]

Copyright also applies to *collected works*, which are collections of individually copyrighted works amassed into larger works, such as anthologies. In such cases, the copyright for the collected work is separate from the copyright for the individual work. The owner of the copyright to the collected work has the right to reproduce the work as a whole, but not to reproduce its individual parts. Copyright also protects *compilations* of facts, as long as they possess the requisite level of originality.

What Cannot Be Copyrighted?

Facts and ideas

Because the primary purpose behind copyright protection is the creation of knowledge, copyright law does not protect facts or ideas. It only protects the unique way that facts or ideas are expressed. Others may use the same information, as long as they express it in a different way. Courts refer to this distinction between what is and is not protected as the idea/expression or fact/expression dichotomy. In practice, it means that a CNN news piece about the president would receive protection for the way the information is conveyed – the words chosen, the arrangement of the facts and selection of imagery to go with them – but not the actual information conveyed. If the contrary were true, we would all have to watch CNN to get the information in CNN's control.[8] The same guidelines apply to creative material. For example, copyright protects the particular lyrics and arrangement of a song, but not the underlying idea expressed through the music. If a songwriter were entitled to control an idea, we might be limited to one song about falling in love and another about breaking up. The Top 40 would look more like the Top 2.

Facts are not protected because "[n]o one may claim originality as to facts."[9] Facts are not authored; they are discovered. In contrast, a compilation of facts may be sufficiently original to justify protection. Writing for the Supreme Court in *Feist Publications, Inc. v. Rural Telephone Service Co.* (1991), Justice O'Connor explained:

> The compilation author typically chooses which facts to include, in what order to
> place them, and how to arrange the collected data so that they may be used effectively
> by readers. These choices as to selection and arrangement, so long as they are made
> independently by the compiler and entail a minimal degree of creativity, are suffi-
> ciently original that Congress may protect such compilations through the copyright
> laws.[10]

Still, in a compilation, copyright subsists only in the parts of the work that are
original, not in the facts themselves. If there is nothing distinctive about the arrangement of the data, no amount of work invested in its assembly will justify copyright
protection.

The Supreme Court illustrated this point in *Feist Publications* when it rejected
the "sweat of the brow" theory that a compiler's hard work put toward collecting
facts deserved protection.[11] Rural Telephone Service Company sued Feist
Publications for republishing parts of its alphabetized telephone directory and was
granted summary judgment on its copyright claim in district court. The Court of
Appeals affirmed the judgment, but the Supreme Court reversed, finding that Rural
Telephone's alphabetical listings displayed no originality worth protection.
Acknowledging that it may seem unfair for others to benefit from a compiler's
labor, the Court explained that the "primary objective of copyright is not to reward
the labor of authors, but '[t]o promote the Progress of Science and useful Arts.'
To this end, copyright assures authors the right to their original expression, but
encourages others to build freely upon the ideas and information conveyed by a
work."[12]

However, the European Union does protect databases. In 1996, the EU passed
the Database Directive[13] to harmonize levels of protection for databases among
member states, some of which protected databases under the copyright rules and
some of which did not. The directive defines a database as a "collection of independent works, data or other materials arranged in a systematic or methodical way and
individually accessible by electronic or other means." It requires member states to
recognize a sui generis (meaning unique or different) right to protect a database
when there has been "qualitatively and/or quantitatively a substantial investment
in either the obtaining, verification or presentation of the contents."[14] The right
allows a database owner to prevent the unauthorized extraction or reuse of all or a
substantial part of the contents of a database.

Procedures, processes, systems, or methods of operation

Copyright does not protect procedures, processes, systems or methods of operation. However, works that fall into these categories may receive protection under
patent law.

Titles and names

Titles and names cannot be copyrighted, which is why so many works carry the same name. However, some titles and names receive protection under trademark law or laws related to unfair competition.

Scenes à faire

Copyright does not protect *scenes à faire*, which are stock or standard expressions of an idea. Some incidents, characters, and settings are indispensable to the treatment of topic and therefore expected to be used repeatedly.[15] In *Data East USA, Inc. v. EPYX, Inc.* (1988), the copyright holder for the electronic game "Karate Champ" won a judgment against the distributor of "World Karate Championship" for copyright infringement. Both games included karate matches in which there were two opponents, one wearing white and the other wearing red, using similar karate moves. The Ninth Circuit reversed the judgment because both games incorporated *scenes à faire*.[16] The appellate court determined that the common features were necessary to the idea of a karate game.

The *scenes à faire* exemption has also been used in the context of computer software to exclude certain elements of a work from copyright protection that are dictated by external constraints on the work's production. The Tenth Circuit explained that "[f]or computer-related applications, these external factors include hardware standards and mechanical specifications, software standards, and compatibility requirements, computer manufacturer design standards, industry programming practices, and practices and demands of the industry being serviced."[17]

U.S. government documents

Copyright protection does not apply to U.S. government works. These are items produced by federal employees in the course of their official duties. Most reports produced by government agencies belong in the public domain and may be used without restrictions. C-SPAN video of House and Senate floor proceedings is also part of the public domain. Its video of other federal government events, like Congressional committee hearings and White House briefings is not, but the network permits public Internet sites to make noncommercial use of it.[18]

Although the U.S. government cannot copyright its own work in the United States, U.S. agencies outside the United States may obtain protection for government works through foreign copyright laws. The U.S. government also may own copyrighted material that is transferred or bequeathed to it.[19] Work prepared for the U.S. government by private contractors may be copyrighted. The owner of the work depends on the terms of the contract. A privately prepared work that includes material from government documents may be copyrighted, but the copyright would not extend to the government work in the document, only to the original material added by the author.

Works produced by state or municipal governments do not necessarily fall into the public domain. As sovereign entities, states and municipalities are responsible for setting their own policies regarding the use of their documents. Sometimes they assert a copyright interest in them.

Works in the public domain

The *public domain* is a conceptual category of works that never had or no longer have copyright protection and therefore are freely available for anyone to use at any time for any purpose. All works enter the public domain when their copyright protection expires. Others are there because their copyright was abandoned or not properly registered or renewed when copyright registration and renewal were required. In 2004, for example, Ludlow Music, Inc. demanded that JibJab Media, the creator of a widely circulated Web animation parodying George Bush and John Kerry to "This Land is Your Land," remove the animation from the Internet and compensate the company for the unlicensed use of its copyrighted song. JibJab enlisted the Electronic Frontier Foundation's help to file for a declaratory judgment, requesting judicial confirmation that its use of the song was fair.[20] While preparing for the case, EFF discovered that the song had been in the public domain since 1973. Woodie Guthrie, the composer, filed the original copyright for the song when copyright protection lasted 28 years, with the option to renew for another 28 years. Ludlow acquired the copyright from Guthrie, but failed to renew it.

The Internet has highlighted an interesting dilemma regarding the public domain. A work in the public domain in one country may still be protected in another country, but freely available in both through the Internet. In 2007, Universal Edition, an Austrian music publisher, bullied a Canadian music student into taking down a collaborative wiki he had established for musical scores whose copyrights had expired in Canada.[21] Within less than two years, the nonprofit site called the International Music Score Library Project (IMSLP) had grown to become the largest public domain music score library on the Internet. UE demanded that the site block European users from accessing it because some of the scores included were still protected in Europe. Canada protects works for 50 years beyond the death of the author, but countries in Europe protect works for an additional 20 years. The site was certainly legal under Canadian law, but if UE were to file a copyright suit in Austria, the outcome would be uncertain. According to Canadian copyright scholar Michael Geist, even if an Austrian court asserted jurisdiction, a Canadian court would probably refuse to uphold the judgment. However, the student removed the site because he couldn't afford to fight a lawsuit or to pay for the technology to block European users.

Who Qualifies for Copyright Protection?

Copyright protection vests in the creator of a work the moment the work is produced. If two or more people produce a work, they are considered to be joint owners of the copyright.

Works prepared by an employee in the scope of his or her employment are considered *works for hire* and belong to the employer. A graphic artist, writer, or Web designer employed by a company to create a work for the company has no right to authorize others to use the work without the permission of his or her employer. A work commissioned by an organization from a freelancer also may be considered a work for hire. But both parties must agree in a signed document before the work commences that it will constitute a work for hire.[22]

In *New York Times Co. v. Tasini* (2001), the Supreme Court held that the *New York Times* violated its freelance writers' distribution rights by making their work available in computer databases that sell access to articles divorced from the newspaper. The *New York Times* owned the compilation right to the particular issues that contained the freelancers' articles, but it did not have the right to use the articles individually for other purposes.[23] The win was short-lived for the freelancers. After its loss, the *Times* simply required them to sign over the electronic rights to their work before the paper would publish it.

Occasionally, it is not clear whether a work's creator is an employee producing a work for hire or an independent contractor who may retain the copyright. For example, in *Community for Creative Non-Violence v. Reid* (CCNV), an organization established to aid the homeless commissioned a sculpture to depict their plight.[24] The artist commissioned to produce the work created it in his studio, where the organization's representatives visited on several occasions to check on the work's progress, providing suggestions regarding its configuration and size. When it was delivered, the organization paid the artist for the work and installed it. Subsequently, both parties filed competing copyright claims. When CCNV sued to determine copyright ownership, the district court found in its favor, concluding that the statue was a work for hire. But the D.C. Court of Appeals reversed, because the statue was not "prepared by an employee within the scope of his or her employment" and the parties had not agreed in writing that it was a work for hire. The Supreme Court came up with the following criteria to determine whether a party hired for a particular job may be categorized as an employee within the meaning of the Act's work for hire provision. Factors to consider include:

- the hiring party's right to control the manner by which the work is done;
- the skill required to complete the work;
- the source of the instruments or tools used to produce the work;

- the location of the work;
- the duration of the business relationship between the parties;
- whether the hiring party may assign additional projects to the hired party;
- the hired party's discretion over when and how long to work;
- the method of payment;
- the hired party's role in hiring and paying assistants;
- whether the work is part of the hiring party's regular business;
- whether the hiring party is in business;
- the provision of employee benefits; and
- the tax treatment of the hired party.[25]

Basing its analysis on these factors, the Supreme Court concluded that Reid was an independent contractor who retained ownership of the copyright.

What Are a Copyright Holder's Exclusive Rights?

Although the word *copyright* implies the right to reproduce a work, copyright law actually encompasses a bundle of individual rights, which are listed in Section 106 of the Copyright Act. Copyright holders have the exclusive right to do or authorize someone else to do any of the following:

1. to reproduce the copyrighted work in copies or phonorecords;*
2. to prepare derivative works† based upon the copyrighted work;
3. to distribute copies or phonorecords of the copyrighted work to the public by sale or other transfer of ownership, or by rental, lease, or lending;
4. in the case of literary, musical, dramatic, and choreographic works, pantomimes, and motion pictures and other audiovisual works, to perform the copyrighted work publicly;
5. in the case of literary, musical, dramatic, and choreographic works, pantomimes, and pictorial, graphic, or sculptural works, including the individual images of a motion picture or other audiovisual work, to display the copyrighted work publicly; and
6. in the case of sound recordings, to perform the copyrighted work publicly by means of a digital audio transmission.

---

* This rather antiquated sounding term actually encompasses any modern sound recording. Section 101 of the Copyright Act defines phonorecords as "material objects in which sounds, other than those accompanying a motion picture or other audiovisual work, are fixed by any method now known or later developed, and from which the sounds can be perceived, reproduced, or otherwise communicated, either directly or with the aid of a machine or device."

† A derivative work is one that has been "recast, transformed, or adapted" from the original. It may include newly edited editions, translations, dramatizations, abridgments, adaptations, compilations, and works republished with new matter added. A derivative is independently copyrightable; its protection begins the moment it is created.

Copyrights are separable. Copyright holders may transfer all or some of the rights to a copyrighted work to others, either through sale or bequeathal in a will. Consequently, the rights to one work may be controlled by more than one person or organization. To be valid the transfer must be in writing and signed by the copyright holder.

The Copyright Act also provides a limited right of attribution and integrity to visual artists. It gives authors of visual works of art, whether or not they are the copyright owners of the work, the right to claim authorship of their works, or alternatively, the right to prevent the association of their names with works they did not create or which have been distorted, mutilated or modified.[26] It also entitles the author of a visual work, subject to some restrictions, to prevent any intentional "distortion, mutilation, or other modification of that work which would be prejudicial to his or her honor or reputation" or "to prevent the destruction of a work of recognized stature."[27]

First sale doctrine

Generally, however, copyright holders have no right to control the physical product embodying their expression once it has been sold. The Copyright Act distinguishes between the physical copy of the work, which anyone may own, and its content, which is exclusively controlled by the copyright owner.[28] Under the *first sale doctrine*, the lawful owner of a copyrighted work may sell, give away, or destroy the particular copy he or she owns without the copyright owner's permission. This policy entitles a CD owner, for example, to sell his or her copy of the CD but does not allow the CD owner to make copies for others from it.

Registering and Protecting Works

Copyright, once protected through state and common law, is now exclusively protected through federal law. It is no longer necessary, however, to register a work officially through the Copyright Office to acquire copyright in it.[29] All works created from 1978 on have been protected upon creation. The United States made this concession in order to join the Berne Convention for the Protection of Literary and Artistic Works. The treaty, originally signed in Berne, Switzerland, in 1886, has 164 member nations who recognize the international validity of each other's copyrights.[30]

Although copyright registration is not required in the United States, certain conveniences and rights accrue from it that make the extra effort and expense worthwhile. To sue for copyright infringement, for example, the work must be registered. It is possible to register a work after the infringement has taken place, but doing so poses a delay and the copyright holder may be limited to an award of actual damages. A copyright holder who registers a work within three months of publication or prior to the infringement of the work may be awarded statutory damages and attorney's fees.

To register a work, the copyright owner must submit a completed application form and $45 fee to the Copyright Office along with two copies of a published work or one copy of an unpublished work to be deposited in the Library of Congress. The Register of Copyrights will issue a certificate of registration to the copyright holder. A certificate issued before or within five years after a work is first published constitutes prima facie evidence of a valid copyright that may be used later in a judicial proceeding should someone else use the work illegally.[31]

Affixing a notice of copyright to a published work is not required for copyright protection but is advisable. It may later serve as evidence in a copyright suit that the alleged infringer's use was not innocent. A copyright notice consists of three elements:

(1)   the letter c in a circle (©) or the word "Copyright," written in its entirety or abbreviated as Copr.;
(2)   the year the work was first published; and
(3)   the name of the copyright owner.

If the copyrighted work is a "phonorecord," then the letter c is replaced with the letter p in a circle accompanied by the year of publication and the copyright holder's name. A copyright notice also may be placed on an unpublished work, as in the following example: Unpublished work © 2008 Ashley Packard.

Because the copyright notice is not required, it is never safe to assume that its absence means a work may be freely used. In general, unless a work is very old, you should assume that it is copyrighted and permission to use it is required. However, identifying the copyright holder for a work is not always easy. Some works are not only missing the copyright information, but also published anonymously or under a pseudonym. The name accompanying the notice of copyright published with the work may no longer be valid if the copyright has changed hands. Also the copyright holders responsible for individual parts of a collected work may not be listed. The best place to begin a search for a copyright holder is through Copyright Office records, which include registration information. The records for newer works are accessible through the Copyright Office's website at http://www.copyright.gov/records/ and searchable by the author, copyright notice, or title.

How long does copyright protection last?

Copyright in a work created since 1978 lasts for the life of the author plus 70 years, expiring at the end of the calendar year.[32] If a work is jointly owned by two or more people, copyright endures 70 years beyond the life of the last surviving author. A work for hire, or a work that is anonymous or pseudonymous, is protected for 95 years after the date of publication or 120 years after the work is created, whichever comes first.

Determining the term of protection for a work created before January 1, 1978, is more complicated. At that time, copyrights were protected for 28 years, with the option to renew another 28 years. But changes in the law extended the renewal period on the second term from 28 to 67 years. As of January 2010, any work published or copyrighted prior to January 1, 1925, has expired.

Congress extended copyright protection prospectively and retrospectively by 20 years in 1998.[33] The extension made American copyright terms consistent with those in the European Union. The EU's Council of Ministers passed a directive in 1993 requiring all EU members to protect their own copyrights for a term equal to the life of the author plus 70 years and foreign copyrights for a term equal to that guaranteed by their own countries.[34] At the time, the duration of U.S. copyright protection complied with the minimum standard required by the Berne Convention – 50 years beyond the life of the author. Congress passed the 20-year extension to ensure that EU countries protected American works as long as their own.

The extension was also politically motivated. Disney lobbied hard for it because the copyrights on its characters Mickey Mouse, Goofy, and Pluto were about to expire.[35] If that happened, the characters would move into the public domain where others could use them for creative purposes. Disney itself has been a tremendous beneficiary of public domain works. It has generated millions in revenue reinterpreting folk tales in the public domain, such as Cinderella and Snow White, and literature in the public domain, such as Victor Hugo's *The Hunchback of Notre Dame* and the Grimm brothers' fairy tales.

Eric Eldred, the publisher of an online repository of public domain works, challenged the constitutionality of the Copyright Term Extension Act in *Eldred v. Ashcroft* (2003).[36] Eldred argued that the law (which extended copyright's duration for the eleventh time) violated the constitutional mandate to protect works for *limited times* and the First Amendment by giving retroactive protection to copyrighted works destined for the public domain. However, the Supreme Court applied a lower level of scrutiny to the law. It found that extending copyright to meet the EU standard was a rational exercise of Congressional authority.

What Is Copyright Infringement?

Reproducing, distributing, publicly displaying, publicly performing, or producing a derivative version of a copyrighted work without the copyright holder's permission constitutes copyright infringement. To succeed in a copyright infringement case, plaintiffs must prove their ownership of the work and that the defendant violated one or more of their exclusive rights. Because there is rarely direct evidence that a person copied a work, courts will settle for circumstantial evidence that the defendant had access to the copyrighted work prior to the creation of his or her own and that there is substantial similarity between them, both in ideas and expression. An exact reproduction is not required.

Those involved in the production of digital media particularly need to understand that a series of steps taken with regard to one work may violate more than one right. For example, making an unauthorized copy of someone else's copyrighted work, altering it, and then distributing it without permission, would violate three of the copyright holder's exclusive rights, each punishable separately.

Misconceptions regarding the derivative right are common. Copyright holders possess the exclusive right to make alternative versions of their work. Finding an image on the Internet and altering it does not create a new work; it creates a derivative work that violates the copyright holder's exclusive right. Although urban myths suggest that altering a work by 20 percent or changing it a certain number of times can protect against suits for copyright infringement, no such formula exists. A good rule of thumb is that if the original work is still recognizable, it can still be considered a derivative version.

Copyright liability

Copyright infringement is a strict liability offense, meaning that intent to infringe has no bearing on a determination of guilt. In *Pinkham v. Sara Lee Corp.* (1992), the Eighth Circuit explained that:

> Once a plaintiff has proven that he or she owns the copyright on a particular work, and that the defendant has infringed upon those "exclusive rights," the defendant is liable for the infringement and this liability is absolute. The defendant's intent is simply not relevant: The defendant is liable even for "innocent" or "accidental" infringements.[37]

The application of strict liability proceeds from the assumption that the infringer, unlike the copyright owner, "has an opportunity to guard against liability for infringement by diligent inquiry, or at least the ability to guard against liability for infringement by an indemnity agreement from his supplier or by an 'errors and omissions' insurance policy."[38]

There are three levels of copyright liability: direct liability, contributory liability, and vicarious liability. Individuals who infringe upon the exclusive rights guaranteed to copyright holders in Section 106 of the Copyright Act are *directly liable* for copyright infringement, whether they were aware of the infringement or not.

Although not part of the Copyright statute, courts have also developed doctrines for contributory liability for copyright infringement. Individuals who "knowingly" induce, cause, or materially contribute to the infringing conduct of others, but who have not actually committed the copyright infringement themselves, may be *contributorily liable* for copyright infringement.[39] A court also may impose liability for contributory infringement on individuals who aid an infringer without knowledge of the infringement, but who should "have reason to know" they are aiding an infringer. For example, in *Religious Technology Center v. Netcom On-Line Communication Services* (1995), a California district judge denied an Internet service provider's request for summary judgment in a copyright infringement suit based on the actions of one of its subscribers.[40] The subscriber was a disgruntled former Church of Scientology minister who began posting the church's secret texts online. Because the plaintiff, the church's publisher, notified Netcom of the infringement and copyright notices were still present on the posts, the court believed there was a legitimate question as to whether Netcom knew or should have known about the subscriber's activity, implicating contributory liability on its part.

Individuals may be *vicariously liable* for copyright infringement if they have the right and ability to supervise the infringing conduct of others, as well as a direct financial interest in the infringement. Knowledge of the infringement is not required. Vicarious liability, which applies to other areas of tort law as well, evolved from the doctrine of respondeat superior, which dictates that the master (employer) is responsible for the actions of the servant (employee). However, it no longer requires an employer-employee relationship, as long as some level of control and financial remuneration is involved.

File trading

Cases involving illegal file sharing can be used to illustrate all three levels of liability. Courts have made it clear that sharing copyrighted music, games, and videos is a form of direct copyright infringement. Over a five-year period, the Recording Industry Association of America filed suit against more than 30,000 file traders. Most of these actions ended in out-of-court settlements, but a few have gone to trial. The most renowned of these cases involved Jammie Thomas, who was fined $1.92 million in 2009 for willfully infringing 24 songs.[41] That is $80,000 per track. Thomas, whom the RIAA alleges traded as many as 1,700 songs on the file sharing network Kazaa, lost her case twice. In 2007, a jury issued a $222,000 verdict against her. But the presiding judge declared a mistrial after learning that his instructions to the jury had been incorrect.[42] The court had been unaware of an earlier precedent within its circuit that infringement of the distribution right requires an *actual* dissemination of a copyrighted work.[43] The judge had instructed the jury that the act of making sound recordings available for electronic distribution without authorization violated the copyright owner's distribution right even without evidence that the file was ever downloaded. Courts in different jurisdictions disagree on whether making a copyrighted work available for download constitutes an actual "distribution" or merely an offer to distribute.[44] However, there is no question that the unauthorized act of uploading or downloading copyrighted music violates the reproduction right. In the second trail Thomas was accused of both illegally uploading and downloading the music. In December of 2008, the RIAA announced its intention to abandon its practice of suing individual file sharers, which had become a public relations fiasco. Instead it plans to work with ISPs to discontinue service to repeat offenders.[45]

Courts consider the provision of file trading services or software to be a form of contributory infringement, if the software provider is aware of the infringement. In *A&M Records v. Napster, Inc.* (2001), the Ninth Circuit found Napster's action of providing a centralized website, where subscribers could find the titles of the music they wanted to download, a contributory and vicarious copyright infringement, even though subscribers downloaded the actual songs from other customer's computers.[46] It was clear to the Ninth Circuit that Napster was not only aware of the infringing activity but facilitated it by channeling subscribers to the music. It was also apparent that, although Napster could have taken actions to restrict the infringement, it did not and that it profited from the service.

Grokster, a West Indies-based software company, was found to have contributorily and vicariously infringed upon on MGM Studios' copyrights by supplying software that enabled Internet users to engage in illegal file trading. Grokster attempted to rely on *Sony Corp. of America v. Universal City Studios, Inc.* (1984) to defeat the claim of contributory infringement. In *Sony*, the Supreme Court held that the distribution of a commercial product, like Sony's video recorder, which was capable of substantial noninfringing uses, would not result in contributory liability for infringement.[47] Although video recorders could be used to make unauthorized copies of televised programs, the court focused on a more common noninfringing use – time shifting.

In *MGM Studios v. Grokster*, however, the Court found that the software was primarily used for infringing purposes and that its distributors had *induced* direct infringement among its users. Distinguishing between the two cases, Justice Souter explained:

> Evidence of active steps … taken to encourage direct infringement, such as advertising an infringing use or instructing how to engage in an infringing use, shows an affirmative intent that the product be used to infringe, and overcomes the law's reluctance to find liability when a defendant merely sells a commercial product suitable for some lawful use.[48]

The Supreme Court also pointed to evidence of vicarious infringement, when it noted that Grokster's profits from advertising increased with the number of users drawn to the service and that the company could have used filtering tools to diminish infringing activity, but did not do so.

Aside from legal differences, *Sony* and *Grokster* also can be distinguished by their real-world economic ramifications. By the time the Court heard *Sony*, videocassette recorders were common in American homes. It would have been difficult to suddenly "outlaw" them. Moreover, Universal Studios had no data indicating that the recorders had caused it direct harm. The software Grokster supplied for peer-to-peer (P2P) file trading was free. Users had not invested hundreds of dollars in the technology. Film studios and music publishers also have data regarding actual damages caused by file trading.

Digital Millennium Copyright Act

Digital media have posed a significant challenge for copyright law because they make it almost effortless to infringe upon others' rights. Lawmakers have responded by passing a series of measures to tighten protection on digital works, the most significant being the Digital Millennium Copyright Act.[49] The DMCA makes it illegal to circumvent digital rights management technology directly or to "import, offer to the public, provide, or otherwise traffic" in any technology, product, or service that can circumvent technological measures used to control access to copyrighted works.[50]

Certain exceptions are allowed. Schools and libraries may circumvent copyright technology to see whether they want to purchase a legitimate copy of a work. Individuals may break the defensive code in a software program in order to reverse engineer it for the purpose of creating another program that works with it. Encryption researchers may circumvent copyright locks "to identify and analyze flaws and vulnerabilities in encryption technologies," as long as the code breaking and any information disseminated regarding it is done for the purpose of advancing the technology rather than facilitating infringement.[51] Exemptions are also provided for those who do security testing for computer networks. Computer users are also allowed to disable technologies used to collect and disseminate personally identifying information about them.

Congress incorporated a "fail safe" provision into the Act to deal with the DMCA's unanticipated impact on legitimate uses of particular categories of copyrighted works. The DMCA authorizes the Librarian of Congress to create limited exemptions to the anti-circumvention provision every three years to spare individuals whose fair use of some copyrighted materials otherwise would be adversely affected. Exemptions created in 2006, allow mobile phone owners to bypass software preventing them from using their phones with competing carriers.[52] Other exemptions allow film professors to circumvent protections on DVDs to create compilations for teaching purposes and let blind people disable controls on electronic books to prevent the read-aloud function or use of screen readers.

The DMCA brought the United States into compliance with the World Intellectual Property Organization Copyright Treaty ("WIPO Treaty"), which requires contracting parties to "provide adequate legal protection and effective legal remedies against the circumvention of effective technological measures" used by copyright holders to restrict unauthorized use of their work.[53] However, its anti-circumvention provision has been controversial because it arguably alters the balance between the rights of copyright holders and copyright users. Critics have claimed that it effectively creates a new right to control access to copyrighted works by prohibiting the circumvention of digital rights management technology used to restrict access to digital works.

Exemption for Internet service providers

The Digital Millennium Copyright Act created an exemption to shield Internet service providers from liability for the infringing actions of their subscribers or for linking to sites that contain infringing information. The DMCA's safe harbor for service providers shields ISPs from liability for "(1) transitory digital network communications; (2) system caching; (3) information residing on systems or networks at the direction of users; and (4) information location tools."[54] The exemption applies as long as the service provider takes no part in editing the material or selecting its audience, has no actual knowledge of the infringement, and gains no financial benefit from the infringing activity. Once service providers learn from copyright holders that material accessible through their systems is infringing, they are required to remove or disable access to it expeditiously. The exemption has consequently come to be known as the DMCA "take-down" provision.

An ISP that disables access to material on the good faith belief that the content is infringing, will not be held liable for any damages that might be caused by the material's removal, even if it later proves not to be infringing. But the service provider is obligated to notify the subscriber that the material has been removed. If the subscriber supplies a counter notification indicating that the material is not infringing, the ISP must forward it to the person who submitted the original notice requesting its removal, informing him or her that access to the material will be restored in 10 days. If the recipient wishes to pursue the matter, he or she must then seek a court order to restrain the subscriber from further infringing the work.

A party who knowingly and materially misrepresents that a document published on an ISP's system is infringing may later be held liable for any damages or legal fees incurred by the alleged infringer or the ISP for the removal of the work.[55] The term *materially* means that the misrepresentation affected the ISP's actions. Such was the case in *Online Policy Group v. Diebold* (2004), when a California federal district court found Diebold Election Systems, a manufacturer of electronic voting machines, guilty of misusing the DMCA to squelch speech.[56] The case began when two Swarthmore College students gained access to Diebold employees' e-mails, acknowledging faults in Diebold voting machines and bugs that made its software vulnerable to hackers, and posted them on various websites. IndyMedia, an online news source, published an article about the e-mails and links to them. Diebold sent cease and desist letters to Swarthmore College, which provided the students' Internet access, and to IndyMedia's access provider, advising them that they would be shielded from a copyright suit by Diebold under the DMCA safe harbor provision as long as they removed the material from their systems. Swarthmore responded to the threat by requiring the students to take the e-mails down. But Online Policy

Group, which provided Internet access for IndyMedia, filed for a declaratory judgment that the material was not infringing and monetary relief based on Diebold's misrepresentation of its copyright claim. Diebold, which never followed through with the suit, told the court that it would not send anymore cease and desist letters regarding the e-mails, so the only question left was whether the plaintiffs had a claim for damages regarding its misrepresentation. Judge Jeremy Fogel believed they did. Pointing out that it would be hard to find a subject more worthy of public interest than memos suggesting that votes might be calculated incorrectly, he concluded that use of the memos was fair. He added that the fact that Diebold never filed a copyright suit against the students suggested that it had tried to use the DMCA "as a sword to suppress publication of embarrassing content rather than as a shield to protect its intellectual property." In a later case, the Ninth Circuit made explicit what was implicit in Judge Fogel's decision, that "there must be a demonstration of some actual knowledge of misrepresentation on the part of the copyright owner" for the provision to apply.[57]

The DMCA also gives copyright holders the right to subpoena Internet service providers to learn the identities of anonymous subscribers who post infringing material.[58] The Recording Industry Association of America has made liberal use of this provision to identify anonymous file traders.

A question yet to be settled is just how far the DMCA's safe harbor provision extends to other Web 2.0 technologies that allow users to upload content. YouTube, for example, considers itself protected by the provision, as long as it observes the law's notice and take-down requests. The video-sharing site owned by Google is awash in infringing videos uploaded by its users. Viacom is suing Google for $1 billion for violating its copyrights.[59] As the owner of MTV, Nickelodeon, Comedy Central, Paramount Studios, and DreamWorks, Viacom says 160,000 of its video clips have been viewed on YouTube 1.5 billion times. The company is arguing that Google promotes YouTube as a tool for infringement, thereby "unlawfully fostering copyright infringement by YouTube users" – essentially an argument based on the inducement theory introduced in *MGM v. Grokster*. It contends that YouTube profits from advertisers who pay to reach users attracted by infringing content. Google argues that the snippets its users upload help promote the original material. The case has the potential to be extremely important and the litigants have the money to take it all the way to the Supreme Court. But many legal commentators speculate it will end in a settlement because neither party would benefit from an either or solution when an arrangement to license the content would benefit both.[60]

Remedies for Copyright Infringement

Because copyright is a federal law, all infringement claims are litigated in federal court. A copyright holder has three years from the date of the infringement to file a civil suit under the Act. If the infringement is on-going, a court may issue a temporary restraining order followed by an injunction to stop it. Courts may also impose civil remedies on infringers that include either (a) the copyright holder's actual damages, along with any profits the infringer may have accrued from the illegal use of the work, or (b) statutory damages that range from $750 to $30,000.[61] If the copyright holder can prove that the infringer's actions were willful, the court may increase statutory damages to a maximum of $150,000 per infringing act. One sign of willfulness is providing false contact information to a domain registry in connection with the infringement.

If the infringer can prove that he or she did not know and further had no reason to know that the material taken was copyrighted, a court may reduce statutory damages to as little as $200.[62] The choice to pursue statutory damages as an alternative to the actual damages belongs to the copyright holder and must be made before the court enters its final judgment.

Criminal infringement

Copyright infringement may also be prosecuted as a criminal offense if the infringement was willful and committed

(A) for purposes of commercial advantage or private financial gain;
(B) by the reproduction or distribution, including by electronic means, during any 180–day period, of 1 or more copies or phonorecords of 1 or more copyrighted works, which have a total retail value of more than $1,000; or
(C) by the distribution of a work being prepared for commercial distribution, by making it available on a computer network accessible to members of the public, if such person knew or should have known that the work was intended for commercial distribution.[63]

A work prepared for commercial distribution would include computer software, motion pictures, music, or other audiovisual works reasonably expected to generate a commercial gain for the copyright holder.

Other actions associated with criminal infringement include placing a fraudulent notice of copyright on someone else's work, fraudulently removing a copyright notice from a copyrighted work and making false representations in an application for copyright registration. These actions may result in a fine of up to $2,500, along with the destruction of infringing copies of a work and any equipment used to produce them.

Willful circumvention of copyright protection systems for commercial or private financial gain will result in the most severe penalties. A person may be fined up to $500,000 or imprisoned up to five years for a first offense. For a subsequent offense, a person may be fined up to $1 million or imprisoned for up to 10 years. The statute of limitations on a criminal offense is five years.

Balancing the Rights of Copyright Owners and Users

Although copyright protects original works of authorship, it has long since been understood that few works are truly original. Therefore it is necessary to find a balance between an author's right to protect expression in a work and the rights of others to draw inspiration from it. "Recognizing that science and art generally rely on works that came before them and rarely spring forth in a vacuum," the Copyright Act limits the rights of a copyright owners regarding works that build upon, reinterpret, and reconceive existing works."[64] It also protects the public's right to use them as the basis for social criticism and political debate.

Fair use

The unauthorized use of a copyrighted work is not always considered an infringement. The Copyright Act provides the right to make fair use of a work, even without permission, under certain circumstances. Favored uses include "criticism, comment, news reporting, teaching (including multiple copies for classroom use), scholarship, or research."[65] But beyond these generalizations, fair use is hard to pin down. There is no predetermined list of what is and is not acceptable to take. Courts determine what constitutes fair use on a case-by-case basis by assessing four factors:

1. the purpose and character of the use, including whether such use is of a commercial nature or is for nonprofit educational purposes;
2. the nature of the copyrighted work;
3. the amount and substantiality of the portion used in relation to the copyrighted work as a whole; and
4. the effect of the use upon the potential market for or value of the copyrighted work.[66]

No one factor is determinative of the outcome. The results of the analysis are weighed together in light of copyright's goals.[67]

In analyzing the first factor, the purpose and character of the use, a court will consider how the protected work was used and whether the use was for commercial or nonprofit purposes. The use of a work is more likely to be considered fair if it is noncommercial. Another important consideration is the degree to which the work is transformative.[68] Keeping in mind that the purpose of copyright law is to foster new knowledge, the work should add "something new, with a further purpose or different character, altering the first with new expression, meaning, or message."[69] If the new work merely supplants the original or contributes nothing to society, it is less apt to be viewed as fair. Transformation is not essential to a finding of fair use, but "the more transformative the new work, the less will be the significance of other factors, like commercialism, that may weigh against a finding of fair use."[70] For example, the Ninth Circuit held that the use of "screen shots" taken from a computer game for the purpose of comparative advertising was fair use because it is socially useful.[71]

The second factor, the nature of the copyrighted work, considers the characteristics of the work itself, for example whether the work is factual or creative, published or unpublished. Courts are more sympathetic to the use of factual works, which serve as building blocks for other factual works, than the unauthorized use of fictional works. Likewise, fair use applies more readily to published works than to unpublished works, based on the assumption that their creators were ready to expose them to the public.[72]

Courts consider the extent of the unauthorized use when they analyze the third factor, the amount and substantiality of the portion of the work used in relation to the whole. Copyright law includes no formula upon which users may rely, no number of words or percentage that it is OK to take. In general, the smaller the use, the more likely it is to be considered fair. But even a small use may be problematic if it constitutes the "heart of the work." For example, the copyright case *Harper & Row, Publishers, Inc. v. Nation Enterprises* (1985) concerned *The Nation* magazine's verbatim use of 300–400 words from former President Gerald Ford's unpublished manuscript.[73] That isn't very much in relation to an entire book. However the section taken constituted the heart of the work – Ford's explanation for pardoning Richard Nixon following the Watergate scandal. Ford's publisher, Harper & Row, sued *The Nation*'s publisher for copyright infringement and won at the district level, but the Second Circuit reversed, finding that *The Nation*'s quotation of Ford's work was a fair use. The Supreme Court disagreed and reversed the decision, pointing to the significance of the particular passages taken, the work's unpublished status and the economic impact of the use on the value of the work.

The actual effect of the unauthorized use on the market value of the work is the fourth and most important factor that courts consider in a fair use analysis. A commercial use that directly impairs the market for a work mitigates against fair use. So does a commercial use that interferes with a copyright holder's ability to capitalize on derivative rights. For example, Harry Potter novelist J. K. Rowling won a permanent injunction against the publisher of the Harry Potter Lexicon, preventing him from publishing an encyclopedia modeled after his successful website based on her novels. Rowling had supported the website but contended that the book would interfere with her plans to pursue a similar project.[74]

But even a noncommercial use can weigh against fair use if it deprives the copyright holder of the work's value. File trading, for example, may not appear to be "commercial" because those engaging in file exchanges are not selling music files. However, file trading allows those who otherwise might have bought the work to avoid paying for it, so it does damage the copyright holder's ability to exploit the market value of the work. The Supreme Court has said that for a noncommercial use to negate fair use "one need only show that if the challenged use should become widespread, it would adversely affect the potential market for the copyrighted work."[75]

Parodies

Parodies, which imitate "the characteristic style of an author or a work for comic effect or ridicule," are normally considered a fair use because they are intended as social or literary criticism. No one listening to Luther Campbell singing "Oh hairy woman, you better shave that stuff," would assume that his mocking parody of "Oh Pretty Woman" was meant to supplant Roy Orbison's work. Yet a lower court did rule against Campbell in a copyright suit because his parody was intended for commercial use. In *Campbell v. Acuff-Rose* (1994) the Supreme Court reversed the decision. It held that a work's commercial purpose should not automatically disqualify it from a finding of fair use when it is unlikely to be taken as a substitute for the original. It has also rejected the argument that a parody's criticism could harm the future derivative value of a work.

For a parody to enjoy fair use, however, it must be perceived as such.[76] The copyrighted work must be the "target" of the satire. An imitation of the copyrighted work's style to spear something else won't do. In *Dr. Seuss Enterprises v. Penguin Books USA, Inc.*, the defendant's poem about O. J. Simpson's trial, titled "Cat NOT in the HAT," did not qualify as a parody of Dr. Suess's work. Although its stanzas imitated the familiar cadence of "Cat in the Hat," the poem commented on Simpson.[77]

In contrast, the photographs artist Tom Forsyth displayed on his website, depicting Barbie in compromising positions among various kitchen implements, were clearly meant to mock the gender stereotype the iconic doll has come to embody. In a series titled "Food Chain Barbie," Forsyth juxtaposed Barbie against the dangers of domesticity by photographing her nude and under attack by kitchen appliances. Barbie's corporate parent, Mattel, was not amused. The company sued the artist for copyright and trademark infringement. The Ninth Circuit Court of Appeals observed that Forsyth's use of Barbie for social criticism was fair. The character and purpose of the use was transformative; although Barbie is a creative work, parodies are generally based on creative works; Forsyth's use of the entire work was not considered excessive because any less would have required him to sever Barbie; and although his series was intended for sale, its commercial purpose did not harm Barbie's market value.[78]

The Eleventh Circuit described a lower court's injunction of *The Wind Done Gone*, a parody of Margaret Mitchell's *Gone With the Wind* written from a slave's perspective, as "at odds with the shared principles of the First Amendment" and "a prior restraint on speech."[79] Mitchell's heirs convinced a Georgia court that the parody would interfere with the market for the original work. The Eleventh Circuit lifted the injunction in *SunTrust Bank v. Houghton Mifflin Co.* (2001), declaring it improbable that fans of Mitchell's romanticized view of the South would be confused by Randall's parody, written to undermine the original book's stereotypes.

Copyright and freedom of expression

The Supreme Court has described copyright as "the engine of free expression," adding that "[b]y establishing a marketable right to the use of one's expression, copyright supplies the economic incentive to create and disseminate ideas."[80] As a general rule, courts recognize no conflict between copyright protection and First Amendment rights. They base this assumption on two factors: fair use and the idea/expression dichotomy. Fair use allows the public to make limited use of others' expression without permission. The idea/expression dichotomy "strike[s] a definitional balance between the First Amendment and the Copyright Act by permitting free communication of facts while still protecting an author's expression."[81]

The Supreme Court explained this rationale in *Harper & Row, Publishers, Inc. v. Nation Enterprises*, in which *The Nation* tried to assert a fair use exception to copyright for matters of public concern. The Supreme Court pointed out that the theory, if accepted, "would expand fair use to effectively destroy any expectation of copyright protection in the work of a public figure. Absent such protection, there would be little incentive to create or profit in financing such memoirs, and the public would be denied an important source of significant historical information."[82]

The Supreme Court also rejected the idea that a First Amendment news exception could trump proprietary rights in *Zacchini v. Scripps Howard Broadcasting Co.* (1977).[83] Hugo Zacchini performed a 15-second "human cannonball" act in an Ohio county fair. A freelance reporter for a local television station filmed the entire act against his wishes, and it was broadcast the same evening as part of a story about the fair. Zacchini sued. His cause of action was based on the "right to publicity value of his performance." Right of publicity is a proprietary right that is protected through state law. Instead of protecting the commercial value of expression in one's work, it protects the commercial value of one's name and likeness. The Supreme Court agreed to review the case, which would normally be exclusively a state matter, because the Ohio Supreme Court based an exception to the right of publicity on the First Amendment right to report matters of public interest. The Ohio court said the media

> must be accorded broad latitude in its choice of how much it presents of each story or incident, and of the emphasis to be given to such presentation. No fixed standard which would bar the press from reporting or depicting either an entire occurrence or an entire discrete part of a public performance can be formulated which would not unduly restrict the "breathing room" in reporting which freedom of the press requires.[84]

The U.S. Supreme Court believed the Ohio court had misapplied constitutional law. It said, "Wherever the line in particular situations is to be drawn between media reports that are protected and those that are not, we are quite sure that the First and Fourteenth Amendments do not immunize the media when they broadcast a performer's entire act without his consent."[85] The case would have been very different, the Court said, if the television station had simply described the act rather than showing it in its entirety. It focused on the market value of the work, observing that if people could see it on television, they had no incentive to pay to see it at the fair. The Supreme Court concluded that while Ohio may privilege the media in such circumstances, the First Amendment did not require it to do so.

Code as speech   The publisher of *2600*, a magazine for hackers, challenged the DMCA as a violation of the First Amendment in *Universal City Studios v. Corley* (2001).[86] Eric Corley wrote an article about the development of "DeCSS," a computer program created by a Norwegian hacker to circumvent the CSS encryption technology used in DVDs, and posted the article on his magazine's website along with a copy of the program. Eight film studios sued him for violating the anti-trafficking provision of the DMCA, which makes it illegal to traffic in technology that can circumvent a technological measure used to protect a copyrighted work. A federal district judge issued a preliminary injunction barring Corley from publishing the computer program or knowingly linking to any other website that posted it. Corley removed the program, but not the links. Challenging the constitutionality of the DMCA, he argued that computer programs are speech protected by the First Amendment. He defended his action of posting the code, saying "in a journalistic world, ... you have to show your evidence ... and particularly in the magazine that I work for, people want to see specifically what it is that we are referring to."[87] The district court judge agreed that computer programs constitute protected speech. But he said the DMCA was targeting the "functional" aspect of that speech rather than its content and was therefore a content-neutral regulation to be evaluated under the intermediate scrutiny test. Under intermediate scrutiny, a regulation is permissible if it "serves a substantial governmental interest, the interest is unrelated to the suppression of free expression, and the regulation is narrowly tailored – meaning that it does not 'burden substantially more speech than is necessary to further the government's legitimate interests.'"[88] The Court of Appeals for the Second Circuit upheld the lower court's injunction, concluding that the "government interest in preventing unauthorized access to encrypted copyrighted material is unquestionably substantial" and regulating DeCSS served that interest.[89]

The Court of Appeals agreed that computer programs, which include code and operational instructions, are protected speech. But it distinguished them from other sets of instructions because computers execute them.

> Unlike a blueprint or a recipe, which cannot yield any functional result without human comprehension of its content, human decision-making, and human action, computer code can instantly cause a computer to accomplish tasks and instantly render the results of those tasks available throughout the world via the Internet. The only human action required to achieve these results can be as limited and instantaneous as a single

click of a mouse. These realities of what code is and what its normal functions are require a First Amendment analysis that treats code as combining nonspeech and speech elements, i.e., functional and expressive elements.[90]

Corley argued that 1201(c)(1) of the DMCA, which provides that "nothing in this section shall affect rights, remedies, limitations or defenses to copyright infringement, including fair use" should be read to allow the circumvention of encryption technology protecting copyrighted material when the material would be put to "fair use." The Court of Appeals rejected that interpretation, indicating instead that the DMCA targets circumvention and is not concerned with the use made of the materials afterward. It also rejected Corley's argument that the DMCA unconstitutionally restricts fair use, noting that there is no constitutional entitlement to fair use.

Linking   Linking, which is intrinsic to the Web, is rarely considered to be infringing. Courts generally agree with U.S. District Court Judge Harry L. Hupp in *Ticketmaster v. Tickets.com* (2000) that "hyperlinking does not itself involve a violation of the Copyright Act (whatever it may do for other claims) since no copying is involved."[91] *Universal v. Corley* was one of the first cases involving a U.S. Court of Appeals to consider linking an infringement. Like other forms of computer code, the court considered hyperlinks to be a form of speech. Because a ban on linking could significantly chill speech, the district court developed a test for linking liability in cases involving circumvention technology. It required clear and convincing evidence that:

> those responsible for the link (a) know at the relevant time that the offending material is on the linked-to site, (b) know that it is circumvention technology that may not lawfully be offered, and (c) create or maintain the link for the purpose of disseminating that technology.[92]

The Court of Appeals neither endorsed nor rejected the test, but stated that proof of intent to harm would not be necessary to overcome First Amendment protection on hyperlinks. The court concluded that it could not avoid the choice between impairing some communication or tolerating decryption and a policy choice between the two was Congress's to make.

In 2003, the Ninth Circuit Court of Appeals upheld a ruling that using thumbnail size images in links on a search engine is a fair use in *Kelly v. Arriba Soft*. The defendant, a search engine named Arriba Soft (now Ditto.com), offers thumbnail images in search results. At one point it also used inline linking so the images were expandable within the website's frame. Inline linking involves the placement of an html link for an image on a website into the page of another website, creating the illusion that the image is part of the second site. Photographer Leslie Kelly sued the search engine for copyright infringement. The district court granted summary judgment in favor of the search engine, finding use of the thumbnail images and inline links to be fair. The Court of Appeals agreed that linking to thumbnail images is fair, based on the transformative use of the images and their public benefit.[93] It concluded that a judgment on the issue of inline linking was premature because neither side had moved for summary judgment on the issue.

Inline linking resurfaced in *Perfect 10 v. Amazon* (2007). Perfect 10 sued Amazon and Google for directly infringing its display and distribution rights by linking to thumbnails and full-size images of its subscription photos of nude models. The district court concluded that the question of infringement in inline linking cases hung on whether the linker stored a copy of the protected work on its server or simply directed others to the original stored on another server via the link.[94] The Court of Appeals agreed. Based on the district court's "server test," Google did not directly infringe on the full-size images, because it simply linked to other pages without storing the images on its servers. It did cache copies of the thumbnails, but in *Kelly v. Arriba Soft* the court had already concluded that was a fair use.

Sampling and mash-ups Sampling involves the incorporation of a portion of a sound recording, video, or photograph into a new work. It is not uncommon for artists to digitally alter a sample before using it. In the context of sound recordings, for example, the sample's tone, pitch, or rhythm may be changed. Sampling is commonly used in rap music, and although generally commercial, it is also transformative. Two federal circuits differ regarding the extent to which sampling is allowed.

In *Newton v. Diamond* (2003), the Ninth Circuit found the Beastie Boys' incorporation of a six-second, three-note segment of James Newton's jazz composition into one of their songs to be a de minimis (trivial) use that did not trigger a copyright violation.[95] A use is considered de minimis only if the average audience is unlikely to recognize its appropriation.

To sample part of a song, a musician must acquire a license to use both the sound recording and the composition because they are distinct works. The Beastie Boys licensed use of the sound recording from EMC Records, but did not license use of the composition from Newton, who retained all rights to it. Newton sued the group for copyright infringement. Although the plaintiff's sound is distinctive, it was not relevant to the court's inquiry because the recording was licensed. The court focused exclusively on the notes taken from the composition, which were less likely to be recognized by the average audience. The Beastie Boys looped the segment repeatedly throughout their song "Pass the Mic," but the relevant question was not the extent to which they used the copied segment, but how much of the original work was taken. The court also considered whether the portion taken was a trivial or substantial element in the original work. It found that the three-note sequence, which appeared only once in Newton's work, was not qualitatively original or quantitatively significant enough to implicate copyright.

In contrast, the Sixth Circuit ruled that any sample used in a work – even if unrecognizable – should be licensed in *Bridgeport Music, Inc. v. Dimension Films* (2005).[96] NWA, the defendant in the case, sampled a three-note, two-second guitar riff from Funkadelic's "Get Off Your Ass and Jam" for its song "100 Miles and Runnin." The group did not have a license to use the music or composition. The district court granted summary judgment on the case in favor of the defendant because it did not believe the defendant's de minimis use constituted infringement. The two-second sample, which was looped and extended to 16 beats, was used five times in the new song. The Court of Appeals reversed. Its decision established a "bright line" rule regarding sampling that where no authorization exists, infringement is established.

A mash-up is a more complex form of sampling that remixes two works into one. Some are more successful than others. Brian Burton's remix of rapper Jay-Z's *The Black Album* with The Beatles' *White Album* to create *The Grey Album* is the most well known. When Burton released his CD, it received critical acclaim from *Rolling Stone* and other publications. He received a cease-and-desist letter from EMI, the record company that owns the rights to The Beatles' sound recordings and Sony/ATV, which owns the rights to The Beatles' compositions. Burton complied with the request to stop distributing the album, but his fans did not. More than 300 websites protested EMI's action for 24 hours on a day they dubbed "Grey Tuesday" – many by distributing the album as a form of civil disobedience.[97] EMI sent cease-and-desist letters to the individual website operators and take-down notices to their Internet service providers. The affair came to represent an incongruity between advances in technology that make digital media creation easier than ever and changes in the law that make copyright more restrictive.

Licensing and music

Digital technology has opened more venues for music, which is now disseminated through webcasts, podcasts, digital cable and satellite, mobile entertainment services, and even ring tones, in addition to the traditional venues of radio and television. But licensing music for these venues has presented challenges for copyright holders and users. Musical pieces are protected by two forms of copyright licenses. One applies to the *musical work*, which is the composition of music and lyrics, generally owned by the songwriter or a music publisher. The other applies to the *sound recording*, or final product produced in a studio by musicians, producers, and sound engineers, which is generally owned by the record company.

Broadcasting or webcasting copyrighted music requires a *performance license* that may be negotiated directly with a copyright owner or indirectly through a performing rights organization that represents the copyright owner. Performing rights organizations keep track of musical performances, collect royalties from them, and redistribute the royalties to the copyright holders they represent. Trade groups such as the American Society of Composers, Authors, and Publishers (ASCAP), Broadcast Music, Inc. (BMI), and SESAC license the performance of compositions and collect royalties for their members who are songwriters, composers, and publishers. Broadcasters or venue owners may pay to license songs individually, but most choose to pay a blanket license fee in return for the right to use any music from the performing rights organization's repertoire. To keep track of the particular songs performed under a blanket license, ASCAP conducts sample and census surveys of networks, stations, and Internet sites that license its music. The licensing fees it collects from bars and restaurants are lumped into a general licensing fund, and copyright holders are paid from the fund at a rate proportional to their featured performances on radio and television.[98]

Until 1995, copyright holders in sound recordings could not collect licensing fees for the performance of their music. With the passage of the Sound Recordings Act of 1995 and the Digital Millennium Copyright Act, Congress created a performance right in sound recordings that are digitally transmitted through noninteractive services. There is still no performance right for sound recordings played by radio and television stations, unless they simulcast on the Web.

Congress opted to deter potential monopolistic behavior by including statutory (compulsory) licenses in the Copyright Act that entitle parties who satisfy certain conditions to exercise some of a copyright holder's exclusive rights without permission, as long as they pay the copyright holder a predetermined licensing fee. Section 114 of the Copyright Act provides a compulsory license to perform sound recordings publicly by digital audio transmission, without the permission of the copyright holder, for a licensing fee. The statutory license applies to noninteractive webcasters and simulcasters, subscription services that provide music over digital cable or satellite television, and satellite radio. There is no licensing scheme for podcasters, because they are considered interactive. Sound Exchange has been designated as the performance rights organization to distribute licensing fees.

A *mechanical* license is required to reproduce a sound recording, for a CD compilation or digital download, for example. The reproduction right in a sound recording must be licensed from the record label, which may license a work at its discretion. But the right to reproduce a musical composition is subject to a statutory license under Section 115 of the Copyright Act. Once a song has been commercially released, others may re-record it without the copyright holder's permission, as long as they pay the copyright holder a licensing fee and their primary purpose is to distribute the music to the public for private use.[99]

To incorporate a musical work into a video, a *synchronization* license is required from the songwriter or publisher. A license to incorporate the sound recording must be obtained from the record label.

The Copyright Royalty Board, a three-judge panel employed by the Library of Congress, sets the royalty fees for statutory licensing. In order to take advantage of a statutory license, the user must first file a "Notice of Use" with the Copyright Office. If the copyright holder is known, the user must send the license fee to him or her directly. If the copyright holder is not known, the licensing fee is paid to the Register of Copyrights in the Copyright Office.

Licensing fees are paid for music regardless of whether any revenue is accrued from use of the music or whether a fraction of the song or the whole song is played. The Copyright Royalty Board made this determination based on the assumption that a station's inability to generate revenue had no relationship to the market value of a copyrighted work. However noncommercial rates are available to webcasters operated by tax-exempt organizations and government entities.

The Creative Commons

WE ♥ CREATIVE COMMONS

© Blender Foundation, www.bigbuckbunny.org
The animated short "Big Buck Bunny" was created using free open source software and released under a Creative Commons license. People can freely reuse and distribute the content as long as it is correctly attributed.

Although copyright provides a bundle of exclusive rights, the copyright holder may not want to exercise them all. In fact, some copyright holders want to share their work with others in order to draw wider exposure to it or to foster the spirit of intellectual creativity.

The nonprofit organization Creative Commons provides a mechanism to allow copyright holders to license certain uses of their work that they consider acceptable, while retaining control over other uses. Some artists license others to reproduce, remix, and distribute their work for noncommercial uses, as long as they receive credit for the original. Others license their work for reproduction and distribution but restrict users from making derivatives from the original. Still others allow their works to be used for derivatives as long as users share alike with others by licensing

their derivatives similarly. Finally, some CC copyright holders allow unlimited use of their work.

The Creative Commons website provides directions for licensing and a search function to locate music, video, photos, and art that can be modified, adapted, and built upon or that can be used for commercial purposes. Creative Commons licenses – expressed as a cc in a circle – are free. They are not meant to serve as a substitute for official registration, but they are legally enforceable and will terminate if abused.

Creative Commons was established in 2001, following the loss of *Eldred v. Ashcroft*, the case that challenged the legitimacy of copyright extensions that kept millions of works out of the public domain for another 20 years. Eric Eldred and his attorney, Stanford law professor Lawrence Lessig, helped to found the organization, along with experts in copyright and computer science. The name alludes to land held in common for cultivation in Northwestern Europe that was privatized during the Enclosure Movement between the 15th and 19th centuries at tremendous cost to the common people who had relied on it for their survival.[100] The reference suggests that creative works do not spring wholly formed from the minds of their creators, but that all works are in some way inspired by earlier works that must be protected from further enclosure.

Questions for Discussion

1. What does a work need to acquire copyright protection in the United States?
2. What cannot be copyrighted?
3. What is fair use? Why is it hard to know if fair use will apply in any particular instance?
4. What is the relationship between copyright law and freedom of expression?

8

Intellectual Property: Patents, Trademarks, and Trade Secrets

Intellectual property is commonly divided into two categories: copyright and industrial property. Copyright, discussed in the previous chapter, protects literary or artistic works. Patent, trademark, and trade secret law protect industrial property, a category that encompasses all digital media devices and products, as well as the words and symbols used to market them.

Although copyright, patent, trademark, and trade secret laws are lumped together within the category of intellectual property, they are all very different. As Richard Stallman, who pioneered the free software movement, has pointed out, they "originated separately, evolved differently, cover different activities, have different rules, and raise different public policy issues."[1] What they do have in common, however, is the challenge they face adapting to the acceleration of technology. All are "in flux" to some extent.

This chapter discusses the application and reach of patent, trademark, and trade secret law. It pays attention to areas that are still in transition, such as the use of trademarks in contextual advertising, metatags, and cybersquatting. It also discusses the fair use of trademarks in social commentary, parodies, and gripe sites.

Patents

Patent law protects inventions, processes, devices, and methods. In the context of digital media, is applies to digital media devices like computers, flash drives, DVD players, and MP3 players, and to some software.

The same section of the U.S. Constitution that directs Congress to protect copyright also empowers it to protect patents by securing inventors' exclusive rights to inventions and discoveries for a limited period of time.[2] Unlike copyright law, however, its duration of protection is much more limited. While copyright protects a work for the life of the creator plus 70 years, patent protection lasts 20 years from the date of application.

Types of patents

There are three types of patents: utility, design, and plant patents.

1. Utility patents apply to the invention or discovery of "any new and useful process, machine, article of manufacture, or composition of matter, or any new and useful improvement thereof."[3]
2. Design patents apply to "new, original and ornamental design for an article of manufacture."[4]
3. Plant patents apply to the invention or discovery and asexual reproduction of new kinds of plants.[5]

Some subject matter cannot be patented. The U.S. Patent and Trademark Office (PTO) will not grant patents for laws of nature, natural phenomena, or abstract ideas. Albert Einstein could not have patented the formula $E = mc^2$, for example.

The PTO used to include business methods within the category of abstract ideas. However, the U.S. Court of Appeals for the Federal Circuit reversed that rule. Courts now interpret utility patents to cover business methods as long as they are computerized, a factor likely to become increasingly important to companies involved in e-commerce.[6]

Registering and protecting patents

Protection for patents, unlike copyrights, is not automatic. Patents must be registered through the PTO to acquire protection. The application must include a sufficiently detailed description of the invention and its use to allow a PTO examiner to determine whether it qualifies for patent protection.

The requirements for patent protection are also a bit more stringent than for copyright protection. Assuming the invention or discovery qualifies for patent protection, the creator must show that it meets three criteria: it must be *novel*, *useful*, and not *obvious*. To preserve its novelty, an inventor must make sure that the invention is not described anywhere in print before the date of the invention or within one year before the application date of the patent. To meet the utility requirement, the invention or discovery must serve a purpose. To be nonobvious, the invention must display some ingenuity. It cannot be something that is simply a common sense solution to a person of ordinary skill in the field.

Applications for patent protection are limited to natural persons. But once the person has acquired the patent, he or she may assign the rights to a corporation or license the patent for use by someone else. A patent registered in the United States will only be effective in the U.S. and U.S. territories. The product or its packaging should carry the word Patented or the abbreviation Pat. along with the patent number to provide notice to potential infringers that the work is protected.

Patent infringement and remedies

Patent infringement applies to "whoever without authority makes, uses, offers to sell, or sells any patented invention, within the United States, or imports into the United States any patented invention during the term of the patent."[7] It also applies to anyone who actively induces infringement.[8]

Patent law offers no statutory provision for fair use.[9] A common law exception for patent infringement has developed for experimental use and research.[10] But the U.S. Court of Appeals for the Federal Circuit has taken a narrow view of it, saying that that the "slightest commercial implication" or "any conduct that is in keeping with the alleged infringer's legitimate business, regardless of commercial implications" is enough to defeat it.[11] It considers the defense "limited to actions performed 'for amusement, to satisfy idle curiosity, or for strictly philosophical inquiry.'"[12]

Patent infringement is a civil violation tried in a federal court. It can be remedied by an injunction to stop the infringement or damages if the plaintiff has been harmed. Actual damages are normally equal to a reasonable royalty for the use made of the invention, along with interest and court costs.[13] If the plaintiff can show that the infringement was willful (committed with knowledge of the patent), the court may triple the damages.

Digitization and patents

Digitization poses less of a challenge to patent law than copyright law, because end users are much less likely to value a patented discovery or process apart from the tangible property produced from it.[14] It is fairly easy for anyone to download a song and reap the benefits from it immediately, but taking the patent for one of the many parts that go into the making of an iPod is not particularly useful for most of us, who may want an iPod, but have no interest in making one.

Consequently, most patent conflicts involving digital media occur among competitors in the manufacture of equipment or software. For example, Internet phone carrier Vonage was sued by Verizon, Sprint Nextel, and AT&T for infringing patents related to Voice over Internet Protocol (VoIP) services, including one for technology that linked the Internet telephone network with ordinary telephones. The combined total to settle the suits, $199 million, nearly drove the company into bankruptcy.[15]

Challenging bad patents

Although the PTO investigates patent applications before approving them, it doesn't have the resources to investigate all of the applications that it receives thoroughly.

As a result, some processes and devices are patented that really shouldn't be. Perhaps the most egregious example is U.S. patent 5,443,036 for "Method of exercising a cat," described as "directing a beam of invisible light produced by a hand-held laser apparatus onto the floor or wall or other opaque surface in the vicinity of the cat, then moving the laser so as to cause the bright pattern of light to move in an irregular way fascinating to cats."[16]

The Electronic Frontier Foundation organized a Patent Busting Program to combat software patents that are not novel. The foundation searches for "prior art," the PTO's term for technology that predates the patent, and asks the PTO to re-examine patents that appear to overreach. One of its requests prompted the PTO to revoke a patent owned by Live Nation, a Clear Channel spinoff, for a method to capture, mix, and burn music from live concerts on a CD for immediate purchase following the show. The patent locked music groups into reliance on the company for the all-in-one service. EFF discovered that another company had produced a similar technology a year before Clear Channel applied for the patent.[17]

Trademarks

Trademark law protects consumers from misleading packaging and advertisements that could confuse them about the source of the products and services they buy.[18] In doing so, it promotes economic efficiencies by reducing consumer search costs and providing incentives among manufacturers to produce quality products and services that consumers will remember.[19] Unlike copyright and patent law, which stimulate the marketplace of ideas by promoting writings and discoveries, trademark law stimulates the economic marketplace by promoting competition.

Types of marks

Trademark law protects the different *marks* companies use to identify their products and services and distinguish them from competitors. A mark may be a name, word, slogan, symbol, picture, or combination of any of these elements. *Trademarks* identify goods already in or intended for commerce. Coca Cola, for example, is distinguished from its competitors not only by its name, but also by its trademarked script, contour bottle, and slogans, such as "Have a Coke and a smile." *Service marks* identify businesses in the service industry. NBC's colorful peacock and three-note chime are examples of registered service marks. *Collective marks*, like the block R used by the National Association of Realtors, identify membership organizations. A related mark intended for use by someone other than the mark's owner, is the *certification mark*. It is used to certify "origin, material, mode of manufacture, quality, accuracy, or other characteristics" of the person's good or service. For example, Wi-Fi® is a registered certification mark of the Wi-Fi Alliance.

Distinctiveness

To acquire trademark protection, a mark must be *distinctive*. Marks considered to be *inherently distinctive* are fanciful, arbitrary, or suggestive:

1. A *fanciful* mark, like Google, is invented specifically for the product or service and is the easiest mark to protect because the name is not associated with anything else.
2. An *arbitrary* mark, like Apple, Inc., is one that has no relationship to the purpose or characteristics of the product or service it represents. There is no obvious connection, for example, between computers and fruit.
3. A *suggestive* mark, like YouTube or Microsoft, hints at the product's function, but is still abstract enough to require some imagination.

Assuming the mark is not already in use or misleadingly similar to another in use, it will qualify for trademark protection if it is inherently distinctive.

Marks that incorporate the name or characteristic of a product or service, like International Business Machines, or the geographic region in which they are sold, like Saint Louis Bread Company, are considered to be merely *descriptive*. A descriptive mark must develop a secondary meaning to earn trademark status. It must conjure up the particular company, not just one that makes business machines sold internationally or bread in St. Louis, in the minds of consumers. Marks based on surnames are also treated as descriptive marks until they acquire secondary meaning. That occurs when people begin to think of the business before the person, such as Dell, Ford, or McDonalds. Courts look for three factors when they are deciding whether a product has acquired secondary meaning: the extent to which the mark has been promoted through advertising, the product's sales and, most importantly, the length of time the mark has been used. Under Section 1052(f) of the Trademark Act, exclusive and continuous use of a mark for five years is prima facie evidence that it is distinctive.

Some marks will not qualify for registration even if they do achieve a secondary meaning. These include words or images that are "immoral, deceptive or scandalous" or which may "disparage or falsely suggest a connection with persons, living or dead, institutions, beliefs, or national symbols."[20] Generic words, like computer or camera, cannot be trademarked because they are part of the public domain and must remain available for others to use to identify their products and services.

Trade dress

Other unregistered aspects of a brand's "total image and overall appearance," such as its packaging, color, size, and shape, may acquire protection under trademark law if their imitation is likely to result in consumer confusion regarding the source of the product or service.[21] Protection for these characteristics is known as *trade dress*.[22] Originally intended to apply to product packaging, trade dress has evolved to include other characteristics that are inherently distinctive or that have acquired distinctiveness through a "secondary meaning." For example, Owen's Corning insulation is associated with a distinctive shade of pink.

Trade dress protection does not extend to functional aspects of a product's packaging or design or other elements that make it particularly useful. An element is functional if it is essential to the purpose of the product or affects its quality or cost.[23] An element is also considered functional if its exclusive use would put competitors at a disadvantage. For example, a court would not recognize the use of frames on a website as a protected element under trade dress.

Acquiring trademark protection

One can acquire common law trademark protection by being the first to use a particular trademark in commerce. However protection for the mark will be limited to the geographic area in which the product is sold. So, for example, the owner of Bayou Design Company in Louisiana may be able to establish the legitimacy of the trademark there, but would not be able to prevent another person from starting a company with the same name in Florida. To acquire protection for the mark nationwide, it must be officially registered through the Patent and Trademark Office.

Registration confers other benefits as well. It makes it easier for others to research the trademark to avoid infringement. It serves as notice to potential infringers that the mark is taken, eliminating the potential for "innocent" infringement. In the event of an infringement, it entitles the mark's owner to sue for trademark infringement in federal court, while providing prima facie evidence of ownership and the exclusive right to use the mark. Certain remedies, such as treble damages for willful infringement and attorney's fees, are also tied to registration.

To avoid wasted time and effort on a mark that is already taken, the application process should begin with a search of existing trademarks. The Patent and Trademark Office offers an electronic search service called Trademark Electronic Search System (TESS), available through its website. If the mark is available, registration can be filed electronically for a $325 application fee.

It takes the Patent and Trademark Office about 15 to 18 months to issue a certificate of registration. A party who claims ownership of a mark may use the TM for trademarks or SM for service marks that are not registered or pending registration. Once the certificate of registration arrives, the mark should be changed to an R enclosed in a circle, ®.

The certificate is good for 10 years, but the trademark owner must file a form in the fifth year asserting its continuous use of the mark. After that, protection is renewable every 10 years and, as long as registration is maintained, may last indefinitely. The trademark for Singer sewing machines, for example, was registered in 1880. Löwenbräu beer first used its lion mark in 1383.

Products sold outside the United States must be trademarked in each country in which they are distributed. However, the owner of a trademark registered or pending registration in the United States is entitled to register the trademark in any of the countries that are members of the Madrid Protocol by filing one "international application" with the International Bureau of the World Property Intellectual Organization, through the U.S. Patent and Trademark Office.

Losing trademark protection

A trademark is considered abandoned when the owner discontinues its use. If the mark has not been used for three consecutive years, its abandonment is inferred. Once a mark is lost, it cannot be re-registered by another party. The mark moves into the public domain.

A trademark also may be lost if its owner allows the trademark to become a generic name for a good or service. A mark must maintain its *distinctiveness* to preserve its protection. Names like aspirin, corn flakes, zipper, thermos, yo-yo, and shredded wheat were trademarks that lost their distinctiveness because they were used as nouns rather than adjectives.

Finally, a mark will be lost if it was fraudulently registered in the first place. The law defines "fraud" as a knowing misrepresentation or concealment of a material fact.

Trademark Act of 1946

Although some aspects of trademark are protected through state and common law, trademark is primarily secured through federal law under the Trademark Act of 1946, also known as the Lanham Act. The statute protects trademark owners against trademark infringement, false designation of origin, and trademark dilution.

Trademark infringement   Trademark infringement occurs when a registered mark is used, without permission of the mark's owner, on a product or in an advertisement for a product or service in a manner that is likely to confuse consumers about the source of the product or service. Specifically, Section 1114 of the Trademark Act prohibits the

> use in commerce [of] any reproduction, counterfeit, copy, or colorable imitation of a registered mark in connection with the sale, offering for sale, distribution, or advertising of any goods or services on or in connection with which such use is likely to cause confusion, or to cause mistake, or to deceive.[24]

False designation of origin   Unregistered marks and trade dress also receive protection under a section of the Act that prohibits false designations of origin. Section 1125 imposes liability on anyone who:

> on or in connection with any goods or services, or any container for goods, uses in commerce any word, term, name, symbol, or device, or any combination thereof, or any false designation of origin, false or misleading description of fact, or false or misleading representation of fact, which –
>
> (A) is likely to cause confusion, or to cause mistake, or to deceive as to the affiliation, connection, or association of such person with another person, or as to the origin, sponsorship, or approval of his or her goods, services, or commercial activities by another person ...[25]

Essentially, in cases involving allegations of trademark infringement or false designation of origin, plaintiffs are required to prove five things:

1. that they possess a valid mark;
2. that the defendant used the mark;
3. that the defendant's use of the mark occurred "in commerce";
4. that the defendant used the mark "in connection with the sale ... or advertising of any goods," and
5. that the defendant used the mark in a manner likely to confuse consumers.[26]

A court will consider each of these factors in order. It will first ask if the plaintiff owns the mark. If the mark is not registered to the plaintiff, the plaintiff will have to demonstrate that he or she has acquired possession of the mark through first use and that the mark is distinctive or has acquired a secondary meaning associated with the plaintiff. Only then will the court consider whether the defendant has used the mark and, if so, whether the use was "in commerce."

Circuits differ regarding their interpretation of *commerce*. The definition provided in the Lanham Act is circular, stating "The word 'commerce' means all commerce which may lawfully be regulated by Congress."[27] Some circuits have chosen to interpret "in commerce" as commercial activity, and therefore assume that trademark infringement and false designation of origin only apply to commercial speech. Other circuits have chosen to interpret "in commerce" to refer to activities that fall within the purview of congressional jurisdiction. This interpretation acknowledges Congress's authority to legislate interstate activity based on the Constitution's commerce clause, which gives it the exclusive right "To regulate commerce with foreign nations, and among the several states ..." These courts have observed that in other sections of the Act Congress has prohibited the "commercial use in commerce of a mark," concluding that trademark infringement and false designation of origin may also apply to noncommercial speech.

The court will then decide whether the mark was used "in connection with a sale, distribution or advertisement of goods and services" (in the case of trademark infringement) or "in connection with any goods or services" (in the case of false designation of origin). If the plaintiff is able to establish each of these factors, the court will consider whether the use was likely to cause confusion among consumers.

To assess the likelihood of confusion, courts consider the following factors:

1. the strength of the plaintiff's mark;
2. the similarity between the plaintiff's mark and the allegedly infringing mark;
3. the similarity between the products and services offered by the plaintiff and defendant;
4. the similarity of the sales methods;
5. the similarity of advertising methods;
6. the defendant's intent, e.g., whether the defendant hopes to gain competitive advantage by associating his product with the plaintiff's established mark; and
7. actual confusion.[28]

Trademark dilution   The Trademark Act has protected consumers from confusion resulting from trademark misuse since 1945, but in 1995, Congress added a layer of protection for trademark owners by amending the Act to prohibit trademark dilution.[29] *Trademark dilution* is "the lessening of the capacity of a famous mark to identify and distinguish goods or services." The Trademark Dilution Act gives owners of famous trademarks the right to prevent others from using them commercially if the use dilutes the distinctive quality of the marks by blurring or tarnishing them. A mark may be *blurred* if its association with a dissimilar product weakens the unique identity of the original. The amendment's legislative history gives "DUPONT shoes, BUICK aspirin, and KODAK pianos" as examples of uses that would be actionable under the legislation.[30] A mark may be *tarnished* if it is associated with an inferior or disreputable product.

A dispute involving the famous Victoria's Secret trademark led to the Supreme Court's landmark decision on trademark dilution. In *Moseley v. V Secret Catalogue, Inc.* (2003), the retail chain sued the owners of an adult novelty shop called Victor's Secret for trademark infringement and dilution. When a recipient of the novelty shop's ad alerted Victoria's Secret to the mark's use, the corporation contacted the store's owners, Victor and Cathy Moseley, requesting they change its name. The Moseleys changed the name to Victor's Little Secret. Victoria's Secret wasn't satisfied and filed for an injunction to prevent the Moseleys from using the name. Finding no likelihood of consumer confusion, the district court granted summary judgment in favor of the Moseleys on the trademark infringement action and proceeded to the trademark dilution claim. The district court concluded that Victor's Little Secret diluted the Victoria's Secret mark by tarnishing it and enjoined the Moseleys from further use of the mark. The Sixth Circuit affirmed the decision, but the Supreme Court reversed.

The Court explained that unlike trademark infringement, which requires the *likelihood* of harm, trademark dilution requires *actual* harm. To prove trademark dilution, the trademark owner must submit evidence demonstrating an actual lessening of the trademark's capacity to identify and distinguish goods or services. While it is not necessary to show lost sales, a plaintiff must submit more than the argument that consumers mentally associate the junior mark with the famous mark. Blurring and tarnishing are not inevitable results of mental association. In the Victoria's Secret case, for example, there was no evidence that people who associated the two marks thought any less of Victoria's Secret.

Remedies

Trademark infringement and false designation of origin   Remedies for trademark infringement and false designation of origin include injunctive relief, fines, and the seizure and destruction of infringing articles that include the mark. Plaintiffs are most likely to request injunctive relief to stop the defendant from further use of the mark without permission. If the infringement is committed innocently by third parties printing or publishing the mark for someone else, plaintiffs are only entitled to injunctive relief.[31]

Courts may award plaintiffs the defendant's profits from the use of the mark, actual damages sustained from the infringement and court costs associated with pursuing the case. In assessing damages, a court may render a judgment for as much as three times the actual damages. In exceptional cases, it may also award attorney's fees to the winning party.[32]

Trademark dilution   Trademark owners will be entitled to injunctive relief only if trademark dilution is willful. In that case, the plaintiff will also be entitled to the infringement remedies described above.

State trademark protection

Trademark protection is also available through state law. Many states have adopted most or all of the International Trademark Association's model state trademark law. The bill, which prohibits infringement and dilution, is similar to federal trademark law but recommends a five-year renewal period. State trademark laws are useful to small businesses that do not sell products or services in interstate or foreign commerce.

Trademark owners who file suit for trademark infringement or dilution usually also assert claims under state unfair competition laws. "Unfair competition" refers to the tort of engaging in business practices meant to confuse consumers. Some states have adopted the Uniform Deceptive Trade Practices Act (UDTPA), a model law to deal with fraudulent business practices related to misidentification of goods and services and false advertising. But most have varying definitions of unfair business practices. Trademarks are also protected at the state level through common law that prohibits "passing off" goods and services as those of another.

Trademark and free speech

Congress never meant trademark infringement and dilution claims to be used to inhibit free speech. In the case of trademark infringement, claims can only succeed if use of the trademark is likely to confuse consumers regarding the source of a product or service. To succeed in a trademark dilution claim, a plaintiff must show that the mark was used commercially and actually diluted by the use. Congress was particularly concerned about protecting speech that might be critical of a product or service when it amended the Trademark Act to prohibit trademark dilution. So it precluded liability for fair uses of trademarks in comparative advertising, parodies, criticism, and commentary, along with references to trademarks in news reporting and commentary.[33]

The incorporation of Playboy's trademarks into a former Playboy Playmate's website was considered a fair use by the Ninth Circuit. Playboy sued Terry Welles for using the "Playboy," "Playmate," and "Playmate of the Year 1981" marks on her website. The district court granted summary judgment in favor of Welles on Playboy's claims of trademark infringement and dilution, false designation of origin, and unfair competition. The Court of Appeals upheld the ruling, concluding that most of Welles's uses constituted a *nominative fair use* of Playboy's marks that served to identify her as a former Playmate without suggesting Playboy's sponsorship of the website.[34] A nominative fair use of a trademark occurs when no term other than the trademark could adequately identify the subject, the trademark is used no more than necessary to identify the subject, and the use does not suggest the trademark holder's sponsorship or endorsement.

A federal district court held that trademark dilution does not apply to the noncommercial expression of political views in *Lucasfilm Ltd. v. High Frontier* (1985).[35] *Star Wars* creator George Lucas filed a trademark dilution suit against political groups that adopted the term "Star Wars" to identify the Reagan Administration's Strategic Defense Initiative. The court dismissed the complaint because the defendants were not using the plaintiff's mark in connection with the sale of goods or services in commerce. It said the defendants were "not engaged in selling anything but ideas … Purveying points of view is not a service."[36]

More recently, a U.S. district judge denied Fox News's request for an injunction to prevent Penguin Books from using its trademarked slogan "fair and balanced" on Al Franken's 2003 book *Lies and the Lying Liars Who Tell Them: A Fair and Balanced Look at the Right*. Fox argued that use of the slogan and its commentator Bill O'Reilly's picture on the cover of the book might trick consumers into believing it was a Fox product. It also argued that the Fox trademark would be tarnished through its association with Franken on the book's cover. The judge said the case had no merit and that the network was "trying to undermine the First Amendment." He also said "fair and balanced" was "unlikely a valid trademark" because it was weak as trademarks go.[37] Fox withdrew the suit.

In most cases, parodies are also protected from trademark dilution claims. In *L.L. Bean v. Drake Publishers* (1987), the First Circuit reversed a ruling against a pornographic magazine that spoofed Bean's catalog with an article called the "Back-to-School-Sex-Catalog."[38] The article, which included bawdy advertisements for new products, was labeled "humor" and "parody" in the table of contents. The district court granted summary judgment to the clothing company on its trademark dilution claim because it thought the piece tarnished Bean's reputation, but the First Circuit reversed. It said "Denying parodists the opportunity to poke fun at symbols and names which have become woven into the fabric of our daily life would constitute a serious curtailment of a protected form of expression."[39]

But in *Mutual of Omaha v. Novak* (1987), an artist's parody of Mutual of Omaha's Indian head logo was considered a trademark infringement.[40] Franklyn Novak produced shirts and mugs advertising nuclear holocaust insurance, which depicted the profile of an emaciated human head wearing a feathered headdress above text that read "Mutant of Omaha." In reference to Wild Kingdom, the television show the company sponsored, some of the items showed a one-eyed tiger accompanied by the title "Mutant of Omaha's Mutant Kingdom." There was no evidence that Novak intended to pass off his goods as Mutual of Omaha's. His art was intended as political commentary on the potential for nuclear war. Surprisingly, however, the company was able to demonstrate consumer confusion regarding the source of the products. Mutual of Omaha submitted a survey as evidence that 40 out of 400 people from several cities believed that Mutual of Omaha had approved the T-shirts and other paraphernalia "to help make people aware of the nuclear war problem." The court's injunction prevented Novak from marketing Mutant of Omaha products, but left other avenues open for his parody in books, magazines, or films.

Our consumer culture is increasingly tied to brand names that appear in songs, movies, and art. Restrictions on their use for commentary and art are bound to raise First Amendment concerns. Kembrew McLeod, the author of *Owning Culture*, wanted to make a statement about the increasing power of intellectual property law to influence discourse, so in 1998 he trademarked the phrase "Freedom of Expression." He submitted the registration as a joke and was very surprised when the Patent and Trademark Office allowed him to register it. McLeod lost the mark because he didn't renew in time. Because a trademark cannot be re-registered by another person, "Freedom of Expression" is appropriately back in the public domain.

Contextual advertising

Contextual advertising, also called key-word advertising or keying, has become a multi-million dollar marketing tool on the Internet. Advertisers pay search engines to show their ads or sponsored links when computer users search for particular "key words." For example, using Google's AdWords program, a digital media studies program can select the key words "digital," "interactive," and "new media" to trigger its ad. Users who type in any of these terms will see the program's sponsored link among their search results. Some businesses select key words that include the names of competitors' trademarks to trigger their ads or sponsored links.

Courts have grappled with whether this practice constitutes trademark infringement. The keywords are used within the search engine's code, rather than displayed on a good or in an advertisement for a good or service. So whether their use constitutes a "use in commerce … in connection with the sale, offering for sale, distribution, or advertising of any goods or services" is a questionable proposition. Key words are not a traditional marketing tactic anticipated by trademark law. Nevertheless, when trademarks are bought and sold for use as key words without the trademark holder's permission, they are being traded commercially.

The second area of disagreement is whether their use is likely to confuse consumers who never see the keywords in the code. Assuming the competitor's sponsored link or ad does not actually incorporate the plaintiff's trademark, people will see it as one of many links or ads among search results. Search engine users are accustomed to selecting the links they want to open from a list of search results. Placing a competitor's link or ad near the plaintiff's link is not likely to confuse them anymore than placing two competing products side by side on a shelf.

At present, the Second and Ninth Circuits appear to be split on the legality of using trademarks as keywords. The Second Circuit does not consider the use of key words that are hidden from the computer user to be a use in commerce for purposes of trademark infringement. In *1-800 Contacts, Inc. v. WhenU.com* (2005), the Court of Appeals dismissed an injunction barring the distributor of a computer program that creates pop-up ads tied to keywords from using the plaintiff's web address.[41] WhenU's software, which is often bundled with freeware Internet users download onto their computers, triggers advertisements that correspond to users' search terms. When computer users accessed the website for 1-800 Contacts, an ad for Vision Direct, the company's competitor, popped up in a separate window on the desktop. 1-800 Contacts, Inc. sued WhenU.com for trademark infringement and dilution. The Second Circuit concluded that as a matter of law WhenU did not "use" 1-800's trademark when it included the company's URL in its software directory of terms that trigger contextual ads. The company's URL, which is similar to its trademark, was never displayed to computer users or placed in an area that was accessible to them, so there was no possibility of confusion. The court stated that

[a] company's internal utilization of a trademark in a way that does not communicate it to the public is analogous to a individual's private thoughts about a trademark. Such conduct simply does not violate the Lanham Act, which is concerned with the use of trademarks in connection with the sale of goods or services in a manner likely to lead to consumer confusion as to the source of such goods or services.[42]

It was significant to the court, however, that WhenU did not sell 1-800's trademark directly to competitors but rather included it in a category of terms that triggered Vision Direct's ad.

In contrast, Google does sells trademarked names directly to companies for use as key words. When Google sold the mark "Rescuecom" through its AdWords program to Rescuecom's competitors, the company sued Google for trademark infringement. A federal district judge in New York dismissed the suit.[43] Relying on the Second Circuit's reasoning in *1-800 Contacts*, the court said "internal use of plaintiff's trademark to trigger sponsored links is not a use of a trademark within the meaning of the Lanham Act ... because there is no allegation that defendant places plaintiff's trademark on any goods, containers, displays, or advertisements, or that its internal use is visible to the public."[44] Other cases in the Second Circuit reached similar conclusions.[45]

In contrast, the Ninth Circuit does consider the practice of keying a trademark to an advertisement to be a use in commerce under the Trademark Act that could confuse consumers. In *Playboy Enterprises v. Netscape Communications Corp.* (2004), Playboy sued Netscape for selling advertisements for adult products and services keyed to a list of search terms that included the Playboy and Playmate trademarks.[46] The district court awarded summary judgment in favor of Netscape, but the Court of Appeals reversed, allowing Playboy's case to go forward. The appellate court focused on the likelihood of consumer confusion, taking it as a given that the search engines had used Playboy's trademarks in commerce. The court observed that when computer users entered the terms Playboy or Playmate into Netscape's search engine, pop-up ads for Playboy's competitors appeared. The ads did not include Playboy's trademarks. But because their source was ambiguous (some just said "click here"), the court concluded that search engine users might have assumed that Playboy sponsored them. However, the Court of Appeals also clarified that if the ads had been clearly labeled, consumer confusion might be averted.

Several district courts have followed the Ninth Circuit's reasoning, either because they were bound to or because they found it persuasive. Google sought a declaratory judgment that as a matter of law its use of trademarks as key words does not constitute a use in commerce for purposes of the trademark law in *Google v. American Blind and Wallpaper Factory* (2005).[47] It cited cases from the Second Circuit that supported its argument. Judge Fogel of the U.S. District Court of the Northern District of California made it clear that sponsored links did not appear likely to confuse consumers, but that he was bound by Ninth Circuit precedent that implicitly suggests key words are used in commerce. He also observed that it was in the public's interest that the matter be resolved through trial. American Blind settled the case with Google before that could happen, citing litigation expenses. The company's decision was likely influenced as well by Judge Fogel's conclusion that its trademarks on the terms "American Blind" and "American Blinds" were unenforceable. The marks were registered after the alleged infringement. If registration occurs after an infringement, the plaintiff must establish that it had a common law interest in the mark before the infringement. The judge accepted Google's argument that when the terms were first used as key words they were merely descriptive and had not yet acquired a secondary meaning.

Google lost its motion to dismiss a similar suit in *Government Employees Insurance Co. v. Google, Inc.* (2004).[48] A federal district court in Virginia held that "when defendants sell rights to link advertising to plaintiff's trademark, defendants are using the trademarks in commerce in a way that may imply that defendants have permission from the trademark holder to do so." In *800-JR Cigar, Inc. v. GoTo.com, Inc.* (2006), a New Jersey district court found that a search engine's sale of key words based on trademarks amounted to a use in commerce because it (1) traded on the value of the plaintiff's marks; (2) steered potential consumers from the plaintiff to its competitors by ranking the links of paid advertisers before 'natural' links and (3) marketed the plaintiff's trademarks through a search term suggestion tool.[49] Courts in Illinois, Minnesota, and Pennsylvania have also found trademarks used as keywords to be a use in commerce.[50]

Google's AdWords program has raised controversy in other countries as well. A Paris District Court ruled that selling trademarks to trigger advertising infringed on Louis Vuitton's trademark and enjoined Google from displaying ads for Vuitton's competitors when Google users entered the trademark into the search engine.[51] The company has also settled or is defending suits in Germany, Israel, Italy, Austria, and Australia.

Metatags

Metatags are words or phrases embedded in a website's code. Search engines use them to either prioritize sites among searches or provide short descriptions of the information included on the site. At least four circuits have found the unauthorized use of trademarks as metatags by competitors to be a trademark infringement.

The Ninth Circuit considered the use of metatags to be a trademark infringement in *Brookfield Communications v. West Coast Entertainment Corp.* (1999).[52] The defendant, a video rental chain, used the plaintiff's "Movie Buff" trademark as a metatag in the coding for its website to affect search results. The court understood that a search engine user would be able to distinguish the website he or she sought from a list of search results that included the competitor's site and that even if the user chose to look at the competitor's site, it was not likely that he or she would be confused about its source. It none the less based its determination that the use of the metatag was infringing on a theory of "initial interest confusion."[53] The theory assumes that by using the plaintiff's trademark to divert people looking for the plaintiff's website, the defendant improperly benefited from good will associated with the plaintiff's mark.[54] The court's reasoning has been criticized because the purpose of the Trademark Act is not to secure the trademark owner's good will, but to avoid confusion among consumers.

The Seventh Circuit adopted the same theory in *Promatek Industries Ltd. v. Equitrac Corp.* (2002), when it upheld an injunction that barred a company from using a competitor's trademark as a metatag. It explained that initial interest confusion occurs "when a customer is lured to a product by the similarity of the mark, even if the customer realizes the true source of the goods before the sale is consummated."[55] In fact, in *Australian Gold, Inc. v. Hatfield* (2006), the Tenth Circuit concluded that the defendant's use of metatags containing the plaintiff's trademark resulted in initial interest confusion despite the defendant's use of a disclaimer on its website. The court reasoned that "a defendant's website disclaimer, proclaiming its real source and disavowing any connection with its competitor, cannot prevent the damage of initial interest confusion, which will already have been done by the misdirection of consumers looking for the plaintiff's websites."[56]

The Eleventh Circuit also held that the unauthorized use of a trademark as a metatag could be an infringement, but its decision can be distinguished from those of the Seventh, Ninth, and Tenth Circuits because the defendant used the plaintiff's mark in a description of its website that accompanied its link, so the mark was no longer hidden in the code.[57]

Metatags used in a site that is not intended to act as a competitor are given more leeway. In *Bihari v. Gross* (2000), the U.S. District Court for the Southern District of New York held that the defendant's use of the plaintiff's trademarks in a "gripe site" was allowed.[58] Craig Gross, who was dissatisfied with the plaintiff's business practices, registered sites called "designscam.com" and "manhattaninteriordesign. com" and embedded Bihari's name as a metatag in the code, so searches for Bihari would pull up his sites. The court pointed out that there was no likelihood of confusion to support a trademark infringement claim. Users searching for information about Bihari would find it – albeit disparaging – in the defendant's site. Moreover, they were not being diverted from Bihari's site because she didn't have one.

Cybersquatting

Entrepreneurial types frequently register domain names with the intent of selling them at a profit. It is legal to register and sell a domain that incorporates a generic term that cannot be trademarked, a distinctive term that has not yet been trademarked (through official registration or regular use), or a term that was formerly trademarked, but that has fallen into the public domain. However, registering a domain that incorporates someone else's trademark, or a term that is confusingly similar to the trademark, with the intent to sell it back to the trademark owner or to profit from the trademark owner's good will is illegal. This practice, known as cybersquatting, has become an international problem. In 2007, the World International Property Organization heard complaints against cybersquatters from 72 countries.

Congress amended the Trademark Act to prevent cybersquatting in 1999. The Anti-Cybersquatting Consumer Protection Act (ACPA) imposes liability on anyone who "registers, traffics in, or uses a domain name" that is identical or confusingly similar to a mark that was distinctive at the time of registration or identical or confusingly similar to a mark that was a famous mark at the time of registration with a "bad faith intent to profit from the mark."[59]

To determine whether someone is operating in bad faith, a court may consider a variety of factors, including:

- the user's trademark rights in the domain name;
- the extent to which the domain includes the legal name of the person or another commonly used to identify the person;
- the person's prior use of the domain name in connection with the legitimate commerce;
- the person's bona fide noncommercial or fair use of the mark in a site that uses the domain name;
- the person's intent to divert traffic from the mark owner's site, either for commercial gain or with the intent to tarnish or disparage the mark, by creating a likelihood of confusion regarding the source of the site;
- the person's offer to transfer, sell, or otherwise assign the domain name to the mark owner or any third party for financial gain or the person's prior pattern of such conduct;
- the person's provision of false contact information when applying for the registration of the domain name or failure to maintain accurate information with the registrar;
- the person's registration or acquisition of multiple domain names which the person knows are identical or confusingly similar to marks of others or dilutive of famous marks; and
- the extent to which the mark incorporated into the domain name is distinctive or famous.[60]

If a court determines that a defendant has violated the ACPA, it may order the defendant to forfeit the domain and transfer it to the rightful owner of the trademark. It also may impose actual or statutory damages, ranging from $1,000 to $100,000.[61] If the violator knowingly provided false contact information to register the site, a court may assume the violation is willful.[62]

One cybersquatter, John Zuccarini, was fined $500,000 for five domains registered in bad faith that were confusingly similar to service marks used by Electronics Boutique, a video games and software retailer.[63] Zuccarini registered domain names that included typos users might make while entering the address for a site – a practice nicknamed typo squatting – and filled them with pay-per-click advertising. Users who stumbled into the sites were forced to click through a plethora of ads before they could escape, each earning Zaccarini 10 to 25 cents per click. He earned between $800,000 and $1 million annually from the thousands of domain names he registered.[64]

The Internet Corporation of Assigned Names and Numbers (ICANN), the organization responsible for the management of the Internet domain name system, has established an arbitration procedure for victims of cybersquatters who would rather avoid the expense and delays associated with trial. Domain registrants agree to standard conditions imposed by ICANN when they register a domain name. Among these is the requirement that the registrant submit to an arbitration proceeding initiated by a trademark holder who believes the domain is confusingly similar to his or her trademark.

Cybersquatting and gripe sites

Some people register domains that incorporate company trademarks to criticize a company rather than to profit from it. Gripe sites have received mixed receptions from courts, depending on their interpretation of the Trademark Act's requirement that the mark be used "in connection with goods or services" before it could be considered infringing or dilutive.

In *United We Stand America v. United We Stand America New York, Inc.* (1997), the Second Circuit reached the surprising conclusion that the nonprofit dissemination of information or opinion could be considered a "service" for purposes of the Trademark Act.[65] The case involved a trademark infringement suit against a breakaway chapter of Ross Perot's campaign organization that continued to use the United We Stand name with a regional distinction.

The Second Circuit suggested that liability for the unauthorized use of a mark should depend on whether it is likely to cause confusion, not whether it is commercial. The defendant argued that its political use of the plaintiff's mark was protected, referencing the *Lucasfilm* decision regarding the use of "Star Wars" in a political context. The Second Circuit said that while it agreed with the outcome of that case, it disagreed with the *Lucasfilm* court's reasoning. "[I]f the court were right that communicating ideas and purveying points of view is not a service subject to the controls established by trademark law, then one who established a learning center would be free to call it Harvard or Yale University."[66]

The Fourth Circuit has also accepted the position that "services" may be interpreted to include "dissemination of information, including purely ideological information."[67] In *People for the Ethical Treatment of Animals v. Doughney* (2001), the appellate court upheld a lower court's grant of summary judgment in favor of an animal rights organization on trademark infringement and cybersquatting claims. The defendant used PETA's mark to create a parody site based on the acronym "People Eating Tasty Animals." The court concluded that

> To use PETA's Mark "in connection with" goods or services, Doughney need not have actually sold or advertised goods or services on the www.peta.org website. Rather, Doughney need only have prevented users from obtaining or using PETA's goods or services, or need only have connected the website to other's goods or services.[68]

It concluded the defendant's use of the mark was likely to prevent some users from reaching PETA's site because upon failing to find it after typing in

PETA.org, they may be angry, frustrated, or under the impression that PETA's site didn't exist.

This argument that the use of a mark that diverts traffic from a plaintiff's site, potentially causing commercial harm, constitutes a use "in connection with" the sale of products and services for purposes of the Lanham Act has also been accepted by the Third Circuit,[69] but rejected by the First,[70] Sixth,[71] and Ninth Circuits.[72]

The Fourth Circuit also found evidence that Doughney's site was used in connection with goods and services because it included links to other sites that sold animal-based products. This argument, which invests the linking site with the characteristics of the linked site, is also accepted in the Sixth Circuit.[73]

The appellate court found the use of PETA's mark in the domain likely to cause confusion on the part of consumers. It rejected the defendant's parody defense because the domain *name* did not indicate a parody. The parody was not apparent until the user clicked on the website and read its content. The court asserted that "A parody must 'convey two simultaneous – and contradictory – messages: that it is the original, but also that it is not the original and is instead a parody.'"[74] The appellate court faulted Doughney for not conveying the messages "simultaneously" in the domain name.

It is likely that the court took such a hard line because the defendant had a history of registering company trademarks as domain names and had allegedly offered to sell the domain to PETA. Doughney also acquired the plaintiff's domain by providing false information to his Internet service provider. The court considered this evidence of bad faith for purposes of the Anti-Cybersquatting Act.

In another case involving a gripe site against Jerry Falwell, the Fourth Circuit acknowledged that a criticism site could be protected. In *Lamparello v. Falwell Ministries* (2005), the Fourth Circuit ruled in favor of the defendant who registered a gripe site, using a domain that was confusingly similar to one owned by Rev. Jerry Falwell, to dispute the minister's claims that gays and lesbians were sinners who could change their ways.[75] The court noted that the defendant's site carried a prominent disclaimer that the site did not belong to Falwell and a link to Falwell's site for those who still wanted it. Lamparello did not use the site to sell goods or services. His links to other organizations included one to a book on Amazon.com, but the link did "not diminish the communicative function of this site."[76]

The Fifth, Sixth, and Ninth Circuits have endorsed the view that the noncommercial use of a trademark as a domain name does not violate the Lanham Act. In *Taubman Co. v. Webfeats* (2003), the Sixth Circuit held that a gripe site that contained no commercial content, advertisements, or links to other commercial sites was a protected form of expression:[77]

> [T]he First Amendment protects critical commentary when there is no confusion as to source, even when it involves the criticism of a business. Such use is not subject to scrutiny under the Lanham Act. In fact, Taubman concedes that [the defendant] is "free to shout 'Taubman Sucks!' from the rooftops …" Essentially, this is what he has

done in his domain name. The rooftops of our past have evolved into the internet domain names of our present. We find that the domain name is a type of public expression, no different in scope than a billboard or a pulpit, and [the defendant] has a First Amendment right to express his opinion about Taubman, and as long as his speech is not commercially misleading, the Lanham Act cannot be summoned to prevent it.[78]

The Fifth Circuit held in *TMI v. Maxwell* (2004) that a gripe site which mixed noncommercial content and commercial content by including a recommendation for one contractor, could still be considered noncommercial because it accepted no payment for advertising, carried no links to other sites, and did not sell products, services, or domain names.[79]

Coming to the same conclusion, the Ninth Circuit warned that the *PETA* court's theory that use of a trademark as a domain name satisfies the Lanham Act by deterring customers from reaching the plaintiff's site "would place most critical, otherwise protected consumer commentary under the restrictions of the Lanham Act."[80]

Trade Secrets

A trade secret is a confidential formula, pattern, compilation, program, device, method, technique, or process that offers its owner an economic advantage over competitors who do not know it. An example would be the Colonel's secret chicken recipe, proprietary research, product development plans, or an invention that has not yet been patented. Protecting trade secrets is thought to encourage research and development that supplements the patent system.[81]

Protecting a trade secret

The best way to protect a trade secret is by keeping it secret. Trade secrets, unlike copyrights, patents, and trademarks, are never registered. Registration requires public disclosure of the information, which would expose the secret. Once a trade secret is divulged to the public, its protection ends.

Some companies expend great effort protecting their trade secrets. Coca-Cola, for example, locks its formula in a bank vault that can only be opened by a resolution from its board of directors. No more than two employees ever know the secret at one time and they are not allowed to fly on the same plane together.[82]

But such extreme measures are not necessary to acquire legal protection. Reasonable precautions for maintaining secrecy include advising employees who work with the information of its trade secret status to prevent them from inadvertently sharing it, limiting access to the information to those who need it, labeling materials "confidential," locking up files when not in use, and maintaining proper computer security.

Companies also commonly require their employees to sign non-disclosure agreements, which are legally enforceable contracts that prevent them from revealing confidential information to third parties. Some firms also require employees to sign non-compete clauses that prevent them from working for direct competitors for a specified period of time after leaving the company.

How long does a trade secret last?

The distinct advantage of trade secret protection is that it is perpetual. So a formula or method that would only be protected for 20 years if it were patented can be held indefinitely. The disadvantage is that once the information is made available to the public, the protection ends.

What legal rights does the trade secret owner have?

Most states have enacted civil legislation that prohibits misappropriation of trade secrets. *Misappropriation* includes the acquisition or disclosure of a trade secret by someone who knows or has reason to know that it was acquired improperly and its use is unauthorized.

Trade secret protection applies if:

- the information derives independent economic value, actual or potential, from not being known to the public or people who could benefit from its disclosure; and
- the owner has made reasonable efforts under the circumstances to maintain its secrecy.

Misappropriation claims do not apply to people who learn about trade secrets independently through separate invention or reverse engineering. In fact, because two parties can own a trade secret separately, a person or company that invests heavily in the reverse engineering of a product or formula may also protect the information it has discovered as a trade secret.

A person damaged by misappropriation of a trade secret may sue for compensation. The statute of limitations for misappropriation is normally three years. If the plaintiff establishes his or her case, the court may issue an award for actual damages for losses incurred that include compensation for the defendant's unjust enrichment from the trade secret. Alternatively, the court can order the defendant to pay a sum equal to reasonable royalties on the use of the information. If the defendant's misappropriation was willful, the court may double the damages.

If the misappropriation has not yet occurred, the trade secret owner can file for an injunction to prevent it. Courts are empowered to enjoin actual or threatened misappropriation of trade secrets for as long as the trade secret remains valid. During the course of the litigation, the court will act to preserve secrecy of the information by granting protective orders, holding in-camera hearings (closed to the public), and sealing records.

The intentional theft of a trade secret is a criminal offense under the Economic Espionage Act of 1996.[83] An individual acting for economic benefit, who steals a trade secret related to or included in a product meant for interstate or foreign commerce, or accepts one knowing it was taken without authorization, may be fined or imprisoned for as much as 10 years. A company may be fined as much as $5,000,000.[84] If the trade secret was stolen for the benefit of a foreign government, an individual may be fined as much as $500,000 or imprisoned up to 15 years. A corporation may be fined up to $10,000,000.[85]

Trade secrets and the Internet

Increasingly, cases filed for misappropriation of trade secrets involve information published on the Internet by bloggers. Apple, Inc. and Ford Motor Company have each sued college students for revealing information about company products on their websites. In both cases, the information was provided to the websites anonymously. Both plaintiffs and defendants assumed that it came from company employees who were bound by confidentiality agreements.

Apple experienced a backlash when it sued the publisher of Think Secret, a Mac enthusiast site that ran news about products in development, for misappropriation of trade secrets.[86] The site had developed a loyal following among Mac users who accused the company of censorship. Apple eventually settled the suit for an unknown sum to get the Harvard student who ran the site to shut it down.

Ford's legal battle with the publisher of an enthusiast site that disclosed its secrets was not resolved so easily. Robert Lane published information about quality issues concerning the Cobra engine, fuel efficiency strategies for the year 2010, and engineering blueprints on his website BlueOvalNews.com. Ford asked the court to enjoin Lane from further publication of its secrets, but the court refused.

The court held that restraining Lane from publishing Ford's trade secrets "would constitute an invalid prior restraint of free speech in violation of the First Amendment."[87] It cited a Sixth Circuit decision in *Procter & Gamble Co. v. Bankers Trust Co.* that overturned an injunction on publication of trade secrets. The Court of Appeals decision directed courts to consider, in cases involving prior restraint of pure speech, whether publication "threaten[s] an interest more fundamental than the First Amendment itself."[88] It explained that "private litigants' interest in protecting their vanity or their commercial self interest simply does not qualify as grounds for imposing a prior restraint."[89]

The court would not impose an injunction on Lane in the absence of a confidentiality agreement or fiduciary duty between the parties. However, it did enjoin

Lane from posting Ford's copyrighted documents and required him to divulge any information he had about the sources of the proprietary information.

Questions for Discussion

1. What is required to get patent, trademark, and trade secret protection?
2. What kinds of marks are inherently distinctive? How does a mark earn distinctiveness if it is not inherently distinctive?
3. What is the difference between trademark infringement and trademark dilution?
4. How can you post a gripe site without being accused of cybersquatting?

9

Defamation

Around the world, countries balance protections for freedom of expression and reputation differently. The United States, which protects freedom of speech and press in the Constitution, tips the balance in favor of expression. Reputation is still considered worthy of protection but must give way if society's need for information is more pressing. This policy choice is evident in the Supreme Court's decision to impose First Amendment constraints on state defamation laws.

Unlike other nations, the United States no longer imposes strict liability upon libel defendants. The Supreme Court has created "a zone of protection for errors of fact" that inevitably occur in publication.[1] Plaintiffs who sue for defamation regarding a matter of public concern must prove negligence or malice on the part of the defendant. The United States is also unique in allowing plaintiffs to sue defendants for libel in only one jurisdiction, regardless of how widely the defamation was published. As a result, media have more protection against defamation in the United States than any other country in the world.

This chapter discusses the elements required to establish a libel claim and defenses that apply in libel suits. It describes how U.S. defamation law differs from that of other countries and the impact that difference has had on the way different types of plaintiffs are treated. Just as importantly, it explains how libel laws apply to media defendants v. nonmedia defendants in a period in which we are all producing digital media products. Finally, it considers the related tort of infliction of emotional distress and its relationship to defamation law.

What Is Defamation?

Defamation is a tort (a civil wrong), regulated through state law, that involves harm to someone's reputation. It occurs when a false communication exposes a person to hatred, contempt, or ridicule, or lowers a person's stature in the community.[2]

The communication may take a variety of forms. It might be a verbal statement in front of a group, an article printed in a publication, an advertisement broadcast on air, a video circulated on YouTube, or a cartoon distributed through e-mail.

Defamation is one of the legal problems writers, editors, and producers commonly face. People do not dismiss harm to their reputations easily. As former Supreme Court Justice Stewart explained, the right to protect one's reputation "reflects no more than our basic concept of the essential dignity and worth of every human being – a concept at the root of any decent system of ordered liberty."[3]

Defamation suits are also very costly. Under the doctrine of respondeat superior, a plaintiff can sue a media company for a defamatory statement made by its employee and generally will because the company is the one with deeper pockets. Juries are empowered to decide the facts of the case, and their decisions occasionally reflect a bias against the media. In 1997, a Texas jury awarded $223 million, the largest award ever, to a Houston brokerage firm that sued the *Wall Street Journal* for libel.[4] The *WSJ* published an article that alleged criminal activity on the company's part. The verdict was set aside in 1999 when a former employee of the brokerage firm came forward with a tape recording of the firm's executives that supported accusations made in the news piece.[5] Many media awards in libel suits are vacated or reduced on appeal. But in the interim, the defendant loses time and money fighting for vindication.

Types of Defamation

Defamation can be subdivided into two categories: libel and slander. *Libel* is defamation in printed or broadcast form. *Slander* refers to spoken words of limited reach. Of the two, libel is considered more damaging because it is fixed and can be circulated broadly. A slanderous statement is transitory in nature, so its potential for damage is presumed to be less severe.

Who Can Be Defamed?

Individuals, as well as corporations and nonprofit organizations, can sue for damage to their reputations. While individuals are considered "natural persons" under the law, a corporation is treated as a "legal person" with standing to sue apart from its officials and stockholders. Some torts, like defamation, apply to natural as well as legal persons; others, like invasion of privacy, apply only to natural persons.

Government entities may not sue for defamation under the theory that the government should not be permitted to use public funds to prevent the public from criticizing it.[6] But government officials are entitled to sue on their own behalf. By necessity, public officials are subject to greater scrutiny than private citizens, so courts require them to meet a higher standard of proof in defamation cases.

On rare occasions plaintiffs find they cannot sue for defamation because they have no reputation left to protect. When *US Weekly* reported that Britney Spears had created a sex tape with her husband, the singer sued the magazine for libel. But a Los Angeles superior court judge dismissed the suit, concluding that because Spears had "put her modern sexuality squarely, and profitably, before the public eye" the allegation was unlikely to be defamatory.[7] Few individuals are "libel proof" for all purposes, however. Courts usually reserve that designation for notorious criminals.[8]

Most states limit defamation claims to the living, but the dead can be libeled in New York, New Jersey, Pennsylvania, and Texas. In these jurisdictions, families are allowed to sue for compensation when the memories of their relatives have been blackened by false statements.

Trade libel

A subcategory of defamation known as trade libel protects the market for particular products that may be harmed by false allegations. Oprah Winfrey, for example, was sued in Texas for disparaging beef. A guest on a "dangerous food" segment of her show suggested that mad cow disease could make AIDS look like the common cold and that the United States was doing too little to protect consumers from tainted beef. Other guests refuted the danger, but when the show was edited for time, some of their assurances were removed. Following a drastic drop in cattle prices after the show, Texas cattle ranchers sued Winfrey for violating the state's False Disparagement of Perishable Food Products Act. The jury ruled in Winfrey's favor because the cattlemen could not prove she had made "knowingly false statements" about them.[9]

SLAPP suits

Companies have been known to use defamation law as a weapon to silence critics via Strategic Lawsuit Against Public Participation suits, more commonly known as SLAPP suits. Courts consider these suits meritless when companies appear to be using the threat of a prolonged legal battle to intimidate legitimate critics. Many states have passed anti-SLAPP statutes that empower courts to dismiss SLAPP suits intended to chill protected expression and award attorneys' fees to the victim.

Elements of Libel

Libel is a combination of six elements: publication, identification, defamation, falsity, fault, and damage. Before an allegation can be considered defamatory, a

judge or jury must be convinced that the statement was of or concerning the plaintiff, that it was harmful to reputation and untrue, that the defendant was at fault,
and that the statement resulted in damage to the plaintiff.

Publication

An accusation must be made public before it can harm someone's reputation. So
the first thing a libel plaintiff must establish in a claim is that the statement in question was published. An article that appears in a printed or online news source is
considered published. So is a story distributed via broadcast, cable, or satellite. But
publication is not exclusive to the mass media. Information may be "published" on
a personal website or blog, or through an e-mail or fax circulated among colleagues.
Technically, the requirement for publication is met when a third person sees the
information.

Identification

Next, the plaintiff must prove the he or she was the subject of the offensive remark.
A statement that cannot be shown to be "of or concerning" the plaintiff will not be
considered harmful to the plaintiff's reputation.

Identification may occur in a variety of ways. A plaintiff who is named is obviously identified, but a name is not required for identification. Any information or
depiction in which the plaintiff is recognizable will do. This could be accomplished
through a picture, cartoon, video, or a sufficiently detailed description. For example,
a reference to "a Scientologist, married to Katie Holmes, who starred in the movie
Mission Impossible" should bring Tom Cruise to mind without using his name.

Group membership is not a sufficient basis for identification, unless a reference
to a group could reasonably be interpreted as referring to specific individuals.
Under the *group libel doctrine*, a plaintiff will not be considered identified if he or
she is referenced solely as a member of a group.[10] For example, a libel suit filed by
67 members of the religious group Falun Gong was dismissed because they could
not prove that articles written by the defendants about "New York-based Falun
Gong practitioners" referenced any of them specifically.[11] In general, courts have
been reluctant to acknowledge "group libel," particularly for groups of 25 or more.

Defamation

After a court is satisfied that the statement in question was published and that the
plaintiff has been identified as its subject, it will consider whether the words themselves could be considered damaging to reputation. The court or jury will look at
the words in light of their ordinary meaning.

Libel can also be subdivided into two categories: libel per se and libel per quod. *Libel per se* is a statement that is obviously damaging to one's reputation (or as courts say, libelous on its face). Suggesting that someone is guilty of a crime, disreputable in business, sexually promiscuous, or suffers from a communicable disease would be considered libel per se. *Libel per quod* is not obvious. Its negative implication depends on innuendo or knowledge of extraneous facts. For example, a California newspaper published a photo of a police officer sitting in his squad car, tilting his head to one side. The accompanying caption described him prowling for traffic violations on a lightly traveled street, adding "his tilted head may suggest something." Readers assumed he was sleeping on duty. Actually, he was writing a citation, a fact the editors knew when they published the caption. Other cases of libel per quod appear completely innocent unless readers happen to have additional information. For example, a meat market ad that included bacon wouldn't raise an eyebrow among readers, unless they happened to know that the butcher was a kosher meat dealer.

A common misconception is that qualifying words like "alleged" or "reportedly" will prevent libel suits. In *Time, Inc. v. Pape* (1971), the Supreme Court said the word "alleged" should not be construed as "a superfluity in published reports of information damaging to reputation."[12] Qualifying words may offer some protection when used as verbs, for example: *Police alleged that Smith was the murderer.* But they should never be used as adjectives: *Smith is the alleged murderer.* Ultimately, however, it is safer and more accurate to use a verifiable statement of fact, such as *Police arrested Smith in connection with the murder.*

Another misconception is that quotation marks will protect a writer from liability for a source's defamatory comments. They will not. Repeating a defamatory remark made by someone else is known as *republication of libel*. The person republishing the libel also bears responsibility for it. Consequently, it is not enough to quote a source accurately. Before publishing information that could be contentious, it is important to check more than one source.

Falsity

A statement that is harmful to reputation, but true, cannot be defamatory. In the United States, libel plaintiffs are obligated to prove the falsity of a statement. It is not the defendant's obligation to prove the statement's truth. One exception to this rule is when proving the falsity of the statement would require the plaintiff to prove the negative – for example, that he or she never cheated or lied.

The jury, as fact finder (or the judge in a bench trial), will determine whether a statement is true or false. However, on appeal, the appellate court has an obligation to examine the evidence as well to make sure that "the judgment does not constitute a forbidden intrusion on the field of free expression."[13]

Absolute accuracy is not essential. Minor flaws in a story that have no bearing on the plaintiff's reputation will not be considered libelous. But small details – such a misspelled name or a missing or wrong middle initial – can be problematic if they point an accusatory finger at the wrong person. For example, a story that Robert A. Smith was arrested for computer fraud might be considered defamatory if Robert B. Smith was the real culprit.

Fault

If the defamation concerns a matter of public interest, the plaintiff must not only prove falsity but also some level of fault on the part of the defendant. The level of fault depends on whether the plaintiff is a public or private figure.

A *public figure* is one who willingly assumes a position in the public arena and has ready access to the media. Certain individuals are considered to be public figures for all purposes. These include celebrities with "pervasive fame and notoriety" and public officials. A public official includes a candidate for public office, an elected official, or an appointed official with substantial responsibility for or control over governmental affairs.[14] Public officials need not be people in high places. Many states consider police officers to be public figures, for example.

A *limited-purpose public figure* is someone who voluntarily thrusts him or herself into the spotlight in regard to a particular issue or controversy and who has effective access to the media to rebut false statements made in relation to that controversy. This would include someone like Cindy Sheehan, who protested the war in Iraq following her son's death.

There is also limited support for an *involuntary limited-purpose public figure* category that would apply to people who are unwitting subjects of media coverage related to events of public interest, such as an air traffic controller on duty during a plane crash.[15] However, while courts have acknowledged this category, its use is exceedingly rare.

In contrast, a *private figure* is an average person who has not voluntarily exposed him or herself to the increased risk of defamation by seeking media attention and who has no special access to the media to refute damaging accusations. Most people fall into this category.

In a defamation suit, plaintiffs who are public figures must prove with clear and convincing evidence that the defendant acted with actual malice. The term actual malice is defined as either knowledge of falsity or reckless disregard for the truth. To prove actual malice, a plaintiff must demonstrate that the defendant made the statement knowing that it was false at the time or "entertained serious doubts" about its truth.[16]

Proving actual malice is very difficult. It requires substantially more than a showing of "extreme departure from professional standards."[17] The first case in which the Supreme Court affirmed a finding of actual malice against a media defendant was *Harte-Hanks Communications v. Connaughton* (1989). The plaintiff was a candidate for a municipal judge position in Hamilton, Ohio, who lost the election after the local newspaper suggested he had used "dirty tricks" to unseat his opponent. The article suggested Connaughton had bribed a woman who witnessed improprieties in his opponent's office to cooperate in an investigation to discredit the incumbent judge. The paper's editors, who endorsed Connaughton's opponent, reported accusations made against him by a source whose veracity was questionable while ignoring Connaughton's denial and contradictory evidence from five other sources. No one from the paper attempted to interview the witness Connaughton was accused of bribing. Nor did anyone listen to the recording Connaughton provided of his meeting with the witness in which she described what she had seen. The Supreme Court concluded that the editors' actions amounted to a "purposeful avoidance of truth" that constituted reckless disregard under the actual malice standard.[18] The case could be read as checklist of behaviors that might support a finding of actual malice: relying on questionable sources, failing to interview relevant sources, ignoring contradictory evidence and denials, accepting improbable notions, and exhibiting obvious prejudice.[19]

Limited-purpose public figures are required to prove actual malice on the part of a defendant if the statement alleged to be libelous was made in relation to an issue or controversy for which the plaintiff sought media attention. In any other circumstance, the plaintiff would be treated like a private figure.

Private figure plaintiffs are not required to prove actual malice in cases involving a matter of public concern, but they are required to establish negligence on the part of the defendant. Negligence equates with dereliction of duty. A negligent person either does something that a reasonable person would not do, or fails to do something that a reasonable person would do. Professional negligence amounts to a failure to follow accepted professional practices. Applied to a journalist, this might include failure to check public records, verify information through other sources, or contact the person defamed before running the story. It would not include the failure to verify facts from a wire service, because wire services are normally trustworthy. A court will also consider the degree to which the story in question was "hot news."[20] Time-sensitive stories offer a narrower window for fact checking.

The Supreme Court has not ruled on whether a private figure is required to prove fault in a libel case that has no public relevance. Some jurisdictions require private plaintiffs to prove some level of fault regardless of the issue. Others require them to prove fault only in matters of public interest.[21]

Damage

In a libel suit, plaintiffs are required to prove damages that go beyond mere embarrassment. These might include loss of income, denial of employment, suffering from documented depression or anxiety, or being shunned by one's colleagues.

Damages may be presumed for public figures who establish actual malice on the part of the defendant in cases of libel per se, but not in libel per quod. Public figure plaintiffs that allege libel per quod must show actual damages because the impact in libel per quod cases is presumed to be limited to the small group of readers or viewers aware of the extraneous facts that make the remark libelous.

Private figures who sue for libel in a case involving a matter of public interest are always expected to prove damages. If they seek actual damages in recompense for their loss, they will have to prove negligence. If they seek punitive damages, they will have to prove actual malice. In contrast, a private plaintiff suing over a matter that does not concern the public interest, may be entitled to an award of presumed and punitive damages without showing actual malice.

Defenses to Libel

Truth

Truth is an absolute defense against libel claims since defamation is false by definition. Courts will look for "substantial truth." Minor inaccuracies will not destroy a truth defense if the overall gist of the story is truthful. What matters is how a person of ordinary intelligence would construe it as a whole.

By the same token, a truth defense will not stand if the individual facts are correct but combined in a manner to create a false impression. In *Richardson v. State-Record Co.* (1998), a South Carolina woman sued a newspaper for publishing an article that, while technically true, libeled her through the omission of information.[22] The plaintiff, Nora Richardson, hit the police chief of Eastover, S.C., with her car. He died one year later. The State Record reported his death in an article titled "Eastover chief dies a year after being hit by car." The article correctly stated that Richardson had seriously injured the chief in the accident and that he had never fully recovered. A follow-up story, titled "Chief's death won't bring new charges against driver," indicated that Richardson would face no more charges because she had already pled guilty and could not be charged twice for the same crime. Each sentence was true, but what the paper neglected to mention was that the chief died of rectal cancer. The court pointed out that the truth defense "must substantially cover the 'gist' or the 'sting' of the defamatory statement."[23]

Opinion

The Supreme Court has not created a separate constitutional protection for opinion in defamation cases.[24] But it has stated that "a statement of opinion relating to matters of public concern, which does not contain a provably false factual connotation, will receive full constitutional protection."[25] In other words, a statement of opinion that cannot be proved true or false will be protected. This protection, according to the Court, is simply an extension of its policy that "a statement on matters of public concern must be provable as false before there can be liability under state defamation law, at least in situations … where a media defendant is involved."[26]

The Supreme Court considered the contours of opinion as a libel defense in *Milkovich v. Lorain Journal Co.* (1990). The petitioner in the case was a high school wrestling coach whose team had been punished following an altercation with another team in which several people were injured. The Ohio High School Athletic Association placed the team on probation for one year. Several of the wrestlers' parents filed suit asking for an injunction preventing enforcement of the association's decision. Milkovich testified during the proceeding. The following day a local columnist implied that Milkovich lied under oath. The trial court granted summary judgment to the paper on the grounds that the article was opinion. The Supreme Court reversed.

It stated that protection does not extend to verifiable statements couched as opinions. In other words, a statement like "In my opinion, Jones is a liar," would not be a protected opinion because the essence of the statement – Jones is a liar – can be proved true or false.[27] The test for protected opinion is whether a reasonable listener would interpret the statement as a fact that could be verified.

Fair comment and criticism

Statements of opinion are also protected under the common law defense of fair comment and criticism. The protection applies to comments on matters of public interest, supported by facts and made without malice, which convey an honest expression of the writer's opinion. The defense, which originated under English common law, was explained by a New York court in *Hoeppner v. Dunkirk* (1930):

> Everyone has a right to comment on matters of public interest and concern, provided they do so fairly and with an honest purpose. Such comments or criticism are not libelous, however severe in their terms, unless they are written maliciously. Thus it has been held that books, prints, pictures, and statuary publicly exhibited, and the architecture or public buildings, and actors and exhibitors, are all the legitimate subjects of newspapers' criticism, and such criticism fairly and honestly made is not libelous, however strong the terms of censure may be.[28]

Fair comment and criticism protected a Louisiana food critic who described a restaurant's "hideous sauces" as "yellow death on duck" and "trout a la green plague."[29] The court ruled that the critic's comments about the sauces reflected his expertise on the subject and that his colorful descriptions were merely hyperbole.

Rhetorical hyperbole

Rhetorical hyperbole – or exaggeration for effect – is protected under common law on the theory that a statement must be provable as false before it can be considered defamatory.[30] Rhetorical hyperbole applies to statements so extreme and overstated that no reader or listener could seriously consider them to imply factual charges.[31] Take, for example, the title "Director of Butt Licking." Virginia Tech's student newspaper printed the appellation under a pull-quote by the university's Vice President of Student Affairs accompanying an article about her efforts to promote a state fellowship program. She sued the paper for libel, claiming she had been accused of "moral turpitude." While acknowledging that the term was "in extremely bad taste," the Virginia Supreme Court upheld a lower court's dismissal of the suit, finding that as a matter of law the phrase could not be defamatory because it was "void of literal meaning" and no reasonable person would accept it as a factual statement about the plaintiff.[32] Although the designation is generally associated with sycophantic behavior, the court found nothing in the article to support the conclusion that the plaintiff's behavior was in any way unprofessional.

In determining whether speech is protected as rhetorical hyperbole, courts consider the context in which it appears. For example, in an emotional debate over the murder of abortion providers, talk show host Geraldo Rivera described Neal Horsley, the creator of the Nuremberg Files website (discussed in chapter 11) that listed the names and addresses of abortion providers and classified them as working, wounded, or deceased, as "an accomplice to homicide." Horsley sued Rivera for libel and a district court in Georgia concluded that Rivera's comments were not protected. The U.S. Court of Appeals for the Eleventh Circuit reversed, concluding that Rivera's statements were rhetorical hyperbole.[33] It said a reasonable viewer would have understood that Rivera's comment was meant to suggest that Horsley was morally culpable for one of the murders, not that he had committed a felony.

The rhetorical hyperbole defense applies to music as well. Record producer Armen Boladian lost a libel suit against musician George Clinton, when the Sixth Circuit held that Clinton's rap lyrics referring to the "sorrows and horrors of Armen's abuse," and describing him as a "disgrace to the species," were rhetorical hyperbole and puerile taunts.[34] Ultimately, the test is whether the audience would take the accusation seriously.

Privilege

Common law also acknowledges a certain level of privilege to make defamatory statements in pursuit of a legal, moral, or social duty. There are three kinds of privileges that serve as protection against libel suits: absolute, fair reporting, and neutral reportage.

Absolute privilege immunizes people in certain positions from liability for defamation. The U.S. Constitution, for example, provides that members of Congress are privileged from suits based on their remarks on the floor of either house.[35] Courts have extended absolute privilege to other officials engaged in public proceedings, such as judges on the bench or city council members during official meetings. The guarantee is intended to provide these officials with a safe zone in which to speak their minds on important public issues. Absolute privilege also applies to public records from government agencies, legislative committee reports,[36] and trial transcripts.[37]

Absolute privilege does not, however, serve as a free pass to say or print anything "off the job." Its protection applies only to officials engaged in their official duties. The case *Hutchinson v. Proxmire* (1979) illustrates the point.[38] Senator William Proxmire invented the Golden Fleece Award to shame people who he believed had fleeced the American public. One of its recipients – a researcher given a federal grant to study aggression in monkeys – sued Proxmire for defamation after Proxmire distributed a news release and newsletters that accused the researcher of making a monkey out of tax payers. While Proxmire's comments on the floor of the Senate and to his staff were protected, his comments in the press releases and newsletters were not because they were not part of the legislative "deliberative process."

The *fair reporting privilege* is a common law defense against libel that protects those who report information from public records or proceedings later alleged to be defamatory. The justification for the privilege is two-fold. First, the public needs access to information regarding the workings of government. Second, information taken from public sources would already have been available to any citizen who could have attended the proceeding or read the public document. However, fair reporting is a qualified privilege that can be overcome. *Time* magazine was denied the privilege for an inaccurate report of a judicial proceeding.[39] To secure it, editors and writers need to report information fairly and accurately.

Some jurisdictions also recognize a common law privilege known as *neutral reportage*. The privilege protects those who report impartial and accurate representations of allegations made by a responsible party or organization against a public official.[40] It is based on the controversial assumption that the accusation itself is newsworthy, regardless of whether it is likely to be true. Some courts have flatly rejected the privilege because it provides no exception for actual malice and has never been recognized by the Supreme Court.[41] Jurisdictions that do recognize neutral reportage require that the reports be based on a "good faith" belief in their accuracy and compiled without additional commentary.

Mitigation of Damages

Printing or broadcasting an apology or a retraction will not serve as a defense to libel, but it may mitigate libel damages and serve as an indication to a court or jury that malice was not intended. However, if the defamatory statement appeared at the beginning of a broadcast, the retraction cannot appear at the end. It must be as conspicuous and prominent as the earlier statement.

Under the mitigation of damages doctrine, plaintiffs who are harmed by a tort are expected to take reasonable steps following the harmful act to minimize their damages. In libel cases, plaintiffs are expected to notify defendants of the libel so the defendant can issue a correction or retract the article. Many states have retraction statutes that shield media defendants who issue a retraction for a libelous statement from punitive damages. Other states bar plaintiffs from seeking punitive damages if they fail to notify defendants about problem material before filing suit.[42] For example, a Georgia court denied punitive damages in a libel suit against an electronic message board owner because the plaintiff failed to seek a retraction before filing suit.[43]

However, the applicability of retraction statutes is not always clear-cut. In many states retraction statutes are specific to certain media, such as newspapers, broadcasts, and periodicals. Courts do not always consider an online publication or website to be a "periodical." A California Court of Appeals held that the term applied to "all ongoing, recurring news publications," including online magazines.[44] But a Wisconsin appellate court would not apply the state's retraction statute to an interactive bulletin board service because communication of messages on the site did not appear at regular intervals.[45]

How Has Defamation Changed?

Before 1964, the U.S. approach to libel was like that of other common law countries. A plaintiff bringing a libel suit was required to show that the defendant's statement was published and that it was defamatory in nature. The plaintiff was not required to prove that the defendant's statement was false or that the defendant had acted with malice. If the defendant could not prove the statement's truth, malice was inferred. The plaintiff was not required to show that the statement damaged his or her reputation. Damages were presumed. A defendant could avoid strict liability by proving that the statement was either true or privileged. A defendant who could show the statement was privileged rebutted the presumption of malice, obligating the plaintiff to prove that the defendant had abused the privilege defense by acting in bad faith or with actual malice.[46]

By applying the First Amendment to defamation in *New York Times v. Sullivan* (1964) and its progeny, the Supreme Court overturned 200 years of settled law.[47] It did so on the theory that a court judgment, even one applying common law, constitutes an exercise of state action. In other areas of law, state action imposing content-based restrictions is presumed to be unconstitutional unless the government can establish that it is justified under strict scrutiny (the requirement that the regulation serve a compelling interest). In *New York Times v. Sullivan*, the Court applied what is essentially the same level of scrutiny but required the plaintiff to bear the burden of showing that the restriction on speech is justified.[48]

The plaintiff in *New York Times v. Sullivan* was a police commissioner who alleged that he had been libeled in a political ad that members of the civil rights movement had placed in the *New York Times*. The ad, which described a civil rights protest at Alabama State College, contained minor inaccuracies. Under common law, false statements of fact were unworthy of protection. The Supreme Court established a new framework for libel when it observed that errors in reporting are inevitable and that a policy of strict liability might discourage the media from covering public issues if they could not guarantee complete accuracy.[49]

The Court wanted to provide "breathing room" for debate, particularly where the actions of public officials were concerned. To that end, it required public officials who sued for libel to prove that the offensive statement was false and that the defendant made it with knowledge of its falsity or reckless disregard of the truth. Actual malice is an exceedingly difficult standard to prove because, in essence, it requires the plaintiff to probe the defendant's state of mind.[50]

New York Times v. Sullivan not only revolutionized libel law; it also had an unexpected impact on commercial speech. Advertisements were not constitutionally protected in 1964. But the ad in *Sullivan* concerned political speech, which has traditionally been accorded the highest protection. Consequently, the case was the first to put advertising under the umbrella of the First Amendment.

The Supreme Court extended the actual malice requirement to public figures in *Curtis Publishing Co. v. Butts* (1967), a case involving a well-known athletic director accused of fixing football games.[51] The Court defined public figures as individuals who are "intimately involved in the resolution of important public questions or, by reason of their fame, shape events in areas of concern to society at large."[52] In his concurring opinion, Chief Justice Warren explained, "[o]ur citizenry has a legitimate and substantial interest in the conduct of such persons, and freedom of the press to engage in uninhibited debate about their involvement in public issues and events is as crucial as it is in the case of public officials …"[53] In an accompanying case, the Supreme Court concluded that a plaintiff also could be classified as a public figure by "thrusting … his personality into the 'vortex' of an important public controversy."[54] The Court later clarified the distinction between general-purpose and limited-purpose public figures. It explained that people who hold positions of pervasive fame or power may be deemed public figures for all purposes. Individuals who voluntarily inject themselves or are drawn into a particular public controversy become public figures for a limited range of issues.[55]

For a short time, the actual malice standard was extended to private figure plaintiffs in libel cases involving "matters of general or public concern."[56] In *Rosenbloom v. Metromedia, Inc.* (1971), a plurality[57] of the Court held that the context of the defamation rather than the notoriety of the plaintiff should determine whether actual malice applied. The decision to impose the actual malice requirement on public officials and figures was intended to prevent holdings that might chill public debate on important issues, so extending the standard to all cases involving matters of public interest seemed to make sense at the time. But the new theory imposed a particular burden on private plaintiffs who were less equipped to fight libelous accusations than public figures.

The Court reversed itself three years later in *Gertz v. Robert Welch, Inc.* (1974).[58] It held that private figure plaintiffs should not be compelled to prove actual malice. Private figures are more vulnerable than public figures. They have not voluntarily assumed a position in the public eye and do not have ready access to the media to refute defamatory statements. However, if the case concerns a matter of public opinion, the defendant is still expected to prove some level of fault, generally negligence, on the part of the medium that printed or broadcast the defamatory statement. If the plaintiff seeks punitive damages, the level of fault rises to actual malice.

Finally, in *Dun & Bradstreet, Inc. v. Greenmoss Builders, Inc.* (1985), the Supreme Court considered how libel should be handled in cases involving private figure plaintiffs who sue over statements that do not involve the public interest. The case concerned a builder's suit against a credit agency that issued false credit reports to the builder's clients. The Court said "not all speech is of equal First Amendment importance."[59] When the issue is private, there "is no threat to the free and robust debate of public issues; there is no potential interference with a meaningful dialogue of ideas concerning self-government; and there is no threat of liability causing a reaction of self-censorship by the press."[60] Consequently, the First Amendment interest in protecting speech is deemed less important and the balance shifts toward protection of the plaintiff's interests.

The Court never resolved whether a private figure plaintiff suing over a private matter should be required to prove falsity and fault. Concurring statements by Chief Justice Burger and Justice White suggested that the Court intended to follow traditional common law principles in private plaintiff/private interest cases that do not require plaintiffs to prove falsity or fault.

The Single Publication Rule

The U.S. approach to defamation differs from other countries in another important respect. Under traditional common and civil law principles, every distribution of a libelous statement constitutes a separate publication and a libel plaintiff is entitled to sue for each one of them. The United States has adopted a "single publication rule," which allows libel plaintiffs to sue only once for libel, eliminating the possibility of multiple libel suits for the same defamatory statement.

The borderless nature of the Internet has highlighted this difference. In Europe, a plaintiff who is defamed in an Internet publication may sue in every country in which the publication may be downloaded, as long as the plaintiff can convince a court that he or she has a reputation to protect there. In the United States, the plaintiff may sue in only one jurisdiction, even if the defamatory statement was published on the Internet or broadcast via satellite and therefore accessible in every state.

Statutes of Limitation

All states impose a statute of limitations on defamation claims. Depending on the jurisdiction, this period ranges from one to three years after the date of publication. The statute of limitations is shorter in some states if the claim is filed against a government entity. California, for example, requires claims against state agencies to be filed within six months.

Courts have rejected the claim that publication on the Web constitutes continuous publication.[61] The statute of limitations on Internet material begins when the information is first published. Updating the website will not affect that unless the particular article alleged to be defamatory is altered.[62]

Criminal Libel

Although they are rarely enforced, statutes criminalizing the communication of a libelous statement are still on the books in fourteen states.[63] Criminal libel is subject to the same constitutional restraints imposed on civil libel. Before a state could successfully prosecute a libel against a public figure, for example, it would have to prove that the defendant acted with actual malice.[64]

In 2002, a jury convicted a news organization of criminal libel for the first time in 30 years. Criminal charges were filed against the *Kansas City News Observer* after it ran an article during the middle of the plaintiff's re-election for a mayoral position in Wyandotte County, Kansas, which implied that she did not meet the residency requirement for the office.[65] The *Observer*'s publisher, David Carson, and editor, Edward Powers – both disbarred attorneys – were known for using the publication to irritate local officials. In fact, the Kansas Supreme Court had to assign a judge from a neighboring county to preside over the trial because all the Wyandotte County judges recused themselves. A special prosecutor was appointed to replace the one who brought charges against Carson and Powers because he too had a contentious history with the paper. Carson and Powers claimed to have gotten their information from unnamed sources, but later admitted to knowing that the mayor lived in the county. A Kansas Court of Appeals upheld the criminal libel verdict in 2004 and the Supreme Court refused to review the decision. The misdemeanor fine was $700 for each.

Criminal libel statutes are more commonly applied to individuals operating websites than journalists. Unfortunately, some cases have involved students who used the Internet to express their frustrations with school. Utah, for example, applied its 100-year-old criminal libel law in a case against Ian Lake, a 16-year-old high school student who disparaged his teachers, principal, and schoolmates on his website. Lake described his principal as a drunk who was having an affair with the school secretary and suggested that one of his teachers was a homosexual leading a double life. Although there were no threats or references to violence on the website, the Beaver County Sheriff's Department arrested Lake and held him in juvenile detention for a week to avoid a "Columbine"-type of incident. When the juvenile court would not dismiss the case, Lake appealed. The Utah Supreme Court held that the statute, which made it a crime to "impeach the honesty, integrity, virtue, or reputation, or publish the natural defects of one who is alive and thereby expose him to public hatred, contempt, or ridicule," was unconstitutional because it presumed malice from the act of making a libelous statement and provided no immunity for truth.[66]

A Colorado judge threw out a case against a University of North Colorado student who doctored a photograph of a finance professor and published it in a satirical publication about the university. Thomas Mink, the editor of *The Howling Pig*, digitally altered a photo of professor Junius Peake to resemble Gene Simmons of the band KISS and added a caption describing its subject as "Junius Puke," a KISS roadie who made a fortune by riding "the tech bubble of the nineties like a $20 whore." Police confiscated Mink's computer and launched an investigation against him for violating a Colorado law that makes it a crime to "impeach the honesty, integrity, virtue, or reputation or expose the natural defects of one who is alive." The judge ordered police to return Mink's computer and barred his prosecution for libel but refused to rule on the constitutionality of the law.[67]

Media v. Non-Media Defendants

The Supreme Court ignored the question of whether there should be a different standard of review for a non-media defendant versus a media defendant in *Dun & Bradstreet, Inc. v. Greenmoss Builders, Inc.* It has since pointed out in two other cases that the issue remains unresolved.[68]

It is unlikely that the Court will make such a distinction. Setting up two different standards of constitutional review would force courts to decide what constitutes a legitimate medium. Courts are loath to make this determination because it puts the government in the position of defining what constitutes real journalism – and by extension who would qualify for freedom of the press. In *Branzburg v. Hayes* (1972), the Court indicated that liberty of the press belongs as much to the "lonely pamphleteer" as it does to the largest publisher. It described freedom of the press as a "fundamental personal right … not confined to newspapers and periodicals."[69] Particularly now, when technology is blurring the line between traditional journalism and citizen journalism, courts are unlikely to distinguish between an individual blogger, podcaster, or videographer and a traditional media defendant.

Recent cases suggest that bloggers and podcasters are entitled to the same level of First Amendment protection in libel cases. For example, a trial court in New York refused to enjoin the host of the podcast "DivorcingDaze" from making further statements about her ex-husband because they were protected by the First Amendment.[70] Likewise, in *New School Communications, Inc. v. Brodkorb* (2007), a Minnesota District Court granted summary judgment to a Republican blogger sued for defamation by a Democratic political advisor because the blogger had followed sound journalistic practices in covering the allegedly defamatory story, including the use of multiple sources.[71]

However, bloggers and podcasters, like traditional media, are equally subject to liability if their statements are libelous. David Milum, the first blogger to lose a libel case, ran a website about politics in Forsyth County, Georgia, on which he accused a local attorney of delivering bribes to a judge from drug dealers. A jury awarded the attorney $50,000 in compensatory damages, later affirmed by a Georgia appellate court.[72]

Following her suspension by a disciplinary committee for stalking a professor, a University of North Dakota student started UNDnews.com, a website that criticized the university and its professors. Her site alleged that the professor had sexually harassed her. He sued her for libel and won $3 million in damages. The former student argued that her statements were privileged. In upholding the award, the North Dakota Supreme Court clarified that while her statements during the disciplinary hearing – a quasi-judicial proceeding – were privileged, she was not free to repeat them on her website.[73]

If Internet posts are used to air private grievances against private figures, the awards can be especially high. A Florida woman who runs an online referral service for parents of troubled teenagers won an $11.3 million libel judgment against a Louisiana woman for posts she made on Internet bulletin boards accusing the plaintiff of being a "crook," a "con artist," and a "fraud." The defendant sought the plaintiff's help in extricating her sons from a boarding school where they were placed by their father. The plaintiff helped in that respect but denied the defendant additional information she requested regarding a student who claimed to have been sexually abused by the same boarding school. The defendant, a Hurricane Katrina victim, did not show up at trial to defend herself. In her absence, the jury awarded the plaintiff $6.3 million in compensatory and $5 million in punitive damages.[74] The defendant, who has no hope of paying the award, appealed it, but the award was upheld in 2007.[75]

Immunity for Interactive Computer Services

The ease with which Internet subscribers can post messages, both on their own websites and through other interactive websites, prompted Congress to carve out a safe harbor provision to protect online service providers from liability for their users' posts.

Section 230 of the Communication Decency Act shields operators of "interactive computer services" from liability for their users' defamatory comments. Congress enacted the provision to overrule *Stratton Oakmont, Inc. v. Prodigy Services Co.* (1995), in which a New York court held that Prodigy, an online service provider, could be considered a publisher vicariously liable for its users' posts.[76] In the United States, a publisher may be held liable for defamatory statements in a publication, but a distributor may not unless the distributor has actual knowledge of the libel. Courts assume that publishers have the opportunity to review the material in their publications before they disseminate it while distributors do not. From the court's perspective, Prodigy appeared to be exercising editorial control over its service by using software to screen out offensive language and a moderator to enforce content guidelines on its bulletin boards and therefore qualified as a publisher.

Congress realized that if interactive services were held liable for their users' posts based on their good-faith attempts to control indecency, none would exercise editorial control. The likely consequence would be an increase in indecency and other offensive content. So it included a safe harbor provision for ISPs in the Communications Decency Act. Section 230 says: "No provider or user of an interactive computer service shall be treated as the publisher or speaker of any information provided by another information content provider."[77] The provision has also been interpreted to apply to interactive websites, forums, listservs, and blogs that allow users to post comments.

A federal court applied Sec. 230 for the first time in *Zeran v. America Online, Inc.* (1995). Kenneth Zeran, the plaintiff, sued AOL because it did not do enough to stop one of its subscribers from anonymously posting hoax advertisements in his name. The ads, which included Zeran's name and number, promoted t-shirts and other paraphernalia supporting the bombing of the Oklahoma federal building in which 168 victims died. The plaintiff was threatened repeatedly following the anonymous posts. When AOL failed to stop them, Zeran sued it for libel. The court concluded that AOL was immune from the suit under the CDA, even though it had been notified of the libel. The Fourth Circuit upheld the decision.[78]

Some sites, like Don'tDateHimGirl and the now defunct Juicy Campus, have taken advantage of the exemption by allowing users to post gossip unchecked. Subjects of these posts are almost powerless to retaliate. Section 230 exempts the website from liability, while its operators shield posters through coding that protects their anonymity. An individual who wanted to pursue a libel claim against a message board poster would have to persuade a court to issue a subpoena for the user's IP address.

Although it is most frequently used to shield ISPs from defamation claims, courts have used Sec. 230 to bar claims for invasion of privacy, misappropriation of trade secrets, and negligence. In 2008, the U.S. Court of Appeals for the Fifth Circuit upheld a Texas court's decision to dismiss negligence claims against MySpace for failing to protect a thirteen-year-old from sexual predators by using age verification software to screen her profile for truthfulness.[79] By lying about her age the girl had circumvented a safety feature that would have prevented the public display of her profile. The court concluded that MySpace was not responsible because it was merely the distributor of third-party content, not a content provider. However, Section 230 does not shield interactive service providers against liability for users' posts if they ignore criminal acts or intellectual property claims.

Photo Illustrations / Digitally Altering Images

Misleading and harmful information can be conveyed through imagery just as easily as through words. Digital imaging software makes it relatively easy to alter an image so that seeing is no longer believing.

The *Final Call*, a Nation of Islam paper, Photoshopped prison attire on a woman whose photo was randomly selected from its archives to illustrate the article "Mothers in Prison, Children in Crisis." The woman, Tatia Morsette, was a successful entertainment promoter who had never been incarcerated. No one tried to identify Morsette before digitally altering a photo of her holding her child while standing beside two other women.

When Morsette complained, the paper published a clarification indicating that the photo illustration was not meant to imply that the women were in prison, but it never apologized. Morsette sued for libel. The jury awarded her $1.3 million, a sum later reduced when punitive damages were taken away because the paper had not intended to harm her.[80]

Crystal Kiesau, a deputy sheriff in Buchanan County, Iowa, sued a fellow deputy for libel and invasion of privacy when he digitally altered her picture to make it appear that she was exposing her breasts. The defendant, Tracey Bantz, downloaded a picture of Kiesau standing with her K-9 dog in front of her sheriff's vehicle from a departmental website, then e-mailed the altered image to others. The jury concluded that the defamation was libel per se, which in Iowa comes with a presumption of damage, falsity, and malice in private figure cases. The Iowa Supreme Court upheld the verdict.[81] It rejected Bantz's argument that Kiesau was a public figure because she was a police officer or a limited public figure because she appeared on the website.

Libel in Fiction

Fiction is often inspired by real life. But changing the names of the "characters" in a real-life story and calling it fiction may lead to a libel claim if the characters are identifiable as real people. A story published in *Seventeen* magazine that was labeled as fiction was found to be defamatory in 1991. The central character, Bryson, who was labeled a "slut," shared characteristics with a girl named Kimberly Bryson who went to school with the author. The Illinois Supreme Court said "The fact that the author used the plaintiff's actual name [made] it reasonable that third persons would interpret the story as referring to the plaintiff despite the fictional label."[82]

In 2008, a New York appellate court judge allowed a libel-in-fiction claim against the producers of Law & Order to move forward, despite the show's disclaimer that it was fiction. Ravi Batra, an Indian-born New York attorney, filed the lawsuit arguing that an episode defamed him. In 2003, the *New York Times* ran an article about Batra, describing his unusual influence among Brooklyn judges. At the time, the district attorney's office was investigating allegations that judgeships could be bought in Brooklyn. A judge charged with corruption hinted that Batra and an associate in his law firm, who were both members of a judicial screening panel, were involved and offered to wear a hidden wire to a meeting with Batra to ask if money could influence the selection process. Nothing incriminating came from the meeting and Batra was never charged with anything, but his business associate was subsequently convicted of extortion in another case and the judge who wore the wire went to jail. Later that year, Law & Order ran an episode that portrayed an Indian-born New York attorney, named Ravi Patel, bribing a Brooklyn judge.[83] A Supreme Court judge in Batra's case said it was possible that viewers would identify the character as Batra based on the character's name, ethnicity, and appearance.[84] She said Batra, who is a limited-purpose public figure due to his connection with the corruption scandal, would have to demonstrate that the episode identified him and that viewers were convinced that parts about him were not fictional.

In an unsuccessful libel suit against the publisher of the book *Primary Colors*, a New York court wrote: "For a fictional character to constitute actionable defamation, the description of the fictional character must be so closely akin to the real person claiming to be defamed that a reader of the book, knowing the real person, would have no difficulty linking the two. Superficial similarities are insufficient."[85]

Satire and Parody

By its nature satire is not only critical of its subjects, who it often names, but also knowingly false. It may also include outrageous fictionalized quotations attributed to the subject, making it a prime target for libel suits. Meanwhile parody ridicules sacred cows through imitation. Both are protected precisely because they are outrageous and therefore unlikely to be taken seriously. The Supreme Court considers satire and parody to be a valuable part of political debate. It has said, "Nothing is more thoroughly democratic than to have the high-and-mighty lampooned and spoofed. An observant electorate may also gain by watching the reactions of objects of satiric comment, noting those who take themselves seriously and those whose self-perspective is somewhat more relaxed."[86]

In *New Times, Inc. v. Isaacks* (2004), a Dallas judge and district attorney sued a newspaper that ran a satirical article about them in its print and online editions.[87] Denton County District Attorney Bruce Isaacks and Juvenile Court Judge Darlene Whitten filed a libel suit against the *Dallas Observer* after it published an article that mocked them for arresting and jailing a 6-year-old girl for writing a book report on Maurice Sendak's classic *Where The Wild Things Are*, that included references to "cannibalism, fanaticism and disorderly conduct." The article was laced with false quotes, including one from Whitten that said: "Any implication of violence in a school situation, even if it was just contained in a first grader's book report, is reason enough for panic and overreaction … it's time for us to stop treating kids like children." A quote attributed to Isaacks said: "We've considered having her certified to stand trial as an adult, but even in Texas there are some limits." It also described authorities reviewing her disciplinary record "which included reprimands for spraying a boy with pineapple juice and sitting on her feet."

The article was intended as a form of commentary on another case involving a 13-year-old boy who was sent to juvenile detention for five days by Whitten for a

Halloween story he wrote that depicted the shooting of a teacher and two students. The seventh grader penned the tale for a class assignment to write a scary story and, in fact, earned a 100 on it. But the principal read it and called juvenile authorities, who sent sheriff's deputies to pull the boy out of school. Issacks declined to prosecute the student but commented that he was a discipline problem and school authorities were "legitimately concerned."

Whitten demanded an apology from the paper but got a snarky clarification instead stating:

> Unfortunately, some people – commonly known as "clueless" or "Judge Darlene Whitten" – did not get, or did not appreciate, the joke behind the news story "Stop the madness," which appeared in last week's *Dallas Observer*.
>
> Here's a clue for our cerebrally challenged readers who thought the story was real: It wasn't. It was a joke. We made it up. Not even Judge Whitten, we hope, would throw a 6-year-old girl in the slammer for writing a book report. Not yet, anyway.[88]

New Times defended the article as rhetorical hyperbole. Lower courts denied summary judgment to the defendants, because they thought it failed "to provide any notice to a reasonable reader that it was a satire or parody."[89] But the Texas Supreme Court dismissed the case. It clarified that "the test is whether the publication could be reasonably understood as describing actual facts."[90] This must be taken from the perspective of a person of ordinary intelligence, not the weakest link. "Thus, the question is not whether some actual readers were mislead, as they inevitably will be, but whether the hypothetical reasonable reader could be."[91] Even though the article bore no disclaimer and was indexed in the news section, the court found plenty of clues that the piece was satiric.

The court rejected the plaintiffs' argument that the article was published with actual malice because defendants knew the statements in it were false. Acceptance of that argument would strip satire of all protection. It also considered the paper's attempt to clarify that the article was satire evidence of a lack of malice.

Intentional Infliction of Emotional Distress

To get around the requirement to show actual malice on the part of the defendant in a libel case, some plaintiffs have opted to sue on other theories, like intentional infliction of emotional distress and false light (an invasion of privacy tort described in the next chapter).

Televangelist Jerry Falwell sued *Hustler* magazine for mocking him in a parody of a Campari Liqueur campaign.[92] Campari ran a series of ads dubbed "My First Time" in which celebrity subjects of the ads recalled their first time to try Campari. *Hustler's* parody, titled "Jerry Falwell talks about his first time," included Falwell's picture and an "interview" in which he recounted his first sexual experience, a drunken liaison in an outhouse with his mother. The ad included the disclaimer "ad parody – not to be taken seriously" at the bottom of the page.[93] Falwell sued. Although the jury found that the ad could not "reasonably be understood as describing actual facts about [Falwell] or actual events in which [he] participated," and was therefore not defamatory, it awarded Falwell damages for intentional infliction of emotional distress.[94] The Fourth Circuit affirmed the verdict, but the Supreme Court reversed.

The Court was concerned that public figures could use the tort of intentional infliction of emotional distress to sidestep actual malice, so it extended actual malice to it.

In most states, the elements required to show intentional infliction of emotional distress are:

- that the defendant's conduct was extreme and outrageous;
- that the defendant either intended or was aware of a high probability that the action would cause emotional distress;
- that the plaintiff suffered severe or extreme emotional distress; and
- that the cause of the suffering is the defendant's conduct.

In *Hustler v. Falwell*, the Supreme Court said those factors were not sufficient in cases involving public figures. It said a standard based on outrageousness, which is inherently subjective, "runs afoul of our longstanding refusal to allow damages to be awarded because the speech in question may have an adverse emotional impact on the audience."[95]

It also said that intent to harm is not sufficient because it had already held that expression motivated by hatred or ill will is protected by the First Amendment.[96] "Debate on public issues will not be uninhibited if the speaker must run the risk that it will be proved in court that he spoke out of hatred; even if he did speak out of hatred, utterances honestly believed contribute to the free interchange of ideas and the ascertainment of truth."[97] A contrary holding would subject political cartoonists and satirists to liability because their criticism is deliberate.

The Court held that "public figures and public officials may not recover for the tort of intentional infliction of emotional distress … without showing … that the publication contains a false statement of fact which was made with 'actual malice.'"[98] By *false statement of fact*, the Court means a false statement that would be taken literally – not a false statement such as the outhouse story. Through its choice to protect *Hustler*'s parody, the Court implicitly rejected the notion that knowledge of falsity in parody or satire constituted actual malice.

In 2007, a federal jury awarded Albert Snyder, the father of a soldier killed in Iraq, $10.9 million for invasion of privacy and intentional infliction of emotional distress in a lawsuit against Fred Phelps, the leader of Westboro Baptist Church. The Kansas-based congregation believes God kills soldiers and allowed the Sept. 11 attacks to punish the United States for tolerating homosexuality. Members of the church picketed at the soldier's funeral with signs that said "Thank God for dead soldiers" and posted derogatory statements about him on their website, GodHatesFags.com. Citing *Hustler Magazine v. Falwell*, the U.S. Court of Appeals for the Fourth Circuit reversed the judgment. The court concluded that the defendant's statements were exaggerated rhetoric about issues of public concern – homosexuals in the military, morality in the United States, and scandals in the Catholic Church – and not statements that could reasonably be interpreted as facts about the soldier or his family. As such, they were protected by the First Amendment.[99]

Questions for Discussion

1. How does the American concept of libel law differ from other common law and civil law countries?
2. What is the difference between a public and private figure plaintiff in a libel case?
3. How does knowledge of falsity differ from reckless disregard of the truth?
4. Why have ISPs been given immunity from their subscribers' libelous posts?

10

Invasion of Privacy

Privacy is the right to control access to information about ourselves. States have described it as a natural right essential to the pursuit of life, liberty, and happiness. But privacy is also a right balanced against society's need for information, which has never been greater.

In general, privacy law has evolved in a piecemeal fashion rather than as a response to a unified policy. Privacy is not mentioned in the U.S. Constitution, but it is included in some state constitutions. A common law right to privacy was first recognized by the Georgia Supreme Court in 1905.[1] By the mid 1930s, the American Law Institute included invasion of privacy as an actionable tort in its distillation of tort law, the *Restatement of Torts*, and more courts began to acknowledge it. Today, most jurisdictions recognize a right to privacy through common or statutory law, but protections vary by jurisdiction and are generally waived if the information revealed is in the public's interest.

This chapter will discuss protections for privacy under common law and through federal and state statues. It will describe the four privacy torts recognized in the *Second Restatement of Torts*: intrusion upon seclusion, public disclosure of private facts, misappropriation of identity for commercial purposes, and portrayal in false light. It will also consider the extent of our right to privacy with regard to digital media at home, at work, and online.

Whose Privacy Is Protected?

Privacy laws protect people from the emotional distress caused by an unexpected intrusion into their private affairs or loss of control over their personal information. Because its emphasis is on protection of feelings, rather than reputation as in defamation law, privacy law applies only to people.[2] Corporations and other organizations that wish to guard their information must do so through intellectual property or contract law.

As a general rule, privacy rights apply only to the living, but there are exceptions. For example, the common law right of publicity, which protects an individual's exclusive right to exploit the market value of his or her identity, may be inherited after death. The U.S. Court of Appeals for the District of Columbia Circuit has also concluded that the privacy exception to the Freedom of Information Act may survive death, if the potential harm inflicted on surviving family members by its release would outweigh the public's interest in the information.[3]

Constitutional Protections for Privacy

While the U.S. Constitution protects speech and press through the First Amendment, there is no equivalent protection for personal privacy. In fact, the word privacy never appears in the Constitution. Consequently, when rights to privacy and expression compete, expression usually emerges as the victor in American jurisprudence.

The Supreme Court has found *penumbral protections* for privacy cast by other amendments. It has observed, for example, that the First Amendment's implied right of association, the Fourth Amendment's prohibition against unreasonable searches and seizures, and the Fifth Amendment's right against self incrimination all suggest an implied right to privacy. Moreover, the Ninth Amendment states that the enumeration of rights in the Constitution "shall not be construed to deny or disparage others retained by the people." The Court has used this theory to strike down statutes that interfere with marital relations and reproductive rights, but it has not extended it to other spheres of privacy protection.[4]

Ten states have included privacy provisions in their constitutions. Some of them protect privacy as an individual right. These include Alaska (Art. I, § 22); California (Art. I, § 1); Florida (Art. I, § 23); Hawaii (Art. I, § 6); and Montana (Art. II, § 10). Others mention a right to privacy within provisions that guard against unreasonable searches and seizures. These are Arizona (Art. II, § 8); Hawaii (Art. I, § 7); Illinois (Art. I, § 6); Louisiana (Art. I, § 5); South Carolina (Art. 1, § 10); and Washington (Art. I, § 7).

Privacy Protection under Common Law

Common law protects people against four invasion of privacy torts: (1) unreasonable intrusions into private affairs, (2) publicity given to private facts, (3) appropriation of a person's name or likenesses, and (4) publication of information that unreasonably places a person in false light.

Most states protect privacy interests under common law. Nebraska, New York, North Dakota, and Wyoming are the exceptions. Nebraska and New York recognize statutory protections for privacy, but do not recognize a common law right to privacy.[5] North Dakota and Wyoming do not recognize invasion of privacy as an actionable tort.

States that recognize common law privacy protections do so in varying degrees. Some states recognize only two or three of the four privacy torts. Consequently, it is important to keep in mind that a decision rendered in one jurisdiction may not be applicable in another. The descriptions provided here offer general guidelines. It is important to understand the law in the particular state in which you work.

Intrusion upon seclusion

Intrusion upon seclusion is what we classically think of as invasion of privacy – the violation of a person's private space. The tort requires an intentional intrusion "upon the solitude or seclusion of another or his private affairs or concerns" that is highly offensive to a reasonable person.[6] The intrusion may be physical, such as trespassing on someone's property to peep in the windows or open the mail. Or it may be electronic, such as the use of a recording or wiretap device or illegal access to phone mail or e-mail. In assessing whether the intrusion could be construed as highly offensive, a court will consider: the degree of intrusion, the intruder's conduct, the circumstances surrounding the intrusion, the intruder's motives, the location or setting of the intrusion, and the plaintiff's reasonable expectation of privacy.[7]

Unlike other privacy torts, intrusion upon seclusion does not depend on the kind of information collected or its publication. It is based solely on the process used to gather information and whether it is highly offensive. Normal reporting practices do not constitute an invasion of privacy. It is fine to ask the subject of a story for an interview; to gather information about the person from neighbors, friends, and enemies; and to search for information through public records.

No expectation of privacy in public   The level of privacy protection accorded under common law depends on the person's reasonable expectation of privacy under the circumstances. There is no expectation of privacy in a public place. It would be perfectly legal, for example, to photograph or video a couple's public display of affection in a city park, or any other activity conducted in plain view, even if the image is captured surreptitiously.

The *standing-in doctrine* allows a person to take a picture or video of anything that occurs out in the open, under the theory that the photographer is standing in for others who would have seen the same thing had they been there. An intrusion cannot be something that the general public is free to view. Based on this principle, a Washington appellate court upheld summary judgment in favor of a news station photographer who videoed his subject through a drugstore window.[8] The court pointed out that the cameraman recorded something that any passerby also could have seen.

The exception to this general rule involves photos that anyone would consider humiliating. In 1964, an Alabama court found that that a newspaper's photo of a woman whose dress had blown up above her waist as she descended from a county fair ride was an invasion of privacy.[9] It noted that although she had given up an expectation of privacy in a public setting, her release did not give the newspaper a right to publish a photo that would cause embarrassment to a person of reasonable sensitivity.

The proliferation of cell phones with cameras has contributed to a more contemporary version of this problem. Worldwide, men are snapping photos under women's skirts, a phenomenon called *upskirting*, or down their shirts, a companion practice called *downblousing*. Thousands of these images wind up on websites like Flickr or photobin.com. More than 25 states now consider it illegal to photograph a person's private parts in a public place.[10] Federal law also prohibits the use of camera equipment to capture an image of an individual's private area without consent when the person has a reasonable expectation of privacy. Within its definition of reasonable expectation of privacy, the law includes "circumstances in which a reasonable person would believe that a private area of the individual would not be visible to the public, regardless of whether that person is in a public or private place."[11]

Full expectation of privacy at home   There is a complete expectation of privacy in one's home. This principle was established in *Dietemann v. Time, Inc.* (1971), which involved an invasion of privacy suit against the publisher of *Life* magazine.[12] Two *Life* reporters, working in conjunction with the Los Angeles District Attorney's office, visited the home of a plumber masquerading as a doctor under the pretense of requiring his medical services. While one was "examined" the other secretly filmed and recorded the plumber's diagnosis. The resulting article, published after his arrest, incorporated quotes and pictures surreptitiously gathered during the visit. The Ninth Circuit held that even though Dietemann had invited the journalists in, he was still entitled to an expectation of privacy within his home. The court determined that "One who invites another to his home or office takes a risk that the visitor may not be what he seems, and that the visitor may repeat all he hears and observes when he leaves. But he does not and should not be required to take the risk that what is heard and seen will be transmitted by photograph or recording …"[13]

Limited expectation of privacy at work   There is a limited right to privacy in one's workplace, depending on the setting. In *Sanders v. ABC* (1999), the Supreme Court of California held that a plaintiff's expectation of privacy in the workplace does not have to be complete in order to sue for intrusion. The case involved a "PrimeTime Live" investigation of a psychic hotline. A reporter for the show obtained a job as a telepsychic and covertly taped conversations with other employees. Two of them sued for intrusion upon seclusion. The court held that "[i]n an office or other workplace to which the general public does not have unfettered access, employees may enjoy a limited, but legitimate, expectation that their conversations and other interactions will not be secretly videotaped by undercover television reporters."[14]

This is true regardless of whether other employees are privy to the conversation. But the court cautioned "we do not hold or imply that investigative journalists necessarily commit a tort by secretly recording events and conversations in offices, stores or other workplaces. Whether a reasonable expectation of privacy is violated by such recording depends on the exact nature of the conduct and all the surrounding circumstances."[15] Some workplaces are too open to the public to suggest a reasonable expectation of privacy.

Company e-mail and phone mail is generally not considered private. If an employer runs the system, it has a right to review content on it – a subject discussed in greater depth later in this chapter.

Expectation of privacy in other areas   There is no comprehensive list of places in which privacy is protected. But in other intrusion cases, courts assumed that individuals had an expectation of privacy in a prison exercise room,[16] hospital room,[17] dressing room,[18] private dining room at a restaurant,[19] and private party.[20]

Courts have also held that people have a reasonable expectation that their social security numbers will be kept private. The New Hampshire Supreme Court observed that a "person's interest in maintaining the privacy of his or her SSN has been recognized by numerous federal and state statutes."[21] Consequently, "the entities to which this information is disclosed and their employees are bound by legal, and, perhaps, contractual constraints to hold SSNs in confidence to ensure that they remain private."[22] The court considered whether the unauthorized release of someone's social security number could be an intrusion upon seclusion in *Remsburg v. Docusearch, Inc.* (2003). The case concerned an information broker's liability for the sale of a woman's social security number to a stalker who murdered her. Liam Youens contacted Docusearch through its website to request Amy Lynn Boyer's social security number and place of employment. Docusearch provided the social security number, gleaned from Boyer's credit report, and place of employment, obtained by a subcontractor who telephoned Boyer and tricked her into providing the information. After acquiring the information, Youens drove to Boyer's workplace, fatally shot her, and then killed himself. Police later learned that Youens, who had become obsessed with Boyer in high school, maintained an online diary about stalking and killing her.

The court said that "a person whose SSN is obtained by an investigator from a credit reporting agency without the person's knowledge or permission may have a cause of action for intrusion upon seclusion for damages caused by the sale of the SSN," if he or she could prove the intrusion would have been offensive to a reasonable person.[23] The fact finder determining whether the intrusion was offensive would have to consider "the degree of intrusion, the context, conduct, and circumstances surrounding the intrusion as well as the intruder's motives and objectives, the setting into which he intrudes, and the expectations of those whose privacy is invaded."[24] Although a work address is generally not considered private information, the court held the information broker could be liable under the state's

Consumer Protection Act for damages caused by its pretext call to get information it used for commercial purposes.

Publicity given to private life

Publicizing information that concerns the private life of another person can be considered an invasion of privacy if the information published (1) would be highly offensive to a reasonable person and (2) is not of legitimate public concern. In determining whether the information is of legitimate public concern, the *Second Restatement of Torts* says "the line is to be drawn when the publicity ceases to be the giving of information to which the public is entitled, and becomes a morbid and sensational prying into private lives for its own sake."[25] The private information shared, such as a medical condition, financial difficulty, sexual preference, or a humiliating experience, must be of a highly personal nature.

Newsworthy information is protected   The context in which the information is revealed is as important as the information itself. The publication of newsworthy information is protected from liability. Whether the information is newsworthy is a matter for a jury (or judge in a bench trial) to decide. Factors affecting that consideration include the public value of the information, the extent of the intrusion into the person's private affairs, and the extent to which the person may have voluntarily assumed a position of public notoriety.

Information must be communicated widely   A private fact communicated to one person or a small group of people does not constitute an invasion of privacy.[26] The word *publicity* differs from the word *publication*. Publication refers to communication of information to a third person. Publicity refers to communication of information to the public at large, or at least to a very large group of people so that the information becomes public knowledge.[27] The means of communication is not important. It may be oral, written, or broadcast. It is the reach of the communication that matters.

The Supreme Court has refused to answer categorically whether the publication of true information may ever be punished consistently with the First Amendment. So courts are reluctant to impose liability on the publication of true facts. Some jurisdictions have refused to recognize the tort. These states include Alaska, Nebraska, New York, North Carolina, North Dakota, Oregon, Virginia, and Wyoming.

Information in public records is not protected   Once information has appeared in a public record it is no longer considered a private fact and is permissible to publish. This is particularly true of information from judicial proceedings. In *Cox Broadcasting v. Cohn* (1975), the Supreme Court considered the constitutionality of a Georgia statute that made it a crime to broadcast a rape victim's name. The Court held that "the First and Fourteenth Amendments command nothing less than that the States may not impose sanctions on the publication of truthful information contained in official court records open to public inspection."[28] It concluded that coverage of judicial proceedings fell within the press's public obligations. Records from criminal proceedings may include information about the defendant as well as the defendant's victims. Civil suits may include medical histories, mental health data, financial information, and intimate details about a person's life required to establish damages. States may not punish individuals for reproducing this information.

In fact, absent a need to further a state interest of the highest order, a medium cannot be punished for publishing truthful information obtained lawfully about a matter of public interest.[29] In *Florida Star v. B.J.F.* (1989), the Supreme Court considered whether a newspaper could be punished under a Florida statute that prohibited publication of a rape victim's identity for revealing a victim's name that was mistakenly included in a police report. The Court held that "[o]nce the government has placed [confidential] information in the public domain, 'reliance must rest upon those who decide what to publish or broadcast,' … and hopes for restitution must rest upon the willingness of the government to compensate victims for their loss of privacy."[30] States that wish to protect the identity of rape victims and juvenile offenders must do so by withholding that information from public records, not by barring the media from using it. However, most media voluntarily withhold that information because they consider it the right thing to do.

The passage of time   Occasionally, the media are sued for doing anniversary or "where are they now" types of stories that rehash information from the lives of individuals who were once publicly known but have since been forgotten. The passage of time will not make information that was once public private again. However, it does not create a license to disclose new information of a private nature about a subject who has attempted to resume a private life.

Appropriation of name or likeness and right of publicity

Appropriation, the oldest invasion of privacy tort, is committed when someone "appropriates to his own use or benefit the name or likeness of another."[31] Most states limit appropriation claims to unauthorized uses for commercial purposes.

As a privacy right, appropriation protects individuals from the emotional distress or embarrassment that might result from having their name or likeness used in an advertisement without their permission. For example, in *Cohen v. Herbal Concepts, Inc.* (1984), a court denied summary judgment to a company that used a picture of the plaintiffs (a mother and her four-year-old daughter) bathing nude in an advertisement for the defendant's cellulite removal product.[32] As private individuals, the plaintiffs were able to assert emotional harm derived from the humiliation of being pictured in the ad.

But appropriation also operates like a property right by protecting an individu-al's exclusive use of his or her name and likeness for economic benefit. Russell Christoff, a model who did a photo shoot for Taster's Choice in 1986, was never called back, so he assumed the company was not interested in using his photo. He was shocked to learn in 2002 that the company had been using his image on its label worldwide for seven years without compensating him. Christoff sued Nestlé, which owns Taster's Choice, for appropriation of his image. A jury awarded him $330,000 in actual damages and $15 million in punitive damages, representing the company's profits from Taster's Choice while Christoff's face was on the jars. A California Court of Appeals reversed because Christoff failed to show that Nestle's $15 million profit was due to his likeness.[33] The court also held that Christoff's suit was time-barred. It applied the single publication rule, normally used for defama-tion, to appropriation, which requires that suits be filed within two years of first publication.[34] In August of 2009, the California Supreme Court agreed that the single publication rule applies to misappropriation claims. But it did not agree that Nestlé's use of Christoff's likeness necessarily constituted a single publication. It remanded the case to a lower court to consider whether the varied uses of Christoff's likeness – on coffee jars, coupons and advertisements – amounted to a single integrated publication.[35]

Average individuals will find it easier to use appropriation to protect their emo-tional interests. It is difficult for private plaintiffs to prove that a defendant's use of their name or likeness appropriated its economic value unless they could claim value in their identities before the use. On the other hand, celebrities find greater success in appropriation's emphasis on property rights. After choosing to live in the public eye, it is hard for them to argue that appropriation of their identities has caused them emotional pain.

Right of publicity   While some states continue to categorize the property interest in identity under privacy law, approximately half recognize a separate tort called "right of publicity." Right of publicity, a tort that emerged in 1953, protects those who suffer economic rather than emotional harm from the appropriation of their identities.[36] To pursue a right of publicity claim a person must be able to show that his or her identity has economic value. The Supreme Court has observed a similarity between right of publicity and copyright law. Not only does right of publicity protect the performer's right to be compensated for his or her work, but it also provides an economic incentive for the performer to invest in the produc-tion of new acts.[37] Like other property rights, right of publicity is transferable. The right can be licensed to third parties and, in some states, bequeathed to others at death.[38]

Right of publicity is distinct from appropriation in that it protects more than name and likeness. It protects all recognizable aspects of a person's personality. Bette Midler, for example, used it to sue a company that hired someone to imper-sonate her voice for an ad to sell cars.[39] Jacqueline Kennedy Onassis used it to prevent a clothing manufacturer from using a look-alike model to evoke her image in an advertisement.[40] Vanna White used it to sue Samsung Electronics for a commercial with a female robot wearing a blond wig and turning letters.[41]

News and information exemption   Courts show broad deference to the First Amendment in appropriation and right of publicity claims involving editorial content. The names and likenesses of individuals may be used for news and information purposes without their permission. If the contrary were true, individuals could use appropriation or right of publicity to stifle public criticism.[42]

Furthermore, the fact that a publication, broadcast, or film is made for profit makes no difference to the "newsworthiness" defense. Although the appropriation tort is meant to punish unauthorized commercial use of a name or image, the term *commercial use* does not refer to use in a commercial medium. A commercial use is an invitation to conduct a transaction.

The news and information exemption is not, however, a license to steal an artist's work. The Supreme Court has held that the First Amendment and right of publicity must be balanced. In *Zacchini v. Scripps-Howard Broadcasting Co.* (1977), for example, the Court rejected a news organization's argument that the First Amendment protected its right to broadcast a performer's entire act without permission.[43]

In right of publicity cases, a public figure can only recover damages for noncommercial speech by proving actual malice by clear and convincing evidence. Clint Eastwood did this in a suit against the *National Enquirer*. The magazine ran an article that it touted as an exclusive with Eastwood. Because Eastwood never gave an interview to the *Enquirer*, or anyone else, he sued under California's right of publicity statute. The article included quotes, scene-setting phrases (such as "he said with a chuckle") that implied the writer and star had conversed, and a byline by an *Enquirer* assistant editor. The court agreed that taken together, the magazine's actions showed an intent to convey a false impression that Eastwood willingly granted an interview to the *Enquirer*.[44]

In contrast, the Ninth Circuit held that *Los Angeles Magazine*'s inclusion of a digitally altered photo of Dustin Hoffman in a fashion spread was protected by the First Amendment. Using digital imaging software, the magazine clothed Hollywood icons Grace Kelly, Marilyn Monroe, and Cary Grant in the latest fall fashions. Hoffman's photo from the film *Tootsie* was updated with a new designer gown. Hoffman won a right of publicity claim against the magazine at the district level, but the Court of Appeals reversed. It found the article's commercial aspects to be "inextricably entwined" with expressive elements that could not be separated "from the fully protected whole."[45] Also, because the magazine referred to its use of digital technology to alter the famous photos, there was no evidence that the defendant intended to mislead the public to believe that Hoffman posed for the picture.

Booth rule   A medium that uses a person's name or likeness for informational purposes is allowed to use the same piece later to advertise itself. This exception to appropriation, known as the Booth Rule, was created by the New York Supreme

Court in *Booth v. Curtis Publishing Co.* (1962).[46] Actress Shirley Booth sued the publishers of *Holiday* magazine for appropriating her image to advertise the magazine. Booth had given the magazine permission to use her image in a travel feature, but had not authorized its use for advertising purposes. The court said media must be able to promote themselves through images that are representative of their content. However, the exception does not allow publications to use such images to advertise other products.

Images as art In general, courts consider the artistic use of an image to be a protected form of expression. However, sorting out what is and is not art may be a challenge. Some states limit the art exemption to transformative rather than duplicative likenesses.[47] Others have limited the exemption to original works, but not reproductions.[48] A New York appellate court rejected a privacy claim by a Hasidic Jew who protested the unauthorized use of his image in a photography exhibit, depicting candid shots of people walking through Times Square.[49] The plaintiff, who never consented to be photographed, objected to the use of his photo based on his religious conviction that it violated the second commandment prohibition against graven images. The court concluded that the images, which were reviewed and exhibited to the artistic community, were art. The fact that the photos were exhibited and sold through a for-profit art gallery did not convert the art into something used for trade purposes.

Portrayal in false light

Publishing information that casts someone in a false light constitutes an invasion of privacy in some jurisdictions. An actionable claim for false light requires that:

1. the information published must be offensive to a reasonable person; and
2. the publisher of the material must be at fault.

In other words, the publisher must have "had knowledge of or acted in reckless disregard as to the falsity of the publicized matter and the false light in which the other would be placed."[50]

The Supreme Court recognized false light in *Time, Inc. v. Hill* (1967), its first privacy case involving the media.[51] The case involved an article published in *Life* magazine about a Broadway play that portrayed a family's experience when it was held hostage by escaped convicts. Although the family was never harmed, the play spiced up the story with violence. The Hill family sued *Life*'s publishers for false light because it represented the play as an accurate portrayal of what happened. The Supreme Court reviewed their claim on the heels of *Rosenbloom v. Metromedia* (1971), a defamation case in which the Court extended the actual malice standard it developed for public officials in *Times v. Sullivan* to matters of public interest.[52] The Court applied the same standard to false light. It held that plaintiffs that sue for false light in matters of public interest must prove the story was published with knowledge of falsity or reckless disregard of the truth. In 1974, the Supreme Court overturned *Rosenbloom* when it held in *Gertz v. Welch* that private figures do not have to prove actual malice in matters of public interest.[53] A few months after *Gertz*, the Court considered another false light case involving a private figure plaintiff and a matter of public interest. The jury in the case had found actual malice on the part of the defendant. The Court did not use the opportunity to decide whether, in light of *Gertz*, a more relaxed standard would have been sufficient. It left states to draw their own conclusions about the appropriate standard to set.[54]

Similarity between false light and defamation   False light claims are often brought in conjunction with defamation claims, but the theory behind false light is different. It is based on emotional distress caused by the false portrayal rather than damage to reputation. Distinguishing between the two concepts, the Minnesota Supreme Court stated: "The primary difference between defamation and false light is that defamation addresses harm to reputation in the external world, while false light protects harm to one's inner self."[55] Minnesota is one of several states that have rejected false light because the tort is too similar to defamation. Others that do not recognize false light include Colorado, Florida, Massachusetts, Missouri, New York, North Carolina, Texas, Virginia, and Wisconsin.[56] States that do not acknowledge false light have concluded that the tort sits in tension with the First Amendment because it offers protection that overlaps defamation without providing defamation's safeguards for speech.

Actual malice for public figures   Public figures must show actual malice in false light cases. In *Solano v. Playgirl* (2002), Baywatch star Jose Solano Jr. sued *Playgirl* for false light after his photo appeared on the magazine's cover between the headlines "Primetime's Sexy Young Stars Exposed" and "12 Sizzling Centerfolds Ready to Score With You."[57] He argued that the cover cast him in a false light by implying both that he agreed to do an interview with the magazine and that he would appear nude inside it. Finding that Solano had established a genuine issue for trial, the Ninth Circuit reversed the district court's order of summary judgment in favor of *Playgirl*. It observed that Solano might be able to prove actual malice by clear and convincing evidence because members of the editorial staff had expressed concern before publication that the cover suggested Solano would appear nude. The case was subsequently settled.

Must be believable   Like defamation, false light must be believable. A court will not find false light in a parody or spoof that no reasonable person would consider factual. A Utah court of appeals granted summary judgment to defendants in a privacy suit filed against Marriott Ownership Resorts by an employee and his spouse over an embarrassing video shown at the company Christmas party.[58] Employees were asked to give a detailed description of a household chore they hate. Later the video was edited to make it appear that they were answering the question "What's sex like with your partner?" The plaintiff was quoted as saying:

The smell. The smell, the smell. And then you go with the goggles. You have to put on the goggles. And then you get the smell through the nose. And as you get into it things start flying all over the place. And the smell. And you get covered in these things.[59]

Another explained that "[i]t's one of those greasy grimy things that you just have to do at least once a year whether you want to or not."[60] Taken together in context, the court concluded that a reasonable person would recognize that the video was a spoof.

"Based on a true story"   False light cases occasionally arise from docudramas that claim to be based on a true story but are partially fictionalized. However, courts are reluctant to find false light in cases in which the overall gist of the story is true.[61] The *Second Restatement of Torts* says of false light claims that:

> The plaintiff's privacy is not invaded when unimportant false statements are made, even when they are made deliberately. It is only when there is such a major misrepresentation of his character, history, activities or beliefs that serious offense may reasonably be expected to be taken by a reasonable man in his position, that there is a cause of action for invasion of privacy.[62]

The family members of the fishing crew depicted in the movie *The Perfect Storm* sued Time Warner for false light and misappropriation. The film included a fictional scene of the captain berating his crew for wanting to go back to shore when threatened by the storm. It also included scenes that briefly portrayed the plaintiffs engaged in invented conversations. The film opened with the statement: "THIS FILM IS BASED ON A TRUE STORY." But a disclaimer at the end added "Dialogue and certain events and characters in the film were created for the purpose of fictionalization." Although most states reject false light claims concerning representations of the deceased, the plaintiffs argued that they had a relational right to sue for false light on behalf of their father, who was vilified in the movie as an obsessed boat caption causing them pain. The Eleventh Circuit did not find the portrayal "sufficiently egregious" to warrant a relational right.[63] The Florida Supreme Court also looked at the case and held that the state misappropriation statute did not apply to the plaintiffs who were depicted in the film because their names and images, while used in a commercial film, were not used to promote a product.[64]

Random photos   False light cases can occur when publishers use unrelated photos and video to illustrate stories. Washington, D.C., pedestrian Linda Duncan sued a television news station for false light after it used her image to illustrate a story on genital herpes. Duncan was walking down a street among a crowd of people when the camera zoomed in on her and an announcer read "For the twenty million Americans who have herpes, it's not a cure."[65]

Defenses to Invasion of Privacy

Newsworthiness

Newsworthiness is a defense for disclosure of private facts, false light, and misappropriation. It is not a defense to intrusion claims, but it is one of the factors considered in intrusion cases when courts try to determine whether an intrusion would be offensive to a reasonable person. The term *newsworthy* is defined as "any information disseminated 'for purposes of education, amusement or enlightenment, when the public may reasonably be expected to have a legitimate interest in what is published.'"[66]

Public figures are usually considered newsworthy and receive less privacy protection than private individuals because they have voluntarily subjected themselves to public scrutiny.

Arrests are always newsworthy, even if the person arrested is later proved innocent. So are victims of crime, accidents, and disasters. William Prosser explained:

> Caught up and entangled in this web of news and public interest are a great many people who have not sought publicity, but indeed, as in the case of any accused criminal, have tried assiduously to avoid it. They have nevertheless lost some part of their right of privacy. The misfortunes of the frantic victim of sexual assault, the woman whose husband is murdered before her eyes, or the innocent bystander who is caught in a raid on a cigar store and mistaken by the police for the proprietor, can be broadcast to the world, and they have no remedy. Such individuals become public figures for a season; and "until they have reverted to the lawful and unexciting life led by the great bulk of the community, they are subject to the privileges which publishers have to satisfy the curiosity of the public as to their leaders, heroes, villains and victims."[67]

However, intimate coverage of victims may cross the line. Although a television station's on-the-scene coverage of a car accident was not considered an invasion of privacy, the Supreme Court of California ruled that its coverage of victims inside a rescue helicopter, where they could claim a reasonable expectation of privacy, could constitute an intrusion upon seclusion and public disclosure of private facts.[68] Courts have found in favor of plaintiffs who sued the media for filming a dying heart attack victim and amplifying a phone conversation in which police notified parents of their son's death.[69]

Public Documents

Publishing or broadcasting information that is available in a public record is not an invasion of privacy because the information is already accessible to anyone willing to comb through public files to get it. Computerization has facilitated the search process.

A surplus of "private" information exists in public documents, such as birth and death certificates, marriage licenses, divorce records, military records, professional licenses, property tax records, and wills.

Consent

A person who willingly provides information for publication or consents to photography or videotaping cannot sue for invasion of privacy later. In fact, some jurisdictions will reject a plaintiff's invasion of privacy claim based on consent, even if the consent was procured by fraud, as long as the activity disclosed is of a commercial rather than a personal or private nature. For example, the Seventh Circuit would not entertain a trespass claim from an eye clinic that gave Primetime Live permission to film cataract operations, even though the show's producers violated their promise not to use hidden cameras or do ambush interviews.[70] Likewise, the U.S. Court for the Eastern District of Michigan granted summary judgment to People for the Ethical Treatment of Animals in a privacy case in which the animal rights organization obtained consent to film animals being euthanized on a chinchilla farm from the owners under false pretenses.[71] It did not consider the defendant's action of placing the video with an article about the farm on its website to be an appropriation because the organization was reporting on a matter of public concern. The fact that the website also collected donations did not transform the use into a commercial endeavor.

Consent to publish intimate or private information, however, may be qualified or conditioned and may even be revoked if done sufficiently in advance of publication.[72] Someone who gives consent for an interview needs to give consent for the publication of the information as well. Consent to publish a private fact may not be assumed from a person's choice to disclose the information to an individual, even an individual in the media. In *Hawkins v. Multimedia, Inc.* (1986), the South Carolina Supreme Court did not infer consent because the plaintiff, who was never informed he would be identified in an article, talked briefly with a reporter.[73]

Also, while consent is a valid defense, there are some circumstances in which it will not apply. People who are minors or mentally handicapped may not give consent on their own behalf. Consent must come from a parent or guardian. Consent may not apply if it was given a long time ago. Consent may be invalidated if the material is changed. For example, consent to use a person's image is not reliable if the image is digitally altered before publication.

Privacy Protection from Federal Statutes

Federal statutes offer specific protections for various pieces of our private lives. They address the federal government's use of records with personal information, state government's handling of driver's license records, and the responsibilities private entities have for electronic communications, financial records, and medical records. Here are some of the most notable:

The Privacy Act – 5 U.S.C. §§ 552a, et seq.

The Privacy Act of 1974 provides limited protection against government collection and disclosure of personal records. The term *record* includes, but is not limited to, information an agency may have about a person's education, financial transactions, medical or employment history, or criminal background. The Act has several functions. It entitles individuals to review government records kept about them and to correct them if necessary.[74] It prevents government agencies from disclosing information about an individual to third parties or other agencies without the individual's written permission, unless the information is part of a public record or falls within one of the Act's exceptions.[75] The Privacy Act also prohibits government agencies from maintaining records regarding people's exercise of their First Amendment rights.[76] Government agencies may not record individuals' participation in demonstrations or Internet petitions, for example.[77]

Electronic Communications Privacy Act – 18 U.S.C. §§ 2510(1), et seq.

The Electronic Communications Privacy Act prevents providers of electronic communication services from divulging the contents of their users' communications. An "electronic communication" is defined as "any transfer of signs, signals, writing, images, sounds, data, or intelligence of any nature transmitted in whole or in part by a wire, radio, electromagnetic, photoelectronic or photooptical system."[78] Title I of the Act amended the federal wiretap statute to include electronic communications. Title II created the Stored Communications Act.

Federal Wiretap Act – 18 U.S.C. §§ 2510–22

The Federal Wiretap Act, as amended by the Electronic Communications Privacy Act, prohibits intentional interception and disclosure of oral, wire or electronic communications. The law applies to the interception of computer files, electronic messages, and phone conversations. It does not apply to electronic communications that are stored on a server. Violators may be fined or imprisoned up to five years.

Stored Communications Act – 18 U.S.C. §§ 2701–11

The Stored Communications Act proscribes unauthorized access to electronic messages stored by Internet service providers or other electronic communication facilities. Congress passed the law as part of the Electronic Communications Privacy

Act to plug a hole in the wiretap statute, which only applies to messages in transit. The Stored Communications Act prohibits anyone from:

1. intentionally accessing, without authorization, a facility through which an electronic communication service is provided; or
2. intentionally exceeding an authorization to access that facility and thereby obtaining, altering, or preventing authorized access to a wire or electronic communication while it is in storage.

Violations are punishable by a fine or one year in prison, or up to five years if the act was committed for commercial advantage, malicious destruction, or private commercial gain.

The Stored Communications Act does not apply to conduct authorized by the entity providing the service or the user of the service who may authorize others to access his or her communications. Nor does it apply to files on electronic systems configured for public access.

In *Konop v. Hawaiian Airlines, Inc.* (2002), the U.S. Court of Appeals for the Ninth Circuit determined that an airline executive violated the Stored Communications Act by using another employee's password to gain access to a pilot's personal, password-protected website criticizing the airline.[79]

Telephone Records and Privacy Protection Act – 18 U.S.C. § 1039(a)

The Telephone Records and Privacy Protection Act of 2006 makes it a criminal offense to obtain confidential phone records under false pretenses, a practice known as *pretexting*. The statute prohibits the knowing and intentional use of false or fraudulent statements or documentation to obtain confidential records from a telecommunications carrier or unauthorized access to those records via the Internet. It also prohibits the unauthorized purchase, transfer, or sale of phone company customer records. The statute applies to cell phone, landline, and voice over Internet protocol (VoIP) records. Violators may be fined or imprisoned up to ten years.

The legislation was inspired by the Hewlett Packard pretexting scandal in which the company's chairwoman hired a team of investigators to spy on HP's board of directors and members of the press to determine the source of information leaked to the media. The investigators used pretexting to obtain the phone records of board members and nine journalists who had written about the company. HP agreed to pay $14.5 million to settle a California civil suit of corporate spying for the fraudulently acquired phone records.

Children's Online Privacy Protection Act – 15 U.S.C. §§ 6501, et seq.

The Children's Online Privacy Protection Act (COPPA) of 1998 authorizes the Federal Trade Commission to regulate Internet sites that collect information from children under the age of 13. Under FTC rules, website operators must post privacy policies and get verifiable consent from a parent or guardian before collecting personal information about a child under 13. The FTC also requires operators to give parents the opportunity to delete the child's personal information and opt-out of future collection or use of the information.

The Federal Trade Commission fined the social networking site Xanga.com $1 million for violating COPPA.[80] The FTC alleged that Xanga allowed 1.7 million users who submitted birthdates indicating they were younger than 13 to create accounts without parental permission and that the site used and disclosed the children's personal information without parental notification or control.

Driver's Privacy Protection Act – 18 U.S.C. §§ 2721, et seq.

The Driver's Privacy Protection Act of 1994 is a federal regulation that bars state departments of motor vehicles from disclosing personal information about drivers without their consent. The statute was modeled on one first implemented by California after a stalker used Department of Motor Vehicle records to track down and kill actress Rebecca Schaefer.

Protection for personal information applies to photos, names, addresses, telephone numbers, social security numbers, driver's license numbers, medical or disability information, and accident reports, but is undermined by 14 exceptions. In 2000, Congress amended the Act to create a class of "highly restricted personal information" that includes photographs, social security numbers, and medical or disability information. This information is also subject to exceptions, but only four. These include use by government agencies; use in connection with any civil, criminal, administrative, or arbitral proceeding; use by any insurer or insurance support organization; and use by an employer or its agent or insurer to obtain or verify information relating to a holder of a commercial driver's license. Under any other circumstances, release of the information would require an individual's consent conveyed in writing or digitally with an electronic signature.

Fair Credit Reporting Act – 15 U.S.C. §§ 1681, et seq.

The Fair Credit Reporting Act of 1970 governs the collection and disclosure of information by consumer credit reporting agencies. The Act requires credit agencies to take steps to maintain the accuracy of credit reports and provide consumers with an opportunity to dispute negative information. It also gives them free access to their reports once a year through the government-authorized website annualcreditreport.com. Companies or organizations that use credit reports for employment purposes are required to notify and obtain the applicant's consent before accessing his or her report. If a negative action is taken based on the credit report, the company is required to inform the applicant of that fact and provide the source of the credit report so the individual can investigate it.

Right to Financial Privacy Act – 12 U.S.C. §§ 3401, et seq.

The Right to Financial Privacy Act of 1978 was passed in response to a Supreme Court decision that found consumers had no right to privacy regarding their financial records held by financial institutions. The Act requires government agencies to provide consumers with notice and an opportunity to object before financial institutions can release copies of private financial records to the government. Usually the information is requested through an administrative summons or subpoena in conjunction with a law enforcement investigation.

Video Privacy Protection Act – 18 U.S.C. § 2710

Congress passed the Video Privacy Act of 1988 after a newspaper published Robert Bork's video rental records during his nomination for Supreme Court justice. The statute imposes civil liability on any video provider who "knowingly discloses, to any person, personally identifiable information concerning any consumer." In addition to prohibiting the release of rental information, it requires video providers to destroy customer records within one year of an account's termination. Records may be released to police or individuals engaged in civil litigation with a valid court order. Consumers whose information has been released in violation of the statute may bring a civil action against the video provider for actual damages of up to $2,500.

A Texas woman has filed a class-action lawsuit against Blockbuster for releasing her video rental records to the social networking site Facebook for use in its Beacon marketing program.[81] Beacon tracks users' online activities offsite and reports their purchases back to their Facebook friends as a newsfeed. It was originally introduced as an opt-out feature until Facebook users rose up en masse to complain that their privacy was being violated. It is now an opt-in program, but the suit claims that Blockbuster continues to share information with Facebook, whether members choose to publish it through Beacon or not.

Privacy Protection Act – 42 U.S.C. §§ 2000aa, et seq.

The Privacy Protection Act of 1980, not to be confused with the Privacy Act, protects newsrooms from illegal searches and seizures of media materials for use as evidence.

Health Insurance Portability and Accountability Act

The Health Insurance Portability and Accountability Act of 1996 (HIPPA) protects "Individually identifiable health information," that relates to:

- an individual's past, present, or future physical or mental health or condition;
- the provision of health care to an individual; or
- the past, present, or future payment for the provision of health care to an individual.[82]

The privacy provision of the Act applies to health plans, health care clearinghouses, and most health care providers who transmit health information in electronic form.

State Statutes

States protect various areas of privacy through statute. Some codify the common law torts of intrusion to seclusion and misappropriation. Others duplicate federal laws that prohibit the interception of electronic communications or the release of medical information. State law also determines whether it is legal to surreptitiously record video and audio.

Surreptitious audio and video recording

Audio recording   Some states consider it OK to record a conversation without informing all parties to it as long as one party involved in the conversation has consented to the recording. That party may be the person doing the recording. These are known as one-party consent states. Other states that require both parties to consent to a recording are known as two-party consent states.

It is illegal to record a person without his or her permission, even in your home, in California, Connecticut, Delaware, Florida, Illinois, Maryland, Massachusetts, Michigan, Montana, New Hampshire, Pennsylvania, and Washington.

If the recording takes place over the telephone between parties in different states, the law that applies is that of the state in which the recording is initiated. It is legal for someone in a one-party state to record someone in a two-party state without permission, but it is not legal for someone in a two-party state to record someone in a one-party state without permission.

However, it is not OK to record a conversation designated for broadcast without giving the other party advanced warning. The Communications Act requires an entity licensed by the FCC to provide notice to any party whom it intends to record for broadcast before the recording is captured.[83] Notice is not required, however, if the recorded party is aware that the conversation will be broadcasted.

Video recording   Certain states also prevent the use of hidden video and still cameras to take pictures without a person's consent. They are Alabama, Delaware, Georgia, Hawaii, Maine, Michigan, New Hampshire, South Dakota, and Utah.

Businesses outside these states have a right to install hidden cameras in their own facilities. But they may not put them in areas where employees and customers have a legitimate expectation of privacy, such as restrooms, locker rooms, or changing rooms.

All states allow people to use hidden video cameras, commonly called nanny cams, in their homes. However, in states in which it is illegal to record someone without permission, the video must be captured without audio.

The freedom to record in one's own home does not extend to landlords who want to spy on their tenants. In *Hamberger v. Eastman* (1964), the New Hampshire Supreme Court found that a landlord who had installed a hidden audio transmitting and recording device in his tenants' bedroom had violated their privacy through intrusion upon seclusion.[84]

Homeowners who install wireless cameras should be aware that an unencrypted signal can be picked up outside the home with a consumer-grade video receiver by anyone within a range of 100 feet. This means that the very tool homeowners install to make them feel safer can become a window into their private lives.

Use of hidden video for reporting   Many excellent investigative journalism pieces that resulted in social reform could not have been as successful without hidden cameras. But that doesn't mean courts assume that journalists are entitled to use them.

ABC lost a suit involving a PrimeTime Live hidden-camera report showing Food Lion selling spoiled meat and rat-gnawed cheese. Although there were inaccuracies in the story, Food Lion chose not to sue for libel because the taped evidence was damning. Instead it focused on the newsgathering practices used. In addition to the hidden cameras, PrimeTime Live's producers used deception to get jobs in Food Lion stores. As a company, Food Lion could not sue for invasion of privacy, so it sued for trespass and fraud. The jury, which never saw the video, awarded Food Lion $5.5 million in compensatory and punitive damages. The Fourth Circuit, which considered Food Lion's suit to be "an end-run" around the First Amendment, reduced the fine to $2: $1 for trespassing and $1 for breaching their legal duty of loyalty to Food Lion as employer.[85]

Publishing Illegally Obtained Information

Sources occasionally give journalists information that is newsworthy but obtained illegally. The Supreme Court has held that the media are not liable for publishing illegally obtained information, as long as the information involves a matter of "public importance" and the media took no part in intercepting it. In *Bartnicki v. Vopper* (2001), the Court considered whether a radio station that aired a tape of an illegally intercepted cellular phone conversation was liable for the broadcast under the federal wiretap statute, which prohibits the disclosure of illegally intercepted communications.[86] The Court considered the statute's two purposes: (1) to discourage theft of communications and (2) to encourage "uninhibited exchange of ideas and information among private parties ..." by preserving their privacy interests. Imposing liability on third parties who might publish the information but who played no role in intercepting it would not serve the first goal. But preventing publication would serve the second goal. Nevertheless, the Court resolved that in light of the nation's commitment to "the principle that debate on public issues should be uninhibited, robust and wide-open," privacy interests must give way when balanced against the interest in publishing matters of public concern.

The First Circuit applied this principle in *Jean v. Massachusetts State Police* (2007), a case in which a political activist sought an injunction to prevent police from forcing her to remove a video from her website that was recorded illegally.[87] Mary Jean maintained a website critical of the local district attorney. In 2006, she posted a video – captured by a "nanny-cam" – of a warrantless search of a man arrested on a misdemeanor charge. Although the tape had been recorded illegally (because it contained secretly recorded audio in a state that barred it), Jean obtained it legally from the man whose home was searched. When police demanded that she take it down, she sought an injunction to bar them from prosecuting her for displaying the video. The Court of Appeals observed that a warrantless search is a matter of public concern and concluded that Jean was likely to win on her First Amendment claim.

Workplace Privacy

About 66 percent of companies surveyed monitor their employees' Internet use, according to a 2007 American Management Association survey.[88] Companies monitor computer use in various ways: 45 percent track keystrokes and web content, 43 percent store and review computer files, and 43 percent retain and review e-mail messages. The survey also showed that 45 percent of employers track the telephone numbers called by employees, 16 percent record phone conversations, and 9 percent review employee phone mail.

Employers monitor employees to guarantee productivity, make sure that trade secrets are not being shared, and prevent their resources from being used for illegal activities. Companies have been held liable for the e-mail actions of their employees.[89] Chevron Corporation, for example, paid a $2.2 million settlement to employees who demonstrated evidence of sexual e-mail harassment.[90]

Employers that provide the network used for communication are largely exempted from liability under the federal Electronic Communications Privacy Act by two statutory exceptions. The service provider exception states:

> It shall not be unlawful … for … a provider of wire or electronic communication service, whose facilities are used in the transmission of a wire communication, to intercept, disclose, or use that communication in the normal course of his employment while engaged in any activity which is a necessary incident to the rendition of his service or to the protection of the rights or property of the provider of that service …[91]

In other words, employers that provide communication networks may tap into them. This provision does not, however, entitle companies that provide Internet service to the public to monitor users' messages beyond what may be necessary for "mechanical or service quality control checks."[92]

Employers that do not provide the communication network may rely on a consent exception that exempts them from liability if they acquire their employees' express or implied consent to monitoring. Some organizations make their employees sign an acknowledgment that the employer may monitor computer usage. Continued use of a computer after being informed of an employer's monitoring policy may be interpreted as implied consent.

Some employees have tried to sue their employers for monitoring their computer activity under the common law tort of intrusion to seclusion. Such cases usually fail because employees have no reasonable expectation of privacy on work computers. A lawsuit brought against an employer who searched an employee's personal computer files was dismissed by a Texas appellate court, which found that the employee had no expectation of privacy on a company-owned computer or to e-mails sent over a company network.[93] Likewise, the U.S. Court of Appeals for the Fourth Circuit found that a government agency's review of an employee's click stream data was not a violation of privacy because the agency's notice that it would "audit, inspect, and/or monitor" employees' use of the Internet, warned employees that they had no reasonable expectation of privacy regarding computer downloads.[94]

Marketplace Privacy

Most individuals are unaware of the type and extent of information that is collected about them when they are using the Internet. It is impossible to know in some instances when private information about online activities is being collected or where the information gathered though online forms and registrations goes. Moreover, the law doesn't prohibit marketers from collecting online data.

The Internet marketing company DoubleClick, Inc. relied on statutory exceptions to the Stored Communications and Wiretap Acts to avoid liability for surreptitiously collecting data from Internet users. DoubleClick, now owned by Google, builds detailed profiles of Internet surfers that it uses to target its clients' banner ads. The company is affiliated with a network of thousands of websites. Through them, it installs cookies on visitors' hard drives. Cookies are small data files that store information that users enter into online forms, their search requests and their movements on a page. When the user comes back and the cookie is activated, DoubleClick uploads this information to its database. When a computer user accesses one of DoubleClick's affiliated websites, the DoubleClick server identifies the user's profile on the cookie to match it with an appropriate ad. In a class action lawsuit, plaintiffs accused DoubleClick of violating the Stored Communications Act by gaining unauthorized access to their communications.[95] But the court accepted DoubleClick's argument that its actions were protected under a statutory exemption that shields "conduct authorized ... by a user of [the wire or electronic communications] service with respect to a communication of or intended for that user."

The company argued that its affiliated websites were users of an "electronic communications service" – the Internet – and that, as users, the websites could access information stored on a facility – the users' hard drives – intended for them or authorize DoubleClick to access information "of or intended for" the websites. The court accepted the novel argument that DoubleClick's actions fell under the Wiretap Act's user exception. Plaintiffs also claimed that DoubleClick had violated the Computer Fraud and Abuse Act (CFAA) (described in chapter 4) by gaining unauthorized access to their computers. The court disagreed because the law, intended for hackers, is predicated on harm to data or computers, which had not occurred.

Information collected through online forms is not protected by privacy laws because it is provided voluntarily. This is so "even if the information is revealed on the assumption that it will be used only for a limited purpose and the confidence placed in the third party will not be betrayed."[96] Consequently, a website that collects information from its users is free to sell it to direct marketers and many do.

None of the common law invasion of privacy torts applies to the collection and sale of information for marketing purposes. It is not an intrusion upon seclusion because people willingly visit sites where information is collected and often provide information to them voluntarily. The information that marketers sell is not a disclosure of private facts because it is either volunteered, or in the case of information gathered surreptitiously through cookies, not considered extremely personal. Nor is the information publicly disclosed, although it is sold to other companies. False light does not apply because the user is not intentionally misrepresented. Nor does misappropriation, which would seem to be the most applicable tort because the information is used for commercial purposes. The New Hampshire Supreme Court explained that "An investigator who sells personal information sells the information for the value of the information itself, not to take advantage of the person's reputation or prestige ..." Consequently, "a person whose personal information is sold does not have a cause of action for appropriation against the investigator who sold the information."[97]

Advertising that tracks users' activities online to deliver ads targeted to their interests is called behavioral advertising. There are no legal restraints on data collection by behavioral marketers. The Federal Trade Commission has told Congress it is "cautiously optimistic that the privacy concerns raised by behavioral advertising can be addressed effectively by industry self-regulation."[98]

In contrast, the European Union passed a Data Protection Directive to give individuals control over their personal data.[99] Marketers cannot collect personal data from EU citizens without informing them first and explaining how the data will be used, nor can they use cookies to surreptitiously track Internet users' surfing habits. They are also prohibited from transferring data to third parties without their customers' permission. Non-European Union nations that offer inadequate safe-guards for data privacy are blocked from doing business with EU citizens. The U.S. Department of Commerce established a Safe Harbor Program to facilitate continued trade. American companies that comply with EU privacy standards may join the program.

Privacy and Social Networking

In social networking sites, like MySpace and Facebook, members exercise their own discretion regarding the amount of information they reveal. They can also determine who has access to the information they provide. Nevertheless, privacy issues have emerged, ranging from stolen information to physical harm.

Using a security hole in MySpace, one hacker accessed half a million images from private MySpace profiles and released them for anyone to download.[100] Meanwhile, third-party games like Mob Wars have lured Facebook subscribers into revealing their social security numbers.[101]

Sexual predators are a danger to young users who reveal too much information. When a 14-year-old girl from Austin, Texas, was raped by a man she met through MySpace, the girl's parents sued News Corp, MySpace's owner, for negligence in failing to take reasonable steps to ensure minors' safety. The Fifth Circuit affirmed a lower court's judgment that their claims were barred by the Communications Decency Act. But negative publicity prompted the social networking site to tighten its policies involving minors.

Then of course there is the data collection that occurs from the sites themselves. Facebook's privacy policy says:

> When you register with Facebook, you provide us with certain personal information, such as your name, your email address, your telephone number, your address, your gender, schools attended and any other personal or preference information that you provide to us …
>
> Facebook may also collect information about you from other sources, such as newspapers, blogs, instant messaging services, and other users of the Facebook service through the operation of the service (e.g., photo tags) in order to provide you with more useful information and a more personalized experience.[102]

When Facebook's Beacon program started reporting subscribers' off-site activities to other users without warning, *02138*, an online magazine for Harvard alumni, decided to teach Facebook's founder, Mark Zuckerberg, a lesson on the value of privacy. It posted Zuckerberg's social security number, his parents' address, and his girlfriend's name. Zuckerberg filed for a temporary restraining order to force the magazine to remove the information, but a federal judge ruled in favor of *02138*. Facebook's Beacon policy changed shortly after.

Anonymity Online

A lot of Internet users value anonymity – a right the Supreme Court has found worthy of protection. It has said an author's decision to remain anonymous, like other decisions concerning omissions or additions to the content of a publication, is an aspect of the freedom of speech protected by the First Amendment.[103]

Without a guarantee of anonymity, distribution of information would be reduced from those who fear official, economic, and social retaliation. In the realm of political speech, the Court imposes a test of exacting scrutiny on government actions affecting anonymous speech. Restrictions must be "narrowly tailored to serve an overriding state interest."[104]

A U.S. district court struck down a Georgia statute that barred the use of pseudonyms online because it was a content-based restriction that was both vague and overbroad. Not only did it "sweep[] protected activity within its proscription," said the court, but it also failed to "define the criminal offense with sufficient definiteness" so that ordinary people could understand what conduct was prohibited.[105]

States do have a compelling interest in preventing anonymous speech that causes harm. In fraud or libel cases, for example, they must decide when it is appropriate to require disclosure of a speaker's name. The leading case on the subject is *Doe v. Cahill* (2005), in which the Delaware Supreme Court developed a test to determine when it is appropriate to unmask an Internet speaker.[106] A plaintiff must (1) make a reasonable effort to notify the anonymous poster that he or she is subject to a subpoena for identity disclosure and (2) submit evidence of a claim sufficient to survive a motion for summary judgment before the court will compel disclosure. Courts in Massachusetts, Pennsylvania, and Texas have adopted this standard.[107] Some states like Arizona, California, New Jersey, and New York impose a balancing test as well.[108] After affirming the evidence is sufficient to support a summary judgment, they balance the strength of the plaintiff's claim against the First Amendment rights of the speaker.

Other states are satisfied if plaintiffs provide some evidence to support their claim in order to learn a speaker's identity. A lower burden is also imposed on plaintiffs in copyright cases, because most courts assume that copyright law does not implicate the First Amendment.

The PATRIOT Act and government surveillance

No discussion of privacy law would be complete without reference to the Patriot Act and government surveillance.

The USA PATRIOT Act is an acronym for the Uniting and Streng- thening America by Providing Appropriate Tools Required to Intercept and Obstruct Terrorism Act. Congress passed the legislation at the height of national fear, only 45 days after the Sept. 11, 2001 terrorist attacks. While the PATRIOT Act gives law enforcement agencies the tools they need to fight criminal activity in the digital age, it has been criticized for its potential to violate Americans' civil liberties.

The Act amended laws discussed in this or other chapters to make it easier for law enforcement officials to conduct electronic surveillance and gain access to private records. Some of the most significant changes were made to the Foreign Intelligence Surveillance Act. FISA prescribes procedures required to conduct electronic surveillance and physical searches of people engaged in espionage or international terrorism on behalf of a foreign power.[109]

Government investigators formerly obtained orders for surveillance from FISA courts when foreign intelligence gathering was the "primary purpose" of the investigation. Now, foreign intelligence need only be a "significant" purpose of the investigation.[110] Consequently, electronic surveillance of Americans – formerly prohibited under FISA – is now allowed if Americans are conversing with foreigners under investigation. This is significant because the standard of proof a court demands for permission to conduct electronic surveillance of Americans under the federal wiretap statute is significantly higher than the standard of proof required for a FISA wiretap.

One of the PATRIOT Act's more controversial provisions expanded roving wiretaps in FISA investigations.[111] Authorities use roving wiretaps to intercept communications made by and to the target of an investigation, rather than to a particular phone or computer. The technique makes sense considering that a subject is likely to use more than one device for communication purposes. However, this form of surveillance will intercept the messages of all others using devices tapped for the investigation.

Another section of the Act, dubbed the "sneak and peek" provision by its critics, eliminated a requirement that authorities notify the subject of a search warrant about the warrant at the time of the search if the court granting the warrant finds reasonable cause to believe that providing immediate notice would have an adverse affect on the criminal investigation.[112] The legislation originally allowed officials to search a person's home or e-mail and inform the person of the search "within a reasonable period," without specifying what reasonable meant. A 2006 amendment requires authorities to notify individuals of secret searches within seven days unless a judge approves an extension.

Section 209 empowers authorities to access voice via a search warrant rather than a wiretap order. Warrants demand a lower standard of proof than that required by the wiretap statute, which requires authorities to show "specific facts to support the belief that a crime has been committed or that items sought are evidence of a crime."

The PATRIOT Act also allows authorities to request a FISA court order to compel third parties to release private financial, medical or educational records they may hold regarding the subject. Initially, individuals who received such an order were prevented from telling anyone about it.[113] A 2006 revision of the statute now entitles them to consult with an attorney without first informing law enforcement. Libraries were shocked to find out that their patrons' records could be subpoenaed. Congress has amended the Act to restrict access to records related to a library's role as an Internet service provider. In some cases, phone, bank, and credit records are accessible to authorities via national security letters (administrative subpoenas) rather than court orders.[114]

The PATRIOT Act also altered the Pen Register and Trap and Trace Statute to extend its application to all electronic communications.[115] Pen registers capture outgoing telephone numbers. Trap and Trace devices, like caller ID boxes, capture incoming numbers. But they do not capture content from phone conversations. The PATRIOT Act revised the definition of pen and trap devices to include the capture of computer routing, addressing, and signaling information. These devices now capture information from e-mails and web searches. They do not target the content of communications, but the information they do collect – e-mail addresses and URLs – reveals more about the character of the communication. Authorities do not need a court order to install these devices. The Attorney General may authorize their use if the information likely to be obtained is relevant to an ongoing investigation to protect against terrorism or clandestine intelligence activities. The law prohibits authorities from using these devices for investigations of American citizens based solely on their First Amendment activities.

Congress passed the PATRIOT Act with a sunset provision that required the Act's renewal in 2005. In 2006, Congress voted to make 14 of its 16 provisions permanent. It will reexamine the roving wiretap and national security letter provisions in 2010. The Obama administration has recommended its extension.

Domestic wiretapping and the Foreign Intelligence Surveillance Act

In 2005, the *New York Times* reported that the National Security Agency was conducting a domestic surveillance program that involved the warrantless interception of e-mails and phone calls made from the United States to foreign parties.[116] President Bush authorized the secret program, which exceeded powers provided by the PATRIOT Act, in 2002. He argued that the program was legal under a 2001 congressional resolution authorizing him to use military force against terrorism. Administration sources credited the program with helping to uncover two suspected terrorist attacks.

The article, which the administration asked the *New York Times* not to run, suggested that AT&T and other telecommunication companies funneled international communications through the NSA, which stored them for data mining. At the time, the law required that wiretaps for communications sent abroad from the United States be obtained through a FISA court order with a particular target in mind. FISA was established in 1978 to curb domestic surveillance abuses by the NSA, the Central Intelligence Agency, and the Federal Bureau of Investigation.

AT&T faced as many as 40 private lawsuits for its complicity with the program. It is not clear how many records were drawn into the program, but estimates reach into the millions. Under the Stored Communications Act, telephone companies can be fined

$1,000 for each consumer whose records are disclosed. In arguing for telecommunication company amnesty, the administration said that the lawsuits could potentially bankrupt the companies.

In 2008, Congress voted to legalize the program and granted amnesty to telephone companies that cooperated with the government.[117] The FISA Amendment Act of 2008 authorizes the government to install wiretapping posts in telephone and Internet facilities inside the United States without a warrant in FISA investigations for up to one week, on the condition that a FISA court is notified when the surveillance begins. A warrant is still required if the investigation targets an American in or outside of the country, but not if the American is called by a foreign target. The blanket authorization expires in 2014.

Questions for Discussion

1. Who is and is not entitled to privacy protection? How do the rules differ from libel law? Why?
2. Why is it not safe to assume that a privacy rule that applies in another state also applies in yours?
3. Where do we have an "expectation of privacy"?
4. If you find a photograph of a cute child on Flickr.com with a creative commons license by the photographer to use the photo for any purpose, is it safe to use the photo commercially?

11

Sex and Violence

Digital media have made it easier than ever to gain access to pornography and violence. Pay-per-view, dial-a-porn, and the Internet spare individuals the embarrassment of having to go in search of the adult materials they want. Video games and simulations go one step further by enabling users to engage in virtual sex and violence. Digital media also make it easier to produce and disseminate adult materials. The pornography industry, which first thrived on the Internet, now complains that amateurs are hurting its business by flooding the Net with homemade images. Meanwhile game companies complain that programmers are modifying, or "modding," their games to make them more violent.

Unrivaled access to this kind of speech has precipitated calls for censorship, reflecting two schools of thought: Some want graphic representations of sex and violence controlled because they are offensive and disturbing. Others believe obscene and violent media should be controlled because they contribute to antisocial behavior. A few media scholars have argued that pornography is associated with abuse of women and children. At the other end of the spectrum are researchers who doubt that violent media have any impact on behavior.

Social scientists have tried to determine the effect of media on human behavior for nearly a century with inconclusive results. Although they have observed correlations between the use of violent media and aggression, they are still at odds over whether cause and effect can be demonstrated outside a laboratory setting. Nevertheless, the popular assumption is that media do have an impact on our behavior. Legislators have responded to this concern by prohibiting the dissemination of obscenity and restricting children's access to indecency. Some states have also imposed restrictions on children's access to violent media. Meanwhile a number of individuals have sued companies that produce violent entertainment thought to have inspired violent acts.

This chapter will discuss the legal restraints that can and cannot be imposed on sex and violence in media products. It will also discuss the extent to which speech used to intimidate others and precipitate violence can be controlled.

Obscenity and Indecency

A central tenet of First Amendment law is that speech cannot be censored because it expresses unpopular ideas or opinions. In fact, Justice Oliver Wendell Holmes wrote "[I]f there is any principle of the Constitution that more imperatively calls for attachment than any other it is the principle of free thought – not free thought for those who agree with us but freedom for the thought that we hate."[1] Obscenity is the exception to that rule. In the United States, obscenity is regulated because it is offensive to others. Indecency, however, is still protected under the First Amendment.

What's the difference?

The primary difference between indecency and obscenity is that one is legal and the other is not. Indecency is constitutionally protected. All media are entitled to use it, although broadcast media must channel it into a period when children are less likely to be in the audience.[2] No medium is entitled to show obscenity. The Supreme Court has categorically denied it First Amendment protection.

However, because indecency and obscenity represent a continuum of adult behavior, it is not always easy to tell where one ends and the other begins. In general indecency encompasses profanity, references to excretory organs, nudity, and implied sexual behavior. Obscenity refers to explicit depictions of actual sexual conduct, masturbation, violent sexual abuse, and child pornography.

For years the Supreme Court struggled to come up with a test for obscenity that would allow communities to restrict what was most offensive without impinging on the rights of adults to produce and have access to material with sexual themes. In *Miller v. California* (1973), the Court produced the three-part test for obscenity now in use:

- an average person, applying contemporary community standards, must find that the material, as a whole, appeals to the prurient interest;
- the material must depict or describe, in a patently offensive way, sexual conduct specifically defined by applicable law; and
- the material, taken as a whole, must lack serious literary, artistic, political, or scientific value.[3]

All three prongs of the test must be met before the material can be declared obscene.

The first two elements of the test are judged by community standards. These can be tricky to establish because people don't like to discuss their sexual interests and stores that sell adult merchandise are reluctant to become involved with an obscenity prosecution. A Florida attorney defending a man charged with disseminating obscenity through the Internet used Google Trends to establish community standards.[4] Google Trends enables users to compare trends in areas based on the volume of searches for particular terms.[5] Lawrence Walters hoped the data would persuade jurors that residents of Santa Rosa County, where the case was to be tried, searched for sexual material on the Internet more frequently than they might have imagined. The data did, in fact, show that people in the area searched for terms like "group sex" and "orgy" more frequently than generic terms like "boating" or "apple pie." After the data became public, the prosecutor offered Walters's client a reduced sentence in exchange for a plea bargain; there was no trial.

Applying community standards to material on the Internet is problematic because it has no geographic boundaries. In *Reno v. ACLU* (1997), the Supreme Court struck down a statute that applied community standards to indecency on the Internet. It observed that "the 'community standards' criterion as applied to the Internet means that any communication available to a nation-wide audience will be judged by the standards of the community most likely to be offended by the message.[6] Five years later, though, when confronted with the opportunity to strike down a law that applied community standards to commercial Internet speech considered harmful to minors, the Court fractured on the issue, leaving them in place.[7]

The second leg of the Miller test requires the material to be "patently offensive." The Supreme Court considered the meaning of patently offensive in *Jenkins v. Georgia* (1974), a case in which a Georgia theater owner was prosecuted for distributing obscene material because he showed the film *Carnal Knowledge*. It concluded that the term encompassed representations or descriptions of "ultimate sexual acts, normal or perverted, actual or simulated" as well as "masturbation, excretory functions and lewd exhibition of the genitals."[8]

Normally obscenity involves explicit or disturbing imagery. However, in *U.S. v. Alpers* (1950), the Supreme Court held that there was no reason the obscenity statute should be limited to visual material.[9] *Alpers* concerned an obscene record album. A more recent case involved a text-only website called Red Rose, which contained fictional stories involving sex with children. The woman who ran the subscription-based site was convicted of transmitting obscenity through interstate commerce in 2008. Hers was the first conviction for obscenity without visual imagery since the *Miller* case. But the Red Rose stories were never exposed to the *Miller* test at trial. An agoraphobic, the defendant pled guilty to avoid trial in exchange for home detention.[10]

The third prong of the Miller test, which considers the literary, artistic, political, or scientific value of the work taken as a whole, is not based on community standards. In *Pope v. Illinois* (1987), the Supreme Court stated "the proper inquiry is … whether a reasonable person would find such value in the material, taken as a whole."[11]

Production and distribution of obscenity

In the United States, it is a felony to knowingly produce obscene material intended for distribution through interstate or foreign commerce, or to knowingly import, transport, or receive obscene materials, through interstate or foreign commerce, via a common carrier, interactive computer service, or the mail.[12] A first offense is punishable by a fine of up to $250,000 or up to five years in prison, or both. If the material is transmitted to a minor under the age of 16, the punishment can increase to 10 years.[13]

By restricting the statute's application to activities that take place through "interstate or foreign commerce," Congress brings obscenity within its jurisdiction to regulate under the Constitution's commerce clause. Congress has also imposed a requirement for *scienter* on obscenity prosecutions, meaning that individuals must know or have reason to know they are committing an illegal act before they can be held liable for it. A law that imposes liability without scienter is known as a strict liability statute. In *Smith v. California* (1959), the Supreme Court struck down a state law that applied strict liability to the distribution of obscenity.[14] The petitioner in the case was a bookstore owner convicted of possessing an obscene book. The Supreme Court reasoned that imposing liability on media distributors who do not have actual knowledge of the character of the material they are distributing would likely burden the First Amendment. Distributors facing strict liability would sell only what they were able to review. The natural result would be a reduction in their inventories, which would deny the public access to constitutionally protected media. This does not mean, however, that a prosecutor must prove that a distributor has actual knowledge that a particular work is obscene. A general knowledge of the material's sexual orientation is sufficient to meet the scienter requirement.

The obscenity statute is somewhat confusing as worded because it also prohibits the transport of "lewd, lascivious … filthy … [and] *indecent*" materials, which are protected. Despite the additional language, the Supreme Court construes the statute to refer solely to obscenity.[15] The statute also criminalizes the transmission of materials related to abortion, including any information about how, where, or from whom one can be obtained. The Justice Department does not enforce these provisions because doing so would violate the First Amendment.[16]

Possession of obscenity

Private possession of obscenity at home is legal. The Supreme Court held that a Georgia statute that criminalized the possession of obscenity violated the First and Fourteenth Amendments in *Stanley v. Georgia* (1969). The Court could see no reason for the statute other than to enforce morality, an inappropriate justification for state action.[17] Writing for the majority, Justice Marshall stated that "[i]f the First Amendment means anything, it means that a State has no business telling a man, sitting alone in his own house, what books he may read or what films he may watch. Our whole constitutional heritage rebels at the thought of giving government the power to control men's minds."[18]

The right to possess obscenity acknowledged in *Stanley v. Georgia* does not create a "correlative right to receive it, transport it, or distribute it."[19] Although the Court

has acknowledged a privacy interest in the home, no "zone of constitutionally protected privacy follows such material when it is moved outside the home."[20]

Child pornography

The obscenity statute criminalizes the act of distributing, receiving, or possessing
obscene depictions of a child engaged in sexual activity transported through interstate or foreign commerce, by any means, including a computer.[21] In 1977, Congress
passed the Protection of Children Against Sexual Exploitation Act, which included
an anti-pandering provision that makes it a crime to advertise, promote, or solicit
child pornography.[22] A first offense in either case is punishable by a fine of $250,000
and imprisonment of 5–20 years. In *New York v. Ferber* (1982), the Supreme Court
upheld a New York law that criminalized the distribution of a sexual performance
by a child under the age of 16.[23] The Court made it clear that such material is
categorically denied First Amendment protection. It also gave lower courts the
leeway to adjust the *Miller* test when material alleged to be obscene includes depictions of children. For example, courts need not consider whether the material
appeals to prurient interest or is patently offensive, and can consider parts of the
work in isolation, rather than assessing the work as a whole.[24]

In *Osborn v. Ohio* (1990), the Court held that possession of child pornography
in the privacy of one's home is a crime.[25] It distinguished the case from *Stanley v.
Georgia*, which concerned a law prohibiting possession of obscenity on the grounds
that it could lead to antisocial conduct. Statutes that ban the possession of child
pornography are not concerned with the morality of the person who possesses the
material, but with the child victimized through its production.

Virtual child pornography

While the transmission of child pornography online is a known problem, no one
knows the extent to which virtual child pornography is. Congress attempted to
address new challenges posed by digital imaging software when it passed the Child
Pornography Prevention Act of 1996. The Act outlawed the possession of virtual
child pornography and material that conveyed the impression of children engaged
in sexual acts. The Free Speech Coalition challenged both provisions as facially
overbroad, not because they actually limited protected speech, but because they had
the potential to. In *Ashcroft et al. v. Free Speech Coalition* (2002), a narrow majority
of the Supreme Court agreed that the ban on virtual child pornography was unconstitutional.[26] Referring to its decision in *New York v. Ferber*, the Court reiterated
that child pornography is illegal because it is the product of sexual abuse, not
because of the ideas it represents. It reasoned that if virtual child pornography is
produced without children, the underlying theory to protect children from harm
doesn't hold. The dissenting justices argued that virtual pornography should be

banned because it could be indistinguishable from the real thing and government should not be put in the position of having to prove that an image is real to get a conviction. In some child pornography cases, the real child is never found, particularly when the images are produced overseas. However, the majority rejected this argument, saying that it "turns the First Amendment upside down ... Protected speech does not become unprotected merely because it resembles the latter. The Constitution requires the reverse."[27]

Most of the justices agreed that the second provision, which banned material that conveyed the impression of minors engaged in sex, was unconstitutional because it would cover protected literary works that included themes of teenage sex and sexual abuse of children. Works like *Romeo and Juliet*, *Traffic*, and *American Beauty* might be considered illegal.

Congress responded with new legislation to allay the Court's concerns. In 2003, it passed the Prosecutorial Remedies and Other Tools to End the Exploitation of Children Today Act. The PROTECT Act amended the obscenity statute to prohibit the production or distribution of *obscene representations* of sexual abuse of children. It also amended the pandering provision to apply to *obscene simulations* of minors engaged in sexually explicit conduct and depictions of actual minors engaged in sexual conduct. This carefully crafted definition exercises the government's right to regulate anything obscene, as well as real child pornography.

As amended by the PROTECT Act, the pandering provision provides that it is illegal to advertise, promote, distribute, or solicit "any material or purported material in a manner that reflects the belief, or that is intended to cause another to believe, that the material or purported material is, or contains child pornography."[28] The Supreme Court upheld the provision against facial overbreadth and vagueness challenges in *United States v. Williams* (2008) by narrowing the Act's construction.[29] The Court interpreted the Act to require proof that the defendant believed he was purveying or soliciting child pornography. If the materials did not include real children, the statute's application would be limited to images that conveyed "sexually explicit conduct." It would not apply to materials in which "sexual intercourse ... is merely suggested," such as R-rated movies. The "portrayal must cause a reasonable viewer to believe that the actors actually engaged in that conduct on camera."[30]

Under these circumstances, the Court concluded that the pandering provision fell within constitutional limits because it (1) targets speech soliciting a crime, (2) requires scienter on the part of the defendant, (3) is limited to those who "communicate in a manner that reflects the belief" that the material is child pornography, and (4) and relies on a definition of sexually explicit conduct similar to definitions upheld in earlier cases.[31] It also held that the statute was not vague because its requirements were clear questions of fact.

It would seem that Congress finally got the wording right, but another factor should be acknowledged. The law allows defendants convicted of violating a statute to challenge it as facially overbroad or vague, based on its potential to harm protected speech in other cases, even if the defendant's actions fall squarely within the

scope of the statute. As Justices Kennedy and Scalia pointed out during oral arguments, the petitioner was clearly guilty of the offense.[32] He had been convicted of
pandering and possession of child pornography after offering an undercover agent
pictures of men molesting his 4-year-old daughter. If the Court had decided to
strike down the provision under which he had been convicted, the pandering charge
against him would have been dropped (although his conviction for possession
would have remained). In this respect, the Court faced a very different situation
than the one in *Ashcroft v. Free Speech Coalition*, in which the petitioner was a First
Amendment proponent challenging a law's potential to curtail speech in hypothetical cases, and in which the cost of striking down the law would be minimal because
Congress would likely revise it.

Age-related record keeping

To make it easier to track the ages of individuals depicted in pornography, Congress
requires producers of pornographic material to document the names and dates of
birth of anyone shown engaging in "actually sexually explicit conduct" and affix a
notice to the material stating the location of the records. The term producer applies
to anyone who creates an image, digitizes or reproduces an image for commercial
distribution, or inserts a digital image on a computer site or service.[33]

This provision of the Child Protection and Obscenity Enforcement Act of 1988
is known in the pornography industry as the "2257 rule," based on its section
number in the United States Code. It was inspired by the child pornography prosecution of two filmmakers who hired Traci Lords to appear in their movies. Lords
was 15 when she started acting in hard-core films. When Congress passed the
PROTECT Act, it extended the age-documentation requirement to sexually explicit
material uploaded to the web. Violators may be punished with a fine or up to five
years in prison.

Regulation of Indecency and Material Harmful to Minors

Many of the regulations Congress and the Federal Communications Commission
have passed to control obscenity have included restrictions on indecency, which is
constitutionally protected. In each case, courts must determine whether the government's interest in protecting children from indecent speech justifies the burden
imposed on adults entitled to receive it, and whether the restriction limits no more
speech than necessary.

The FCC regulates indecency transmitted by broadcasters because broadcast
media are considered pervasive and uniquely accessible to children. It does not
regulate indecency transmitted through cable or satellite because individuals who
subscribe to these services are presumed to have selected the content. FCC oversight
of these media is discussed thoroughly in chapter 3, so it is not necessary to repeat

it here. But one point is better covered in this chapter. Although indecency is permitted on cable and satellite channels, obscenity is not. Criminal sanctions may be applied to anyone who "utters any obscene language or distributes any obscene matter by means of cable television or subscription services on television."[34] Nevertheless, a lot of programming on adult channels includes real, not simulated sex, which far exceeds the FCC's definition of indecency. This occurs because the Commission's policy is not to proscribe adult programming unless it is found to be "unlawful pursuant to statute or regulation."[35] If the FCC suspects a programmer of transmitting obscenity, it will refer the matter to the Justice Department for criminal prosecution, but it will not act until the material has been adjudicated and found to be obscene under the *Miller* test.

Dial-a-porn

As a telecommunications service, dial-a-porn also falls under the FCC's jurisdiction. In 1998, Congress amended the Communications Act to ban obscene and indecent interstate commercial telephone transmissions. Reiterating the distinction between obscene and indecent content, the Supreme Court upheld the ban on obscene phone messages, but struck down the provision barring indecency in *Sable Communication of California v. FCC* (1989).[36] The Court distinguished dial-a-porn from broadcast content, pointing out that dial-a-porn does not enter the home uninvited. A user must take affirmative action to gain access to the service. It concluded that narrower restrictions on these services could protect minors from indecent speech without imposing a complete ban. Following the decision, the FCC adopted regulations that permitted dial-a-porn to offer indecent content as long as its distributors restricted access to it through the use of credit card authorization, access codes, or scrambling of transmissions.[37]

Indecency on the Internet

The government has been trying to figure out how to protect children from indecency on the Internet since 1996. Two of the laws it has passed, the Communications Decency Act and the Children's Online Protection Act – both targeted at websites – have been struck down. Another, the Children's Internet Protection Act – targeted at libraries – has been upheld.

Communications Decency Act   Congress passed the Communications Decency Act as part of the Telecommunications Act of 1996. The law made it illegal to transmit material over the Internet that was obscene or indecent by community standards if it was accessible to minors. The American Civil Liberties Union (ACLU) challenged the Act the day it was signed into law on behalf of websites that provided information about venereal disease and prison rape. The ACLU argued that the

Act was unconstitutionally overbroad because it banned protected speech and burdened websites that had no mechanism for restricting access to minors. The government defended the Act by analogizing websites that provided indecent content to dial-a-porn services. It suggested they could defend themselves by restricting access to Internet users with credits cards or some other mechanism available to adults. The Supreme Court observed that the rule would burden nonprofit information providers who could not afford to implement such restrictions. The Court held that the indecency provision was both unconstitutionally vague and overbroad. Its decision in *ACLU v. Reno* (1997) is especially significant because it unanimously held that the Internet is entitled to full First Amendment protection.[38]

Children's Online Protection Act   Congress went back to the drawing board when the Communications Decency Act was struck down and emerged with a revised version that it hoped would pass constitutional muster: the Children's Online Protection Act (COPA). The 1998 Act applied only to commercial websites that knowingly transmitted material "harmful to minors." Congress applied the Miller test, adding the words "with respect to minors," to define harmful to minors as material that:

(A)   the average person, applying contemporary community standards, would find, taking the material as a whole and with respect to minors, is designed to appeal to, or is designed to pander to, the prurient interest;
(B)   depicts, describes, or represents, in a manner patently offensive with respect to minors, an actual or simulated sexual act or sexual contact, an actual or simulated normal or perverted sexual act, or a lewd exhibition of the genitals or post-pubescent female breast; and
(C)   taken as a whole, lacks serious literary, artistic, political, or scientific value for minors.[39]

A commercial website could avoid prosecution by restricting access to adults through the use of credit cards or adult access codes.

The ACLU and the Electronic Privacy Information Center challenged COPA's constitutionality and won. The law spent the next 10 years in limbo as the government appealed the case. A federal district court in Philadelphia issued an injunction barring enforcement of the statute because it would deny adults access to speech they were entitled to receive and impose financial burdens on speakers (by requiring credit card or access codes) that might lead them to self-censor to avoid the additional cost. The Third Circuit upheld the injunction, but on a different basis. It concluded that "[b]ecause of the peculiar geography-free nature of cyberspace, [COPA's] community standards test would essentially require every web communication to abide by the most restrictive community's standards."[40] The Supreme Court concluded that COPA could not be struck down for its use of community standards. The Court's plurality opinion suggests that the justices could not come to an agreement on the issue. But the Court suggested COPA might be unconstitutional for other reasons. It upheld the injunction and sent the case back down to the district level for a broader review of First Amendment considerations.[41] The lower court held that COPA was unconstitutional because it did not use the least restrictive means to curb harmful speech and Third Circuit upheld the ruling.[42] The Supreme Court reviewed the case a second time, upholding the injunction on its enforcement based on the law's "potential for extraordinary harm and a serious chill upon protected speech."[43] It remanded the case again, asking the district court to consider whether there were less restrictive alternatives to the law. The lower court determined that filters installed by parents represented a less restrictive alternative and struck the law down again. In 2008, the Third Circuit upheld its decision for the third time, finding the Act "impermissibly overbroad and vague."[44] The Supreme Court struck the final blow in 2009 when it refused to review the decision.[45]

Children's Internet Protection Act   In 2000, Congress passed the Children's Internet Protection Act, which ties federal funding for Internet access in public libraries and schools to the installation of filtering software to block material that is obscene, child pornography, or "harmful to minors" on all computers connected to the Internet.[46] Most libraries already used filters on computers in the children's section. The American Library Association (ALA) challenged the law's application to public libraries as a violation of the First Amendment because filters are inexact and block material adults are constitutionally entitled to receive – some of it unrelated to sexual content. The law specifies that adult patrons can ask librarians to remove a filter from a computer they are using for "bona fide research or other lawful purposes."[47] The ALA argued that this puts adults in the position of justifying what they want to read to a librarian.

By a 6–3 margin, the Supreme Court upheld the law in *United States v. American Library Association* (2003). It determined that the government's interest in protecting children outweighed the burden the law imposed on adult patrons. It also stated that libraries that wish to offer their patrons unfettered Internet access may still do so if they choose not to accept federal funding.

Truth in Domain Names Act

Congress passed the Truth in Domain Names Act in 2003 to thwart the use of misleading domain names to pull Internet users into pornographic websites.[48] Knowingly using a deceptive domain name to lure a person into viewing obscene material is punishable by a fine or two years in prison. If the domain name is used to deceive a child into viewing material "harmful to minors," the punishment increases to four years.

Domain names that include the words sex or porn obviously aren't meant to mislead, but websites like Teltubbies.com and Bobthebiulder.com, which contain misspellings that children are likely to make, would certainly qualify. John Zuccarini, the first person convicted of violating the law, registered sites with typos that redirected users' browsers to pay-per-click advertising sites, some with ads for free access to pornography.[49]

State Internet regulation

States are entitled to prohibit the distribution of indecent material to minors. In *Ginsburg v. New York* (1968), the Supreme Court held that a state may classify some forms of sexual expression that would not be obscene for adults as harmful to minors in order to protect their psychological and ethical development. It upheld a statute that made it a crime to knowingly sell to minors any depiction of nudity that

(i)   predominantly appeals to the prurient, shameful or morbid interest of minors,

(ii)   is patently offensive to prevailing standards in the adult community as a whole with respect to what is suitable material for minors, and

(iii) is utterly without redeeming social importance for minors."[50]

However, regulating indecency on the Internet at the state level presents a problem. In *ACLU v. Johnson* (1999), the Tenth Circuit upheld an injunction barring New Mexico from enforcing a state statute that criminalized the dissemination of material "harmful to a minor" via computer.[51] The appellate court relied heavily on the Supreme Court's analysis of the Communications Decency Act in *Reno v. ACLU* to conclude that New Mexico's statute unconstitutionally burdened adult speech. The appellate court also agreed with the district court that the state violated the constitution's commerce clause by: (1) regulating conduct that occurred outside of the state, (2) unreasonably burdening interstate and foreign commerce, and (3) subjecting interstate uses of the Internet to state regulation. The Tenth Circuit pointed out that "the nature of the Internet forecloses the argument that a statute such [as this] applies only to intrastate communications. Even if it is limited to one-on-one e-mail communications … there is no guarantee that a message from one New Mexican to another New Mexican will not travel through other states en route."

Violence

Sex and violence are usually grouped together among media sins, but legally they are very treated differently. Courts are much more reluctant to uphold content-based regulations targeted at violent speech or to impose liability on content producers for the harm that supposedly results from it.

© Semihundido, http://everystockphoto.com/photo.php?imageId=2730875
Although more than 1,000 studies – including reports from the Surgeon General's Office – have shown a link between media violence and aggression in some children, many researchers dispute the assertion that violent media causes violence.

Controlling access to violent speech

Fear engendered by high school shootings in Littleton, Colo., and Paducah, Ky., prompted states and communities to take a closer look at the types of video games, websites, music, and movies the shooters were consuming. Multiple states reacted by passing laws that prohibited the sale of violent video games to minors. States assumed they could act to protect minors from violence under the same theory that allows them to protect minors from exposure to indecency.

Indianapolis, for example, passed an ordinance that required arcade owners to label video game machines that were harmful to minors, partition them off from other games, and limit minors' access to them unless they were accompanied by a parent or guardian. The ordinance relied on a derivative of the *Ginsburg* and *Miller* tests to define what was "harmful to minors" as a game that:

(A) "predominantly appeals to minors' morbid interest in violence or minors' prurient interest in sex,"

(B) "is patently offensive to prevailing standards in the adult community as a whole with respect to what is suitable material for persons under the age of eighteen (18) years," and
(C) "lacks serious literary, artistic, political or scientific value as a whole for persons under" that age, and contains either "graphic violence" or "strong sexual content."[52]

The American Amusement Machine Association sought an injunction to prevent the city from enforcing the ordinance and the U.S. Court of Appeals for the Seventh Circuit granted it. Judge Richard Posner, the author of almost 40 books and one of the most respected legal minds in the country, wrote the opinion for the court. He noted that while the ordinance "bracketed violence with sex," they are distinct categories with different concerns. Obscenity has traditionally been regulated on the basis that it is offensive to society, not that it causes harm. In contrast, the Indianapolis ordinance regulated violent video games primarily on the belief that they cultivate aggressive behavior that could lead players to harm others. The ordinance also presupposed that exposure to violence could be psychologically harmful to the players themselves. Government entities have the right to issue content-based regulations to prohibit violent speech, such as threats or fighting words that lead to breaches of the peace, because they precipitate real violence. But the regulation of violent imagery is another matter because there is no conclusive evidence that violent imagery causes real violence. The government also regulates indecent speech based on the theory that it causes psychological harm to children. Although this is a theory that is accepted at face value, Judge Posner rejected the notion that children are psychologically harmed by violence, based on a lack of conclusive evidence. Noting that violence is a universal theme in literature and that children have First Amendment rights, Judge Posner stated that the evidence "must be compelling and not merely plausible" that violent speech is harmful to justify restricting children from it.[53]

Posner's opinion laid the intellectual foundation for others to follow. Similar laws regulating minors' access to violent content in games have been enjoined from enforcement or struck down in Minnesota,[54] Michigan,[55] Illinois,[56] Washington,[57] St. Louis, Mo.,[58] California,[59] Louisiana,[60] and Oklahoma.[61]

Imposing liability on producers' violent media

Although there is inconclusive evidence that violent media cause violence, it is undisputed that people occasionally model behavior they observe in media in violent crimes. For example, three teen-aged fans of the heavy-metal band Slayer murdered a 15-year-old girl as part of a satanic ritual, following instructions in the band's songs *Altar of Sacrifice*, *Kill Again*, and *Necrophiliac*.[62] In another case, two boys killed their mother and disposed of her body using a technique they learned from a mobster on the HBO series *The Sopranos*.[63] Some individuals have committed suicide after taking the lyrics of songs too seriously. Families of victims in copycat cases occasionally sue media producers on theories of negligence or incitement to violence.

Negligence representations of violence

The families of three children murdered in a Kentucky high school shooting attempted to prove that violent media producers were partly to blame because they negligently disseminated their products to impressionable youths who were led to commit violent acts. In 1997, Michael Carneal, a 14-year-old at Heath High School in Paducah, Kentucky, shot eight of his fellow students, killing three. He was arrested and convicted of murder. A subsequent investigation revealed that Carneal visited pornographic websites; watched *The Basketball Diaries*, a movie that depicted a student shooting his classmates; and played first-person shooter video games, such as *Doom, Quake, Castle Wolfenstein, Mech Warrior, Resident Evil, Redneck Rampage,* and *Final Fantasy.*

In *James v. Meow Media, Inc.* (2002), families of the murdered children sued the producers of these media for negligence, product liability, and racketeering.[64] The plaintiffs claimed the defendants were negligent because they knew or should have known that distribution of such material to Carneal and other young people posed an unreasonable risk to others. They argued that the defendants' violent media desensitized Carneal and caused him to commit violent acts.

A plaintiff who wants to prove that a media producer has been negligent must show: (1) that the defendant owed a duty of care to the plaintiff, (2) that the defendant breached that duty of care, and (3) that the defendant's breach was the proximate cause of the plaintiff's damages. To prove that the defendant owed a duty of care, the plaintiff must show that harm caused by the media product was foreseeable.

The district court concluded that Carneal's actions were not sufficiently foreseeable to trigger a duty on the defendants' part to protect third parties from consumers of their media. It added that even if the defendants had owed a duty of care, Carneal's actions were the superceding cause of the victims' deaths. A superceding cause exists when an event occurs after the defendant's initial action that substantially causes the harm.

The plaintiffs also made the novel argument that violent elements in the film, video games, and websites were defects in the media products distributed by the producers who were subject to product liability laws. The court concluded that "thoughts, ideas and images" portrayed in these media were not products, and therefore the defendants could not be held liable for their defects. Product liability would only apply if the cassettes or DVDs malfunctioned. Finally, it rejected the plaintiffs' argument that the websites were engaged in a pattern of racketeering by distributing obscene material to minors. It did not see the connection between Carneal's violent actions and the material on the pornography sites and would not apply obscenity law to the violent sites because obscenity jurisprudence is generally applied to material of a sexual nature.[65]

A civil suit filed against media producers following the 1999 Columbine High School shootings was almost identical in scope to *James v. Meow Media*. Before killing twelve students and one teacher at their Littleton, Colorado, high school, Dylan Klebold and Eric Harris immersed themselves in the same video games, pornography sites, and film that Carneal had enjoyed. In fact, Klebold and Harris wore the same clothing on the day of the shooting that the central character in *The Basketball Diaries* had worn when he shot his victims. In *Sanders v. Acclaim Entertainment, Inc.* (2002), the family of the teacher Klebold and Harris murdered filed negligence, product liability, and racketeering claims against the same media producers sued in the Kentucky case as well as others.[66]

A federal district judge in Colorado dismissed the negligence claim, concluding that the defendants owed no duty of care to the Columbine victims. While

Grand Theft Auto games have sparked lawsuits related to sex and violence. Families of two police officers and dispatcher killed by an Alabama teen who played *Grand Theft Auto: Vice City* obsessively sued the game's maker, Take-Two Interactive, in 2005, alleging that the game trained him to kill. After his capture, the shooter reportedly told police, "Life is like a video game. Everybody's got to die sometime." The court granted summary judgment to Take-Two in 2009. But the same year Take-Two settled a $20 million class action suit over claims that *Grand Theft Auto: San Andreas* contained a hidden sex game.

acknowledging that the defendants "might have speculated that their motion picture or video games had the potential to stimulate an idiosyncratic reaction in the mind of some disturbed individuals," he noted that "speculative possibility ... is not enough to create a legal duty.[67] He also agreed that product liability claims were inapplicable to intangible thoughts, ideas, images, and messages.

Other courts have reached similar conclusions. In *Davidson v. Time Warner* (1997), a federal district court in Texas dismissed a negligence claim filed by the widow of a state trooper who was fatally shot when he stopped the driver of a stolen car.[68] The killer was listening to rap songs by Tupac Shakur, one of which described violence against police. California and Georgia courts dismissed negligence claims against Ozzy Osbourne filed by the parents of teenaged boys who killed themselves while listening to Osbourne's song "Suicide Solution."[69]

Incitement to Violence

Incitement refers to the use of speech to arouse others to criminal activity. It is a criminal violation, not a tort, and as such brings the added worry that the state might be engaging in official censorship or that the defendant could be imprisoned. The Supreme Court established the modern test for incitement to violence in *Brandenburg v. Ohio* (1969).[70] The case involved the prosecution of a Ku Klux Klan leader who was convicted for violating Ohio's criminal syndicalism statute, which prohibited "advocat[ing] ... crime, sabotage, violence, or unlawful methods of terrorism as a means of ... reform." At a Klan rally, Brandenburg was televised saying "We're not a revengent [sic] organization, but if our President, our Congress, our Supreme Court, continues to suppress the white, Caucasian race, it's possible that there might have to be some revengeance [sic] taken ... We are marching on Congress July the Fourth, four hundred thousand strong."[71]

The Supreme Court, which had spent the last 50 years considering the outer boundaries of speech threatening the government, reversed the decision, holding that abstract advocacy of violence must be distinguished from advocacy of imminent lawless action. It concluded that only speech "directed toward inciting or producing imminent lawless action and likely to incite or produce such action" could be denied First Amendment protection.[72] The words "directed toward" refer to intent. In other words, speech does not qualify as unlawful incitement unless harm is intended, imminent, and likely to occur. Although *Brandenburg* was meant to apply in criminal cases involving political speech rather than entertainment, courts have applied its "intent" requirement in civil tort cases.

The Louisiana Court of Appeals applied the Brandenburg test in *Byers v. Edmondson* (1999), a lawsuit against Oliver Stone, Warner Brothers, and other producers of the film *Natural Born Killers* filed by the victim of a couple on a murderous romp inspired by the movie.[73] The victim, Patsy Byers, was shot by Sarah Edmondson during an armed robbery of the convenience store in which Byers worked as a clerk. Edmondson and her boyfriend, Benjamin Darrus, set out from Oklahoma on a crime spree after taking LSD and watching the movie over and over.

Darrus murdered a man in Mississippi. After they were arrested, Edmondson told police that Darrus called her "his Mallory," alluding to the female character in the movie.

Byers claimed that the defendants knew or should have known that the movie "would cause and inspire people such as the defendants to commit crimes."[74] As evidence, she depended on a comment made by Oliver Stone following the movie's premiere that "The most pacifist people in the world said they came out of the movie and wanted to kill somebody."[75]

A Louisiana Court of Appeals surprised media watchers by refusing to dismiss the suit. It held that Byers had stated a valid cause of action and could proceed with the suit if she could prove intent on the part of the defendants. The court concluded that the film would lose its First Amendment protection if the plaintiffs could prove that the film incited imminent lawless activity. Byers also alleged that *Natural Born Killers* was excepted from First Amendment protection as a form of obscenity, but the appellate court did not address the allegation.

On remand, however, the trial court granted summary judgment to the defendants because plaintiffs' evidence was not sufficient to establish intent. The Louisiana Court of Appeals, now having apparently watched the movie, upheld the district court's summary judgment on appeal, but for a different reason.[76] It held that intent was immaterial in the case because *Natural Born Killers* was not inciteful speech. It explained that "Edmondson and Darrus may very well have been inspired to imitate the actions of Mickey and Mallory Knox, but the film does not direct or encourage them to take such actions. Accordingly, as a matter of law … *Natural Born Killers* cannot be considered inciteful speech" removed from First Amendment protection."[77]

The judge in *Sanders v. Acclaim Entertainment* also briefly considered whether *Brandenburg* applied to the Colorado case and concluded that it did not.[78] The plaintiffs did not allege that the media producers intended Klebold and Harris to react violently to their work, the reaction was not likely, and it was not imminent.

Had it gone to trial, *Rice v. Paladin Enterprises* (1997), better known as the "Hit man case," might have been an exception.[79] The plaintiffs in the case claimed that the publishers of the book *Hit Man: A Technical Manual for Independent Contractors* aided and abetted murder by printing instructions that a contract killer used to kill their family members.

Lawrence Horn hired James Perry to murder his ex-wife, his eight-year-old quadriplegic son, and his son's nurse, so he could collect a $2 million settlement paid to his son for injuries that had left him paralyzed. Perry followed the instructions in the manual to the letter. Both were convicted of murder.

The lower court granted summary judgment in favor of the publisher because it considered the plaintiffs' claim to be barred by the First Amendment, but the U.S. Court of Appeals for the Fourth Circuit reversed, explaining that "speech – even speech by the press – that constitutes criminal aiding and abetting does not enjoy the protection of the First Amendment."[80] The court observed that by Paladin's own admission, it intended through its marketing campaign, "to attract and assist criminals and would-be criminals who desire information and instructions on how to commit crimes," and also that *Hit Man* actually "would be used, upon receipt, by criminals and would-be criminals to plan and execute the crime of murder for hire."[81]

The court described Paladin's manual as "the antithesis of speech protected under *Brandenburg*" because it constituted "advocacy and teaching of concrete action," the "preparation … for violent action and [the] steeling … to such action." Paladin settled the case after the court's opinion rather than bring it to a jury.

Hate Speech

The United States is one of the few democratic nations that protects hate speech. Justice Louis Brandeis expressed a common view in the United States about unpopular speech – that when the malady is falsehood or bias "the remedy to be applied is more speech, not enforced silence."[82] One exception to the rule is *fighting words*, which may be regulated to avoid a disturbance of the peace. These are "words that people of common intelligence would know would be likely to cause a fight."[83] Because the doctrine only applies to face-to-face confrontations likely to ensue in violence, it has no bearing on digital media.[84] Hate speech filtered through a website, text message, e-mail, or television program does not constitute fighting words and is protected by the First Amendment.

Action motivated by hate is not protected, however. Almost all states and the federal government have enacted some form of legislation meant to counter hate crimes motivated by personal characteristics, such as race, color, religion, national origin, ethnicity, gender, disability, or sexual orientation. The federal statute, for example, allows juries to triple the punishment for a crime if they find that it was motivated by the victim's personal characteristics.[85]

Threats

Speech meant to harass or threaten is not protected. It is a criminal violation to transmit in interstate or foreign commerce any threat to kidnap or injure another person.[86]

Threats are open to interpretation, of course. Some are overt; others are implied. Most threats are expressions of momentary anger and would never be realized, as in "I'm going to kill my boss if he asks me to work on the weekend again." What matters is whether the threat, regardless of its character, is a statement that a reasonable person would foresee as likely to be interpreted by those to whom the maker communicates the statement as a serious expression of intent to harm.

The Supreme Court concluded that threats fall outside the realm of protected speech in *Watts v. United States* (1969).[87] But it also warned that law enforcement officers have to be careful because threats are often characterized by hyperbole. In *Watts*, an 18-year-old Vietnam war protester said to fellow demonstrators, "If they ever make me carry a rifle, the first man I want to get in my sights is L.B.J. [President Lyndon Baines Johnson]." He was arrested for violating a federal statute that makes it a felony to "knowingly and willfully … make any threat to take the life of, to kidnap, or to inflict bodily harm upon the President of the United States."[88] Only six years had passed since President John F. Kennedy's assassination, so the Court took death threats against the president seriously, but it also realized that threats must be examined in context. It said "a statute such as this one, which makes criminal a form of pure speech, must be interpreted with the commands of the First Amendment clearly in mind. What is a threat must be distinguished from what is constitutionally protected speech."[89]

The context of the speech determined the outcome in *Planned Parenthood of the Columbia/Willamette v. American Coalition of Life Activists* (2002), better known as the Nuremberg Files case.[90] A Portland, Oregon, jury ordered defendants, a coalition of abortion protesters, to pay $109 million in damages for threatening four abortion providers by circulating their names and addresses on "wanted"-style posters and a website the doctors described as a hit list. Neither the posters nor the website explicitly threatened violence against the doctors, but the plaintiffs successfully argued that they constituted true threats when viewed in context of a wave of violence against abortion providers.

During the 10 years preceding the case, there were 39 bombings, 99 acid attacks, 7 murders, and 16 attempted murders of doctors and clinic workers, according to the National Abortion Federation.[91] Four of those murdered were doctors. Three of them had been identified on similar wanted-style posters. The last to die was Barnett Slepian, whose name appeared on the Nuremberg Files website, along with 200 other abortion providers. The names of murdered doctors appeared on the list with a line through them. The names of injured doctors appeared shaded in gray. Slepian's name was crossed off the site only hours after his murder.

Plaintiffs brought the suit under the Freedom of Access to Clinic Entrances Act, which creates a right of action against whoever by "threat of force … intentionally … intimidates … any person because that person is or has been … providing reproductive health services." In March of 2001, a three-judge panel on the Ninth Circuit reversed the lower court's decision in favor of the plaintiffs. In its view, the district court allowed the jury to find ACLA liable for putting the doctors in harm's way by focusing too much on the context of the speech, which involved violent acts by third parties, and too little on the content, which never directly authorized or threatened harm. The court focused more on the issue of incitement. But that decision was short lived.

The plaintiffs requested the whole court to re-evaluate the case in an en banc hearing. The full court affirmed the lower court's verdict. The majority opinion, written by Judge Pamela Rymer, explained that "If ACLA had merely endorsed or encouraged the violent actions of others, its speech would be protected [under incitement law]. However "by replicating the poster pattern that preceded the elimination of [other] doctors … ACLA was not staking out a position of debate but of threatened demise. This turns the First Amendment on its head."[92]

Cyberstalking

Online harassment, dubbed cyberstalking, is also a violation of law. Cyberstalking not only covers personal actions to harass a victim, but also the encouragement of third parties to harass the victim. For example, stalkers have impersonated their victims in chat rooms and posted the names, phone numbers, and addresses of victims on electronic bulletin boards soliciting sexual attention.

In an attempt to curb cyberstalking, Congress amended the telephone harassment statute to include Internet communications in 2005. The statute makes it a crime to use, in interstate or foreign communications, "a telecommunications device, whether or not conversation or communication ensues, to annoy or threaten someone anonymously.[93]

The federal stalking law has also been adapted to the computer age. It now applies to anyone who, with the intent to harm, uses "… any interactive computer service … to engage in a course of conduct that causes substantial emotional distress" to a person in another state or U.S. jurisdiction or to place that person "in reasonable fear of the death or serious bodily injury" to him or herself, an immediate family member, a spouse, or intimate partner.[94]

Both of these laws only work if the stalking takes place across state lines. When it occurs in one state, the victim has to rely on state law.[95] In 1999, Gary S. Dellapenta was sentenced to six years in prison under California's cyberstalking law. The former security guard, who was angered when his victim rebuffed his attention at church, posted Internet personal ads in her name, indicating that she fantasized about being raped. The ads included her home address and directions to disable her alarm system. Six men visited her home before police learned Dellapenta was behind the harassment and arrested him.

The Indiana Supreme Court overturned delinquency charges filed against a 14-year-old Indiana girl who posted expletive-laced comments about her principal on a fake MySpace profile that a friend created in his name.[96] A lower court had held that the girl's actions, if carried out by an adult, would have violated Indiana's Harassment-Cyberstalking law. It was clear from the student's posts that she was angry because her principal had criticized her piercings:

"hey you piece of greencastle s**t. what the f**k do you think of me know (sic) that you cant [sic] control me? Huh? ha ha ha guess what ill [sic] wear my f**king piercings all day long and to school and you cant [sic] do s**t about it! ha ha f**king ha! stupid bastard.

Unfortunately, in true teen drama queen fashion, she added to the rant: "die … gobert … die" and "F**K MR. GOBERT AND GC SCHOOLS!"

Under the Indiana statute, it is an offense to "with intent to harass, annoy, or alarm another person but with no intent of legitimate communication: …

> (4)　use a computer network … or other form of electronic communication to
> > (A)　communicate with a person; or
> > (B)　transmit an obscene message or indecent or profane words to a person …"[97]

The site's creator had limited access to it to 26 MySpace "friends." The Indiana Supreme Court pointed out that in order to violate the statute's intent requirement "common sense informs that the person must have a subjective expectation that the offending conduct will likely come to the attention of the person targeted for the harassment."[98] There was no evidence to show that the petitioner had any reason to expect that the principal would learn about the site or read it. In fact, he only became aware of the girl's posts because one of the students with access to the site showed him a printout from it. The girl had also created a site of her own that was publicly accessible. But her comments on it – aside from its title, which associated the principal's name with another expletive – were a reaction to her friend's punishment for the private profile. The Indiana Supreme Court found the girl's page to be "legitimate communication of her anger and criticism" of the principal and school regarding the disciplinary actions it took against her friend for her private profile.[99]

Could hacker laws cover harassment?　A federal prosecutor filed charges under the Computer Fraud and Abuse Act, a law normally reserved for computer hackers, against a Missouri woman who taunted a 13-year-old girl on MySpace until she committed suicide. Megan Meier, an insecure teen who suffered from depression, developed a MySpace friendship with 16-year-old Josh Evans, who seemed wonderful at first but then turned on her cruelly. Megan's parents later learned that Josh Evans never existed. Lori Drew, the mother of one of the Megan's former friends, got an employee to create the fake profile so she could learn what Megan was saying online about her daughter. The mother, daughter, and employee sent Josh's messages, the last one telling Megan that the world would be a better place without her.

Missouri, which has since passed a cyberstalking law, was powerless to charge Drew with anything because she had not broken the law there. When the case attracted national attention, Drew was indicted by a federal prosecutor in California, where MySpace's servers are located, for accessing protected computers without authorization to get information used to inflict emotional distress on the girl.[100] The government based its case on the notion that violating MySpace's terms of service, requiring that subscribers provide "truthful and accurate registration information" and "refrain from promoting information that is false or misleading," amounted to an "unauthorized access" of MySpace in violation of the law. A jury cleared Drew of felony computer-hacking charges, but convicted her of three counts of misdemeanor computer fraud.[101] The judge later acquitted Drew of the charges, reasoning that the case was really one of breach of contract and that convicting someone for violating a website's terms of service empoweres the site's owner to determine what is a crime.[102]

Questions for Discussion

1. What is the difference between indecency and obscenity?
2. Why is it legal to possess obscenity in the home, but not to download it at home over the Internet?
3. What is the difference in the approach that American courts take regarding indecency and violent speech and their potential impact on children?
4. Are the makers of violent films, games, and music lyrics liable to the families of victims harmed by people inspired to act violently after using such media? Why or why not?

12

Commercial Speech and Antitrust Law

At one point, purely commercial speech was considered to be unworthy of First Amendment protection.[1] Although this is no longer true, commercial speech is still afforded "lesser protection" than other forms of speech.[2] Unlike political speech, which is considered core to the First Amendment, commercial speech can be suppressed if it is misleading, overreaching, or an invasion of privacy.

The Supreme Court initially based this notion on the "'common sense' distinction between speech proposing a commercial transaction, which occurs in an area traditionally subject to government regulation, and other varieties of speech."[3] As its view on commercial speech developed further it suggested that the First Amendment protects advertising's "informational function." When advertising is false or misleading, it is not serving an informational function and is therefore not protected.

The regulatory agency with the largest impact on commercial speech is the Federal Trade Commission. It serves a dual role by protecting consumers against unfair or deceptive practices and companies from anticompetitive practices and mergers. Occasionally, as in the case of Sirius and XM radio, it is called on to make decisions about mergers in communication companies that not only threaten to have an impact on competition but also on diversity of expression.

This chapter will examine the meaning of commercial speech, the principal legal test that applies to it, policies and restrictions related to advertising, and anti-trust action intended to preserve speech.

Advertising and First Amendment Protection

Advertising earned First Amendment protection through its association with political speech. The Supreme Court first held that a political ad alleged to have been defamatory was protected speech in *New York Times v. Sullivan* (1964).[4] The ad in question, written by a group of African American ministers as a commentary on a civil rights demonstration in Alabama, would now be described as an "advertorial." The Court acted again ten years later to protect advertising in *Bigelow v. Virginia* (1974), a case that concerned the right to advertise legal abortion services.[5] It held that speech is not devoid of First Amendment protection simply because it appears in the form of advertising. But it was not until 1976 that the Court protected advertising for its own sake. In *Virginia State Bd. of Pharmacy v. Virginia Citizens Consumer Council, Inc.* – a case concerning the right to advertise drug prices – the Court held that there is not only a right to advertise but a reciprocal right to receive advertisements.[6] It stated that in a free-enterprise economy "the allocation of our resources at large will be made through numerous private economic decisions. It is a matter of public interest that those decisions, in the aggregate, be intelligent and well informed. To this end, the free flow of commercial information is indispensable."[7]

Advertising is not beyond regulation, however. The government may impose reasonable time, place, and manner restrictions on commercial speech. It can control advertising that is deceptive or misleading or that promotes transactions that are themselves illegal. It also may subject commercial speech disseminated through broadcast media to certain requirements or restrictions based on its scarcity and pervasiveness rationale.

The Court crystallized its policy on commercial speech in the landmark case *Central Hudson Gas & Electric Company v. Public Service Commission* (1980). It concluded that commercial speech is afforded less protection than other speech and that its protection "turns on the nature both of the expression and of the governmental interests served by its regulation."[8] The case concerned the constitutionality of a New York Public Service Commission rule, passed during an energy shortage, which prohibited advertising that promoted energy consumption.

The Supreme Court used *Central Hudson* to establish a four-part test to evaluate the constitutionality of regulations applied to truthful commercial speech. A court must determine that:

1. the expression concerns a lawful activity and is not misleading;
2. the governmental interest in the regulation is substantial;
3. the regulation directly advances that interest; and
4. the regulation is no more extensive than necessary to serve that interest.[9]

The first prong is an entry-level consideration. Commercial speech that is false or misleading or that promotes an activity that is illegal is not protected. Unprotected speech may be regulated constitutionally. So there would be no need to employ the rest of the test.

After reviewing the Central Hudson case based on these criteria, the Court concluded that while the state's interest in energy conservation was substantial and advanced by the regulation, the regulation was overly extensive. A complete ban on advertising burdened too much protected speech. For example, it prevented the petitioner from advertising energy-efficient appliances. In that respect, the regulation violated the First and Fourteenth Amendments.

The right to reject advertising

Just as the First Amendment protects the right to advertise, it protects the right to reject advertising. The Supreme Court has said that the term free speech comprises "the decision of both what to say and what not to say."[10] Requiring a medium to accept advertising it does not want to run would be a form of compelled speech.

The Supreme Court held that there is no right of access to broadcast media in *CBS v. Democratic National Committee* (1973).[11] The DNC requested a declaratory ruling from the Federal Communications Commission stating that broadcasters had no right to refuse to sell time to responsible entities who wanted to solicit funds or comment on public issues. The FCC rejected its request. The Supreme Court upheld the FCC's decision. It pointed out that forcing a private medium to accept advertising would interfere with producers' rights to exercise editorial control over the content of the medium and require them to sacrifice other content they would have preferred to run in the space or time occupied by the compelled ad.

This case, along with another in which the Supreme Court held that there is no right of access to newspapers, has come to stand for the proposition that there is no right of access to private media.[12] This principle also applies to the Internet. A Delaware district court dismissed a suit against Google, Yahoo! Inc., and Microsoft Corp. for refusing to run ads for particular websites in *Langdon v. Google, Inc.* (2007).[13] Christopher Langdon sued the search engines when they declined to run ads for his websites criticizing North Carolina's attorney general and the Chinese government. Filing on his own behalf, Langdon alleged that the defendants' refusal to run his ads violated his First Amendment rights and constituted fraud because Google refused his ads for reasons that were not stated in its content policy. The court pointed out that, as private entities, the search engines could not violate the plaintiff's First Amendment rights. However, a court order compelling the defendants to run Langdon's ads would violate their First Amendment rights. The defendants were also entitled under Section 230 of the Communications Decency Act to refuse objectionable content.

However, the media may not reject advertising for discriminatory reasons.[14] Nor can they refuse advertising in violation of antitrust laws, discussed later in this chapter.[15] Broadcast media are also required to accept advertisements from federal candidates before an election and to provide equal access to other candidates should they choose to run state or local ads.

The FTC and Advertising Regulation

The primary agency responsible for controlling deceptive ads is the Federal Trade Commission. The FTC was created in 1914 to regulate unfair competition, but in

1938 its role was expanded to include consumer protection. The agency draws its power to prohibit deceptive advertising from Section 5 of the Federal Trade Commission Act, which states that "unfair or deceptive acts or practices in or affecting commerce … are … declared unlawful."[16]

Unfair acts or practices

Normally consumers survey product or service options, compare costs and benefits, and make their own choices. An unfair practice would impede consumers' ability to make their own decisions effectively. An ad or business practice is considered unfair if it injures consumers, violates established public policy, and is unethical or unscrupulous.

The act must injure consumers An act found to be unfairly injurious must meet three tests. The injury must be substantial; it must not be outweighed by any countervailing benefits to consumers or competition that the practice produces; and it must be one that consumers themselves could not reasonably have avoided. Substantial injury usually involves monetary harm. But the injury may also involve unwarranted health or safety risks. The FTC is not likely to consider the emotional impact of an advertisement, and therefore is generally not concerned about whether consumers simply find advertising offensive.

The act must violate public policy A finding of unfairness requires that the act or practice violate public policy "established by statute, common law, industry practice, or otherwise." The Commission is principally focused on injury and uses the violation of public policy requirement primarily as further evidence of injury. Reliance on public policy also serves as an external indicator of what constitutes injury. For example, the Commission has relied on the First Amendment decisions upholding consumers' right to receive information.

The act must be unethical or unscrupulous The FTC also considers whether the conduct was immoral, unethical, oppressive, or unscrupulous. The Commission has observed that conduct that is truly immoral or unscrupulous is usually injurious or violative of public policy, so it never relies on the third element as an independent indicator of unfairness.[17]

Deceptive advertising

The FTC considers three factors when determining whether an advertisement is deceptive: whether the ad contains a representation, omission, or practice that is likely to mislead; how a consumer acting reasonably in the circumstances would be likely to interpret the ad; and whether the ad's deception is material.

There must be a representation, omission, or practice likely to mislead   Deceptive ads may include false oral or written misrepresentations about a product or service, omissions meant to lead consumers to false conclusions, misleading price claims, and false warranties. Advertisers that make particular claims, whether explicitly stated or simply implied, must have a "reasonable basis" for them. The level of evidence required depends on the claim made. The FTC is most concerned about health and safety claims. It requires advertisers to support health and safety claims with "competent and reliable scientific evidence" gathered through studies and tests conducted using appropriate methodologies and evaluated by qualified reviewers.

The act or practice must be considered from a reasonable consumer's perspective   When assessing an ad, the FTC looks at it from the perspective of a "reasonable person" – not someone who is overly sensitive or gullible. If the ad could be interpreted in more than one way by a reasonable person, one of which is false, the seller will be held liable for the false interpretation.

The agency also considers the ad from the perspective of its intended audience. If the ad is targeted toward children, the FTC will consider the ad from the perspective of a reasonable child, who due to lack of age or experience would be less qualified than an adult to filter exaggerated claims. If the ad is targeted toward people who are sick, overweight, or elderly, the FTC will consider the ad from the perspective of audiences who may be more vulnerable to magic cures or scams.

When assessing an advertisement, the FTC considers the ad in its entirety, rather than divorcing particular words or phrases from the whole. Disclaimers in mouse print or spoken at lightning speed at the end of an ad will not be accorded any weight if the rest of the ad implies something else. Disclosures that qualify a claim must be displayed "clearly and conspicuously." If a disclosure is made through a hyperlink, the link should be prominently displayed near the claim. The FTC also considers the fact that people skim ads and websites, so accurate information in the text of an ad may not make up for a deceptive headline.

The representation, omission, or practice must be material   Deceptive statements or omissions are considered material if they are likely to affect a consumer's purchasing decision. Certain categories are presumptively material. These include implied claims, if there is evidence to show that the seller intended to make an implied claim, and express claims about a product's performance, features, safety, price, or effectiveness. In contrast, subjective statements, regarding taste, smell, or appearance, are considered subject to consumer interpretation and are much less likely to attract the FTC's attention.

According the agency's Statement on Deception, "A finding of materiality is also a finding that injury is likely to exist because of the representation, omission, sales practice, or marketing technique … Injury exists if consumers would have chosen differently but for the deception."[18]

FTC Actions against False Advertising

Consumers who spot deceptive advertising can file a complaint with the FTC, which will investigate the ad and respond to it with the action it considers appropriate. The Commission's preferred course of action in false advertising cases is to seek voluntary compliance with the law though a consent order. A consent order is a negotiated settlement in which the advertiser agrees to refrain from further deception without having to admit any wrongdoing. For example, in a consent agreement with the FTC, WebTV agreed to stop advertising that it could offer people the same level of Internet access and content through their TVs that they could achieve through a computer.[19] Consent orders carry the force of law. Violation of the order can result in a fine of $11,000 per ad per day.

If the advertiser does not agree to stop the offending ad, the FTC will issue an administrative complaint against it and the case will go before an administrative law judge within the agency. In an administrative proceeding, parties present evidence and witnesses as they would in a trial, and the administrative law judge acts as fact finder. At the end of the proceeding, the administrative judge issues an initial decision, stating the facts and relevant law. The Commission then makes its final determination to dismiss the case or issue a cease and desist order. Cease and desist orders, which remain in force for 20 years, require an advertiser to discontinue a particular practice and avoid further deception. An advertiser has 60 days to comply with the order or launch an appeal in the federal court system. The advertiser may petition a U.S. Court of Appeals to review the Commission's decision, either in the circuit in which the company is based or where the alleged deception was carried out.

If a fraudulent act is particularly egregious and ongoing, the FTC may go straight to federal court to file a complaint against the advertiser. For example, in *FTC v. Accusearch, Inc.* (2008), the Commission asked for an injunction to stop an information broker from selling consumer telephone records to third parties without the consumers' knowledge.[20] The company advertised on its website that it could deliver anyone's phone records for a fee, and it did after obtaining them through illegal methods. A Wyoming district court permanently enjoined the company from selling or advertising the sale of telephone records and made it return $200,000 in ill-gotten profits.

Courts may also demand corrective advertising in false advertising cases, impose civil fines, and require defendants to pay restitution. In 2008, a federal district judge in Atlanta ordered online pharmaceutical companies to pay the FTC $15.8 million in restitution to consumers duped into spending that much on the defendants' weight loss drugs and erectile dysfunction remedies.[21] The products, advertised as "clinically proven" to reduce overall fat by 40–70 percent and to remedy erective dysfunction in 90 percent of cases, had never been tested in clinical trials. Judge Pannell said the companies "dispensed deception to those with the greatest need to believe it."[22]

Endorsements and testimonials

Endorsements and testimonials are common in advertisements and the FTC has enacted rules for their use. Expert endorsements may only come from someone truly qualified to give an opinion on the subject.[23] Dr. Packard, the professor, would not be allowed to give an opinion on the effectiveness of a particular drug, for example. If the endorser is connected to the seller in a manner that may influence the endorsement, that connection must be revealed. Consumers expect experts and celebrities to be paid for endorsing a product, so it is not necessary to disclose that information. However, if the expert or celebrity endorser will share profits from the sale of the product, consumers should be informed.[24] A person who is paid to endorse a product may not claim that the endorsement is freely given. If the endorser claims to use the product, he or she must in fact use it. Likewise, advertisements that claim to be using endorsements by actual consumers must be using the statements of actual consumers.

Testimonials must reflect customers' typical experience with a product.[25] It is not enough simply to say that results may vary. Claims made about the effectiveness of a drug or device must be substantiated. Testimonials cannot be used to mislead consumers. For example, a testimonial cannot make claims about a product that the manufacturer cannot legally make.[26]

Subliminal advertising

Subliminal advertising is supposed to act on consumers subconsciously by transmitting messages to them below the threshold of their awareness. Although it has never been proved to be effective, the FTC does not allow subliminal advertising because the practice is deceptive. The Federal Communications Commission also has a policy against subliminal advertising because the agency considers it "contrary to the public interest."[27] Nevertheless, advertisers occasionally use it. Examples have been cited in films, on television, in print, and now flash advertisements on the Internet.

Subliminal advertising was an issue in the 2000 presidential election when Senators Ron Wyden and John Breaux asked the FCC to investigate commercials that attacked Al Gore's prescription drug proposal while displaying the word RATS for one-thirtieth of a second longer than the rest of word BUREAUCRATS. The agency questioned 179 stations that aired the ad, finding that they either did not know the word was there or knew that it was there but assumed that because it was visible it did not constitute subliminal advertising. The Commission determined that no further action was warranted on its part because it could only punish the stations, not the opposing campaign for placing the ad.

Vance v. Judas Priest (1990) presents the most in-depth discussion of subliminal messaging.[28] The plaintiffs were parents of two boys who made a suicide pact while listening to the Judas Priest album *Stained Glass*. One succeeded in killing himself; the other was gravely injured. A song on the album called "Better by you, better than me" contained the hidden words "do it." A federal district court in Nevada ruled that subliminal messages are not protected by the First Amendment and constitute an invasion of privacy if they are intended to manipulate the recipient's behavior. However, because the plaintiffs did not prove that the defendants intended to put subliminal messages in the album and scientific evidence did not support the effectiveness of subliminal messages, the court ruled in favor of the defendants.

Advertisements and Foreseeable Harm

Normally the company advertising a particular product or service is responsible for false or deceptive advertising, but third parties such as advertising agencies and web designers may be held liable for false advertising as well if they contribute to the ad's preparation or are aware that its content is deceptive or unfair. The FTC considers it the duty of advertising agencies and web designers to verify the information used to substantiate claims in ads. It will hold them responsible if they know or *should have known* that the claims were false. Accepting a client's assurance that the ads are substantiated is not enough.

Publishers and broadcasters are rarely held liable for advertising unless they take part in the production of the ad or it is obvious from the ad's content that it is likely to cause harm. Courts assume that publishers do not have a duty to investigate the claims of advertisers because requiring them to bear that burden would draw time and attention away from their own speech.

Ohio's First District Court of Appeals reiterated this point in *Amann v. Clear Channel Communications, Inc.* (2006).[29] The appellate court upheld a lower court's grant of summary judgment in favor of Clear Channel on claims that the company negligently failed to verify the content of its advertisements and committed negligent misrepresentation by airing a false ad on a Cincinnati radio station. The advertisements at issue promoted a "guaranteed 10% income plus plan" that turned out to be a fraudulent investment scheme. The appellate court held that Clear Channel had no duty to investigate claims made in the ad. It also held that running the ad was not a negligent misrepresentation on Clear Channel's part because the tort of negligent misrepresentation, which involves supplying false information for the guidance of others in their business transactions, requires a defendant to intentionally direct information to a specific or limited group of people rather than a general audience.

Although a medium has no duty to investigate claims in an ad, it can be held liable for publishing an advertisement that "on its face, and without the need for investigation, makes it apparent that there is a substantial danger of harm to the public."[30]

In *Braun v. Soldier of Fortune* (1992), the Eleventh Circuit upheld a $4.3 million award against the magazine for negligently publishing an ad for a contract killer.

The ad read: "GUN FOR HIRE: 37-year-old professional mercenary desires jobs. Vietnam veteran. Discrete and very private. Body guard, courier, and other special skills. All jobs considered." Two men who read the ad hired the mercenary to kill their business associate, Richard Braun. The victim's son, Michael Braun, was also wounded in the attack. The Court of Appeals held that the First Amendment permits liability for the negligent publication of an ad that poses a clearly identifiable and unreasonable risk.

False Advertising and the Lanham Act

While the FTC enforces its rules intended to protect the public at large, private citizens and companies harmed by unfair competition may sue for false advertising under Section 43(a)(1) of the Lanham Act – the same provision that prohibits false designation of origin in trademark cases. The statute provides a civil claim against anyone who "uses in commerce … any false of misleading representation of fact, which … in commercial advertising or promotion, misrepresents the nature, characteristics, qualities, or geographic origin of his or her or another person's goods, services or commercial activities."[31] The false claims may pertain to the advertiser's product or the competitor's product and may be comparative or noncomparative.

To successfully prove a claim under the Lanham Act, a plaintiff must establish that the defendant made:

1. a false or misleading statement of fact about a product;
2. such statement either deceived, or had the capacity to deceive a substantial segment of potential consumers;
3. the deception is material, in that it is likely to influence the consumer's purchasing decision;
4. the product is in interstate commerce; and
5. the plaintiff has been or is likely to be injured as a result of the statement at issue.[32]

The Lanham Act empowers courts to issue injunctions to stop false advertising. A plaintiff also may recover monetary damages if he or she can show that consumers relied on the false advertising to the detriment of the plaintiff's business or, alternatively, that the defendant deliberately published false comparative claims.[33] A plaintiff who can show willfulness or bad faith on the part of the defendant, may be awarded the defendant's profits from the false advertising.[34] A court may also demand that the defendant do corrective advertising to counteract false claims.

Because the focus of the Lanham Act is unfair competition, it is not meant to provide a private cause of action for consumers hurt by false advertising. Consumers who want to pursue independent claims normally do so through state consumer protection acts.

Categories of falsity

Courts categorize misleading advertisements as literal falsity, implied falsity, and puffery. *Literal falsity* involves false statements of fact. *Implied falsity* refers to statements that are literally true, but which are phrased in a misleading way. *Puffery* describes exaggeration and subjective claims that no consumer would be likely to take as fact. The first two categories are illegal, but the third is not.

Literally false statements are classified as either *establishment claims*, in which the defendant has based the advertised claim on some evidence (e.g. "Tests prove" or "studies show" …) or *bald claims* in which the defendant has made an unsupported assertion.[35] To establish the falsity of an ad with an establishment claim, a plaintiff must show that the defendant's studies do not sufficiently support the claim.[36] To establish the falsity of an ad with a bald claim, the plaintiff must disprove the claim.[37] A plaintiff who can prove that an advertisement is literally false will not be required to show that consumers were actually deceived by it.

If the falsity in an ad is only implied, however, the plaintiff will have to provide evidence that the advertisement is capable of misleading the public. Plaintiffs usually do this by submitting surveys that show consumers received the implied false message from the ad. Some circuits require the plaintiff to show that the ad actually deceived consumers. Others are satisfied with a showing that the ad had a tendency to deceive.

Sometimes it is difficult to tell whether an advertisement should be classified as literal or implied falsity. *Time Warner Cable, Inc. v. DIRECTV, Inc.* (2007) addressed this problem.[38] Time Warner sued DIRECTV for false advertising, contending that the satellite provider's advertising campaign promoting its high-definition programming made the literally false claim that cable HD service is inferior to satellite HD service. A district court, which agreed, awarded summary judgment to Time Warner on its claim and enjoined DIRECTV from further use of the campaign. DIRECTV appealed, arguing that its television commercials were not literally false because they did not explicitly state that DIRECTV's HD programming was superior to any other cable provider's service.

The U.S. Court of Appeals for the Second Circuit reviewed two of DIRECTV's television advertisements. The first, starring Jessica Simpson as Daisy Duke from the movie *Dukes of Hazzard*, went like this:

Simpson: Y'all ready to order?
Hey, 253 straight days at the gym to get this body and you're not gonna watch me on
    DIRECTV HD?
You're just not gonna get the best picture out of some fancy big screen TV without
    DIRECTV.
It's broadcast in 1080i. I totally don't know what that means, but I want it.

The commercial originally ran with an accompanying tagline that read "for picture quality that beats cable, you've got to get DIRECTV." When Time Warner complained, the tagline was changed to: "For an HD picture that can't be beat, get

DIRECTV." The Second Circuit found the ad likely to be proven literally false. Writing for the court, Judge Straub said "These statements make the explicit assertion that it is impossible to obtain 'the best picture' – i.e., a '1080i'-resolution picture – from any source other than DIRECTV. This claim is flatly untrue."[39]

DIRECTV's second television ad, which follows, was a take-off on the science fiction series *Star Trek*, with William Shatner reprising his role as Captain Kirk:

> Mr. Chekov: Should we raise our shields, Captain?
> Captain Kirk: At ease, Mr. Chekov.
> Again with the shields, I wish he'd just relax and enjoy the amazing picture clarity of
>   the DIRECTV HD we just hooked up.
> With what Starfleet just ponied up for this big screen TV, settling for cable would be
>   illogical.

The ad was followed by the same revised tagline: "For an HD picture that can't be beat, get DIRECTV."

The Second Circuit, acknowledged that the Shatner ad was more ambiguous because it did not make an explicitly false assertion. In determining whether the ad could be interpreted as literally false, it chose to adopt the "false by necessary implication" doctrine. The First, Third, Fourth, and Ninth Circuits have already accepted the doctrine, which requires courts to analyze advertising messages in context. The Second Circuit held that "an advertisement can be literally false even though it does not explicitly make a false assertion, if the words or images, considered in context, necessarily and unambiguously imply a false message.[40] However, it warned that "if the language or graphic is susceptible to more than one reasonable interpretation, the advertisement cannot be literally false."[41] Applying the "false by necessary implication" doctrine, the Court of Appeals affirmed the district court's conclusion that the statement "settling for cable would be illogical," *in context with the rest of the ad*, amounted to a false claim that cable's HD service is inferior to DIRECTV's HD service.

Although DIRECTV's television ads did not name Time Warner explicitly, the Second Circuit upheld the lower court's injunction against it. In a market in which Time Warner was the only cable alternative, it would be obvious to viewers that the comparative ads were directed toward it. However, the Court of Appeals reversed the injunction as it applied to DIRECTV's Internet advertisements, because it considered them to be "non-actionable puffery" described below.

Puffery

Puffery involves the use of subjective statements that are not capable of measurement, such as "Downy makes your clothes smell April fresh," the meaning of which is open to anyone's interpretation. It also includes hyperbole consumers are unlikely to believe, such as one game maker's boast that it made "The Most Advanced Home Gaming System in the Universe."[42] Papa John's protected puffery – "Better Ingredients. Better Pizza" – was both opinion and exaggeration.[43] The FTC's stance on puffery is to ignore it as long as it does not imply a statement of fact and consumers are unlikely to take it seriously.[44] Courts also consider puffery OK as long as it doesn't cross the line into believability.

Puffery is almost always described in verbal terms. The Second Circuit's opinion on puffery in *Time Warner v. DIRECTV* was significant because it addressed the use of visual puffery. The Court of Appeals held that puffery includes "visual depictions that, while factually inaccurate, are so grossly exaggerated that no reasonable consumer would rely on them in navigating the marketplace."[45]

DIRECTV's banner advertisements for high-definition satellite service began with an image that was impossible to discern because it was so highly pixilated accompanied by the slogan "SOURCE MATTERS." After a moment, the pixilated image split. One side of the screen, labeled DIRECTV, was crystal clear. The opposite side, labeled "OTHER TV," remained pixilated and distorted. Viewers were prompted to "Find out why DIRECTV's picture beats cable." The Court of Appeals found that it would be "difficult to imagine that any consumer, whatever the level of sophistication, would actually be fooled" by the exaggerated imagery.[46]

False Advertising and State Law

All states have consumer protection laws to protect against unfair and deceptive trade practices. Consumers may use these laws to recover damages when they are harmed by false advertising. Businesses and individuals may use them in lieu of the Lanham Act to seek redress for deceptive competitive practices that do not involve interstate commerce. State laws also empower attorneys general to investigate claims on behalf of the public. Attorneys general from 32 states sued the manufacturers of the nutritional supplement Airborne for making unsubstantiated claims that the product could ward off colds. They reached a multi-state settlement for $7 million in December of 2008.[47] Without admitting guilt, the company also agreed to a $23.3 million settlement in a separate class action suit for false advertising in California.[48] Both suits occurred after ABC reported that the lone study demonstrating Airborne's effectiveness was conducted without doctors or scientists.

Advertising "Sin" Products and Services

Essentially, if a service or product is legal, advertising it must be legal as well, but it took the Supreme Court a while to come to that conclusion. For many years, the government has tried to control what might be called "sin" products and services – that are immoral or unhealthy, like gambling, alcohol, and tobacco products – by controlling advertisements for them.

In *Posadas de Puerto Rico Associates v. Tourism Company of Puerto Rico* (1986), the Court considered whether Puerto Rico could prevent its casinos from promoting themselves in Puerto Rico or using the word "casino" on paraphernalia, such as matchbooks and napkins.[49] The local government legalized gambling to attract the tourist trade but banned casinos from promoting their services to Puerto Ricans. A local casino sued, claiming the law violated the First Amendment by suppressing commercial speech. The Supreme Court took the position that if Puerto Rico had the power to restrict casino gambling, it must have the power to ban advertisements for casino gambling.

The Court overruled *Posadas* in 1996, finding that it "clearly erred in concluding that it was 'up to the legislature' to choose suppression over a less speech-restrictive policy."[50] In *44 Liquormart, Inc. v. Rhode Island*, the Court said "The *Posadas* majority's conclusion on that point cannot be reconciled with the unbroken line of prior cases striking down similarly broad regulations on truthful, nonmisleading advertising when non-speech-related alternatives were available."[51]

Advertisements for alcohol

The *44 Liquormart* case concerned a challenge to a Rhode Island law that prevented retailers from advertising the price of alcoholic beverages. The state had also

"Disarrono: Pass the pleasure around" by Gabor Tarko, http://www.gabortarko.com/QT720/ disaronno.htm
The liquor industry ended its voluntary ban on broadcast advertising in 1996. This Disaronno ad, first aired in the United States in 2003, was banned in the United Kingdom for violating the Advertising Standards Authority guidelines prohibiting a link between sexual pleasure and alcohol consumption.

banned publishers and broadcasters from accepting ads that contained liquor prices.

Applying the *Central Hudson* test, the Court struck down the statute as a violation of the First Amendment. It did not think that a blanket ban on advertising alcohol prices directly advanced the state's interest in reducing alcohol consumption. Moreover, even if the state could establish a link, the regulation was not narrowly tailored.

There has never been a government ban on broadcast advertising of distilled spirits, but the liquor industry imposed a voluntary ban on radio advertising in 1936 and on television advertising in 1948. The Distilled Spirits Council of the United States, the industry's trade group, voted to lift the ban in 1996. NBC became the first network to broadcast ads for distilled spirits in 2001. There are no legal limits on beer advertising, but the beer industry has adopted a voluntary rule limiting advertising to media in which 70 percent of the audience is above the legal drinking age.

In addition to the Federal Trade Commission's power to regulate false advertising generally, the Federal Alcohol Administration Act prohibits statements in alcohol advertisements "that are disparaging of a competitor's products or are false, misleading, obscene, or indecent."[52]

Advertisements for cigarettes

Advertisements for cigarettes, small cigars, and smokeless tobacco products are prohibited on any medium that falls within the FCC's jurisdiction.[53] The ban, imposed by the Federal Cigarette Labeling and Advertising Act, applies to broadcast, cable, and satellite media. It also requires that ads placed in other U.S. media for cigarettes and smokeless tobacco products include the same kinds of health warnings that appear on the products' packaging.[54]

In June of 2009, Congress gave the Food and Drug Administration authority to regulate tobacco.[55] The legislation empowers the FDA to ban most outdoor advertising and impose restrictions on the use of lettering, trademarks, colors and other imagery in advertisements. New warnings would also take up the top half of packaging, pushing branding to the bottom. Two of the three largest cigarette manufacturers, R.J. Reynolds Tobacco Co. and Lorillard Inc., filed suit against the FDA. They claim that advertising and labeling restrictions violate their First Amendment rights by leaving them too few avenues for speech.[56]

Tobacco advertising was significantly curtailed in 1998 by a court settlement between major tobacco companies and 46 states' attorneys general who sued the industry to recover public health costs related to smoking illnesses. Tobacco companies are prevented from marketing their products to children through the use of cartoon characters, apparel with brand-name logos, and brand-name sponsorships of concerts and games with a significant youth audience. The settlement also prohibits payments to promote tobacco products in movies, TV shows, and video games and limits use of ads on billboards and public transit.

Advertisements for lotteries and casinos

Electronic media may not carry advertisements for certain types of lotteries and chance-based schemes that offer prizes in exchange for money or some other consideration.[57] It is generally illegal to broadcast advertisements for lotteries unless:

1. the lottery is state-sponsored and the advertisements appear on a station in that state or another that conducts such a lottery;
2. the gambling is sponsored by an Indian tribe pursuant to the Indian Gaming Regulatory Act; or
3. the lottery is conducted, with state permission, by a not-for-profit or government organization, or by a commercial organization as an occasional promotional activity ancillary to its regular business.[58]

Casino advertising, which was formerly banned on broadcast television, is now legal, regardless of where the station or cable system is located.[59]

By 2003, advertisements for Internet gambling were ubiquitous on television and the Internet. At that point, the Justice Department voiced its view that providing online gambling services is illegal and that accepting advertisements from them may be constituted as aiding and abetting an illegal activity.[60] In 2004, U.S. marshals seized more than $2 million from the Discovery Network in advertising revenue prepaid by Paradise Poker because the money was generated from illegal online gaming and intended for its further promotion.[61] In 2006, the *Sporting News* settled with the Justice Department for $7.2 million to avoid criminal charges for advertising online gambling.

Advertising to Children

Because children can influence their parents' purchasing decisions and have some discretionary income of their own, they are a target audience for advertising. But their inexperience makes them more vulnerable to advertising and therefore worthy of greater protection. The Children's Television Act of 1990 limits advertising in broadcast television programs produced for children 12 and younger to 10.5 minutes of commercials per hour on weekends and 12 minutes of commercials per hour on weekdays.[62] If a program includes an advertisement for a product associated with the program – for example, an ad for Jimmy Neutron toys during the Jimmy Neutron show – the FCC will regard the show as a "program-length" advertisement.

Because the FCC is concerned that young children may not be able to distinguish between some programming and commercial content, it requires the insertion of "bumpers" between programs and ads.[63] Statements like "We'll be right back after these messages," cue children that a commercial is coming. This requirement also suggests, although it has not yet been tested, that product placement and embedded advertising is prohibited in children's programming.

The display of website addresses in programming for children 12 and under is permitted only if the website meets the following criteria:

- it offers a substantial amount of bona fide program-related or other noncommercial content;
- it is not primarily intended for commercial purposes, including either e-commerce or advertising;
- the home page and other menu pages are clearly labeled to distinguish the non-commercial from the commercial sections; and
- the page of the Web site to which viewers are directed is not used for e-commerce, advertising, or other commercial purposes …[64]

If a program character is being used to sell a product on the website, referred to as host-selling, the character must appear in a commercial section of the website that is clearly separated from the noncommercial section.

The Children's Online Privacy Protection Act also requires that websites obtain verifiable parental consent before collecting personal information from children under 13. The rule applies to commercial websites and online services for children and to general websites that know they are collecting information from a child.

Advertising Intrusions

Limitations on commercial speech have been put in place in an effort to safeguard personal privacy and productivity and to curtail fraudulent marketing practices. Recent legislation has imposed restrictions on telemarketing, junk faxes, and spam in particular.

Telemarketing

The Federal Trade Commission prescribes rules against deceptive telemarketing under the Telemarketing and Consumer Fraud and Abuse Prevention Act.[65] The rules require telemarketers to promptly disclose the purpose of the call as well as the nature and price of any goods and services. It prohibits telemarketers from calling people before 8 a.m. or after 9 p.m. or calling people who have stated previously that they do not wish to receive calls from the seller or charitable organization.[66] The FTC implemented the National Do-Not-Call registry to make it easier for people to refuse telemarketing calls.[67] Telemarketers are required to "scrub" their call lists every 31 days to ensure they do not contain numbers placed on the registry.[68]

The FTC also prescribes rules to prohibit deceptive ads for those 900 numbers that charge by the minute.[69] Ads for pay-for-call services must clearly and conspicuously disclose the cost of using the number. They may not target children under 12, unless they offer educational services, and are prohibited from targeting individuals under 18 without stating that consent to use the service is required by a parent or guardian.

Junk faxes

The Telephone Consumer Protection Act prohibits the use of "any telephone facsimile machine, computer, or other device to send an unsolicited advertisement to a telephone facsimile machine."[70] The law applies to unsolicited advertisements sent to personal and business home numbers. The Junk Fax Prevention Act of 2005 amended the law to allow unsolicited faxes to people with whom the sender has an established business relationship.[71] However, the Act also establishes a process receivers may use to opt out of future transmissions. Senders must include contact information on the fax that receivers can use to stop the communications and honor such requests within 30 days.

Spam

Junk e-mail, or spam, outpaced legitimate e-mail for the first time in 2003. To get the problem under control, Congress passed the Controlling the Assault of Non-Solicited Pornography and Marketing Act, better known as the CAN-SPAM Act.[72] The statute provides civil and criminal penalties for false of deceptive commercial e-mail.

The CAN-SPAM Act prohibits marketers from using materially false or misleading header information or subject lines in commercial e-mails. It requires that commercial e-mails be labeled as advertisements and include a functioning return e-mail address or Internet link that recipients can use to opt out of additional messages. Senders have 10 business days to honor a recipient's request and are barred from selling or transferring the person's e-mail address to others. Commercial e-mails must also include the physical location of the sender. Each violation (in other words, each e-mail sent) is punishable by a fine of up to $250, not to exceed $2 million.

Sexually oriented commercial e-mail may not be transmitted to recipients who have not given their prior consent for it. The FTC requires sexually oriented spam to include the warning "SEXUALLY-EXPLICIT" in the subject heading. When opened the initially viewable content must include only the following:

- the phrase "SEXUALLY-EXPLICIT";
- clear and conspicuous identification that the message is an advertisement;
- notice of the opportunity to decline further messages from the sender;
- a functioning return e-mail address or link to decline the messages.[73]

Violations are punishable by fines or imprisonment of up to 5 years.

The statute also directed the FCC to develop rules to prohibit wireless spam, which is not only annoying but costly to receive.[74] The FCC has since banned the transmission of commercial text messages that include an Internet domain name (the @ symbol) to mobile devices. The ban does not apply to messages from commercial senders who already have an established business relationship with the consumer through prior transactions; however, even these retailers must provide an opportunity to opt out of their messages. The FCC does not prohibit commercial text messages transmitted solely to mobile numbers without the inclusion of an Internet address. However, short-message-service spam can be punished if the receiver has included the number on the national Do-Not-Call list.

The Department of Justice can pursue criminal penalties against spammers who commit fraud by knowingly:

- accessing a computer without authorization, and intentionally initiating the transmission of multiple commercial electronic mail messages through it;
- using a protected computer to transmit multiple commercial e-mails, with the intent to deceive or mislead recipients;
- falsifying header information in multiple commercial e-mails;
- registering or using information that materially falsifies the identity of the actual registrant, for five or more e-mail accounts or two or more domain names, and using them to transmit multiple commercial e-mails; or
- falsely representing oneself as the registrant or the legitimate successor to the registrant of 5 or more Internet Protocol addresses, and using them to transmit multiple commercial e-mails.[75]

The term "multiple" refers to more than 100 messages sent in a 24-hour period, 1,000 messages in a 30-day period, or 10,000 messages in a 1-year period.

By the time Congress enacted the CAN-SPAM Act, many states had already developed their own anti-spam laws. The federal statute supercedes state laws, except for provisions that prohibit falsity or deception in any part of a message.[76]

Political Advertising

Unlike other forms of commercial speech, political advertising is fully protected. Consequently, campaign ads are prone to exaggeration and falsehoods. The media serve as a deterrent against political deception to the extent that they are willing to embarrass politicians by exposing false claims made about their opponents. Campaigns have sidestepped this problem, however, by allowing special interest groups to initiate deceptive attack ads. When the ads were exposed, candidates denied responsibility for them.

Congress inhibited this practice when it passed the Bipartisan Campaign Reform Act of 2002, otherwise known as the McCain-Feingold Act. The legislation required candidates for federal office to take responsibility for advertisements placed on their behalf.[77] Television advertisements must now include a visual image of the candidate and a printed statement, indicating that the candidate has approved the message and that the candidate's authorized committee paid for it. Radio advertisements must include a personal audio statement in which candidates identify themselves and the office they are seeking and indicate that they have approved the advertisement.

The legislation also attempted to eliminate loopholes used to get around campaign contribution restrictions. The Federal Election Campaign Act of 1971 placed limits on contributions to candidates in federal elections. An individual or group may donate no more than $2,300 to any one candidate, while political committees must limit their contributions to $5,000. However, "soft money" contributions that were not used to directly influence an election for a particular candidate were left relatively unrestricted. Soft money can be used for get-out-the-vote campaigns, political party ads, legislative activity ads, and issue ads that name a particular candidate as long as there is no call to either elect or vote against the candidate. Corporations, unions, and other organizations that sought to influence campaigns bypassed restrictions on individual contributions by donating soft money to political parties and political action committees that, in turn, used the money to help individual candidates.

The McCain-Feingold Act amended the law to place restrictions on soft money contributions that politicians and political parties could solicit, spend or donate to special interest groups. Interest groups known as 527 committees (based on the section of the tax code that relates to them) may continue to solicit funds for issue advertising. But they may not coordinate their activities with candidates or hide their role in advertising anymore.

The statute created a new term: "electioneering communication," which encompasses any "broadcast, cable, or satellite communication" that identifies a candidate for federal office, airs within 30 days of a primary or 60 days of an election, and targets a relevant electorate. Any individual or group that spends more than $10,000 on electioneering communication must file disclosure statements with the Federal Election Commission. Individuals who contribute more than $1,000 to a group purchasing electioneering communications also must file a disclosure statement. The statute also treats any disbursements for electioneering communications coordinated with a candidate or party as contributions to, and expenditures by, the candidate or party.

Although campaign contributions may not seem like a form of expression, the two are closely connected in politics because money is required to purchase advertising. In *Buckley v. Valeo* (1976), the Supreme Court held that while limits on campaign expenditures are problematic because they curtail a candidate's speech, limits on direct contributions to candidates "entai[l] only a marginal restriction upon the contributor's ability to engage in free communication ..."[78] It added that contribution limits further an important governmental interest: "preventing 'both the actual corruption threatened by large financial contributions and the eroding of public confidence in the electoral process through the appearance of corruption.'"[79]

The McCain-Feingold Act's limits on soft money contributions were challenged as a violation of the First Amendment in *McConnell v. Federal Election Commission* (2003).[80] By a narrow margin, the Supreme Court upheld most of the law's provisions. The Court concluded that limitations on the use of soft money were not overbroad because they met a sufficiently important government interest: "avoiding corruption and the appearance of corruption."[81] It also found that disclosure requirements related to electioneering communications fostered the government's interest in providing the electorate with information, deterring corruption and gathering data necessary to enforce substantive electioneering restrictions.

In a separate case, the Court also considered the rights of corporations and unions to participate in electioneering communication. Congress has prohibited corporations and unions from spending general funds on political ads that advocate the election of a particular candidate within 30 days of a primary or 60 days of a general election. Corporations and unions may run issue ads as long as they are not "the functional equivalent of express advocacy."[82] The Supreme Court has clarified that "an ad is the functional equivalent of express advocacy only if the ad is susceptible of no reasonable interpretation other than as an appeal to vote for or against a specific candidate."[83]

Internet communications and political activity

Campaign finance laws extend to communications on the Internet. If individuals or groups purchase Internet ads for a particular candidate, the expense will be counted as part of the $2,300 contribution individuals or groups can make to one candidate.

A publisher's cost for news reporting is not considered a campaign contribution or expenditure.[84] A media exemption applies to entities that offer news and commentary on the Internet, "including web sites or any other Internet or electronic publication."[85] The Federal Election Commission considers the exemption applicable to bloggers.[86]

Individuals who communicate about elections on the Internet are also exempt from contribution restrictions as long as their actions are uncompensated. They may, with or without a candidate's knowledge, send and forward electronic mail, blog, hyperlink to a website, or create a website supporting a candidate.

Does commercial speech include public relations?

The government can regulate commercial speech for truth, but what about public relations? This was the question in *Nike v. Kasky* (2003).[87] When Nike was accused of using sweatshops in underprivileged countries to produce its products, it defended its labor practices in press releases and letters to the media. Activist Mark Kasky, who argued that Nike's claims were untrue, sued the company under California laws prohibiting false advertising and unfair competition.

A California district court accepted Nike's argument that its statements were part of an ongoing political controversy and therefore deserving of full First Amendment protection. It dismissed the case and a California appellate court upheld the dismissal. But in 2002 the California Supreme Court reversed. A majority of the court accepted Kasky's argument that company speech carried out through public relations is conducted for the purpose of promoting a company's image so that the public will want to buy its products or services. In that respect, PR appears to be commercial speech. The court held that speech should be considered commercial if it is (1) conducted by a commercial speaker, (2) to an intended audience of potential customers, and (3) the content of the message is commercial in character.[88] The court's test was a modified version of one applied by the

Supreme Court in *Bolger v. Youngs Drug Products Corp.* (1983) to analyze expression that contains both political and commercial elements.[89]

Nike's attorney argued that treating press releases and letters as the equivalent of advertising would limit companies' First Amendment rights to engage in political speech. Taking the opposite perspective, the California Supreme Court pointed out that if companies' press releases and letters were fully protected speech, companies could misrepresent their actions in them with impunity. This was not a novel idea on the part of the California Court. The U.S. Supreme Court has stated that "[a]dvertisers should not be permitted to immunize false or misleading product information from government regulation simply by including references to public issues."[90]

The U.S. Supreme Court initially granted certiorari to review the case and then changed its mind, indicating that a decision on its part would be premature because California courts had not yet decided whether Nike's speech was false. The case was remanded back for that determination but never went to trial. Kasky settled with Nike in exchange for the company's donation of $1.5 million to the Washington, D.C.-based Fair Labor Association. Meanwhile, the California Supreme Court's decision regarding PR as commercial speech stands and could be applied again.

Antitrust Law

Antitrust laws prevent anticompetitive behavior that has a negative impact on the marketplace. In a properly functioning economy, market competition provides incentives to offer consumers better goods at lower prices. Within the communication sector, antitrust laws serve another function. They ensure that media consumers receive access to a diversity of "media voices." There are three federal antitrust laws: the Sherman Act, the Clayton Act, and the Federal Trade Commission Act.

The Sherman Act

Congress passed the Sherman Act in 1890 to break up monopolies and trusts (combinations of firms colluding to reduce competition) when it became apparent that single companies were controlling entire markets. The Sherman Act prevents "every contract, combination in the form of trust or otherwise, or conspiracy, in restraint of trade or commerce."[91] The statute empowered the government to break up monopolies like Standard Oil (Exxon's forerunner) and the American Tobacco Company. In 1982, it was used to break up AT&T's monopoly on the telephone system. In the 1990s, the Justice Department used it to go after Microsoft.

The Sherman Act does not ban monopolies per se. It bans attempts and conspiracies to monopolize an industry. A company may reach a superior market position by offering a better product, through particularly effective management, or simply through historic accident. It is only when a company reaches power through improper conduct or attempts to wield its power in an exclusionary or predatory way that it violates the Sherman Act.

Likewise, the Sherman Act does not require the government to take the term monopoly literally. It does not have to wait until a single firm dominates an industry to act. It is sufficient that the firm have "significant or durable market power" – in other words, "the long term ability to raise price or exclude competitors."[92] Courts normally require that a company hold a 50 percent market share of an industry in a particular geographic area before considering its monopolistic potential.

The Clayton Act   In 1914, Congress passed the Clayton Act to close loopholes in the Sherman Act that allowed companies to continue to engage in monopolistic practices. The Clayton Act prohibits a variety of monopolistic behaviors including:

- exclusive sales contracts, which require buyers to purchase certain commodities from one seller;
- price discrimination, which occurs when sellers charge buyers different prices for the same commodity;
- predatory pricing, in which sellers cut their prices below costs temporarily to undercut their competitors and drive them from the market;
- tying agreements, which involves conditioning the sale of a particular commodity on the buyer's agreement to purchase a second product; and
- interlocking directorates, which occurs when competing corporations have at least one director in common on their boards of directors.[93]

The Clayton Act also empowered the government to review and evaluate mergers and acquisitions that were likely to have a detrimental impact on competition. Companies are required to notify the Federal Trade Commission and the Justice Department, before entering into mergers valued at more than $50 million. These agencies have dual jurisdiction over mergers. They will consider a deal potentially harmful if the merger is likely to lead to a more concentrated market that impedes the entry of competing firms in the near term.

The Federal Trade Commission Act

Federal Trade Commission Act, also passed in 1914, was established to prevent "persons, partnerships or corporations" from engaging in unfair competition.[94] The law applies to corporations and other for-profit entities. However, the FTC will exercise its jurisdiction over non-profits as well if their activities are substantially dedicated to providing economic benefits to their for-profit members.[95]

The FTC's Bureau of Competition has the power to challenge mergers and acquisitions that are likely to violate antitrust laws. It is particularly interested in industries likely to affect a substantial portion of the population, such as health care, pharmaceuticals, professional services, food, energy, and certain high-tech industries like computer technology and Internet services.

The FTC prefers to obtain voluntary compliance from individuals or corporations accused of violating antitrust law. As in false advertising cases, it will begin by drawing up a consent order that the company can sign, agreeing to discontinue the behavior without having to admit any wrongdoing. If the company violates the consent order, the FTC may pursue civil penalties or injunctive relief in a federal court.

If the FTC cannot reach a consent order, it will file an administrative complaint to initiate a formal proceeding before an administrative law judge within the agency. The administrative judge will issue a preliminary decision based on the facts presented and the applicable law. The Commission will issue the final order, which may be contested before a U.S. Court of Appeals.

The FTC takes some cases directly to federal court, particularly if an injunction is needed quickly to prevent a particular action. It might, for example, request an injunction to block a proposed merger until it has the opportunity to fully investigate the merger's implications.

Shared antitrust jurisdiction

The Federal Trade Commission shares responsibility for the enforcement of antitrust laws with the Justice Department's Antitrust Division. Both agencies review mergers with anticompetitive potential. While the FTC pursues civil actions in antitrust violations, the Justice Department pursues criminal sanctions when they are necessary. It has primary jurisdiction over antitrust actions involving telecommunications, banks, railroads, and airlines.

The Federal Communications Commission shares the responsibility of evaluating proposed mergers among telecommunications companies with the FTC and Justice Department. Its responsibility is to ensure that such firms continue to operate in the public convenience, interest, and necessity.

State antitrust law

States also have antitrust laws that can be used to control intrastate anticompetitive behavior. These are enforced by the attorney general's office. State attorneys general also may bring federal antitrust suits on behalf of their state's residents.

Individual civil claims

Businesses and individuals harmed by anticompetitive behavior have standing to sue under the Sherman and Clayton Acts. They also may seek injunctive relief or civil damages under state antitrust laws.

Microsoft

Microsoft has been the target of antitrust investigations in the United States and the European Union. In 1998, the U.S. Department of Justice, 20 states, and the District of Columbia sued Microsoft for antitrust violations. The software giant was accused of abusing its dominant position to drive out competing browsers by tying licensing agreements for its Windows operating system to the use of its Internet Explorer browser. The company also intertwined Explorer's code with the Windows operating system so it worked better with Windows than competing browsers users might install later.

Microsoft reached a settlement with the DOJ and some of the states that was affirmed by a federal court in 2002. The company agreed not to discriminate against computer manufacturers that preinstall software that competes with Microsoft applications, prevent them from replacing Microsoft software, or stop them from adding icons for other software to Windows' desktop. But the settlement did not require Microsoft to remove any of its software code from Windows' operating system. Nine states refused to sign the agreement because they considered it insufficient.

The European Union's second-highest tribunal, the Court of First Instance, upheld a decision by the European Commission to impose a $1.44 billion fine on Microsoft for its failure to comply with a 2004 antitrust judgment.[96] In the EU case, Microsoft was penalized for tying the use of its Windows Media Player to its operating software. Microsoft was ordered to make a version of its Windows operating system without its media player and to share information with rival companies that produced competing networking software intended to work with Windows.

Antitrust law and the media

Although it is not always apparent from increasing levels of media consolidation, antitrust laws do apply to the media. In *Associated Press v. United States* (1945), the Supreme Court rejected the argument that the First Amendment immunized media from antitrust laws.[97] AP's bylaws, requiring members to transmit local news to AP and no one else, presented a serious obstacle for new papers that were excluded from AP membership. The problem was compounded by a system that allowed AP members to deny membership to new competitors. When the Justice Department accused AP of violating the Sherman Act, AP argued that its actions were protected by freedom of the press. The Supreme Court observed that the irony of that argument was that it would prevent the government from protecting that freedom. It concluded that the First Amendment provides "powerful reasons" for the application of antitrust laws to the media. Writing for the majority, Justice Black said, "Freedom to publish is guaranteed by the Constitution, but freedom to combine to keep others from publishing is not."[98]

The Court had already shown its willingness to step in to prevent media monopolies in *NBC v. United States* (1943).[99] In that case, the Court upheld the FCC's Chain Broadcasting Restrictions, which required NBC to divest itself of one of its networks because its hold on broadcasting had become too great.

In 1951, the Supreme Court held that a medium's right to refuse advertising did not extend to practices intended to drive out its competition.[100] The petitioner in *Lorain Journal Company v. United States* was an Ohio newspaper that refused to carry ads from businesses that also advertised on a local radio station. The Court held that a publisher's decision to reject advertising from businesses that also purchased ads from a competing media operation was an antitrust violation.

The FCC and the Court continued to express their commitment to ensuring diversity in media and the right of access to information through the 1960s and 1970s. In *Red Lion v. FCC* (1969), Justice Byron White said "It is the purpose of the First Amendment to preserve an uninhibited marketplace of ideas in which truth will ultimately prevail, rather than to countenance monopolization of that market, whether it be by the government itself or a private licensee …"[101]

Yet the public perception is that government agencies handle media consolidation too lightly. In the 1980s and 1990s, the government moved in a deregulatory direction, eliminating ownership restrictions that resulted in greater media consolidation. In the twenty-first century, that trend toward consolidation now encompasses new media technologies. For example, the FTC and Justice Department approved News Corporation's $580 million acquisition of the social networking site MySpace.com in 2005 and Google's $1.65 billion purchase of the video site YouTube in 2006. The FTC, FCC, and Justice Department approved a merger between Sirius and XM in 2008 that will create one satellite radio provider. A key factor in the decision was that both companies were struggling to build a sufficient audience base to stay afloat. Under the circumstances, the agencies thought it unlikely that the merger would enable Sirius-XM to increase prices for satellite radio.

However, the agencies did require Clear Channel to divest 48 of its radio stations before agreeing to its sale for $19.5 billion to two equity firms, Thomas H. Lee Partners and Bain Capital, which own Cumulus Media Partners and Univision Communications. The Justice Department said the divestitures in Cincinnati, Houston, Las Vegas, and San Francisco were necessary to protect advertisers who, otherwise, would face higher prices due to reduced competition. Its decision was not surprising because Clear Channel, which went from no more than 40 stations before the Telecommunications Act eliminated radio ownership restrictions to 1,200 stations, had become a symbol of media consolidation.

Contracts and electronic signatures

A contract is an agreement between two or more people that involves a promise by one party in exchange for a counter promise by the other. Online contracts are now just as enforceable as contracts created on paper. This means that when you enter a website and click on a button that says I ACCEPT, your acceptance to the site's terms is binding.

Congress passed the Electronic Signatures in Global and National Commerce ("E-SIGN") Act to facilitate electronic commerce.[102] The federal statute, in effect since 2000, vests electronic signatures and documents with the same legal force of traditional signatures and printed documents. It defines *signature* broadly as "an electronic sound, symbol, or process, attached to or logically associated with a contract or other record and executed or adopted by a person with the intent to sign the record."[103] The term *process* can be understood to mean a click on an OK or an I ACCEPT button.

In order to be enforceable, a contract must include at least two things:

a consideration (a benefit exchanged for something) and some level of equality between the parties. Clickwrap agreements don't leave room for negotiation. A user either accepts the terms or is denied the service or access to a particular site sought through the agreement.

Nevertheless they have been upheld by courts, which see them as vital to the function of electronic commerce. In *Feldman v. Google* (2007), a lawyer whose firm purchased pay-per-click advertising from Google sued the search engine for negligence because the company failed to protect him from "click fraud."[104] Click fraud occurs when individuals maliciously click on a competitor's ad repeatedly to drain the competitor's advertising budget. The Click Fraud Network estimated in 2008 that more than 16 percent of advertising clicks on search engines were fraudulent.[105] In fact, in 2006, Google agreed to a $90 million settlement to end a class action lawsuit against it emanating from its failure to prevent click fraud.[106]

Lawrence Feldman had assented to Google's terms of agreement, specifying that the forum for any legal action between them would be California and that California law would apply. Feldman, who filed suit in Pennsylvania, argued that Google's contract should not be enforced because he was not given notice of its terms and the contract was unconscionable, meaning it was characterized by unequal bargaining positions or hidden terms.

The court determined that Feldman was given reasonable notice of the terms through Google's scroll-down window, and that by clicking on a button that said "Yes, I agree to the terms above" he had assented to them. Internet users do not always read the terms in these agreements because they are impatient to move forward. One study conducted in 2002 estimated that 90 percent of Internet users did not complete them and 64 percent agreed to them without reading anything at all.[107] But that doesn't make them any less binding. While recognizing that the contract was one-sided, the court did not con-sider Google's terms to be unconscionable because Feldman still had the choice to advertise elsewhere.

Moreover, a website's terms may be binding on others who access the site using someone else's account. In *Motise v. America Online* (2004), Michael Motise filed suit against AOL in New York for releasing his private information to a third party who used it illegally. AOL motioned to dismiss the case because its terms of service specified that legal actions must be filed in Virginia. The plaintiff argued that he never agreed to those terms because he was using his step-father's account. The court considered the plaintiff to be the account holder's sub-licensee. It said "Any other conclusion would permit individuals to avoid the Defendant's Terms of Service simply by having third parties create accounts and then using them as the Plaintiff did."[108]

Certain agreements still require paper. These include wills, adoption papers, divorces, evictions, notices canceling insurance or utilities, court orders, and product recalls.[109]

Questions for Discussion

1. What justification has the Supreme Court given for granting lesser First Amendment protection to commercial speech?
2. How does the Federal Trade Commission deal with false advertising?
3. How do literal falsity, implied falsity, and puffery differ? Which are illegal?
4. Should public relations be fully protected by the First Amendment, even if it is false, or should it be treated like advertising?

Table of Cases

Glossary

Actual damages – An award given to the plaintiff in compensation for a loss or injury, also known as compensatory damages.

Actual malice – A standard of fault in defamation cases. Plaintiffs are required to prove that the defendant published the defamation with knowledge of its falsity or reckless disregard of its truth.

Appellant – The party who files an appeal in a civil or criminal case after losing a case at the trial level.

Appellee – The party who must respond to an appeal in a civil or criminal case.

Applied challenge – A challenge to a law based on its effect on a particular party.

Class-action lawsuit – A lawsuit filed on behalf of particular population that might have been harmed by the defendant company.

Common law – A body of law based on court decisions.

Concurring opinion – An opinion by an appellate court judge that agrees with the majority regarding the holding, but arrives at its conclusion through different reasoning.

Contempt of court – Failure to obey a court order or to exercise proper decorum in the courtroom.

Declaratory judgment – A court order in a civil case explaining the rights and responsibilities of the parties in the case, without awarding them damages or requiring them to take a particular action.

Defendant – The party against whom a civil suit is filed or a crime is prosecuted.

Deposition – A pre-trial legal proceeding in which witnesses are asked questions under oath before a court reporter.

Dissenting opinion – An opinion by an appellate court judge that disagrees with the opinion supported by the majority of the court.

Discovery – The process that opposing parties undertake before a civil trial begins to acquire relevant information and documents from each other in an attempt to learn all pertinent facts that might affect the litigation and avoid surprises at trial.

DSL – An acronym for direct subscriber line, a two-way data connection that provides broadband access through telephone lines.

Electromagnetic spectrum – The range of radiation through which signals of all types are transmitted. The spectrum is divided into frequencies ranging from cosmic-ray photons, gamma rays, x-rays, ultraviolet radiation, visible light, infrared radiation, microwaves, and radio waves.

En banc – A court of appeals sits *en banc* when all (or most) of the justices hear a case together. Appellate cases are normally assigned to a three-judge panel.

Equity – A system of law that furnishes remedies for wrongs that would not be recognized under common law or for which there is no adequate remedy under common law.

Facial challenge – A challenge to a law based on its potential effect because the law is either overbroad or vague or both.

Grand jury – A group of citizens impaneled for a period of time, usually one year, to determine whether the evidence presented by a prosecutor warrants an indictment. Grand jury hearings are closed to the public.

Indictment – A formal accusation charging someone with a crime.

Injunction – A court order rendered through equity law that requires a defendant to take a particular action or to refrain from a particular action.

Incorporation doctrine – A legal doctrine that applies parts of the Bill of Rights, originally meant to serve as a constraint on federal power, to the states through the Due Process clause of the Fourteenth Amendment. Prior to the Fourteenth Amendment's ratification, the Supreme Court interpreted the First Amendment as applicable only to the federal government.

Intermediate scrutiny – A middle level of judicial review that courts employ when a government regulation burdens a constitutional right, usually in pursuit of some other goal. In a First Amendment context, it applies to content-neutral regulations that burden speech. To withstand review, the regulation must further an important government interest through means that are substantially related to the goal and burden no more speech than necessary.

Interrogatives – Written questions that parties in a civil suit answer under oath prior to trial.

Jurisdiction – A court's authority to hear a particular case, based on its subject matter and the geographic region in which the case is filed.

Legislative history – All documents, such as committee reports, floor debates, and transcripts of hearings, that accrue during the enactment of a law. Courts turn to a statute's legislative history, also known as its statutory construction, when they are trying to interpret ambiguous wording.

Majority opinion – The dominant opinion expressed by an appellate court, which provides the holding.

P2P – the acronym for the peer-to-peer communication model that describes an informal network formed among Internet users who exchange files directly from each other's hard drives.

Plaintiff – A party who files a civil suit against a defendant.

Plurality opinion – The controlling opinion in an appellate court when there is no clear majority.

Police power – The legal authority reserved for the states under the Tenth Amendment to preserve and protect the health, safety, and welfare of their citizens. The power of the federal government to prosecute crimes is limited by the Constitution to certain areas, such as commerce.

Pretexting – The act of misrepresenting one's identity or purpose to acquire personal data about someone else.

Prima facie – A Latin legal term meaning "on first face" or "on first look." In a prima facie case, the evidence is sufficient to establish a presumption of fact.

Prior restraint – A form of censorship that takes place before material is published. Prior restraint is considered a more egregious form of censorship than punishment after publication.

Public domain – A term applied to a range of works that are not protected under intellectual property law and are therefore free to be used in any way.

Punitive damages – An award given to the plaintiff in addition to actual damages, which serves as additional punishment for the defendant's actions.

Precedent (binding and persuasive) – A legal principle drawn from a court decision that provides authority for judges deciding similar cases later. A binding precedent is one that a court must follow. A persuasive precedent is one that is issued in another jurisdiction which the court may be persuaded to follow, but may also reject.

Obiter dictum – The part of a court's opinion that provides explanation and analogy, as opposed to the holding, which provides the court's decision. It is known as dicta in its plural form.

Overbreadth doctrine – A doctrine stipulating that a law may be struck down as unconstitutional if it has the potential to proscribe a substantial amount of protected speech along with its proscription on unprotected speech.

Petitioner – The party who petitions a court for the opportunity to appeal a lower court's decision when the court has the prerogative to accept or deny the appeal.

Rational basis test – The lowest level of judicial scrutiny applied in cases in which no fundamental right appears to be threatened. To withstand review, the government must show that the restriction is a reasonable means of achieving a legitimate government goal.

Respondent – The party who is required to answer a petition for appeal.

Respondeat superior – A Latin term that means "let the master answer" for the deeds of the servant. The common law doctrine holds that employers are liable for injuries caused by employees acting on their behalf. The theory allows plaintiffs to probe deeper pockets.

Scienter – Knowledge of wrongdoing.

Service of process – Providing notice that legal action is forthcoming by providing the opposing party with a copy of the complaint.

Sovereign – A legally independent body, such as a state or a nation.

Strict liability – Liability incurred regardless of scienter.

Strict scrutiny – The highest level of judicial review applied by courts when the government imposes restrictions impinging on a constitutional right. It is applied, for example, when the government restricts speech based on the ideas it conveys. To withstand review, the restriction must be justified by a compelling government interest, be narrowly tailored to achieve that interest, and use the least restrictive means to achieve that interest.

Summary judgment – A decision rendered by a court in favor of either the plaintiff or the defendant in a civil suit where the evidence presented suggests that the party would win at trial.

Stare decisis – The common law doctrine that precedents are to be followed.

Vagueness doctrine – A doctrine stipulating that a law may be voided for vagueness if it is not drafted clearly enough to give a reasonable person of average intelligence notice of what constitutes a crime.

Voir dire – The process used for jury selection in which attorneys question prospective jurors to assess their suitability.

Writ of certiorari – A formal petition to a court to hear an appeal.

Notes

1 Introduction to the Legal System

1 The U.S. Constitution declares its supremacy in Article XI: "This Constitution … shall be the supreme Law of the Land; and the Judges in every State shall be bound thereby, any Thing in the Constitution or Laws of any State to the Contrary notwithstanding."

2 5 U.S.C. § 551 et seq. (2007).

3 5 U.S.C. § 706(2)(A) (2007).

4 Motor Vehicle Mfrs. Ass'n of U.S., Inc. v. State Farm Mut. Auto. Ins. Co., 463 U.S. 29, 43 (1983) (citing Burlington Truck Lines, Inc. v. United States, 371 U.S. 156, 168 (1962)).

5 *Id.*

6 Mutual Film Corporation v. Industrial Commission of Ohio, 236 U.S. 230 (1915).

7 Joseph Burstyn, Inc. v. Wilson, 343 U.S. 495 (1952).

8 James G. Apple and Robert P. Deyling, *A Primer on the Civil Law System* (Federal Judicial Center, 1995) 1, available at www.fjc.gov/public/pdf.nsf/lookup/CivilLaw.pdf/$file/CivilLaw.pdf.

9 *Id.* (citing John P. Dawson, *Oracles of the Law* (William S. Hein & Co., 1968) 103, 123).

10 *Id.* at 5.

11 Doerr v. Mobile Oil Co., 774 So.2d 119 (La. 2000) (citing Dennis, J. L., Interpretation and Application of the Civil Code and the Evaluation of Judicial Precedent, 54 LA. L. REV. 1, 15 (1993)).

12 Pronunciation for this word varies, but the most common versions are "ser-she-or-ary," "ser-shah-rair-eye," and "ser-shah-rair-ee."

13 Robert A. Carp and Ronald Stidham, *Judicial Process in America* (CQ Press, 4th edn. 1998) 67.

14 *Id.* at 71.

15 *In re* North (Omnibus Order), 16 F.3d 1234, 1242 (D.C. Cir., Spec. Div., 1994) (quoting Douglas Oil Co. v. Petrol Stops Northwest, 441 U.S. 211, 218–19 (1979)).

16 *See* Edmondson v. Leesville Concrete Co., 500 U.S. 614 (1991) and J.E.B. v. Alabama *ex rel.* T.B., 511 U.S. 127 (1994).

17 Daniel E. Hall, *Criminal Law and Procedure* (Delmar Cengage Learning, 5th ed. 2009) 490.

18 *Id.* at 184.

19 The Seventh Amendment is not deemed sufficiently fundamental to apply at the state level through the Fourteenth Amendment's due process clause. Thus defendants do not have a constitutional right to a jury in a state civil trial. *See* Curtis v. Loether, 415 U.S. 189, 198 (1974) and Dairy Queen v. Wood, 369 U.S. 469, 471–72 (1962).

20 Curtis v. Loether, 415 U.S. 189, 196 (1974).

21 *Id.*

22 Comment, Pre-Trial Disclosure in Criminal Cases, 60 Yale L.J. 626–46 (Apr., 1951).

23 Fed. R. Civ. P. 56.

24 *See* Johnson & Johnson Vision Care v. 1-800 Contacts, Inc., 299 F.3d 1242, 1246–47 (11th Cir. 2002).

25 5 U.S. 137 (1803).

26 14 U.S. 304 (1816).

2 Freedom of Expression

1 Leonard W. Levy ed., *Judicial Review and the Supreme Court* (Harper & Row, 1967) 141.

2 Konigsberg v. State Bar of California, 366 U.S. 36, 61 (1961) (Black, J., dissenting) ("[T]he First Amendment's unequivocal command that there shall be no abridgment of the rights of free speech and assembly shows that the men who drafted our Bill of Rights did all the 'balancing' that was to be done in this field.")

3 Barron v. The Mayor and City Council of Baltimore, 32 U.S. (7 Pet.) 243 (1933).

4 Gitlow v. New York, 268 U.S. 652 (1925).

5 Gideon v. Wainwright, 372 U.S. 335 (1963).

6 *Id.* at 341–42.

7 *See* Balzac v. Porto Rico, 258 U.S. 298, 313–14 (1922), DeRoburt v. Gannett Co., 83 F.R.D. 574, 577–78 (D. Haw. 1979).

8 *See* Kwong Hai Chew v. Colding, 344 U.S. 590 (1953) (holding that aliens who lawfully enter and are residing in the United States are entitled to rights guaranteed by the Constitution, including rights protected by the First Amendment); Bridges v. Wixon, 326 U.S. 135 (1945) (holding that aliens residing in the United States are accorded freedom of speech and of press).

9 William Blackstone, *Commentaries on the Laws of England* (1769).

10 An Act for the Punishment of Certain Crimes against the United States (Sedition Act), July 14, 1798 ch. 74, 1 Stat. 5.

11 Levy, *supra* note 27, at 143.

12 283 U.S. 697 (1931).

13 *Id.* at 713.

14 403 U.S. 713 (1971).

15 *Id.* at 730 (Stewart, J., concurring).

16 United States v. The Progressive, 467 F. Supp. 990, 994 (1979).

17 437 U.S. 539 (1976).

18 *Id.* at 562.

19 Procter & Gamble Company v. Banker's Trust Company, 78 F.3d 219, 226 (1996).

20 *Id.* (citing *In re* Providence Journal Co., 820 F.2d 1342, 1351 (1st Cir. 1986)).

21 *Id.* at 227.

22 Bank Julius Baer & Co. Ltd. v. Wikileaks, 535 F. Supp. 2d 980 (N.D. Cal. 2008).

23 *Id.*

24 Mike Masnick, Photo of Streisand Home Becomes an Internet Hit, Techdirt, June 24, 2003, at http://www.techdirt.com/articles/20030624/1231228.shtml.

25 California Coastal Records Project, Streisand Estate, Malibu (Sept. 23, 2002) http://www.californiacoastline.org/cgi-bin/image.cgi?image=3850&mode=sequential &flags=0.

26 539 U.S. 113, 119 (2003) (citations omitted).

27 Broadrick v. Oklahoma, 413 U.S. 601, 615 (1973).

28 Connally v. General Construction Co., 269 U.S. 385, 391 (1926).

29 521 U.S. 844 (1997).

30 Martin Rimm, Marketing Pornography on the Information Superhighway, 83 Georgetown L.J. 1849 (1995). *See also* Philip Elmer-DeWitt, On a Screen Near You: Cyberporn, *Time*, July 3, 1995. The original study is posted online at http://www.sics. se/~psm/kr9512-001.html.

31 Reno v. American Civil Liberties Union, 521 U.S. 844 (1997).

32 *Id.* at 864–85.

33 Ark. Educ. Television Comm'n v. Forbes, 523 U.S. 666, 677 (1998).

34 Perry Education Association v. Perry Local Educators' Association, 460 U.S. 37 (1983).

35 Hague v. CIO, 307 U.S. 496, 515 (1939).

36 Perry Education Association v. Perry Local Educators' Association, 460 U.S. at 45.

37 United States v. Grace, 461 U.S. 171 (1983).

38 Computerxpress, Inc. v. Jackson, 93 Cal. App. 4th 993, 1006 (2001) (citing Hatch v. Superior Court, 80 Cal. App. 4th 170, 94 Cal. Rptr. 2d 453 (2000).

39 New.net, Inc. v. Lavasoft, 356 F. Supp. 2d 1090, 1107 (C.D. Cal. 2004) (citing Global Telemedia Intern., Inc. v. Doe 1, 132 F. Supp. 2d 1261, 1264 (C.D. Cal. 2001); *see also* MCSi, Inc. v. Woods, 290 F. Supp. 2d 1030, 2003 (N.D. Cal. 2003) (holding that a web chat room is a public forum).

40 United States v. Am. Library Ass'n., Inc., 539 U.S. 194, 199 (2003).

41 518 U.S. 727, 776–77 (1996) (Souter, J., concurring).

42 *Id.* at 802–03 (Kennedy, J., concurring in part, concurring in judgment in part, dissenting in part).

43 Putnam Pit v. City of Cookeville, 221 F.3d 834 (6th Cir. 2000) (quoting Perry Educ. Ass'n v. Perry Local Educators' Ass'n, 460 U.S. 37, 45 (1983)). *See also* Loving v. Boren, 956 F. Supp. 953, 955 (W.D. Okla. 1997), *aff'd*, 133 F.3d 771 (10th Cir. 1998) (holding that University of Oklahoma's computers and Internet services did not constitute a public forum.)

44 *Id.* at 843.

45 *Id.* at 843–44.

46 *See* Perry Educ. Ass'n. v. Perry Local Educators' Assn., 460 U.S. at 46.

47 *See* Cornelius v. NAACP Legal Defense & Ed. Fund, Inc., 473 U.S. 788, 806 (1985).

48 Rosenburger v. Rector and Visitors of the University of Virginia, 515 U.S. 819, 830 (1995).

49 Dan Hunter, Cyberspace as Place and the Tragedy of the Digital Anticommons, 91 CAL. L. REV. 439, 491 (2003).

50 521 U.S. 844, 890 (O'Connor, J., concurring in the judgment in part and dissenting in part).

51 Spence v. Washington, 418 U.S. 405, 410–11 (1974).

52 Hurley v. Irish-American Gay, Lesbian & Bisexual Group of Boston, 515 U.S. 557, 569 (1995).

53 391 U.S. 367, 377 (1968).

54 273 F.3d 429 (2d Cir. 2001).

55 17 U.S.C. §§ 1201(a)(2), (b)(1) (2007).

56 Universal City Studios, Inc. v. Corley, 273 F.3d at 447.

57 *See* Killion, Porter v. Ascension Parish School Bd., 393 F.3d 608, 615 (5th Cir. 2004) (holding that art created off campus is protected by the First Amendment).

58 *See*, e.g., Layshock v. Hermitage School District, 412 F. Supp. 2d 502 (2006).

59 J.S. v. Bethlehem Area School District, 807 A.2d 803 (Pa. 2002).

60 393 U.S. 503, 506 (1969).

61 30 F. Supp. 2d 1175 (E.D. Mo. 1998).

62 *Id.* at 1180.

63 569 Pa. 638, 807 A.2d 847 (Pa. 2002).

64 *See* Bethel School District No. 403 v. Fraser, 478 U.S. 675, 682 (1986).

65 *See* Hazelwood School District v. Kuhlmeier, 484 U.S. 260, 273 (1988).

66 127 S.Ct. 2618 (2007).

67 *Id.* at 2636.

68 Hurley v. Irish-American Gay, Lesbian and Bisexual Group of Boston, 515 U.S. 557, 573 (1995) (quoting Pacific Gas & Electric Co. v. Public Utilities Comm'n of Cal., 475 U.S. 1, 16 (1986)).

69 *See* West Virginia Bd. of Ed. v. Barnette, 319 U.S. 624, 633–34 (1943), Wooley v. Maynard, 430 U.S. 705, 713–17, (1977), and BSA v. Dale, 530 U.S. 640, 653 (2000).

70 Alexander Meiklejohn, *Free Speech and Its Relation to Self-Government* (1948). Reprinted by The Lawbook Exchange, Ltd. (2004).

71 Stromberg v. California, 283 U.S. 359, 369 (1931).

72 Vincent Blasi, The Checking Value in First Amendment Theory, AM. B. FOUND. RES. J. (1977) 521.

73 Louis D. Brandeis, *Other People's Money and How the Banker's Use it* (Frederick A. Stokes Co., 1914) 92.

74 Whitney v. California, 274 U.S. 357, 375 (1927) (Brandeis, J., concurring).

75 *See* C. Edwin Baker, Scope of the First Amendment Freedom of Speech, 25 UCLA L. REV. 964, 965–91 (1978) and Thomas I. Emerson, *The System of Freedom of Expression* (Random House, 1970) 6.

76 *See* M. Redish, Self-Realization, Democracy and Freedom of Expression: A Reply to Professor Baker, 130 U. PA. L. REV. 678, 684 (1982).

77 *See* Thomas I. Emerson, Towards a General Theory of the First Amendment, 72 YALE L.J. 877, 879–80 (1963).

78 *See* Kent Greenawalt, Free Speech Justifications, 89 COLUM. L. REV. 119, 145–46 (1987).

79 Abrams v. United States, 250 U.S. 616 (1919).

80 *Id.* at 630 (Holmes, J., dissenting).

81 Noam Cohen, Editing – and re-editing – Sarah Palin's Wikipedia entry, *International Herald Tribune*, Sept. 1, 2008, at http://www.iht.com/articles/2008/09/01/business/link.php.

3 Telecommunications Regulation

1 Pub. L. 104-104, 110 Stat. 56 (codified in various sections of 47 U.S.C.).

2 47 U.S.C. § 161 (2006).

3 Pub. L. No. 73-416, 48 Stat. 1064 (1934), codified in various section of Title 47 of the United States Code.

4 47 U.S.C. § 303(f) (2006).

5 Federal Communications Commission, http://www.fcc.gov/aboutus.html (last visited Oct. 2, 2008).

6 In the matter of Sponsorship Identification Rules and Embedded Advertising, 73 Fed. Reg. 143 (proposed June 26, 2008) (to be codified at 47 C.F.R. parts 73 and 76).

7 10 F.3d 875 (D.C. Cir. 1993).

8 Anne Broache, FCC's wireless airwaves sale raises $19.6 billion, CNet, March 18, 2008, at http://news.cnet.com/8301-10784_3-9897297-7.html.

9 47 U.S.C. § 301 (2006).

10 A colorful spectrum allocation chart is available at www.ntia.doc.gov/osmhome/allochrt.pdf.

11 319 U.S. 190 (1943).

12 *Id.* at 226–27.

13 395 U.S. 367 (1969).

14 *Id.* at 390.

15 *See* Miami Herald Publishing Co. v. Tornillo, 418 U.S. 241, 248 (1974) and CBS v. Democratic National Committee, 412 U.S. 94, 121–31 (1973).

16 In the matter of Repeal or Modification of the Personal Attack and Political Editorial Rules, 15 F.C.C.R. 20697 (2000).

17 Radio-Television News Dirs. Ass'n v. FCC, 184 F.3d 872, 881 (D.C. Cir. 1999).

18 Radio-Television News Dirs. Ass'n v. FCC, 229 F.3d 269 (D.C. Cir. 2000).

19 438 U.S. 726 (1978).

20 56 F.C.C.2d 94, 99 (1975).

21 FCC v. Pacifica Foundation, 438 U.S. 726, 748–49 (1978).

22 In the Matter of Industry Guidance on the Commission's Case Law Interpreting 18 U.S.C. § 1464 and Enforcement Policies Regarding Broadcast Indecency, 16 F.C.C.R. 7999, 8003, ¶ 10 (April 6, 2001).

23 CBS Corporation v. FCC, 535 F.3d 167, 174 (2008).

24 *In re* Complaints Against Various Broadcast Licensees Regarding Their Airing of the "Golden Globe Awards" Program, 19 F.C.C.R. 4975, 4977 (March 18, 2004) (Memorandum Opinion and Order).

25 489 F.3d 444 (2d Cir. 2007), *cert. granted*, 128 S.Ct. 1647 (U.S., Mar. 17, 2008).

26 C-SPAN persuaded the judges to allow cameras to film the court in session. The video is on YouTube at http://youtube.com/watch?v=QdCsup3zqyA&feature=user.

27 Federal Communications Commission v. Fox Television Stations, 129 S.Ct. 1800 (April 28, 2009).

28 47 U.S.C. § 503 (2006).

29 *In re* Complaints Against Various Television Licensees Concerning Their February 1, 2004 Broadcast of the Super Bowl XXXVIII Halftime Show, 21 F.C.C.R. 2760 (2006) (Forfeiture Order).

30 535 F.3d 167 (2008).

31 Broadcast of telephone conversations, 47 C.F.R. § 73.1206.

32 In the matter of Rejoynetwork, LLC, File Nos. EB-06-IH-1772 and EB-06-IH-1748, ¶ 12, Rel. Oct. 16, 2008 (Forfeiture Order).

33 Station-Initiated Telephone Calls which Fail to Comply with Section 73.1206 of the Rules, Public Notice, 35 F.C.C.2d 940, 941 (1972).

34 In the matter of WXDJ Licensing, File No. EB-03-IH-0275, Rel. Nov. 24, 2004 (Forfeiture Order).

35 Tough call pays off for cranks, *The Age*, July 24, 2003, at http://www.theage.com.au/articles/2003/07/24/1058853184719.html.

36 Broadcast hoaxes, 47 C.F.R. 73.1217.

37 47 U.S.C. § 503(b) (2006).

38 Report on Broadcast Localism and Notice of Proposed Rulemaking, MB Dkt. No. 04-233, FCC 07-218, Released Jan. 24, 2008.

39 FCC Media Bureau, The Public and Broadcasting (July 1999), at http://www.fcc.gov/mb/audio/decdoc/public_and_broadcasting.html#OBSCENE.

40 47 C.F.R. § 73.671.

41 Columbia Broadcasting System v. Democratic National Committee, 412 U.S. 94 (1973).

42 Reasonable access, 47 C.F.R. § 73.1944.

43 47 U.S.C. § 312(a)(7).

44 *See* 47 C.F.R. § 73.1941 (for broadcast rules), 47 C.F.R. § 76.205 (for cable rules) and 47 C.F.R. § 25.701 (DBS rules).

45 47 U.S.C. 315 (2006).

46 Becker v. FCC, 95 F.3d 75 (D.C. Cir. 1996).

47 319 U.S. 190 (1943).

48 47 U.S.C. § 317; 47 C.F.R. §§ 73.1212 and 76.1615.

49 47 C.F.R. § 73.1212(f).

50 Federal Communications Commission, last visited Oct. 3, 2008 at http://www.fcc.gov/mb/facts/csgen.html.

51 United States v. Southwestern Cable Co., 392 U.S. 157, 158 (1968).

52 Public Law 102-385, 106 Stat. 1460 (1992) (codified in scattered sections of 47 U.S.C.).

53 Turner Broadcasting System, Inc. v. FCC, 512 U.S. 622, 643 (1994) ("Turner I").

54 Turner Broadcasting System, Inc. v. FCC, 520 U.S. 180, 189 (1997) ("Turner II") (citing United States v. O'Brien, 391 U.S. 367, 377 (1968)).

55 Signal carriage obligations, 47 C.F.R. § 76.56.

56 *In re* Carriage of digital Television Broadcast Signals: Amendment to Part 76 of the Commission's Rules, Declaratory Order, CS Dkt. No. 98-120, FCC 08-224 (Rel. Sept. 26, 2008).

57 47 U.S.C. § 553 (2006).

58 Denver Area Educational Telecommunications Consortium, Inc. v. FCC, 518 U.S. 727 (1996).

59 512 U.S. 622 (1994).

60 518 U.S. 727 (1996).

61 *Id.* 744–45.

62 529 U.S. 803 (2000).

63 National Association of Broadcasters v. FCC, 740 F.2d 1190 (D.C. Cir. 1984).

64 Subscription Video, 2 F.C.C.R. 1001 (1987) (report and order), *aff'd*, Nat'l Ass'n For Better Broadcasting v. FCC, 849 F.2d 665 (D.C. Cir. 1988).

65 National Ass'n for Better Broadcasting, 849 F.2d 665, 667–68 (D.C. Cir. 1988).

66 Satellite Broadcasting and Communications Asso. v. FCC, 275 F.3d 337, 353 (4th Cir. 2001).

67 John Eggerton, FCC Allows Satellite-TV Providers to Phase In HD, *Broadcasting & Cable*, March 27, 2008.

68 47 U.S.C. § 335(b)(1) (2006).

69 Time Warner Entertainment v. FCC, 93 F.3d 957, 975 (D.C. Cir. 1996).

70 Commission Implements Satellite Home Viewer Improvement Act Sports Blackout and Program Exclusivity Rule Provisions for Satellite Carriers [FCC news release], Oct. 27, 2000, at http://www.fcc.gov/mb/shva/.

71 275 F.3d 337, 353 (4th Cir. 2001).

72 Petition of Public Knowledge, et. al. for Declaratory Ruling Stating that Text Messaging and Short Codes are Title II Services or are Title I Services Subject to Section 202 Nondiscrimination Rules, WC Dkt. No. 08-7, Dec. 11, 2007, available at www.publicknowledge.org/node/1372.

73 John Eggerton, Flood of Filings Challenges FCC's Cross-Ownership Decision, *Broadcasting & Cable*, March 10, 2008, at http://www.broadcastingcable.com/article/CA6539888.html.

4   Internet Regulation

1 The InterNic website provides a helpful explanation of the domain name system's organization and function at http://www.internic.net/faqs/authoritative-dns.html.

2 Affirmation of Commitments by the U.S. Department of Commerce and the Internet Corporation for Assigned Names and Numbers, Sept. 30, 2009, at http://www.icann.org/en/announcements/announcement-30sep09-en.htm#affirmation.

3 Introducing IANA, http://beta.iana.org/about/.

4 National Telecommunications and Information Administration, U.S. Principles on the Internet's Domain Name and Addressing System, http://www.ntia.doc.gov/ntiahome/domainname (follow "II. U.S. Principles" hyperlink).

5 Michael Geist, How the next billion will reshape the Internet, *The Toronto Star*, Dec. 10, 2007, at B05.

6 Jay Baage, IGF: The future of the Internet is in Asia, on cell phones, *Digital Media Wire*, Oct. 30, 2006, http://www.dmwmedia.com/news/2006/10/30/igf-the-future-of-the-internet-is-in-asia-on-cell-phones.

7 Catherine Rampell, A script for every surfer: responding to criticism from the non-English-speaking world, the U.S. firm that oversees the Internet will test domains in foreign characters, *The Washington Post*, Oct. 11, 2007, at D01.

8 Gavin Knight, Technology: Kremlin eyes Internet control. … The Russian government is looking to create a Cyrillic Internet, but is it just another case of Big Brother controlling its citizens? *The Guardian*, Jan. 3, 2008, at 6.

9   *See* Internet Governance Forum Mandate at http://www.intgovforum.org/mandate.
    htm.

10 Pub. L. 108-482, 118 Stat. 3916 (2004) (codified as amended at 15 U.S.C. § 1117 and
    17 U.S.C. § 504(c)).

11 International Telecommunications Union, Telecommunication/ICT Markets and
    Trends in Africa 21 (2007), http://www.itu.int/ITU-D/ict/statistics/material/af_
    report07.pdf.

12 Race to the Bottom, Human Rights Watch, Vol. 18, No. 8(c), August 2006, yaleglobal.
    yale.edu/sites/default/files/pdf/china-web.pdf.

13 A corporate struggle to do the right thing in China. Judgment call. Four professionals
    offer expert advice, *Financial Times* (London), Nov. 7, 2007, 18.

14 *See* § 86 of the German Criminal Code and § 4(1) JMStV (The Interstate Treaty for
    the protection of human dignity and the protection of minors in the media) (cited in
    Jonathan L. Zittrain and John G. Palfrey Jr., Internet Filtering: The Politics and
    Mechanisms of Control, in Ronald J. Deibert et al. ed., *Access Denied: The Practice and
    Policy of Internet Filtering* (MIT Press, 2007) 7, http://opennet.net/node/957 (follow
    "Chapter 2: Internet Filtering" hyperlink).

15 47 U.S.C. § 153 (43).

16 47 U.S.C. § 153 (20).

17 Brand X Internet Servs. v. FCC, 345 F.3d 1120, 1132 (9th Cir. 2003).

18 545 U.S. 967 (2005).

19 Declan McCullagh, FCC probably can't police Comcast's BitTorrent throttling, CNet,
    July 28, 2008, at http://news.cnet.com/8301-13578_3-10000821-38.html.

20 *See* 47 U.S.C.S. §§ 253(a) and (d) (2006).

21 541 U.S. 125 (2004).

22 AR Code § 23-17-409; CO SB 05-152, FL SB 1322, IA Statute § 388.10, MN Stat. Ann
    § 237.19, Revised Statutes of MO § 392.410(7), NE LB 645, NV Statutes § 268.086,
    PA House Bill 30, SC Code § 58-9-2600, TN HB 1403, TX Pub. Util. Code § 54.201
    et seq, UT Code § 10–18, VA Code § 15.2-2160, VA Code § 56-265.4:4, Revised Code
    of WA § 54.16.330, WI Act 278.

23 VT Act 79; NJ ACS 804.

24 E911 Service, 47 C.F.R. § 9.5.

25 FCC, Voice over Internet Protocol, http://www.fcc.gov/voip/ (last visited Oct. 4,
    2008).

26 Minnesota PUC v. FCC, 483 F.3d 570 (8th Cir. 2007).

27 Computer Security Institute / FBI Computer Crime & Security Survey (2008), follow
    link to CSI survey on http://www.gocsi.com/. Organizations surveyed included U.S.
    corporations, government agencies, financial institutions, medical institutions and
    universities.

28 Ledger poisons Google, *Virus Bulletin: Fighting malware and spam*, Jan. 24, 2008,
    http://www.virusbtn.com/news/2008/01_24.xml (last visited Oct. 4, 2008).

29 Federal Desktop Core Configuration, National Vulnerability Database, http://fdcc.
    nist.gov/ (last visited Oct. 4, 2008).

30 Identify Theft Resource Center, Facts and Statistics, April 30, 2007, http://www.
    idtheftcenter.org/artman2/publish/m_facts/Facts_and_Statistics.shtml.

31 Anti-Phishing Working Group, APWG Phishing Trends Activity Report for December
    2007, http://www.antiphishing.org/index.html.

32 *Id.*

33 Robert Louis B. Stevenson, Plugging the Phishing Hole: Legislation v. Technology, 2005 Duke L. & Tech. Rev. 0006, ¶ 3, at http://www.law.duke.edu/journals/dltr/articles/2005dltr0006.html.

34 *Id.*

35 Jonathan J. Rusch, Phishing and Federal Law Enforcement, U.S. Department of Justice, Aug. 6, 2004, http://www.abanet.org/adminlaw/annual2004/Phishing/PhishingABAAug2004Rusch.ppt.

36 Michelle Dello, Pharming Out-Scams Phishing, Wired.com, March 14, 2005, http://www.wired.com/techbiz/it/news/2005/03/66853.

37 OpenDNS, PhishTank Annual Report 4 (Oct. 9, 2007), www.phishtank.com/images/PhishTank_Annual_Report_10-9-07.pdf.

38 Anti-Phishing Working Group, http://www.antiphishing.org/ (last visited Oct. 4, 2008).

39 *Supra* n. 216.

40 Council of Europe, Convention on Cybercrime, Budapest, Nov. 23, 2001, CETS No. 185, http://conventions.coe.int/Treaty/en/Treaties/Html/185.htm.

41 Council of Europe, Convention on Cybercrime, CETS No. 185, http://conventions.coe.int/Treaty/Commun/ChercheSig.asp?NT=185&CM=&DF=&CL=ENG   (last visited Oct. 4, 2008).

42 Yuri Kageyama, *Japanese police arrest alleged spammer*, MSNBC.com, Jan. 25, 2008.

43 Additional Protocol to the Convention on cybercrime concerning the criminalization of acts of a racist and xenophobic nature committed through computer systems (Nov. 7, 2002). Council of Europe Treaty Office, Strasbourg, Jan. 28, 2003, CETS No. 189, http://conventions.coe.int/Treaty/en/Treaties/Html/189.htm.

44 eBay Inc. v. Bidder's Edge, Inc., 100 F. Supp. 2d 1058, 1069–70 (N.D. Cal. 2000).

45 Register.com, Inc. v. Verio, Inc., 126 F. Supp. 2d 238, 248–51 (S.D.N.Y. 2000).

46 *Id.* at 251.

47 Dan Hunter, Cyberspace as Place and the Tragedy of the Digital Anticommons, 91 Cal. L. Rev. 439 (2003); Mark A. Lemley, Place and Cyberspace, 91 Cal. L. Rev. 521 (2003).

48 Hunter, 91 Cal. L. Rev. at 486.

49 Intel Corporation v. Hamidi, 30 Cal. 4th 1342, 1363 (2003).

50 *Id.* at 1347.

51 *Id.* at 1364.

52 Panel Report, United States – Measures Affecting the Cross-Border Supply of Gambling and Betting Services: Recourse to Article 21.5 of the DSU by Antigua and Barbuda, WT/DS285/R (April 20, 2005), as modified by Appellate Body Report, WT/DS285/AB/R, DSR 2005:XII, 5797.

53 U.S. Online Gamblers Doubled in 2005; Only 19% Think It's Illegal, *Digitalmediawire*, May 11, 2006, http://www.dmwmedia.com/news/2006/05/11/report-u-s-online-gamblers-doubled-in-2005-only-19-think-its-illegal.

54 Nancy Zuckerbrod, Bill Passed to Limit Internet Gambling, CBS News, Jul. 12, 2006.

55 720 Ill. Comp. Stat. 5/28-1(a)(12) (2006), La. Rev. Stat. Ann. § 14:90.3, Nev. Op. Atty. Gen. No. 38, 2000 WL 33171886 (requiring permission from the Nevada Gaming Commission), Or. Rev. Stat. § 167.109, S.D. Codified Laws § 22–25A-7 (2004), Wash. Rev. Code § 9.46.240 (2006).

56 109 Pub. L. 109-347, Title VIII (Oct. 13, 2006) (codified at 31 U.S.C. §§ 5301, 5361–67).

57 18 U.S.C. § 1084 (2006).

58 18 U.S.C. §§ 1952, 1955 (2006).

59 *See* United States v. Sacco, 491 F.2d 995, 998–1001 (9th Cir. 1974) and United States v. Lee, 173 F.3d 809, 810–11 (11th Cir.1999) ("if Congress, or a committee thereof, makes legislative findings that a statute regulates activities with a substantial effect on commerce, a court may not override those findings unless they lack a rational basis").

60 Panel Report, United States – Measures Affecting the Cross-Border Supply of Gambling and Betting Services: Recourse to Article 21.5 of the DSU by Antigua and Barbuda, WT/DS285/RW (Mar. 30, 2007).

61 Humphrey v. Viacom, Inc., No. 06-2768 (DMC), 2007 WL 1797648 (D. N.J. June 20, 2007).

62 Panel Report, United States – Measures Affecting the Cross-Border Supply of Gambling and Betting Services: Recourse to Article 21.5 of the DSU by Antigua and Barbuda, WT/DS285/R (April 20, 2005), as modified by Appellate Body Report, WT/DS285/AB/R, DSR 2005:XII, 5797.

63 James Kanter and Gary Rivlin, WTO gives Antigua right to violate U.S. copyrights in gambling dispute, *Int'l Herald Tribune*, Dec. 21, 2007, http://www.iht.com/articles/2007/12/21/business/wto.php.

64 Bragg v. Linden Research, Inc., 487 F. Supp. 2d 593 (E.D. Pa. 2007).

65 Hernandez v. Internet Gaming Entertainment, No. 07-CIV-21403 (S.D. Fla. 2008).

66 Dutch Court Convicts 2 of Stealing Virtual Items, MSNBC.com, Oct. 21, 2008.

67 Emma Thomasson, Dutch police Arrest Teenage Online Furniture Thief, Reuters UK, Nov. 14, 2007, http://uk.reuters.com/article/oddlyEnoughNews/idUKL1453844620071114.

68 Mari Yamaguchi, Angry Online Divorcee 'Kills' Virtual Ex-Hubby, MSNBC.com, Oct. 23, 2008, http://www.msnbc.msn.com/id/27337812/.

69 Jeff W. Le Blanc, The Pursuit of Virtual Life, Liberty, and Happiness and its Economic and Legal Recognition in the Real World, 9 Fla. Coastal L. Rev. 255 (2008).

70 Real Taxes for Real Money Made by Online Game Players, *Wall Street Journal*, Oct. 31, 2008.

5 Conflict of Laws

1 Helicopteros Nacionales de Columbia v. Hall, 466 U.S. 408, 427 (1984).

2 International Shoe Co. v. Washington, 326 U.S. 310, 316 (1945).

3 Hanson v. Denckla, 357 U.S. 235, 253 (1958) and World-Wide Volkswagen v. Woodson, 444 U.S. 286, 297 (1980).

4 465 U.S. 783 (1984).

5 Helicopteros Nacionales de Columbia v. Hall, 466 U.S. at 415.

6 465 U.S. 770 (1984).

7 *Id.* at 780.

8 28 U.S.C. § 1332 (2007).

9 28 U.S.C. § 1251 (2007).

10 In the United States, this principle is codified at 28 U.S.C. § 1404(a) ("For the convenience of parties and witnesses, in the interest of justice, a district court may

transfer any civil action to any other district or division where it might have been brought.").

11　Piper Aircraft Co. v. Reyno, 454 U.S. 235, 247 (1981).

12　*Id.* at 254.

13　*Id.* at 255–56 (citations omitted).

14　Inset Systems, Inc. v. Instruction Set, Inc., 937 F. Supp. 161, 165 (D. Conn. 1996).

15　Zippo Mfg. Co. v. Zippo Dot Com, Inc., 952 F. Supp. 1119, 1124 (W.D. Pa. 1997).

16　*See,* e.g., Toys "R" Us, Inc. v. Step Two, S.A., 318 F.3d 446, 453 (3rd Cir. 2003) (describing it as the "seminal authority regarding personal jurisdiction" involving websites); ALS Scan, Inc. v. Digital Serv. Consultants, Inc., 293 F.3d 707, 713–14 (4th Cir. 2002); Cybersell, Inc. v. Cybersell, Inc., 130 F.3d 414, 418 (9th Cir. 1997).

17　5 Cal. 4th 1054 (2005).

18　315 F. 3d 256 (4th Cir. 2002).

19　395 N.J. Super. 380, 387 (App. Div. 2007).

20　*See,* e.g., Bible and Gospel Trust v. Wyman, 354 F. Supp. 2d 1025 (D. Minn. 2005); Medinah Mining, Inc. v. Amunategui, 237 F. Supp. 2d 1132 (D. Nev. 2002); Burleson v. Toback, 391 F. Supp. 2d 401 (M.D. N.C. 2005); Barrett v. Catacombs Press, 44 F. Supp. 2d 717 (E.D. Pa. 1999); Novak v. Benn, 896 So.2d 513 (Ala. Civ. App. 2004).

21　Restatement (Second) of Conflict of Laws § 145 (1971).

22　*Id.* at §§ 6, 145.

23　Griffis v. Luban, 646 N.W.2d 527, 535 (Minn. 2002).

24　Restatement (Third) of the Foreign Relations Law of the United States § 401 cmt. a (1987).

25　*Id.* at § 401(b).

26　*Id.* at § 421(2).

27　Ronald Brand, Community Competence for Matters of Judicial Cooperation at The Hague Conference on Private International Law: A View From the United States, 21 Journal of Law & Commerce 191, 199–205 (2002).

28　Dow Jones & Co., Inc. v. Gutnick, [2002] HCA 56 ¶ 9 (Austl.) at http://www.austlii. edu.au/ (enter Dow Jones v. Gutnick in search operator; then follow hyperlink for "10. Dow Jones & Company Inc v. Gutnick, [2002] HCA 56").

29　*Id.* at ¶ 26.

30　*Id.* at ¶ 27.

31　Lewis and others v. King, [2004] EWCA Civ. 1329, ¶ 29 (Eng.) (quoting Dow Jones & Co. Inc. v. Gutnick, [2002] HCA 56 ¶ 39).

32　*Id.* at ¶ 34.

33　Berezovsky v. Michaels, [2001] EWCA Civ. 409; Berezovsky v. Michaels, [2000] 2 All ER 986 (affirming Berezovsky v. Michaels, [1999] EMLR 278 (Eng.) at http://www.publications.parliament.uk/pa/ld199900/ldjudgmt/jd000511/bere-1.htm.

34　Michael Freedman, Dark force, Forbes.com, May 21, 2007, http://www.forbes.com/business/forbes/2007/0521/130.html.

35　Burke v. NYP Holdings, Inc., 2005 BCSC 1287 (Can.).

36　Bangoura v. Washington Post, [2005] O.J. No. 3849 (Can).

37　*Id.* at ¶ 5.

38　Jenner v. Sun Oil Company Limited et al., [1952] O.R. 240 (Ont. H.C.) (Can.).

39　Restatement (Third) of the Foreign Relations Law of the United States § 401(a) (1987).

40 David J. Gerber, Symposium: Prescriptive Authority: Global Markets as a Challenge to National Regulatory Systems, 26 Hous. J. Int'l L. 287, 290 (2004).

41 Restatement (Third) of the Foreign Relations Law of the United States § 402 (1987).

42 *Id.* at § 404.

43 Ayelet Ben-Ezer and Ariel L. Bendor, Conceptualizing Yahoo! v. L.C.R.A.: Private Law, Constitutional Review and International Conflict of Laws, 25 Cardozo L. Rev. 2089, 2109 (2004).

44 Restatement (Third) of the Foreign Relations Law of the United States § 403 cmt. a (1987).

45 *See* Uniform Foreign-Country Money Judgments Recognition Act § 4 (2005) (updating the Uniform Foreign Money Judgments Recognition Act of 1962, which codified prevalent common law rules regarding the recognition of money judgments).

46 *See*, e.g., Telnikoff v. Matusevitch, 702 A.2d 230 (Md. 1997) (in which the Maryland Court of Appeals determined that enforcing a foreign libel judgment that lacked the same speech protections the U.S. gives plaintiffs in libel cases would effectively chill protected speech.)

47 433 F.3d 1199 (9th Cir. 2006) (en banc), *cert denied*, 126 S.Ct. 2332, 164 L. Ed. 2d 841 (2006).

48 Association Union des Etudiants Juifs de France v. Yahoo!, Inc, High Court of Paris, May 22, 2000, Interim Court Order No. 00/05308, 00/05309, translated at http://www.juriscom.net/txt/jurisfr/cti/yauctions20000522.htm.

49 Yahoo! Inc. v. La Ligue Contre Le Racisme et L'Antisemitisme, 145 F. Supp. 2d 1168 (N.D. Cal. 2001).

50 28 U.S.C. § 2201 ("[A]ny court of the United States, upon the filing of an appropriate pleading, may declare the rights and other legal relations of any interested party seeking such declaration, whether or not further relief is or could be sought. Any such declaration shall have the force and effect of a final judgment or decree and shall be reviewable as such.").

51 Yahoo! Inc. v. La Ligue Contre le Racisme et L'Antisemitisme, 433 F.3d 1199, 1205 (9th Cir. 2006) (en banc).

52 2008 N.Y. Laws ch. 66.

53 H.R. 5814, 110th Cong. (2008).

54 S. 449, 111th Cong. (2009).

55 BGHZ 46, 212 (Case Az.: 1 StR 184/00) decided on Dec. 12, 2000.

56 Directive 2000/31/EC of the European Parliament and of the Council of 8 June 2000 on certain legal aspects of information society services, in particular electronic commerce, in the Internal Market, O.J. L 178/4, 17/07/2000 pp. 0001–0016, http://eurlex.europa.eu/LexUriServ/site/en/oj/2000/l_178/l_17820000717en00010016.pdf.

57 Directive of the European Parliament and of the Council Amending Council Directive on the coordination of certain provisions laid down by law, regulation or administrative action in Member States concerning the pursuit of television broadcasting activities, 89/552/EEC, COM (2007) 170; 2005/0260 (COD), Final (May 22, 2007).

58 Hague Conference on Private International Law, Summary of the outcome of the discussion in Commission II of the first part of the diplomatic conference (June 2001), www.uspto.gov/go/dcom/olia/interimhague_508.pdf.

59 Council Regulation (EC) No. 44/2001 on Jurisdiction and the Recognition and Enforcement of Judgments in Civil and Commercial Matters, O.J. L 12/1, Art. 5, 16 (Dec. 22, 2000).

60 Convention on the Law Applicable to Contractual Obligations (June 19, 1980), O.J. L 266 (Sept. 10, 1980).

61 Telephone interview with Diane Wallis, Vice President, European Union Parliament, June 21, 2007.

62 Joseph W. Goodman, The pros and cons of online dispute resolution: An assessment of cyber-mediation websites, 2003 Duke L. & Tech. Rev. 4, ¶ 18.

63 E-mail from George Freeman, Asst. General Counsel, *New York Times* (July 31, 2007) (on file with the author).

64 Dow Jones & Company, Inc. v. Gutnick M3/2002 (May 28, 2002) at 70, http://www.austlii.edu.au/au/other/hca/transcripts/2002/M3/2.html.

65 Editorial, A blow to online freedom, *New York Times*, Dec. 11, 2002, at A34.

66 E-mail from Kurt Wimmer, Senior Vice President and Counsel, Gannett Co. (July 24, 2007) (on file with the author).

6   Information Access and Protection

1 eBizMBA, 30 Most Popular Blogs (August 2008) http://www.ebizmba.com/articles/popular-blogs.

2 Kleindienst v. Mandel, 408 U.S. 753, 762 (1972).

3 ARTICLE 19, Access to information: An instrumental right for empowerment 9 (2007, July), www.article19.org/pdfs/publications/ati-empowerment-right.pdf.

4 Christopher Kedzie, The third waves, in B. Kahin and C. Nesson eds., *Borders in Cyberspace* (1997) 115.

5 5 U.S.C. § 552 (2007).

6 *Id.* at § 552(f)(1).

7 Tax Analysts v. United States Dep't of Justice, 845 F.2d 1060, 1069 (D.C. Cir. 1988), *aff'd*, 492 U.S. 136 (1989)).

8 OpenTheGovernment.org, Secrecy Report Card, Sec 1:1 (2008), http://www.openthegovernment.org/.

9 U.S. Department of Defense v. Federal Labor Relations Authority, 510 U.S. 487 (1994).

10 National Archives and Records Administration v. Favish, 541 U.S. 157, 171–72 (2004) (citation omitted).

11 The Justice Department maintains a page that links to other agency sites at http://www.usdoj.gov/oip/other_age.htm. The Reporter's Committee for Freedom of the Press offers a letter generator on its website at http://www.rcfp.org/foi_letter/generate.php.

12 Marks v. United States (Dep't of Justice), 578 F.2d 261 (9th Cir. 1978).

13 5 U.S.C. § 552(a)(4)(A)(ii) (2007).

14 *Id.*

15 *Id.*

16 *Id.* at § 552(a)(6)(C)(iii).

17 *Id.* at § 552(4)(iii).

18   *Id.* § 552(a)(6)(E)(v).

19   *Id.* § 552(a)(6)(C)(ii).

20   George Landau, Quantum leaps: Computer journalism takes off, Columbia Journalism Review, May/June 1992, http://backissues.cjrarchives.org/year/92/3/quantum.asp.

21   *See* United States Department of State v. Ray, 502 U.S. 164 (1991); Department of Air Force v. Rose, 425 U.S. 352 (1976).

22   United States Department of Justice Office of Information and Privacy FOIA Post, New attorney general FOIA memorandum issued ¶ 10, Oct. 15, 2001, http://www.usdoj.gov/oip/foiapost/2001foiapost19.htm.

23   *Id.* at ¶ 11.

24   OpenTheGovernment.org, Secrecy Report Card, Sec 1:8 (2007), http://www.openthegovernment.org/.

25   Pub L. No. 110-175, 121 Stat. 2524 (2007).

26   Chrysler Corp. v. Brown, 441 U.S. 281, 293 (1979).

27   Vaughn v. Rosen, 523 F.2d 1136, 1141 (D.C. Cir. 1975).

28   5 U.S.C. § 552(a) (2006).

29   Soucie v. David, 448 F.2d 1067, 1077 (D.C. Cir. 1971).

30   S. Rep. No. 813, 89th Cong., 1st Sess. 9 (1965).

31   Roy A. Schotland, Re-examining the Freedom of Information Act's exemption 8: Does it give an unduly "full service" exemption for bank examination reports and related materials, 9 Administrative Law Journal of the American University 43 (1995).

32   Mays v. DEA, 234 F.3d 1324, 1327 (D.C. Cir. 2000).

33   Phillippi v. CIA, 546 F.2d 1009, 1013 (D.C. Cir. 1976).

34   People for Amer. Way Found. v. NSA/Cent. Sec. Serv., 462 F. Supp. 2d 21(D.D.C. 2006) (finding National Security Agency's refusal to confirm or deny existence of national security documents sought by a non-profit organization proper because doing either would cause harm under the Freedom of Information exception.).

35   Robert H. Moll, Department of Justice memorandum, "Glomar" responses to Freedom of Information Act (FOIA) requests (Sept. 4, 1998), http://www.doi.gov/foia/glomar.htm.

36   Kissinger v. Reporters Committee for Freedom of the Press, 445 U.S. 136, 156 (1980).

37   Louis Fisher, Politics and Policy: Executive privilege and the Bush administration: essay: Congressional access to information: Using legislative will and leverage, 52 DUKE L.J. 323 (2002).

38   Paul Kane, West Wing Aides Cited for Contempt; Refusal to Testify Prompts House Action, *Washington Post*, Feb. 15, 2008, at A4.

39   Committee on the Judiciary, U.S. House of Representatives v. Harriet Miers, Civil Action No. 08-0409 (JDB) 156 (D.D.C. 2008); 2008 U.S. Dist. LEXIS 58050.

40   44 U.S.C. § 2203(a) (2006).

41   *Id.* § 2201(1).

42   Exec. Order No. 13489, Presidential Records, 74 Fed. Reg. 4667 (Jan. 21, 2009).

43   A history of the litigation is documented at http://www.gwu.edu/~nsarchiv/news/20080417/chron.htm.

44   Thomas, http://thomas.loc.gov/.

45   PACER, http://pacer.psc.uscourts.gov/.

46   Links to all state public information laws can be found at http://www.nfoic.org/foi-center/state-foi-laws.html.

47   North Dakota, Florida, California, Louisiana, Michigan, Mississippi, New Hampshire, Ohio, Rhode Island, and Montana.

48   Iowa, North Carolina, Virginia, Montana, New Jersey, West Virginia, Texas, Nebraska, Nevada, Arkansas, Georgia, California, District of Columbia, Indiana, Vermont, Connecticut, Florida, Idaho, Mississippi, Ohio, Rhode Island, and Utah.

49   *See* Raycom National, Inc. v. Campbell, 361 F. Supp. 2d 679 (N.D. Ohio 2004); The Baltimore Sun Co. v. Ehrlich, 356 F. Supp. 2d 577 (D. Md. 2005); Snyder v. Ringgold, 40 F. Supp.2d 714 (D. Md. 1999) (Snyder II); *see also* Snyder v. Ringgold, No. 97-1358, 1998 U.S. App. LEXIS 562 (4th Cir. 1998).

50   Youngstown Publishing Company v. McKelvey, Case No. 4:05 CV 00625, 2005 U.S. Dist. LEXIS 9476, at *19 (N.D. Ohio 2005).

51   532 U.S. 514 (2001).

52   18 U.S.C. § 2511(1)(c) (2007).

53   *Bartnicki*, 532 U.S. at 533.

54   *Id.* at 534.

55   403 U.S. 713.

56   Karl H. Schmid, Journalist's Privilege in Criminal Proceedings: An Analysis of United States Courts of Appeals' Decisions from 1973 to 1999, 39 Am. Crim. L. Rev. 1441, 1448 (2002).

57   Cohen v. Cowles Media Co., 501 U.S. 663 (1991).

58   Ventura v. Cincinnati Enquirer, 396 F.3d 784, 791 (2005).

59   Alicia Upano, Will a history of government using journalists repeat itself under the Department of Homeland Security? 27 The News Media & the Law 10 (Winter 2003).

60   First Amendment Center, State of the First Amendment 2008, http://www.firstamendmentcenter.org/pdf/SOFA2008survey.pdf.

61   *In re* Grand Jury Subpoena, Judith Miller, 397 F.3d 964, 993 (D.C. Cir. 2005) (Tatel, J., concurring).

62   28 U.S.C. § 1826(a) (2007).

63   H.R. 2101, 110 Cong. (2007).

64   O'Neill v. Oakgrove Construction Inc., 71 N.Y.S.2d 521 (1988).

65   408 U.S. 665 (1972).

66   *Id.* at 697.

67   *Id.* at 690.

68   *Id.* at 692.

69   *Id.* at 695.

70   *Id.* at 743 (Stewart, J., dissenting).

71   *Id.* at 710 (Powell, J., concurring).

72   *Id.* at 710.

73   McKevitt v. Pallasch, 339 F.3d 530, 531–32 (7th Cir. 2003) ("A large number of cases conclude, rather surprisingly in light of Branzburg, that there is a reporter's privilege, though they do not agree on its scope. A few cases refuse to recognize the privilege … Our court has not taken sides."

74   *In re* Grand Jury Subpoena Duces Tecum, 112 F.3d 910, 918 (8th Cir. 1997).

75   Fed. R. Evid. 501.

76   120 Cong. Rec. H 12253-54 (daily ed. Dec. 18, 1974).

77   Policy with regard to the issuance of subpoenas to members of the news media, 28 C.F.R. § 50.10.

78   408 U.S. 665, 743 (1972) (Stewart, J., dissenting).

79   David Von Drehle, FBI's No. 2 Was 'Deep Throat': Mark Felt Ends 30-Year Mystery of The Post's Watergate Source, *Washington Post*, June 1, 2005, at A1.

80   Assembly Joint Resolution No. 24, at 4 (adopted Aug. 30, 2007), info.sen.ca.gov/pub/07-08/bill/asm/ab_0001-0050/ajr_24_bill_20070904_enrolled.pdf.

81   Joseph Wilson, What I Didn't Find in Africa, *New York Times*, July 6, 2003, at Sec. 4, 9.

82   Robert Novak, The Mission to Niger, *Chicago Sun-Times*, July 14, 2003, at 3.

83   50 U.S.C. § 421 (criminalizing disclosure of the identity of a covert agent by anyone having had authorized access to classified information).

84   *In re* Grand Jury Subpoena (Miller), 397 F.3d 964 (2005).

85   Brief for the States of Okla. et al. as Amici Curiae Supporting Petitioners at 7, Miller v. United States, 545 U.S. 1150 (2005) (Nos. 04-1507 and 04-1508), 2005 WL 1317523, at 7.

86   *In re* Grand Jury Subpoena (Miller), 397 F.3d at 1000 (Tatel, J., concurring).

87   *Id.*

88   *See*, e.g., Miller v. Transamerican Press, 621 F.2d 721, 725 (5th Cir. 1980).

89   Branzburg v. Hayes, 408 U.S. 665, 704 (1972).

90   *Id.* at 703 (quoting Lovell v. Griffin, 303 U.S. 444, 450 (1938)).

91   Amanda Lenhart and Susannah Fox, Bloggers: A portrait of the internet's new storytellers, Pew Internet & American Life Project (July 19, 2006), http://www.pewinternet.org/PPF/r/186/report_display.asp

92   *In re* Grand Jury Subpoena, 397 F.3d 964, 968–72, 979 (D.C.C. 2005) (Sentelle, J, concurring).

93   *In re* Madden, Titan Sports v. Turner Broadcasting Systems, 151 F.3d 125 (3rd Cir. 1998).

94   O'Grady v. Superior Court of Santa Clara County, 139 Cal. App. 4th 1423 (2006).

95   Apple Computer, Inc. v. Doe 1, 74 U.S.P.Q.2d (BNA) 1191, 33 Media L. Rep. (BNA) 1449 (Cal. Santa Clara County Super. Ct. Mar. 11, 2005), petition for appeal filed sub nom. O'Grady, et al. v. Apple Computer, Inc., No. H028579 (Sixth App. Dist. filed March 22, 2005).

96   18 U.S.C. § 2702(a)(1) (2007).

97   O'Grady v. Superior Court of Santa Clara County, 139 Cal. App. 4th at 1451.

98   Cal. Const. art. I, § 2(в).

99   O'Grady v. Superior Court of Santa Clara County, 139 Cal. App. 4th at 1467.

100 Texas Free Flow of Information Act, Tex. Civ. Prac. & Rem. Code § 22.021, Tex. Code Crim. Proc. art. 38.11 (2009).

101 Samantha Fredrickson, Guarding the unnamed writers of the Internet, *The News Media & The Law*, Nov. 1, 2008, at 34.

102 Doty v. Molnar, DV07-22 (Mont. 13th Jud. Dist. 2008).

103 Beard v. The Portland Mercury, CV 0803 0693 (Ore. 5th Jud. Dist. 2008).

104 *In re* Grand Jury Subpoenas (Leggett), 29 Media L. Rep. 2301 (BNA) (5th Cir. 2001) (unpublished).

105 Zurcher v. Stanford Daily, 436 U.S. 547 (1978).

106 S. Rep. No. 96-874, at 4 (1980), reprinted in 1980 U.S.C.C.A.N. 3950 (explaining that Congress meant the Act to provide "the press and certain other persons not suspected

of committing a crime with protections not provided currently by the Fourth Amendment").

107   42 U.S.C. § 2000aa (2006) (emphasis added).
108   *See* Steve Jackson Games v. United States, 816 F. Supp. 432 (W.D. Tex. 1993), appeal filed on other grounds, 36 F.3d 457 (5th Cir. 1993).

7 Intellectual Property: Copyright

1   17 U.S.C. § 102(a) (2007).
2   Feist Publications, Inc. v. Rural Telephone Service Co., 499 U.S. 340, 345 (1991).
3   17 U.S.C. § 101 (2007).
4   *Id.* § 102(a).
5   *Id.* at 358.
6   *Id.* at 362 (citing 1 M. Nimmer and D. Nimmer, Copyright 1.08[C]1 (1990) and Burrow-Giles Lithographic Co. v. Sarony, 111 U.S. 53, 59–60 (1884)).
7   17 U.S.C. § 120(a).
8   *See,* e.g., International News Service v. Associated Press, 248 U.S. 215, 234 (1918) (indicating that "the news element – the information respecting current events contained in the literary production – is not the creation of the writer, but is a report of matters that ordinarily are publici juris; it is the history of the day.")
9   Feist Publications, Inc. v. Rural Telephone Service Co., 499 U.S. 340, 347 (1991).
10   *Id.* at 348.
11   *Id.* at 353.
12   *Id.* at 350 (citations omitted).
13   Directive 96/9/EC of the European Parliament and of the Council of 11 March 1996 on the legal protection of databases, O.J. L 077, 27/03/1996 pp. 0020–0028 at http://eur-lex.europa.eu/LexUriServ/LexUriServ.do?uri=CELEX:31996L0009:EN:HTML.
14   *Id.* at ch. 3, art. 7(1).
15   Atari, Inc. v. N. Am. Philips Consumer Elecs. Corp., 672 F.2d 607, 616 (7th Cir. 1982).
16   Data East USA, Inc. v. EPYX, Inc., 862 F.2d 204 (1988).
17   Mitel, Inc. v. Iqtel, Inc., 124 F.3d 1366, 1375 (10th Cir. 1997).
18   C-SPAN policies on use of its video can be found on its website at http://www.c-span.org/about/copyright.asp (last visited Oct. 8, 2008).
19   17 U.S.C. § 105 (2007).
20   Fred von Lohmann, This Song Belongs to You and Me, Electronic Frontier Foundation, Aug. 24, 2004, http://www.eff.org/deeplinks/2004/08/song-belongs-you-and-me, and JibJab Media v. Ludlow Music ("This Land" Parody), Electronic Frontier Foundation, http://www.eff.org/cases/jibjab-media-inc-v-ludlow-music-inc.
21   Michael Geist, Music takedown strikes the wrong chord, *The Toronto Star*, Oct. 29, 2007, at B3.
22   17 U.S.C. § 101(2) (2007).
23   533 U.S. 438 (2001).
24   490 U.S. 730 (1989).
25   *Id.* at 751–52.
26   17 U.S.C. § 106A(a) (2007).

27 *Id.*

28 *Id.* § 202.

29 *Id.* § 408.

30 Berne Convention Implementation Act of 1988, Pub. L. 100-568, 102 Stat. 2853.

31 17 U.S.C. § 410 (2007).

32 *Id.* §§ 302, 305.

33 Sonny Bono Copyright Term Extension Act. *See* Pub. L. 105-298 (Oct. 27, 1998).

34 *See* Jenny Dixon, The Copyright Term Extension Act: Is Life Plus Seventy Too Much?, 18 HASTINGS COMM. ENT. L.J. 945, 968 (1996) (citing Council Directive 93/98, 1993 O.J. (L 290)).

35 *See* Christina Gifford, Note: The Sonny Bono Copyright Term Extension Act, 30 U. MEM L. REV. 363, 398 (2000) (indicating that ten of 13 sponsors for the House bill and eight of 12 sponsors for the Senate bill received contributions from Disney.).

36 537 U.S. 186 (2003).

37 Pinkham v. Sara Lee Corp., 983 F.2d 824, 828 (1992).

38 *Id.* at 829 (quoting 3 Melville B. Nimmer and David Nimmer, Nimmer on Copyright § 13.08 at 139 (1992)).

39 Gershwin Publishing Corp. v. Columbia Artists Management, Inc., 443 F.2d 1159, 1162 (2d Cir. 1971).

40 907 F. Supp. 1361 (N.D. Cal. 1995).

41 Virgin Records v. Thomas (formerly Capitol Records v. Thomas), CV-*06-1497* (MJD/RLE) (D. Minn. 2009).

42 Capitol Records v. Thomas, CV-06-1497 (MJD/RLE) (D. Minn. 2007).

43 National Car Rental System, Inc. v. Computer Associates Int'l, Inc., 991 F.2d 426, 434 (8th Cir. 1993) (citing 2 Nimmer on Copyright §8.11[A], at 8-124.1).

44 *See* Atlantic Recording Corp. v. Howell, 554 F. Supp. 2d 976 (D. Ariz. 2008) (making available recordings for distribution is not actionable under copyright law); London-Sire v. Doe, 542 F. Supp. 2d 153 (D. Mass. 2008) (holding that "merely exposing music files to the internet is not copyright infringement"). *But see* Elektra v. Barker, 551 F. Supp. 2d 234 (S.D. N.Y. 2008) (offering to distribute files on a file sharing network can implicate the distribution right.); Warner Bros. Records, Inc. v. Payne, Civil Action No. W-06-CA-051, 2006 WL 2844415, at *3–4 (W.D. Tex. July 17, 2006) ("Listing unauthorized copies of sound recordings using an online file-sharing system constitutes an offer to distribute those works, thereby violating a copyright owner's exclusive right of distribution.").

45 Sarah McBride, Music Industry to Abandon Mass Suits, *Wall Street Journal*, Dec. 18, 2008, at B1.

46 239 F.3d 1004, 1011–14 (2001); *See also* Hotaling v. Church of Jesus Christ of Latter-Day Saints, 118 F.3d 199 (4th Cir. 1997) (holding that making a work available online violates its owner's distribution right).

47 464 U.S. 417 (1984).

48 MGM Studios v. Grokster, 545 U.S. 913, 936 (2005) (citations omitted).

49 Pub. L. No. 105-304, 112 Stat. 2860 (Oct. 28, 1998), codified at 17 U.S.C. § 1201, et seq.

50 17 U.S.C. §§ 1201(a)(b) (2007).

51 *Id.* § 1201(g).

52 Rulemaking on Exemptions from Prohibition on Circumvention of Technological Measures that Control Access to Copyrighted Works, U.S. Copyright Office, http://www.copyright.gov/1201/ (last visited Oct. 11, 2008).

53 WIPO Treaty, Apr. 12, 1997, art. 11, S. Treaty Doc. No. 105-17 (1997), 1997 WL 447232.

54 17 U.S.C. §§ 512(a)(b)(c)(d).

55 *Id.* § 512(f).

56 337 F. Supp. 2d 1195 (2004).

57 Rossi v. Motion Picture Association of America, 391 F.3d 1000, 1005 (9th Cir. 2004).

58 17 U.S.C. § 512 (h).

59 Viacom International, Inc. v. YouTube, Inc., No.1:2007cv02103 (S.D. N.Y. March 13, 2007). To follow the case's progression, go to http://news.justia.com/cases/featured/new-york/nysdce/1:2007cv02103/302164/.

60 *See*, e.g., Erika Morphy, Viacom v. Google Wends Its Way Through Legal Fog, *Tech. News World*, May 28, 2008, at http://www.technewsworld.com/story/63187.html?welcome=1212698989.

61 17 U.S.C. § 504(a), (c)(1) (2007).

62 *Id.* § 504(c)(2).

63 *Id.* § 506(a)(1).

64 Mattel v. Walking Mountain Productions, 353 F.3d 792 (2003).

65 17 U.S.C. § 107 (2007).

66 *Id.*

67 Campbell v. Acuff-Rose Music, Inc., 510 U.S. 569, 578 (1994).

68 *Id.* at 584.

69 *Id.* at 579.

70 *Id.* at 579.

71 Sony Computer Entertainment America, Inc. v. Bleem, 214 F.3d 1022 (9th Cir. 2000).

72 Salinger v. Random House, Inc., 811 F.2d 90, 97 (2d Cir. 1987).

73 471 U.S. 539 (1985).

74 Warner Bros. Entertainment, Inc. v. RDR Books, O7 Civ. 9667 (RPP) (S.D. N.Y. 2008).

75 Sony Corp. of America v. Universal City Studios, Inc., 464 U.S. 417, 451 (1984).

76 Campbell v. Acuff-Rose Music, Inc., 510 U.S. 569, 582 (1994).

77 Dr. Seuss Enterprises, L.P. v. Penguin Books USA, Inc., 109 F.3d 1394, 1401 (9th Cir. 1997).

78 Mattel v. Walking Mountain Productions, 353 F.3d 792 (9th Cir. 2003); 2004 U.S. Dist. LEXIS 12469 (D. Cal. 2004).

79 SunTrust Bank v. Houghton Mifflin Co., 268 F.3d 1257, 1276 (11th Cir. 2001).

80 Harper & Row Publishers, Inc., v. Nation Enterprises, 471 U.S. 539, 558 (1985).

81 *Id.* at 556 (quoting appellate decision at 723 F.2d 195, 203 (1983)).

82 *Id.* at 557.

83 433 U.S. 562 (1977).

84 Zacchini v. Scripps Howard Broadcasting Co., 47 Ohio St. 2d 224, 235 (1976).

85 Zacchini v. Scripps Howard Broadcasting Co., 433 U.S. 562, 575 (1977).

86 273 F.3d 429 (2001).

87 *Id.* at 339 (citing trial transcript).

88 *Id.* at 450 (citing Turner Broadcasting System, Inc. v. FCC, 512 U.S. 622, 662 (1994)).
89 *Id.* at 454.
90 *Id.* at 451.
91 Ticketmaster Corp. v. Tickets.com, Inc., 2000 U.S. Dist. LEXIS 4553, 6 (C.D. Cal., March 27, 2000) (unpublished opinion).
92 Universal v. Reimerdes, 111 F. Supp. 2d 346, 341 (S.D.N.Y. 2000).
93 Kelly v. Arriba Soft Corp, 336 F.3d 811, 818–22 (9th Cir. 2003).
94 Perfect 10 v. Amazon, 508 F.3d 1146 (2007) (citing Perfect 10 v. Google, Inc, 416 F. Supp. 2d 828, 843–45 (C.D. Cal. 2006)).
95 Newton v. Diamond, 388 F.3d 1189 (2003).
96 410 F.3d 792 (6th Cir. 2005).
97 Bill Werde, Defiant Downloads Rise from Underground, *New York Times*, Feb. 25, 2004, at E3.
98 In 1998, Congress drastically reduced the amount of licensing fees collected from restaurants and other small businesses that use radio or television to supply music for their customers when it passed the Fairness in Music Licensing Act. The Act exempted approximately 70 percent of food and drinking establishments from paying licensing fees, as long as the establishment is less than 3,750 square feet and does not retransmit the music.
99 17 U.S.C. § 115(a)(2) (2007).
100 *See* James Boyle, The Second Enclosure Movement and the Construction of the Public Domain, Law and Contemporary Problems, 66 Law & Contemp. Probs. 33 (Winter/Spring 2003) (analogizing copyright's impact on the public domain to the English Enclosure Movement). Professor Boyle is also a founding member of the Creative Commons.

8   Intellectual Property: Patents, Trademarks, and Trade Secrets

1 Richard Stallman, Did You Say "Intellectual Property"? It's a Seductive Mirage, GNU Operating System, http://www.gnu.org/philosophy/not-ipr.html (last visited June 11, 2008).
2 U.S. Const., art. 1, § 8.
3 35 U.S.C. §101 (2006).
4 *Id.* § 171.
5 *Id.* § 161.
6 *See* State Street Bank & Trust v. Signature Financial Group, Inc., 149 F.3d 1368 (Fed. Cir. 1998).
7 35 U.S.C. § 271(a) (2006).
8 *Id.* § 271(b).
9 *Id.* § 271(e).
10 *See* Lorelei R. De Larena, What Copyright Teaches Patent Law About "Fair Use" and Why Universities Are Ignoring the Lesson, 84 Ore. L. Rev. 779, 790 (2005).
11 Madey v. Duke University, 307 F.3d 1351, 1362 (Fed. Cir. 2002) (quoting Embrex, Inc. v. Serv. Eng'g Corp., 216 F.3d 1343, 1353 (Fed. Cir. 2000) (Rader, J., concurring)).

12   *Id.* (quoting Embrex, 216 F.3d at 1349).

13   35 U.S.C. § 274.

14   *See* Robert E. Thomas, Vanquishing Copyright Pirates and Patent Trolls: The Divergent Evolution of Copyright and Patent Laws, 43 Am. Bus. L.J. 689, 702 (2006).

15   Verizon Services Corp. v. Vonage Holdings Corp. 503 F.3d 1295 (Fed. Cir. 2007); Amol Sharma, Vonage Says Patent Suits Could Lead to Bankruptcy, *Wall Street Journal*, April 18, 2007, at A2.

16   *See* U.S. Patent No. 5,443,036 (issued Aug. 22, 1995).

17   Max Hefflinger, U.S. Patent Office to Revoke Instant Live Concert CD Patent, *Digital Media Wire*, March 12, 2007, http://www.dmwmedia.com/news/2007/03/13/u-s-patent-office-to-revoke-instant-live-concert-cd-patent.

18   Margreth Barrett, Internet Trademark Suits and the Demise of "Trademark Use," 39 U.C. Davis L. Rev. 371, 376 (2006).

19   *Id.*

20   15 U.S.C. § 1052(a) (2007).

21   *See* Blue Bell Bio-Medical v. Cin-Bad, Inc., 864 F.2d 1253, 1256 (5th Cir. 1989); John J. Harland Co. v. Clarke Checks, Inc., 711 F.2d 966, 980 (11th Cir. 1983).

22   Section 43(a) of the Lanham Act, codified at 15 U.S.C. § 1125(a)(3).

23   *See* TrafFix Devices, Inc. v. Mktg. Displays, Inc., 532 U.S. 23 (2001).

24   15 U.S.C. § 1114(1) (2007).

25   *Id.* § 1125(a)(1)(A).

26   *See* North American Medical Corp. v. Axiom Worldwide, Inc., 522 F.3d 1211, 1218 (11th Cir. 2008) (citing 1-800 Contacts, Inc. v. WhenU.com, Inc., 414 F.3d 400, 406–07 (2d Cir. 2005); People for Ethical Treatment of Animals v. Doughney, 263 F.3d 359, 364 (4th Cir. 2001).

27   15 U.S.C. § 1127 (2007).

28   Alliance Metals, Inc. of Atlanta v. Hinely Indus., Inc., 222 F.3d 895, 907 (11th Cir. 2000).

29   15 U.S.C. §§ 1125(c), 1127 (2007).

30   Victor Moseley v. V. Secret Catalogue, 537 U.S. 418, 431 (2003) (citing H. R. Rep. No. 104-374, 1030 (1995)).

31   15 U.S.C. § 1114(1)(b)(2) (2007).

32   *Id.* § 1117.

33   *Id.* § 1125 (c)(4).

34   Playboy Enterprises, Inc. v. Terri Welles, Inc., 279 F.3d 796 (9th Cir. 2002).

35   622 F. Supp. 931 (D.D.C. 1985).

36   *Id.* at 934.

37   Susan Saulny, In Courtroom, Laughter at Fox and a Victory for Al Franken, *New York Times*, Aug. 23, 2003, at B1.

38   L.L. Bean, Inc. v. Drake Publishers, Inc., 811 F.2d 26 (1st Cir. 1987).

39   *Id.* at 34.

40   836 F.2d 397 (8th Cir. 1987).

41   414 F.3d 400 (2d Cir. 2005).

42   *Id.* at 409 (a section quoted less often was the Second Circuit's observation that WhenU did not link its ads to specific trademarks, but to categories of products and services).

43   Rescuecom Corporation v. Google, Inc., 456 F. Supp. 2d 393 (N.D. N.Y. 2006).

44 *Id.* at 403.
45 *See*, e.g., Merck & Co., Inc. v. Mediplan Health Consulting, Inc., 425 F. Supp. 2d 402 (S.D. N.Y. 2006); FragranceNet.com v. FragranceX.com, Inc. 493 F. Supp. 2d 545 (E.D. N.Y. 2007).
46 354 F.3d 1020 (9th Cir. 2004).
47 Case No. C03-05340-F (N.D. Cal., March 30, 2005, settled Aug. 31, 2007).
48 330 F. Supp. 2d 700 (E.D. Va. 2004).
49 437 F. Supp. 2d 273, 285 (D. N.J. 2006) *See also* Buying for the Home, LLC v. Humble Abode L.L.C., 459 F. Supp. 2d 310 (D. N.J. 2006) (finding that the purchase of trademarks as key words satisfied the Lanham Act's commercial use requirement).
50 *See* Int'l Profit Assocs v. Paisola, 461 F. Supp. 2d 672 (N.D. Ill. 2006) (finding trademark use in keywords likely to cause confusion); Edina Realty, Inc. v. TheMLSOnline. Com, 2006 U.S. Dist. LEXIS 13775, 2006 WL 737064 (D. Minn. 2006); J.G. Wentworth, S.S.C. v. Settlement Funding LLC, 2007 U.S. Dist. LEXIS 288, 2007 WL 30115 (E.D. Pa. 2007).
51 Mark Hefflinger, French Court: Google Breached Louis Vuitton Trademark Rights, *Digital Media Wire*, Feb. 7, 2005, http://www.dmwmedia.com/news/2005/02/07/french-court-google-breached-louis-vuitton-trademark-rights.
52 174 F.3d 1036 (9th Cir. 1999).
53 *Id.* at 1062.
54 *Id.*
55 Promatek Industries Ltd. v. Equitrac Corp., 300 F.3d 808 (7th Cir. 2002).
56 436 F.3d 1228, 1240 (2006).
57 North American Medical Corp. v. Axiom Worldwide, Inc., 522 F.3d 1211 (11th Cir. 2008).
58 119 F. Supp. 2d 309 (S.D. N.Y. 2000).
59 15 U.S.C. § 1125(d)(1)(A).
60 *Id.* § 1125(d)(1)(B)(i).
61 *Id.* § 1117(d).
62 *Id.* § 1117.
63 Electronics Boutique Holdings Corp. v. Zuccarini, No. 00-4055, 2000 U.S. Dist. LEXIS 15719 (E.D. Pa. 2000).
64 *See* Shields v. Zuccarini, No.00-494, 2000 U.S. Dist. LEXIS 15223 (E.D. Pa. 2000).
65 128 F.3d 86 (2d Cir. 1997).
66 *Id.* at 91.
67 People for the Ethical Treatment of Animals, Inc., v. Doughney, 263 F.3d 359 (4th Cir. 2001).
68 *Id.* at 365.
69 *See* Jews for Jesus v. Brodsky, 993 F. Supp. 282, 309 (D. N.J. 1998) ("The conduct of the Defendant is not only designed to, but is likely to, prevent some Internet users from reaching the Internet site of the Plaintiff Organization … As such, the conduct of the Defendant is 'in connection with goods and services' as that term is used in Section 1125(a)."), *aff'd*, 159 F.3d 1351; 1998 U.S. App. LEXIS 18889 (3d Cir. 1998) (decision without published opinion).
70 *See* Int'l Ass'n of Machinists & Aerospace Workers v. Winship Green Nursing Home, 103 F.3d 196 (1st Cir. 1996) (rejecting the argument that defendant's use of mark in manner that impedes plaintiff's sale or offering of services constitutes use "in connection with any goods or services").

71 *See* Taubman Co. v. Webfeats, 319 F.3d 770, 777 (6th Cir. 2003) (questioning reasoning in Planned Parenthood).

72 *See* Nissan Motor Co. v. Nissan Computer Corp., 378 F.3d 1002 (9th Cir. 2004) (rejecting "effect on commerce" test for commercial use) and Bosley Medical Institute, Inc. v. Steven Kremer, 403 F.3d 672, 674 (2005).

73 Taubman Co. v. Webfeats, 319 F.3d at 775 (although defendant's linking was "extremely minimal," it was sufficient to constitute a use "in connection with the sale or advertising of a good or service.").

74 People for the Ethical Treatment of Animals v. Doughney, 263 F.3d at 366 (citing Cliffs Notes, Inc. v. Bantam Doubleday Dell Publ. Group, Inc., 886 F.2d 490, 494 (2d Cir. 1989)).

75 420 F.3d 309 (4th Cir. 2005).

76 *Id.* at 320.

77 319 F.3d 770, 774 (6th Cir. 2003).

78 *Id.* at 778.

79 368 F.3d 433, 438 (5th Cir. 2004).

80 Bosley Medical Institute v. Kramer, 403 F.3d 672, 679 (2005).

81 *See* Ford Motor Co. v. Lane, 67 F. Supp. 2d 745, 749 (E.D. Mich. 1999).

82 *See* Coca-Cola Bottling Co. v. Coca-Cola Co., 107 F.R.D. 288 (Del. 1995).

83 18 U.S.C. § 1831.

84 *Id.* § 1832.

85 *Id.* § 1831.

86 Apple Computer, Inc. v. DePlume, et al., Case No. 1-05-CV-033341 (Cal. Santa Clara County Super. Ct. filed Jan. 4, 2005).

87 Ford Motor Co. v. Lane, 67 F. Supp. 2d 745, 746 (E.D. Mich. 1999).

88 78 F.3d 219, 227 (6th Cir. 1996).

89 *Id.* at 225.

9   Defamation

1 Time, Inc. v. Pape, 401 U.S. 279 (1971).

2 Restatement (Second) of Torts § 581A cmt. f (1977).

3 Rosenblatt v. Baer, 383 U.S. 75, 92 (1966) (concurring opinion).

4 MMAR Group, Inc. v. Dow Jones & Co., Civ. No. H-95-1262 (S.D. Tex. 1997).

5 MMAR Group, Inc. v. Dow Jones & Co., 187 F.R.D. 282; 1999 U.S. Dist. LEXIS 14941 (1999).

6 *See* New York Times v. Sullivan, 376 U.S. 254, 291 (1964) (holding that prosecutions for libel against the government have no place in the American system of jurisprudence); *See also* Klein v. Port Arthur Independent School District, 92 S.W.3d 889; 2002 Tex. App. LEXIS 8966 (2002) (affirming summary judgment in favor of a blogger sued by the Port Arthur School District for writing about a gang fight at a local prom because government entities cannot sue for defamation.)

7 Judge dismisses Britney Spears' libel suit, MSNBC.com, Nov. 7, 2006, http://www.msnbc.msn.com/id/15595990/

8 *See*, e.g., Thomas v. Telegraph Publishing Company, 155 N.H. 314 (N.H. 2007) (in which the New Hampshire Supreme Court found that a repeat criminal was not libel proof because he had not been made notorious through prior publicity of his crimes).

9   Texas Beef Group v. Winfrey, 11 F. Supp. 2d 858 (1998), *aff'd*, 201 F.3d 680 (5th Cir. 2000).

10 *See* Church of Scientology Int'l v. Time Warner, 806 F. Supp. 1157, 1160 (S.D. N.Y. 1992).

11 Friends of Falun Gong v. Pacific Cultural Enterprise, Inc., 288 F. Supp. 2d 273, *aff'd*, 2004 U.S. App. LEXIS 16419 (2d Cir. N.Y., Aug. 9, 2004).

12 401 U.S. 279, 292 (1971).

13 Bose Corp. v. Consumers Union of United States, Inc., 466 U.S. 485, 499 (1984) (quoting New York Times v. Sullivan, 376 U.S. 254, 284–86 (1964)).

14 *See* Rosenblatt v. Baer, 383 U.S. 75 (1966).

15 *See* Dameron v. Washington Magazine, Inc., 779 F.2d 736, 737 (D.C. Cir. 1985) (concerning an air traffic controller who became an involuntary, limited-purpose public figure due to his role in a major public occurrence). *But see* Wells v. Liddy, 186 F.3d 505 (4th Cir. 1999) (setting a higher standard to ensure that involuntary limited public figures are "exceedingly rare").

16 *See* Time, Inc. v. Pape, 401 U.S. 279, 292 (1971).

17 Harte-Hanks Communications v. Connaughton, 491 U.S. 657, 664 (1989).

18 *Id.* at 684–85.

19 *Id.* at 691–92.

20 *See* Curtis Publishing Co. v. Butts, 388 U.S. 130 (1967).

21 *See* Lyrissa Barnett Lidsky and R. George Wright, *Freedom of the Press: A Reference Guide to the United States Constitution* (Praeger Publishers 2004) 73–75.

22 330 S.C. 562, 499 S.E.2d 822 (Ct. App. 1998).

23 *Id.* at 566.

24 Milkovich v. Lorain Journal Co., 497 U.S. 1, 21 (1990).

25 *Id.* at 20.

26 *Id.* at 20–21.

27 *Id.* at 19.

28 Hoeppner v. Dunkirk Pr. Co., 254 N.Y. 95 (1930).

29 Mashburn v. Collin, 355 So.2d 879 (La. 1977).

30 *See* Greenbelt Cooperative Publishing Assn. v. Bresler, 398 U.S. 6 (1970) (finding that a plaintiff characterized as blackmailing the city during a zoning negotiation was not libeled because the term was rhetorical hyperbole); Underwager v. Channel 9 Australia, 69 F.3d 361, 366–67 (9th Cir. 1995).

31 *See* Milkovich v. Lorain Journal Co., 497 U.S. 1, 20 (1990).

32 Yeagle v. Collegiate Times, 497 S.E.2d 136 (Va. 02/27/1998).

33 Horsley v. Rivera, 292 F.3d 695, 698, 702 (11th Cir. 2002).

34 Boladian v. UMG Recordings, Inc., 123 F. App'x 165, 2005 U.S. App. LEXIS 68 (6th Cir. 2005).

35 U.S. Const., art. 1, § 6.

36 Doe v. McMillan, 412 U.S. 306, 307–10 (1973).

37 Brown & Williamson v. Jacobson, 713 F.2d 262 (7th Cir. 1983).

38 443 U.S. 111 (1979).

39 Time, Inc. v. Firestone, 424 U.S. 448 (1976).

40 *See, e.g.,* Edwards v. National Audubon Society, 556 F.2d 113 (2d Cir. 1977).

41 *See* Kyu Ho Youm, Recent Rulings Weaken Neutral Reportage Defense, 27 NEWSPAPER RES. J. 58 (2006).

42 *See* Edward Seaton, The Uniform Corrections Act: A way out of the libel litigation nightmare, AM. SOC. OF NEWSPAPER EDITORS, July 17, 1998, http://www.asne.org/index.cfm?ID=613 (last visited Oct. 11, 2008).

43 Mathis v. Cannon, 276 Ga. 16; 573 S.E.2d 376 (Ga. 2002).

44 O'Grady v. Superior Court of Santa Clara County, 139 Cal. App. 4th 1423 (Cal. App. 2006).

45 It's in the Cards, Inc. v. Fuschetto, 535 N.W.2d 11 (Wis. Ct. App. 1995).

46 *See* Steven W. Workman, Note: Reports on public proceedings and documents: Absolutely protected by constitutional privilege, 1985 U. ILL. L. REV. 1059 (1985).

47 Dun & Bradstreet, Inc. v. Greenmoss Builders, Inc., 472 U.S. 749, 766 (1985) (White, J., concurring).

48 *See* David A. Anderson, First Amendment Limitations on Tort Law, 69 BROOKLYN L. REV. 755, 767, 771 (2004).

49 New York Times v. Sullivan, 376 U.S. 254, 270–72 (1964).

50 *See* Herbert v. Lando, 441 U.S. 153 (1979).

51 388 U.S. 130 (1967).

52 *Id.* at 167 (Warren, C.J., concurring).

53 *Id.* at 164 (Warren, C.J., concurring).

54 *Id.* at 155.

55 Gertz v. Robert Welch, Inc., 418 U.S. 323, 351 (1974).

56 Rosenbloom v. Metromedia, Inc., 403 U.S. 29, 48 (1971).

57 A plurality opinion is the controlling opinion when no majority exists.

58 418 U.S. 323 (1974).

59 Dun & Bradstreet, Inc. v. Greenmoss Builders, Inc., 472 U.S. 749, 758 (1985).

60 *Id.* at 760.

61 *See* Nationwide Biweekly Administration, Inc., v. Belo Corp., 512 F.3d 137 (5th Cir. 2007); Oja v. U.S. Army Corp. of Engineers, 440 F.3d 1122 (9th Cir. 2006); Van Buskirk v. N.Y. Times Co., 325 F.3d 87 (2nd Cir. 2003).

62 *See*, e.g., Firth v. State, 98 N.Y.2d 365, 371 (2002) (finding that an unrelated modification to a website did not constitute a republication).

63 *See* Bill Kenworthy and Beth Chesterman, Criminal-libel Statutes, State by State, First Amendment Center Online, Aug. 10, 2006, http://www.firstamendmentcenter.org/analysis.aspx?id=17263.

64 *See* Garrison v. Louisiana, 379 U.S. 64 (1964).

65 Felicity Barringer, A criminal defamation verdict roils politics in Kansas City, Kan., *New York Times*, July 29, 2002, at C7.

66 *In re* I.M.L. v. State of Utah, 2002 UT 110 (2002).

67 Editor of Satirical Web Site Won't Face Libel Charge, Associated Press, Jan. 20, 2004 available at http://www.usatoday.com/tech/news/2004-01-20-howling-legal_x.htm.

68 Milkovich v. Lorain Journal Co., 497 U.S. 1, 20, n. 6 (1990); Philadelphia Newspapers v. Hepps, 475 U.S. 767, 779, n. 4 (1986).

69 408 U.S. 665, 704 (1972).

70 *See* Leslie Kaufman, When the Ex Writes a Blog, The Dirtiest Laundry Is Aired, *New York Times*, April 18, 2008, at A1.

71 New School Communications, Inc. v. Brodkorb, CX-06-006432, slip op., at 3–4 (Minn. Dist. Ct., 1st Dist., Mar. 6, 2007).

72 Milum v. Banks, 283 Ga. App. 864 (2007).

73   Wagner v. Miskin, 2003 ND 69, 660 N.W.2d 593 (N.D. May 6, 2003). *See also* Kono v. Meeker, No. 06-1554, 2007 Iowa App. LEXIS 1277 (Iowa App. Dec. 12, 2007) (upholding a libel judgment against two California antique dealers who described an Ohio client as a "flat-out liar, thief and cheat" after a business disagreement); Laughman v. Selmeier, No. A02-08401 (Ohio C.P. jury verdict Feb. 23, 2003) (in which a nurse accused on a patient's website of sexually assaulting him was awarded a $1,125,000 libel judgment); and Omega World Travel v. Mummagraphics, Inc., No. 05-122 (E.D. Va. jury verdict April 27, 2007) (in which the website www.cruises.com won a $2.3 million libel judgment against the operator of www.sueaspammer.com for listing the company as a spammer on the site. The jury award was reduced to $110,000).

74   Scheff v. Bock, No. CACE03022837 (Fla. Cir. Ct. default verdict Sept. 19, 2006).

75   Bock v. Scheff, 991 So.2d 1043 (Fla. 4th Dist. 2008).

76   1995 N.Y. Misc. LEXIS 229; 1995 WL 323710 (N.Y. Sup. Ct. May 24, 1995).

77   47 U.S.C. § 230(c)(1) (2006).

78   Zeran v. American Online, Inc., 129 F.3d 327, 330 (4th Cir. 1997).

79   Doe v. MySpace, 528 F.3d 413 (5th Cir. 2008).

80   Morsette v. "Final Call," 90 N.Y.2d 777 (1997).

81   Kiesau v. Bantz, 686 N.W.2d 164 (Iowa 2004).

82   Bryson v. News America Publications, Inc., 174 Ill.2d 77, 97, 672 N.E.2d 1207 (Ill. 1996).

83   *See* Dan Slater, Libel-in-Fiction Claim, Rarely Successful, Survives Summary Judgment, *Wall Street Journal*, March 20, 2008, http://blogs.wsj.com/law/2008/03/20/libel-in-fiction-claim-rarely-successful-survives-summary-judgment/.

84   Batra v. Wolf, 116059/04; 2008 N.Y. Misc. LEXIS 1933 (March 14, 2008).

85   Carter-Clark v. Random House, Inc., 196 Misc.2d 1011, 768 N.Y.S.2d 290 (2003).

86   Falwell v. Flynt, 805 F.2d 484, 487 (1986).

87   146 S.W.3d 144; 2004 Tex. LEXIS 787 (2004).

88   *Id.* at 149 (citing Patrick Williams, Buzz, *Dallas Observer*, Nov. 18–24, 1999, at 9).

89   *Id.* at 150 (citing lower court decision at 91 S.W.3d 844, 857, 859 (2002)).

90   *Id.* at 157 (citing Pring v. Penthouse Int'l, Ltd., 695 F.2d 438, 442 (10th Cir. 1982)).

91   *Id.*

92   Hustler Magazine, Inc. v. Falwell, 485 U.S. 46 (1988). A transcript of the oral argument is at http://www.oyez.org/cases/1980-1989/1987/1987_86_1278/argument/.

93   *Id.* at 49.

94   *Id.* at 57 (quoting appendix to petition for certiorari).

95   *Id.* at 55.

96   Garrison v. Louisiana, 379 U.S. 64 (1964).

97   *Id.* at 73.

98   *Id.* at 56.

99   Snyder v. Phelps, No. 08-1026 (4th Cir. Sept. 24, 2009).

10   Invasion of Privacy

1   *See* Pavesich v. New England Life Ins. Co., 122 Ga. 190, 50 S.E. 68 (Ga. 1905).

2   *See*, e.g., L. Cohen & Co. v. Dun & Bradstreet, Inc., 629 F. Supp. 1425, 1430 (D. Conn. 1986) (privacy law concerns "the reputational interests of individuals rather than the

less substantial reputational interests of corporations."); Ion Equip. Corp. v. Nelson, 110 Cal. App. 3d 868 (1980) ("A corporation is a fictitious person and has no 'feelings' which may be injured in the sense of the tort."); Felsher v. University of Evansville, 755 N.E.2d 589 (Ind. Sup. Ct. 2001) (a university could not rely on a privacy tort to sue a former faculty member who faked websites and e-mails in his colleagues' names, but they could).

3   *See* Accuracy in Media v. National Park Service, 194 F.3d 120 (D.C. Cir. 1999) (recognizing a privacy interest in the family members of former Deputy White House Counsel Vince Foster, thought to have committed suicide, to prevent access to photos taken at the scene of his death and autopsy. Media plaintiffs, who suspected foul play in Foster's death, filed a Freedom of Information Act request for the photos.)

4   *See* Griswold v. Connecticut, 381 U.S. 479 (1965) (striking down a Connecticut law that prevented the use of contraceptives) and Roe v. Wade, 410 U.S. 113 (1973) (striking down a Texas law that criminalized abortion).

5   *See* Roberson v. Rochester Folding Box Co., 64 N.E. 442, 447 (N.Y. 1902); Brunson v. Ranks Army Store, 73 N.W.2d 803, 806 (Neb. 1955).

6   RESTATEMENT (SECOND) OF TORTS § 652B (1977).

7   *See* Miller v. NBC, 232 Cal. Rptr. 668, 679 (Ct. App. 1986).

8   Marks v. King Broadcasting, 27 Wash. App. 344, 356, 618 P.2d 512 (1980) (finding in favor of a TV news photographer, who videoed a pharmacist accused of Medicare fraud through a pharmacy window when he refused to come out for an interview).

9   Daily Times Democrat v. Graham, 276 Ala. 380 (1964).

10 Video Voyeurism Laws, National Center for Victims of Crime, http://www.ncvc.org.

11 18 U.S.C. § 1801(b)(5)(B).

12 Dietemann v. Time, Inc., 449 F.2d 245 (9th Cir. 1971).

13 *Id.* at 249.

14 Sanders v. ABC, 20 Cal. 4th 907, 911, 1100 (1999).

15 *Id.*

16 *See* Huskey v. National Broadcasting Co., Inc. 632 F. Supp. 1282 (N.D. Ill. 1986).

17 *See* Berthiaume v. Pratt, 365 A.2d 792, 795 (Maine 1976) (a surgeon who had treated cancer patient committed actionable intrusion by photographing him in hospital bed against his will as he lay dying).

18 *See* Doe by Doe v. B.P.S. Guard Services, Inc., 945 F.2d 1422 (8th Cir. 1991).

19 *See* Stessman v. Am. Black Hawk Broadcasting, 416 N.W.2d 685, 687 (Iowa 1987).

20 *See* Rafferty v. Hartford Courant Co., 416 A.2d 1215, 1216, 1220 (Conn. Super. Ct. 1980).

21 Helen Remsburg, Administratrix of the Estate of Amy Lynn Boyer v. Docusearch, Inc., 149 N.H. 148, 156 (N.H. 2003).

22 *Id.*

23 *Id.* at 157.

24 *Id.* at 156 (citing Bauer v. Ford Motor Credit Co., 149 F. Supp. 2d 1106, 1109 (D. Minn. 2001).

25 RESTATEMENT (SECOND) OF TORTS § 652D cmt. h (1977).

26 *Id.* § 652D, cmt. a.

27 *Id.*

28 Cox Broadcasting Co. v. Cohn, 420 U.S. 469, 495 (1975).

29 Florida Star v. B.J.F., 491 U.S. 524 (1989).

30 *Id.* at 538.

31 Restatement (Second) of Torts § 652B (1977).

32 472 N.E.2d 307 (N.Y. 1984).

33 Christoff v. Nestlé USA, Inc., 152 Cal. App. 4th 1439 (2007).

34 Christoff v. Nestlé USA, Inc., 169 P.3d 888 (Cal. 2007).

35 Christoff v. Nestlé USA, Inc., No. S155242 (Cal. Aug. 17, 2009).

36 *See* Haelan Laboratories, Inc. v. Topps Chewing Gum, Inc., 202 F.2d 866, 868 (1953).

37 *See* Zacchini v. Scripps-Howard Broadcasting Co, 433 U.S. 562, 573, 576 (1977).

38 California, Florida, Illinois, Indiana, Kentucky, Nebraska, Nevada, Ohio, Oklahoma, Tennessee, Texas, Virginia, and Washington.

39 Midler v. Ford Motor Co., 849 F.2d 460 (9th Cir. 1988).

40 Onassis v. Christian Dior, Inc., 472 N.Y.S.2d 254 (Spec. Term. 1984)

41 White v. Samsung Elecs. Am., 971 F.2d 1395 (9th Cir. 1992).

42 *See, e.g.,* Taylor v. NBC, No. BC 110922 (Cal. Super. Ct. Sept. 29, 1994).

43 433 U.S. 562 (1977).

44 Eastwood v. National Enquirer, 123 F.3d 1249 (1997).

45 Hoffman v. Capital Cities/ABC, Inc., 255 F.3d 1180 (2001).

46 11 N.Y.S.2d 907 (1962).

47 *See, e.g.,* Comedy III Productions, Inc. v. Gary Saderup, Inc., 25 Cal. 4th 387 (2001).

48 *See* Martin Luther King, Jr. Center for Social Change, Inc. v. American Heritage Products, Inc., 250 GA 135 (1982).

49 Nussenzweig v. DiCorcia, 2006 NY slip op. 50171U; 6 N.Y. Misc. LEXIS 230 (Feb. 8, 2006).

50 Restatement (Second) of Torts § 652E (1977).

51 385 U.S. 374 (1967).

52 403 U.S. 29 (1971).

53 418 U.S. 323 (1974).

54 *See* Cantrell v. Forest City Publishing Co., 419 U.S. 245 (1974).

55 Lake v. Wal-Mart Stores, Inc., 582 N.W.2d 231, 235 (Minn. 1998) (recognizing causes of action in tort for intrusion upon seclusion, appropriation, and publication of private facts, but not false light).

56 Denver Publishing Co. v. Bueno, 54 P.3d 893 (Colo. 2002); Jews for Jesus v. Rapp, 36 Media L. Rep. 2540, 2008 Fla. LEXIS 2010 (Fla. Oct. 23, 2008); Sullivan v. Pulitzer Broadcasting Co., 709 S.W.2d 475, 478–80 (Mo. 1986) (Missouri will not recognize false light in cases unrelated to defamation but has left open the possibility that it might recognize false light in "an appropriate case."); Renwick v. News and Observer Pub. Co., 312 S.E.2d 405, 411 (N.C. 1984); Cain v. The Hearst Corporation, 878 S.W.2d 577 (Tex. 1994); WJLA-TV v. Levin, 564 S.E.2d 383, 395 n. 5 (Va. 2002). *See also* Jacqueline Hanson Dee, Comment, The Absence of False Light from the Wisconsin Privacy Statute, 66 Marq. L. Rev. 99, 99–112 (1982).

57 Solano v. Playgirl, Inc., 292 F.3d 1078 (9th Cir. 2002).

58 Stein v. Marriott Ownership Resorts, Inc., 944 P.2d 374 (Utah App. 1997).

59 *Id.* at 376.

60 *Id.*

61 *See, e.g.,* Seale v. Gramercy Pictures, 964 F. Supp. 918, 925–31 (E.D. Pa. 1997) (holding that plaintiff could not support false light claims and that his right to publicity was not violated because his likeness was not used for a commercial purpose).

62 RESTATEMENT (SECOND) OF TORTS § 652E, cmt. c. (1977).

63 Tyne v. Time Warner Entm't Co., 336 F.3d 1286 (11th Cir. 2003).

64 Tyne v. Time Warner Entm't Co., L.P., 901 So.2d 802, 2005 Fla. LEXIS 728 (Fla., 2005).

65 Duncan v. WJLA-TV, 10 M.L.R. (BNA) 1385 (D.D.C. 1984).

66 See RESTATEMENT (SECOND) OF TORTS § 652D, Comment j (1977).

67 W. Prosser, *The Law of Torts* (4th edn. 1971) 824–26.

68 Shulman v. Group W. Prods., 955 P.2d 469 (Cal. 1998).

69 *See* Marich v. MGM/UA Telecommunications, 113 Cal. App. 4th 415 (2003).

70 Desnick v. Am. Broadcasting Companies, 44 F.3d 1345, 1351 (7th Cir. 1995). *But see* Braun v. Flynt, 726 F.2d 245, 255 (5th Cir. 1984) (Fraudulently induced consent is the "legal equivalent of no consent.").

71 Ouderkirk v. People for the Ethical Treatment of Animals, No. 05-10111, 2007 U.S. Dist. LEXIS 29451 (E.D. Mich. 2007).

72 *See* Virgil v. Time, Inc., 527 F.2d 1122, 1127 (9th Cir. 1975).

73 288 S.C. 569, 571 (S.C. 1986).

74 5 U.S.C. § 552(d)(1) (2007).

75 *Id.* § 552a(b).

76 *Id.* § 552(e)(7).

77 *See* J. Roderick MacArthur Found. v. FBI, 102 F.3d 600 (D.C. Cir. 1996).

78 *Id.* § 2510(12).

79 302 F.3d 868 (9th Cir. 2002).

80 Bob Sullivan, FTC fines Xanga for violating kids' privacy, MSNBC, Sept. 7, 2006, at http://www.msnbc.msn.com/id/14718350/.

81 Harris v. Blockbuster Inc., Case No. 08-CV-155 (E.D. Texas), filed April 9, 2008.

82 Public Law 104-191 (1996), codified in various section of the United States Code.

83 Broadcast of Telephone Conversations, 47 C.F.R. § 73.1206.

84 106 N.H. 107 (1964).

85 Food Lion, Inc. v. Capital Cities/ABC, Inc., 194 F.3d 505, 512 (4th Cir. 1999).

86 532 U.S. 514 (2001); *but see* Peavy v. WFAA-TV, Inc., 221 F.3d 158 (5th Cir. 2000) (holding that a reporter who encouraged a man to make illegal recordings of his neighbor's cordless phone conversations, heard over a police scanner, was not protected by the First Amendment from liability for disclosing the information under the Federal Wiretap Act).

87 492 F.3d 24, 35 (1st Cir. 2007).

88 American Marketing Association and ePolicy Institute, 2007 Electronic Monitoring & Surveillance Survey, http://press.amanet.org/press-releases/177/2007-electronic-monitoring-surveillance-survey/. (A total of 304 U.S. companies participated: 27% represent companies employing 100 or fewer workers, 101–500 employees (27%), 501–1,000 (12%), 1,001–2,500 (12%), 2,501–5,000 (10%), and 5,001 or more (12%)).

89 *See* Burlington Industries, Inc. v. Ellerth, 524 U.S. 742 (1998); Faragher v. City of Boca Raton, 524 U.S. 775 (1998).

90 John Yaukey, Firms Crack Down on E-Mail, *USA Today*, June 28, 2000, at 2B.

91 18 U.S.C. § 2511 (2)(a)(i) (2007).

92 *Id.*

93 McLaren v. Microsoft Corp., No. 05-97-00824-CV (Tex. Ct. App. 5th Dist. 1999), 1999 Tex. App. LEXIS 4103 at *4.

94 United States v. Simons, 206 F.3d 392, 396 (4th Cir. 2000).

95   *In re* Doubleclick, Inc. Privacy Litigation, 154 F. Supp. 2d 497 (S.D. N.Y. 2001).

96   United States v. Miller, 425 U.S. 435, 443 (1976).

97   Remsburg v. Docusearch, Inc., 149 N.H. 148, 158 (N.H. 2003).

98   Prepared Statement by the Federal Trade Commission on Behavioral Advertising, Before the Senate Committee on Commerce, Science and Transportation, July 9, 2008, www.ftc.gov/os/2008/07/P085400behavioralad.pdf.

99   European Union Directive 95/46/EC of the European Parliament and of the Council art. 4, EU O.J. L, 1995.

100 Kevin Poulsen, Pillaged MySpace Photos Show Up in Massive BitTorrent Download, Wired, Jan. 23, 2008, http://www.wired.com/politics/security/news/2008/01/myspace_torrent.

101 Facebook Games Could Lead To Identity Theft, WBAL-TV, July 6, 2008.

102 Facebook Privacy Policy, The Information We Collect, www.facebook.com/policy.php (last visited Jan. 30, 2009).

103 *See* MacIntyre v. Ohio Elections Commission, 514 U.S. 334 (1995) (striking down an election law against anonymous campaign literature).

104 *Id.* at 347.

105 ACLU v. Miller, 977 F. Supp. 1228 (N.D. Ga. 1997) (citing M.S. News Co. v. Casado, 721 F.2d 1281, 1287 (10th Cir. 1983) and Kolender v. Lawson, 461 U.S. 352, 357 (1983)).

106 884 A.2d 451 (Del. 2005).

107 *See* McMann v. Doe, 460 F. Supp. 2d 259 (D. Mass. 2006); Reunion Industries v. Doe, 2007 WL 1453491 (Pa. Com. Pl. 2007); *In re* Does 1-10, 2007 WL 4328204 (Tex. App. 2007).

108 *See* Mobilisa v. Doe, 170 P.3d 712 (Ariz. Ct. App. 2007); Columbia Insurance v. Seescandy.com, 185 F.R.D. 573 (N.D. Cal. 1999); Dendrite v. Doe, 775 A.2d 756 (N.J. App. Div. 2001); Greenbaum v. Google, 845 N.Y.S.2d 695 (N.Y. Sup. Ct. 2007).

109 50 U.S.C. § 1801 et seq. (2006).

110 Pub. L. No. 107-56, § 218, 115 Stat. 272, 291 (2001).

111 50 U.S.C. § 1805(c)(1).

112 18 U.S.C. § 3103(a).

113 50 U.S.C. § 1861(d).

114 *Id.* § 1861(a).

115 18 U.S.C. § 3121(c) (2007).

116 James Risen and Eric Lichtblau, Bush Lets U.S. Spy on Callers Without Courts, *New York Times*, Dec. 16, 2005, at A1.

117 FISA Amendment Act of 2008, Public L. No. 110-261.

11   Sex and Violence

1   United States v. Schwimmer, 279 U.S. 644, 654–55 (1929) (Holmes, J, dissenting).

2   Action for Children's Television v. FCC ("ACT III"), 11 F.3d 170, 178 (D.C. Cir. 1993).

3   413 U.S. 15 (1973).

4   Matt Richtel, What's Obscene? Defendant Says Google Data Offers a Gauge, *New York Times*, June 24, 2008 at A1.

5   Trends.google.com.

6   Reno v. ACLU, 521 U.S. 844, 877–78 (1997).

7   *See* Ashcroft v. ACLU, 535 U.S. 564, 584–85 (2002).

8   Jenkins v. Georgia, 418 U.S. 153, 160 (1974).

9   338 U.S. 680 (1950).

10   U.S. v. Fletcher, No. CR 06-329 (W.D. Pa. Aug. 7, 2008).

11   481 U.S. 497, 500–1 (1987).

12   18 U.S.C. §§ 1461, 1462, 1465 (2007).

13   *Id.* § 1470.

14   361 U.S. 147 (1959).

15   *See* Hamling v. United States 418 U.S. 87, 114 (1974): United States v. Orito, 413 U.S. 139, 145 (1973).

16   *See* Janet Reno, Statement on Justice Department Policy Concerning Abortion Speech, Feb. 9, 1996, at http://www.ciec.org/trial/abort_speech.html.

17   394 U.S. 557 (1969).

18   *Id.* at 565.

19   United States v. Orito, 413 U.S. 139, 141–43 (1973). *See also* United States v. 12 200-Ft. Reels of Super 8mm Film, 413 U.S. 123 (1973).

20   *Id.* at 141–42.

21   18 U.S.C. § 1466A (2007).

22   *Id.* § 2252A(a)(3)(B).

23   458 U.S. 747 (1982).

24   *Id.* at 763–65.

25   495 U.S. 103 (1990).

26   535 U.S. 234 (2002).

27   *Id.* at 254–55.

28   18 U.S.C. §2252(a)(3)(B) (2007).

29   128 S.Ct. 1830 (2008).

30   *Id.* at 1840–41.

31   128 S.Ct. 1830 (2008).

32   Transcript of oral argument at 39, 44, 128 S.Ct. 1830 (2008) (No. 06-694), available at www.supremecourtus.gov/oral_arguments/argument_transcripts/06-694.pdf

33   18 U.S.C. § 2257(h)(2).

34   18 U.S.C. § 1468 (2007).

35   *In re* Litigation Recovery Trust, Memorandum Opinion and Order, 17 F.C.C.R. 21852, ¶ 9 (2002).

36   492 U.S. 115 (1989).

37   Restrictions on Obscene or Indecent Telephone Message Services, 47 C.F.R. § 64.201(c) (1987).

38   521 U.S. 844 (1999).

39   47 U.S.C. § 231(e)(2)(B) (2006).

40   ACLU v. Reno, 217 F.3d 162, 175 (3rd Cir. 2000).

41   Ashcroft v. ACLU, 535 U.S. 564 (2002).

42   ACLU v. Ashcroft, 322 F.3d 240 (3d Cir. Pa., 2003).

43   Ashcroft v. ACLU, 542 U.S. 656, 671 (2004).

44   ACLU v. Mukasey, 534 F.3d 181 (3rd Cir. July 22, 2008), *aff'g* ACLU v. Gonzales, 478 F. Supp. 2d 775 (E.D. Pa., 2007).

45   Mukasey v. ACLU, 2009 U.S. LEXIS 598 (Jan. 21, 2009).

46 47 U.S.C. § 254(h)(6) (2006).

47 *Id.*

48 18 U.S.C. § 2252B (2007).

49 U.S. Department of Justice, 'Cyberscammer' Sentenced to 30 Months for Using Deceptive Internet Names to Mislead Minors to X-Rated Sites, Feb. 26, 2004, http://www.usdoj.gov/criminal/cybercrime/zuccariniSent.htm.

50 Ginsburg v. New York, 390 U.S. 629, 633 (1968).

51 194 F.3d 1149 (10th Cir. 1999); *See also* PSINET v. Chapman, 167 F. Supp. 2d 878 (W.D. Va. 2001) (holding that a Virginia law barring Internet material "harmful to juveniles" violated the First Amendment and the Constitution's Commerce Clause).

52 American Amusement Machine Association v. Kendrick, 244 F.3d 572, 573 (7th Cir. 2001).

53 *Id.* at 576.

54 *See* Electronic Software Association v. Hatch, 443 F. Supp. 2d 1065 (D. Minn. 2006), *aff'd*, 519 F.3d 768 (8th Cir. 2008).

55 *See* ESA v. Granholm, 426 F. Supp. 2d 646 (E.D. Mich. 2006).

56 *See* ESA v. Blagojevich, 469 F.3d 641 (7th Cir. 2006).

57 *See* Video Software Dealers v. Maleng, 325 F. Supp. 2d 1180 (W.D. Wash. 2004).

58 *See* Interactive Digital Software Association v. St. Louis County, 329 F.3d 954 (8th Cir. 2003).

59 *See* Video Software Dealers Association v. Schwarzenegger, 401 F. Supp. 2d 1034 (N.D. Cal. 2007).

60 *See* ESA v. Foti, 451 F. Supp. 2d 823 (M.D. La., 2006).

61 *See* Entertainment Merchants Association v. Henry, 2007 U.S. Dist. LEXIS 69139 (W.D. Okla., 2007).

62 Pahler v. Slayer, 29 Media L. Rep. 2627 (Cal. Super. Ct. 2001).

63 People v. Bautista, 2006 Cal. App. Unpub. LEXIS 11714 (Dec. 28, 2006).

64 300 F.3d 683 (6th Cir. 2002).

65 *See also* United States v. Thoma, 726 F.2d 1191, 1200 (7th Cir. 1984) (holding that obscenity jurisprudence does not apply to depictions of violence).

66 188 F. Supp. 2d 1264, 1272 (2002).

67 *Id.* at 1272.

68 25 Media L. Rep. 1705 (1997).

69 *See* McCollum v. CBS, 202 Cal. App. 3d 989 (1988); Waller v. Osbourne, 763 F. Supp. 1144 (1991).

70 395 U.S. 444 (1969).

71 *Id.* at 447.

72 *Id.* at 447.

73 Byers v. Edmondson, 712 So.2d 681 (La. Ct. App. 1998), *cert. denied*, 526 U.S. 1005 (1999).

74 *Id.* at 684.

75 Robert O'Neil, *The First Amendment and Civil Liability* (2001) 157.

76 Byers v. Edmondson, 826 So.2d 551 (La. App. 2002).

77 *Id.* at 557.

78 188 F. Supp. 2d 1264, 1279 (D. Colo. 2002).

79 128 F.3d 233 (4th Cir. 1997), *cert. denied*, 523 U.S. 1074 (1998).

80 *Id.* at 242.

81 *Id*. at 241 (quoting parties Joint Statement of Facts, at 58–62).

82 Whitney v. California, 274 U.S. 357, 377 (1927) (Brandeis, J, concurring).

83 Chaplinsky v. New Hampshire, 315 U.S. 568 (1942) (finding fighting words to be of "such slight social value" as to be unworthy of First Amendment protection).

84 *See* Gooding v. Wilson, 405 U.S. 518 (1972) (finding that fighting words must be limited to face-to-face conflicts, involving words "that have a direct tendency to cause acts of violence by the person to whom, individually, the remark is addressed.").

85 18 U.S.C.S. Appx § 3A1.1 (Lexis-Nexis 2008).

86 18 U.S.C. § 875 (2007).

87 394 U.S. 705 (1969).

88 18 U.S.C. § 871(a) (2007).

89 Watts v. United States, 394 U.S. 705, 707 (1969).

90 244. F.3d 1007 (9th Cir. 2001), *reh'g en banc granted*, 290 F.3d 1058 (9th Cir. 2002).

91 National Abortion Federation, NAF Violence and Disruption Statistics, www. prochoice.org/pubs_research/publications/downloads/about_abortion/violence_ statistics.pdf.

92 Planned Parenthood of the Columbia/Willamette v. American Coalition of Life Activists, 290 F.3d at 1086.

93 47 U.S.C. § 223(a)(1)(C) (2006).

94 18 U.S.C. § 2261A (2007).

95 National Conference of State Legislatures, State Computer Harassment or "Cyber-stalking" Laws, Last updated Dec. 17, 2007, at http://www.ncsl.org/programs/lis/cip/ stalk99.htm (last visited Oct. 11, 2008).

96 A.B. v. State of Indiana, No. 67S01-0709-JV-373 (Ind. Sup. Ct. May 13, 2008).

97 Indiana Code § 35-45-2-2(a)(4) (2004).

98 A.B. v. State of Indiana, No. 67S01-0709-JV-373 at *4.

99 *Id*. at *7.

100 U.S. v. Drew, Crim. No. 08- 00582 (C.D. Cal. indictment filed May 15, 2008).

101 Kim Zetter, Lori Drew Not Guilty of Felonies in Landmark Cyberbullying Trial, Wired.com, Nov. 26, 2008, http://blog.wired.com/27bstroke6/2008/11/lori-drew-pla-5.html.

102 Kim Zetter, Judge Acquits Lori Drew in Cyberbullying Case, Overrules Jury, *Wired*, July 2, 2009, at http://www.wired.com/threatlevel/2009/07/drew_court/.

12 Commercial Speech and Antitrust Law

1 *See* Valentine v. Chrestensen, 316 U.S. 52 (1942).

2 *See* Central Hudson Gas & Electric Company v. Public Service Commission, 447 U.S. 557, 563 (1980).

3 *Id*. at 562 (quoting Ohralik v. Ohio State Bar Ass'n, 436 U.S. 447, 455–56, (1978)).

4 376 U.S. 254 (1964).

5 421 U.S. 809 (1975).

6 425 U.S. 748 (1976).

7 *Id*. at 765.

8 *Central Hudson*, 447 U.S. at 563 (1980).

9 *Id*. at 566.

10   Riley v. National Fed'n of the Blind of North Carolina, 487 U.S. 781, 796–97 (1987).

11   412 U.S. 94 (1973); *see also* Clark County Sch. Dist. v. Planned Parenthood, 941 F.2d 817, 824 (9th Cir. 1991) (holding that advertising space in school newspapers and yearbooks is not a public forum and schools may reject advertising).

12   *See* Miami Herald Publg. Co. v. Tornillo, 418 U.S. 241 (1974) (upholding a publisher's right to refuse to run editorial replies).

13   474 F. Supp. 2d 622 (D. Del. 2007).

14   *See* Pittsburgh Press Co. v. Pitt. Commn. of Human Rel., 413 U.S. 376, 391 (1973) (prohibiting a publication from carrying advertisements for jobs in sex-designated columns).

15   *See* Lorain J. Co. v. U.S., 342 U.S. 143, 155–56 (1951); Home Placement Serv. v. Providence J. Co., 682 F.2d 274, 281 (1st Cir. 1982).

16   15 U.S.C. § 45(a) (2007).

17   FTC Policy Statement on Unfairness, Dec. 17, 1980, appended to International Harvester Co., 104 F.T.C. 949, 1070 (1984). *See also* 15 U.S.C. § 45(n).

18   F.C.C. Policy Statement on Deception, appended to Cliffdale Associates, Inc., 103 F.T.C. 110, 174 (1984) ¶ 33, http://www.ftc.gov/bcp/policystmt/ad-decept.htm.

19   *See, In re* WEBTV Networks, Inc., FTC Docket No. C- 3988 (Dec. 8, 2000) (consent order).

20   Civil Action No. 06-CV-0105 (D. Wyo. 2008); FTC File No. 052 3126.

21   Federal Trade Commission v. National Urological Group, No. 1:04-cv-3294-CAP (N.D. Ga. June 4, 2008).

22   *Id.* at *98.

23   Expert endorsements, 16 C.F.R. § 255.3.

24   Disclosure of material connections, 16 C.F.R. § 255.5.

25   Consumer endorsements, 16 C.F.R. § 255.2.

26   General considerations, 16 C.F.R. § 255.1.

27   See Public Notice Concerning the Broadcast of Information By Means of "Subliminal Perception" Techniques, 44 F.C.C. 2d 1016, 1017 (1974).

28   Vance v. Judas Priest, No. 86-5844/86-3939, 1990 WL 130920 (D. Nev. Aug. 24, 1990).

29   165 Ohio App. 3d 291(2006).

30   968 F.2d 1110, 1119 (11th Cir. 1992).

31   15 U.S.C. § 1125(a)(1) (2007).

32   *See* Pizza Hut, Inc. v. Papa John's International, Inc., 227 F.3d 489, 495 (5th Cir. 2000).

33   *See* U-Haul International, Inc. v. Jartran, Inc., 793 F.2d 1034 (9th Cir. 1986).

34   *See* ALPO Petfoods, Inc. v. Ralstan Purina Co., 997 F.2d 949 (D.C. Cir. 1993).

35   *See* BASF Corp. v. Old World Trading Co., 41 F.3d 1081 (7th Cir. 1994); Johnson & Johnson-Merck Consumer Pharms. Co. v. Rhone-Poulenc Rorer Pharms., Inc., 19 F.3d 125, 129–30 (3d Cir. 1994).

36   *See* Southland Sod Farms v. Stover Seed Co., 108 F.3d 1134, 1144 (9th Cir. 1997); EFCO Corp. v. Symons Corp., 219 F.3d 734, 740 (8th Cir. 2000).

37   *See* United Industries Corp. v. Clorox Co., 140 F.3d 1175, 1182 (8th Cir. 1998).

38   497 F.3d 144 (2007).

39   *Id.* at 154.

40   *Id.* at 148.

41   *Id.* at 158.

42   *See* Atari Corp. v. 3DO Co., No. C 94-20298 RMW (EAI), 1994 WL 723601, at 1 (N.D. Cal. May 16, 1994).

43 Pizza Hut, Inc. v. Papa John's International, 227 F.3d 489 (5th Cir. 2000).

44 FTC Policy Statement on Deception, U.S.S.G. § 2B1.1(b)(7) (Nov. 1, 2001).

45 Time Warner Cable v. DIRECTV, 497 F.3d 144, 148 (2d Cir. 2007).

46 *Id.* at 160.

47 State settles suit against Airborne Health, Milwaukee Bus. J., Dec. 16, 2008.

48 $23.3M Settlement in Airborne False Ad Suit, FindLaw, March 4, 2008, http://commonlaw.findlaw.com/2008/03/233m-settlement.html.

49 478 U.S. 328 (1986).

50 517 U.S. 484, 509 (1996).

51 *Id.* at 509–10.

52 27 U.S.C. §§ 205(e)(4), (f)(4) (2007).

53 15 U.S.C. §§ 1331–41, 4402 (2007).

54 Billboard ads for smokeless tobacco products are excepted from the rule.

55 Family Smoking Prevention and Tobacco Control Act, Public Law 111-31, June 22, 2009.

56 Commonwealth Brands, Inc. v. FDA, 1:2009cv00117 (W.D. Ky filed Aug. 31, 2009).

57 *See* 18 U.S.C. § 1343 (2007).

58 *See* FCC Consumer Facts, Broadcasting, Contests, Lotteries and Solicitation of Funds, http://www.fcc.gov/cgb/consumerfacts/contests.html (last visited Oct. 12, 2008).

59 *See* Greater New Orleans Broadcasting Ass'n v. United States, 527 U.S. 173 (1999).

60 *See* Correspondence from John G. Malcolm, Deputy Asst. Attorney General, Criminal Division, United States Department of Justice (06.11.03). A copy of the letter can be viewed at http://www.igamingnews.com/articles/files/ NAB_letter-030611.pdf.

61 *See* Matt Richtel, U.S. Steps Up Push Against Online Casinos by Seizing Cash, *New York Times*, May 31, 2004, C1.

62 47 U.S.C. § 303a. Ads for other children's programs are not included in that limit.

63 Policies and Rules Concerning Children's Television Programming, 6 FCC Rcd. 2111, 2117–18 (1991).

64 Children's Educational Television: FCC Consumer Facts, http://www.fcc.gov/cgb/consumerfacts/childtv.html (last visited Oct. 11, 2008).

65 15 U.S.C. § 1601 et seq. (2007).

66 Abusive telemarketing acts or practices, 16 C.F.R. Part 310.4(c).

67 Individuals can register home and cellular phones online at www.donotcall.gov.

68 16 C.F.R. Part 310.4(b)(3)(iv).

69 15 U.S.C. § 5711 (a)(1) (2007).

70 47 U.S.C. § 227 (2006).

71 Restrictions on telephone solicitation, 47 C.F.R. § 64.1200.

72 Public Law 108-187, 117 Statute 2699, codified at 15 U.S.C. §§ 7701-13, 18 U.S.C. 1037 and 28 U.S.C 994.

73 Requirement to place warning labels on commercial electronic mail that contains sexually oriented material, 16 C.F.R. § 316.4.

74 Restrictions on mobile service commercial messages, 47 C.F.R. § 64.3100.

75 18 U.S.C. § 1037 (2007).

76 15 U.S.C. § 7707(b) (2007).

77 Pub. L. No. 107-155, Mar. 27, 2002 (amending the Federal Election Campaign Act of 1971 (2 U.S.C. § 434)).

78   424 U.S. 1, 20–21 (1976).

79   *Id.* (citing Federal Election Comm'n v. National Right to Work Comm., 459 U.S. 197 1982)).

80   540 U.S. 93 (2003).

81   *Id.* at 153.

82   Federal Election Commission v. Wisconsin Right to Life, 127 S.Ct. 2652, 2007 U.S. LEXIS 8515, ***6 (2007).

83   *Id.*

84   *See* 2 U.S.C. § 431(9)(B)(i) (2007).

85   11 C.F.R. §§ 100.73, 100.132.

86   Federal Election Commission, Internet Communications and Activity, http://www. fec.gov/pages/brochures/internetcomm.shtml#press (last visited Jan. 30, 2009).

87   27 Cal. 4th 939 (2002).

88   *Id.* at 961.

89   463 U.S. 60, 66–67 (1983).

90   *Id.* at 67–68.

91   15 U.S.C. §§ 1–7 (2007).

92   FTC Guide to Antitrust Laws, Single Firm Conduct: Monopolization Defined, FTC website, http://www.ftc.gov/bc/antitrust/monopolization_defined.shtm (last visited Oct. 11, 2008).

93   15 U.S.C. §§ 12–27 (2007).

94   *Id.* § 45(a)(2).

95   California Dental Ass'n v. Federal Trade Commission, 526 U.S. 756 (1999).

96   Case T-201/04, Microsoft Corp. v. European Commission, O.J. C 269 (2007), available at http://curia.europa.eu/jurisp/cgi-bin/form.pl?lang=EN&Submit=rechercher&num aff=T-201/04

97   326 U.S. 1 (1945).

98   *Id.* at 20.

99   319 U.S. 190 (1943).

100   *See* Lorain Journal Company v. United States, 342 U.S. 143 (1951).

101   395 U.S. 367, 390 (1969).

102   15 U.S.C. § 7001 et. seq. (2007).

103   *Id.* § 7006.

104   Feldman v. Google, 513 F. Supp. 2d 229 (E.D. Pa. 2007).

105   Click Fraud Network, Click Fraud Index (2008), http://clickfraudnetwork.com/ content/ClickFraudIndex.aspx.

106   Lane's Gifts and Collectibles v. Google, Inc., No. CV-2005-052-1 (Miller Co., Ark. Cir. Ct. 2006).

107   Adam Gatt, The enforceability of click-wrap agreements, 18 COMPUTER L. & SECURITY REP., 404–10 (2002).

108   Motise v. America Online, 346 F. Supp. 2d 563, 566 (S.D. N.Y. 2004).

109   15 U.S.C. § 7003 (2007).

Index